The Art of Collaboration

PICKARD CHILTON

The Art of Collaboration

MICHAEL J. CROSBIE

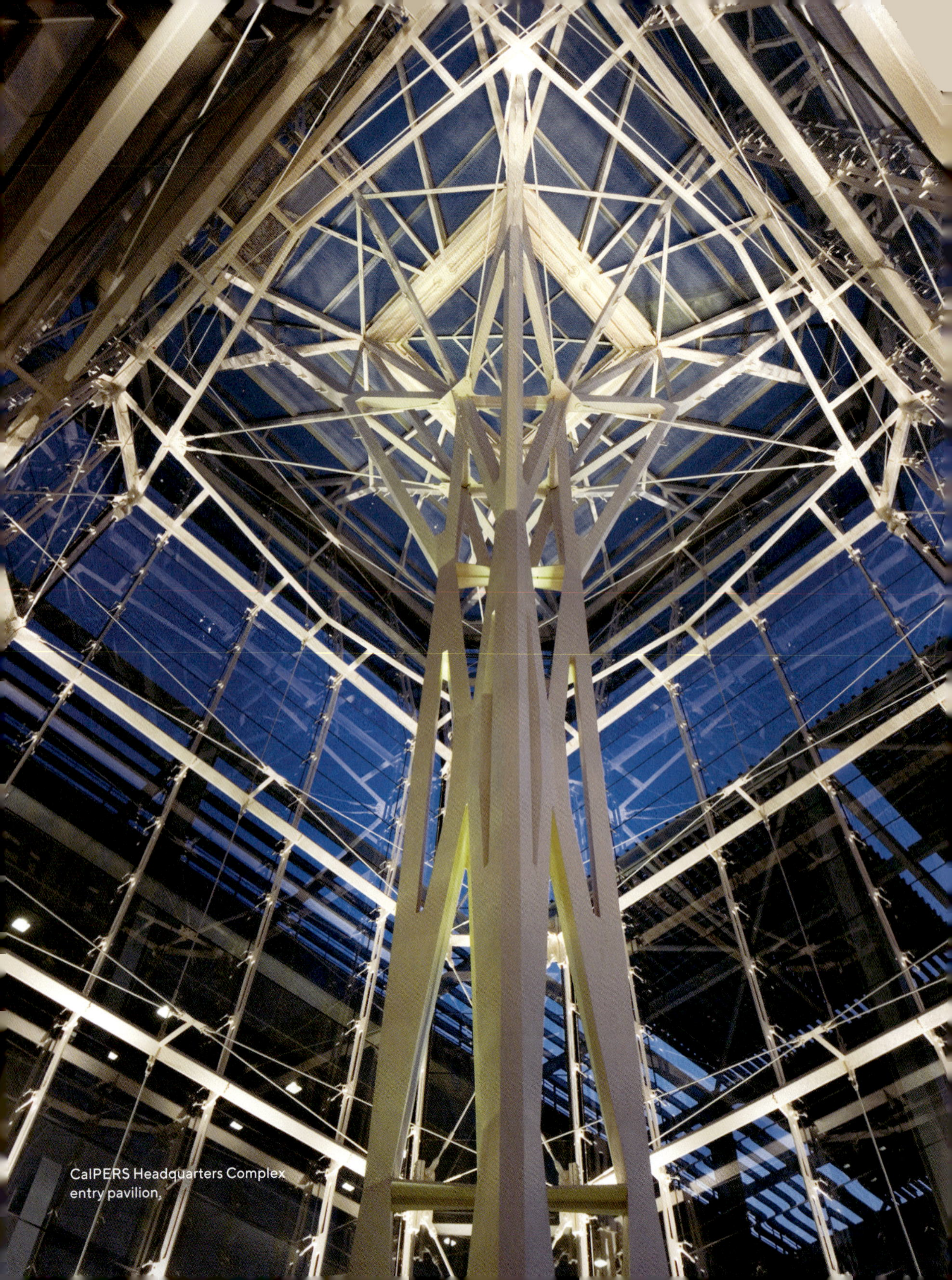

CalPERS Headquarters Complex
entry pavilion.

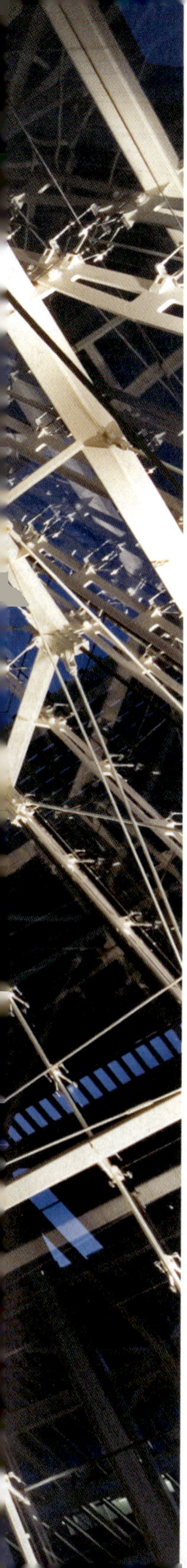

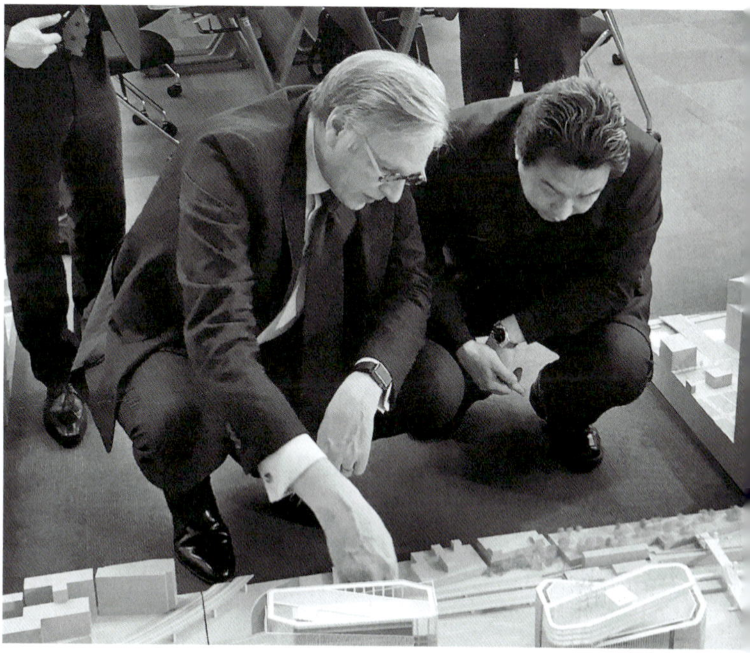

Principal William Chilton reviews the Global Gateway Shinagawa model during a project review meeting in Tokyo.

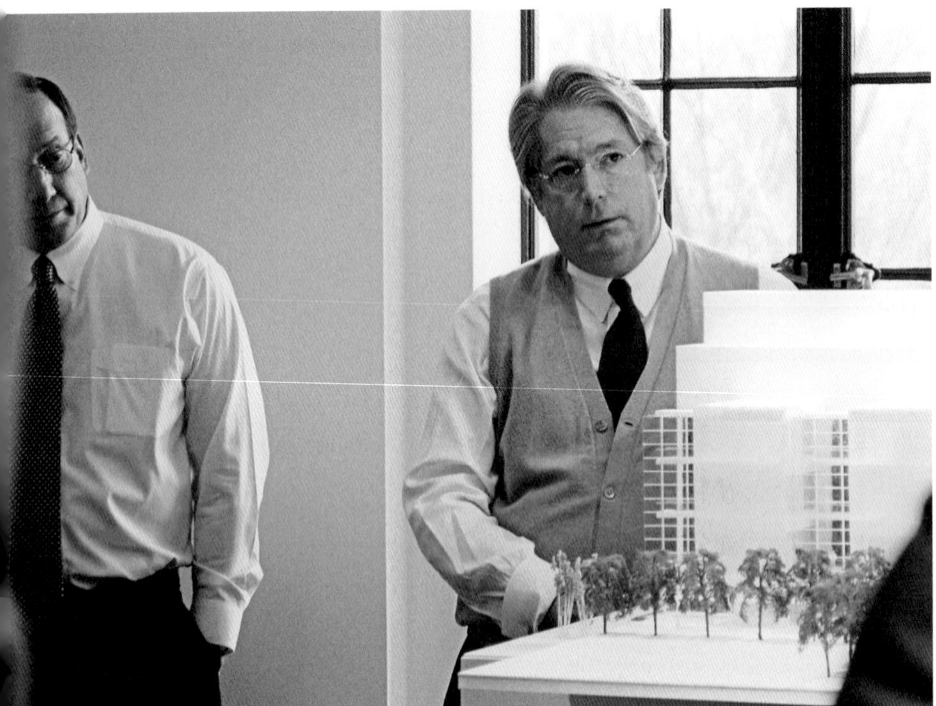

Hines's Jerry Lea and Principal Jon Pickard in milestone Design Development presentation with the Devon Energy client in studio.

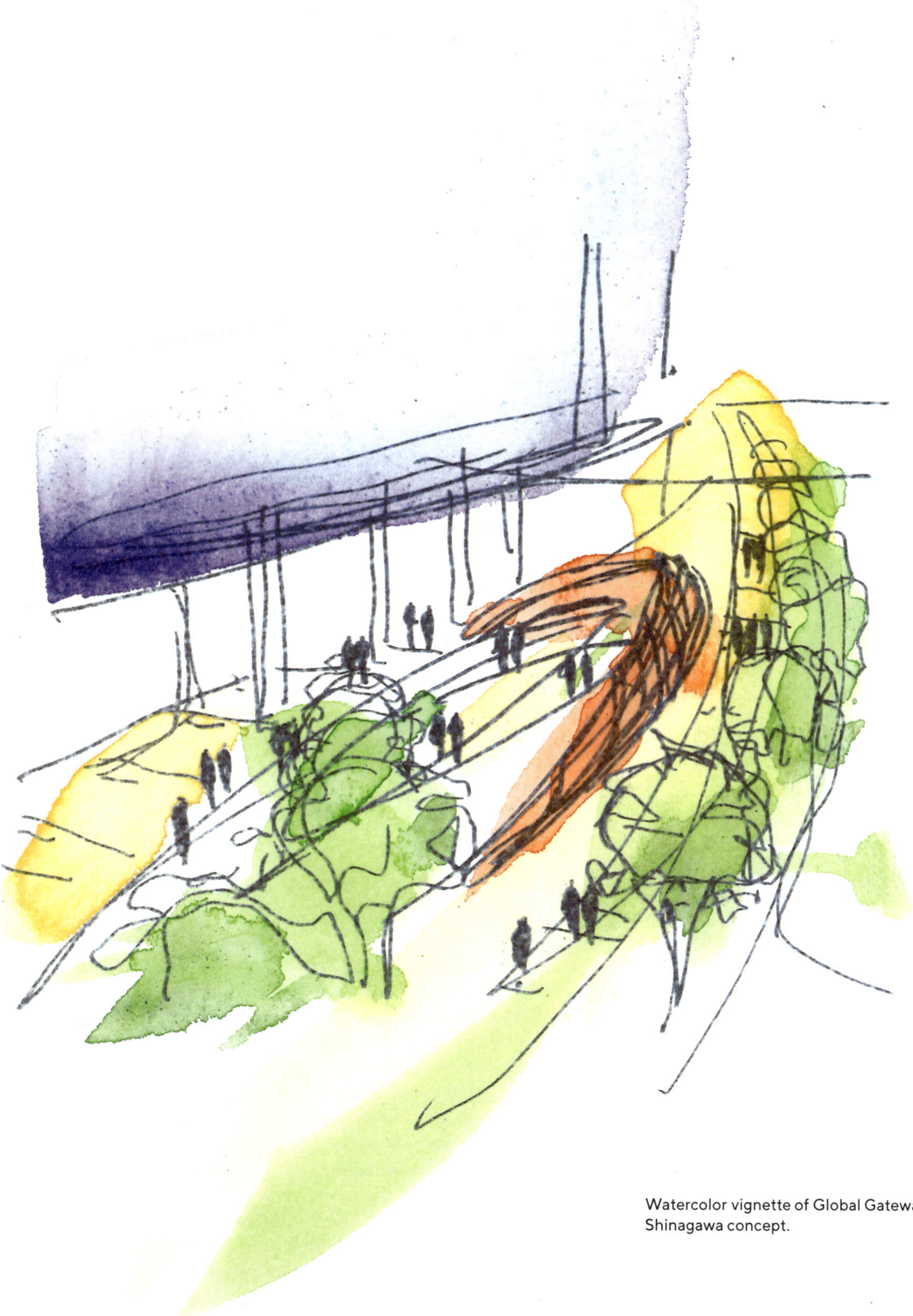

Watercolor vignette of Global Gateway Shinagawa concept.

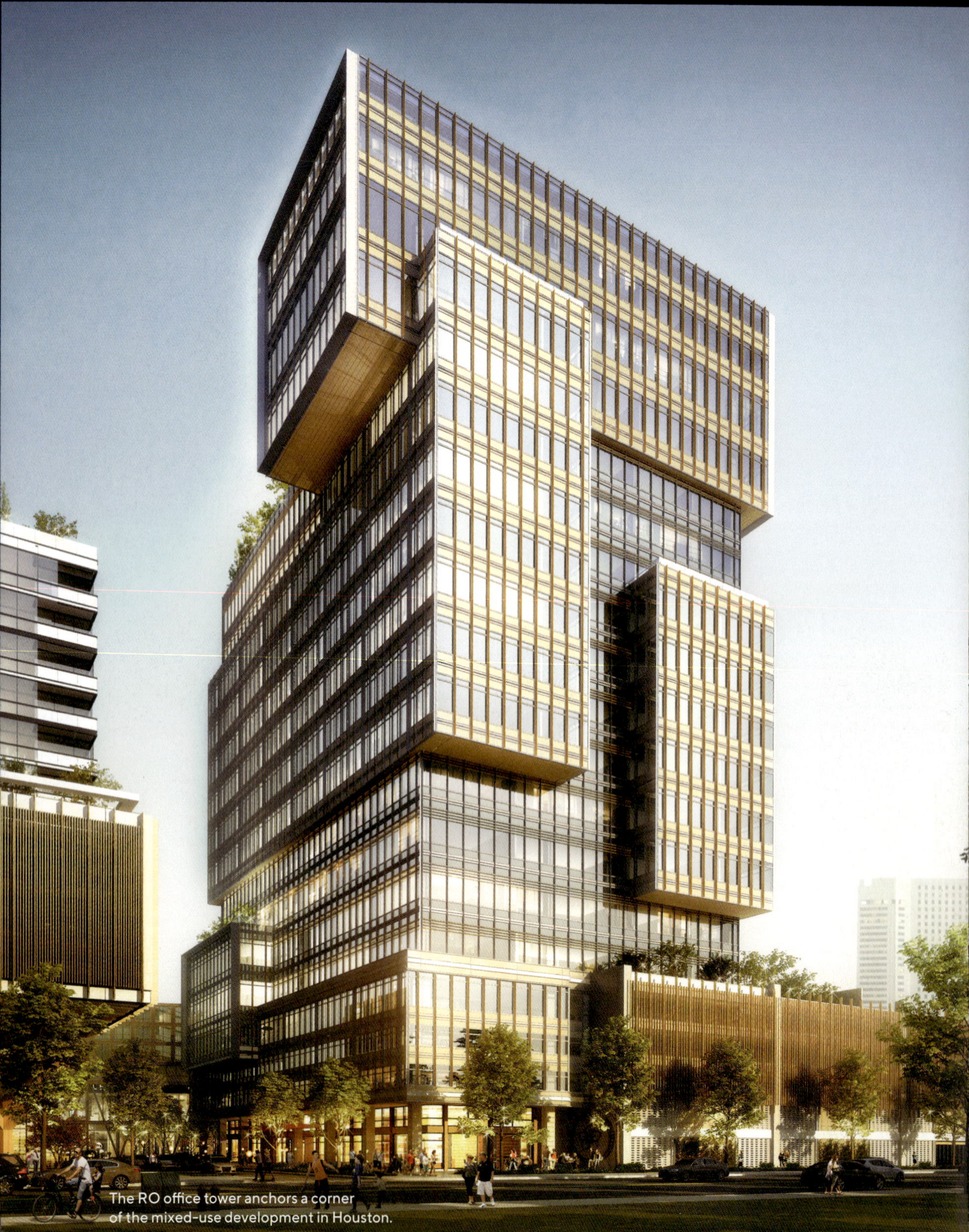

The RO office tower anchors a corner of the mixed-use development in Houston.

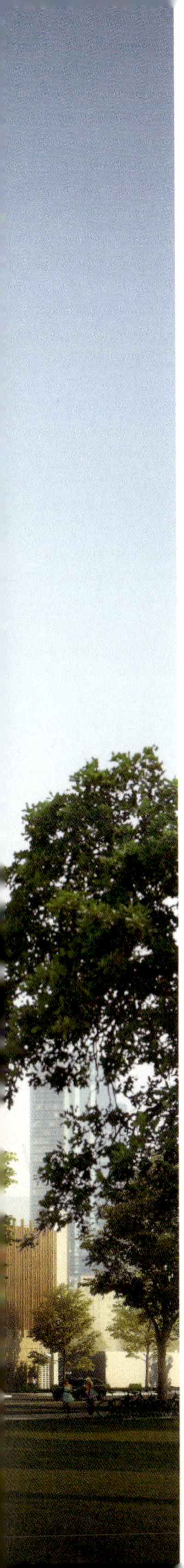

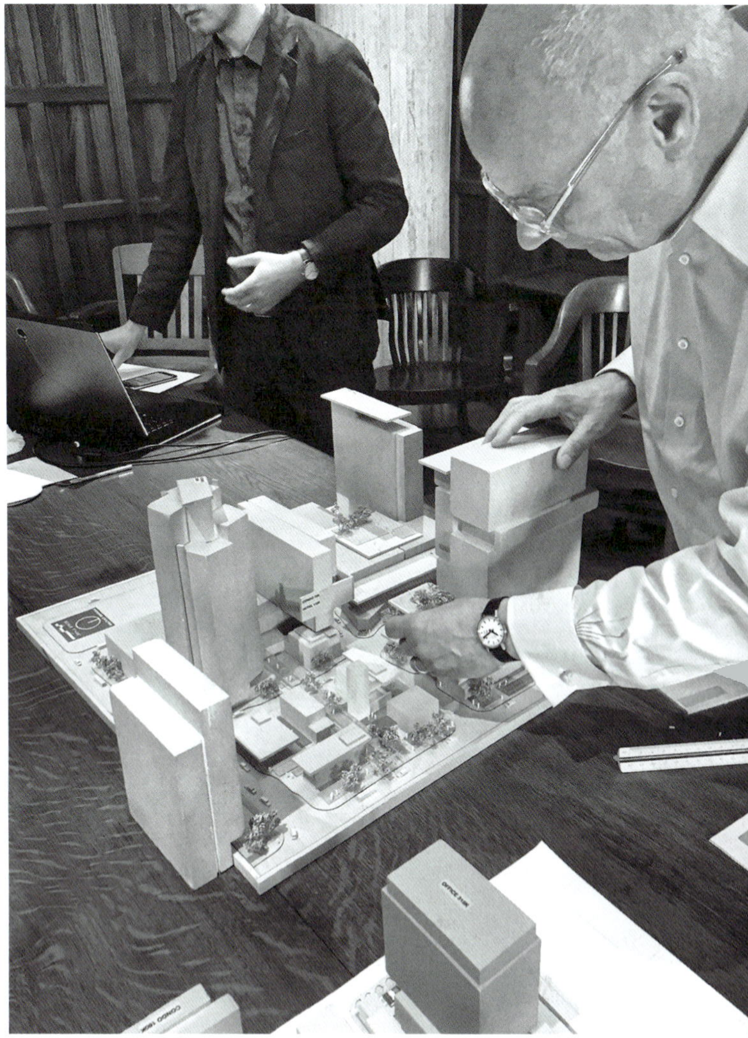

Principal Anthony Markese prepares a site model for a presentation to The RO client.

Contents

Foreword

Reflecting the Client's Values

Cesar Pelli

Every good work of architecture is a product of collaboration with your client. The collaboration between the architect and the client, and communication between them, are often the most important factors in creating a piece of architecture that responds to their needs, that can become part of a city, that is a reflection of the client's values (which architecture should always be). Sometimes your clients become friends, but that is not the objective, and it's not even necessary in creating a successful project. However, developing a friendship with a client is part of building trust, and trust is often the key that unlocks a client's innermost desires for the building. Trust, built from friendship, allows you a glimpse into how the client views him or herself. And that knowledge is critical for the architect engaged in the design.

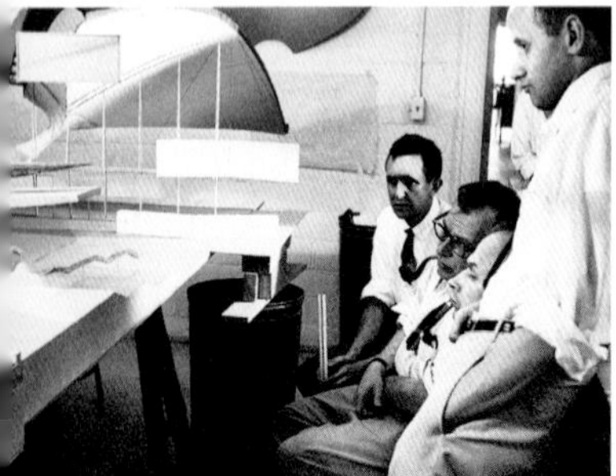

When I was a young architect just out of school, the most important experiences I had were those practicing with Eero Saarinen in Bloomfield Hills, Michigan. Eero had an incredible focus, an amazing drive. He was consumed with making architecture that was just the right response to his clients' needs. He's attributed with describing this as "the style for the job," which he might have said, or not (Eero was not very verbal). But the value behind that phrase was important

Cesar Pelli, Eero Saarinen, Leon Yulkowski, and Kevin Roche with model of TWA Flight Center in Saarinen studio.

to Eero and to the architecture he created. He approached every design as a new journey in architecture, and in discovering the client in the design.

Pickard Chilton is part of this tradition and this legacy. Jon Pickard, while in practice with me, was very adept at communicating with clients and developing a relationship with them that made them collaborators. Together with his colleagues William Chilton and Anthony Markese, they have shared this critical skill throughout their studio. In this way I see Pickard Chilton as heirs of my own approach to architecture, which in large measure I learned from Eero: How to develop a feel for a project, the right direction, rapport with your client collaborators (who might also become friends). These are the most important values for any architect to have.

New Haven, Connecticut
May 10, 2019

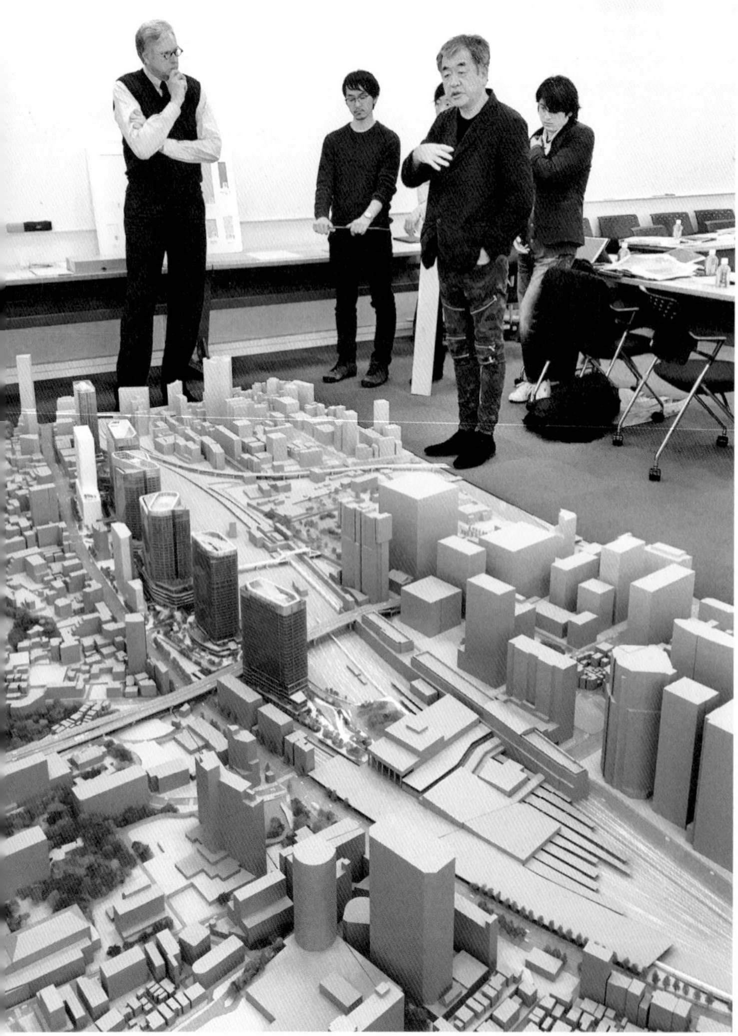

Kengo Kuma with William Chilton at Global Gateway Shinagawa master plan presentation in Tokyo.

Preface

Lessons for Clients and Their Architects

Thomas Fisher

The exceptional client relationships that Pickard Chilton builds and maintains make me think of the two times in my life that I've been a client of architects, and what I learned in the process. I was educated as an architect, have worked in architecture offices, written about architecture my entire career, and now teach in an architecture school. But having been a client—once as the dean during the expansion and renovation of our college, and most recently as a homeowner for the design and construction of our new house — I realized that sharing some of my experiences might have some value for those thinking about (or about to take on) the role of the client.

Be Frank

The success of Pickard Chilton has a lot to do with the amazing talent of the firm's designers, having created one remarkable building after another for a very long time. But that success also comes down to one word: "Listen." The architects of Pickard Chilton listen to their clients and act upon what they hear. This requires, however, that the clients are frank with their architects. My experience as a client reminded me of what my father, a clinical psychologist, used to say about the role of patients in psychotherapy: they had to be candid and tell their therapists what they needed to hear, however revealing that might be.

Architecture is not just about bricks and mortar. It is also about the spaces that people need in order to do their work and live their lives. And architects have to know not just how much space is required, but also what the client wishes the new space to encourage, enable, and inspire. When I was the client for our college's expansion, the architects had a list of our space needs and the area requirements of each. But the best aspects of our building came from conversations I had with the architects about what I hoped the expanded college would become, and the role the architecture would play in the education of our students. The more honest and open our clients are, the better the final outcome.

Be Open

That openness needs to continue throughout the design process. Design is an amazing experience, in which we see our goals translated into form. During that process, unexpected ideas and unconventional solutions also arise. As a client, it can be tempting to resist a design direction you didn't anticipate, as often happened with my wife during the design of our house. She had a certain idea of what the house should be like and when new and better ideas emerged as the design progressed, she tended to react negatively to them. But as the process continued and she saw the clear advantages of what she had initially rejected, she came around, so much so that some of the things in the design that she least liked at first are now her favorite aspects.

Openness goes both ways. Good architects remain open to clients' ideas. One story in this book relates how a client suggested the use of stone in the building, an idea that the design principal admits he had real doubts about. But Pickard Chilton remained open to stone and successfully incorporated it into the design—recognizing that the client's suggestion was "brilliant," in the words of the principal.

Openness has long characterized modern architecture, with its expansive use of glass and uncluttered, flowing spaces. But the openness of modern architects — and modern clients — to each other's ideas might be equally important and just as significant a break from the past.

Be Patient

The creative process also demands patience—it's not a linear path or a fast process, despite how it sometimes gets portrayed in movies or pop culture. Designers are more like the explorers of unknown territory, on a purposeful journey, but one that requires taking one step back on occasion in order to keep moving forward, reinvestigating possibilities previously passed by in a continual search for the best route to reach the client's goals. The looping quality of the design process can unnerve those not used to it. My wife, educated as an architectural historian but unfamiliar with the design process, often asked during the design of our house why we were revisiting things we had already dismissed. It was a good question, and all I could say was: be patient, it will all work out. When you have good architects, like Pickard Chilton, building collaborative relationships with their clients, it inevitably does.

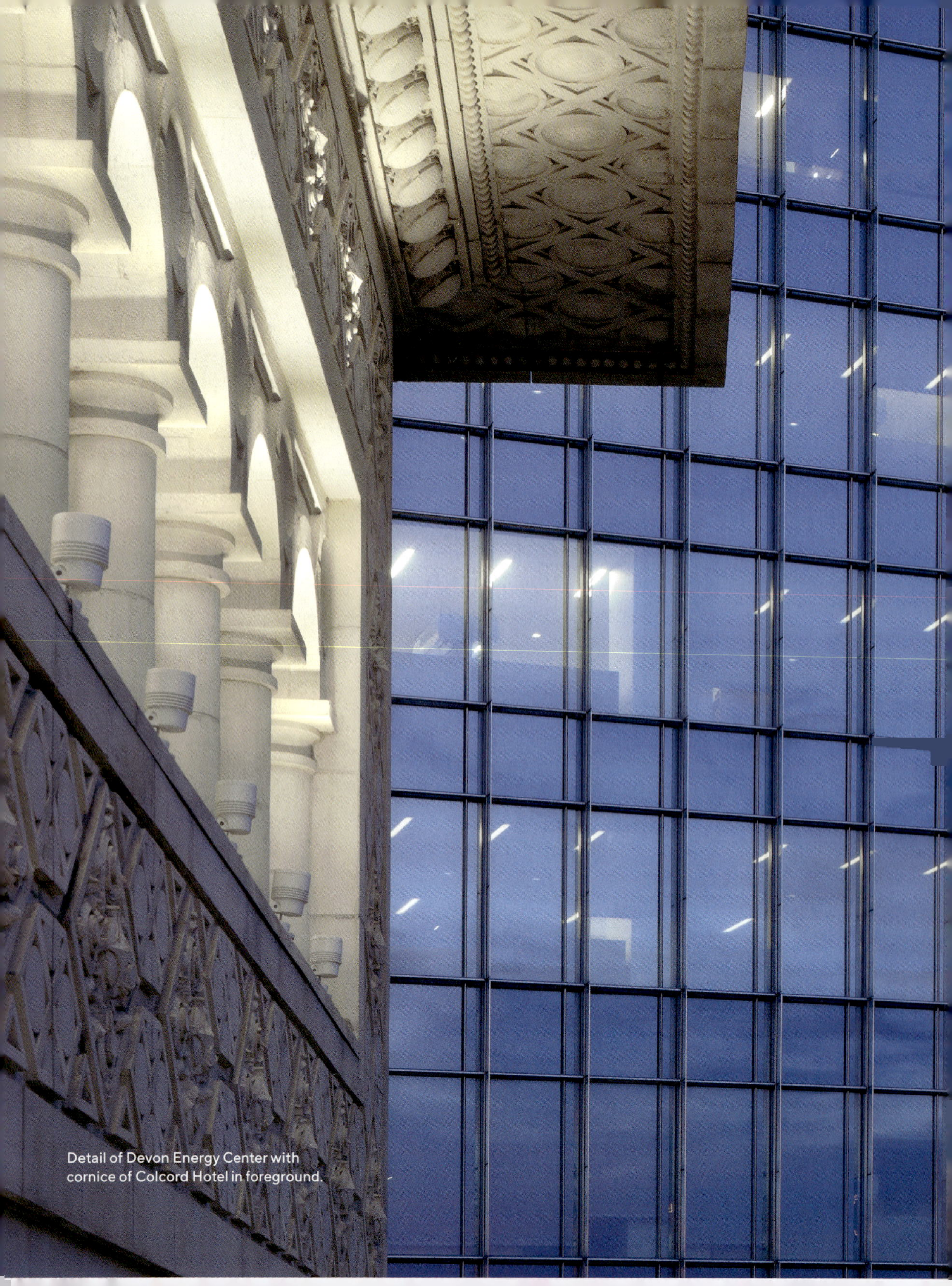

Detail of Devon Energy Center with cornice of Colcord Hotel in foreground.

Introduction

The Art of Collaboration

Michael J. Crosbie

The success or failure of the design and creation of a contemporary work of architecture depends upon something typically not discussed in architectural education, rarely considered in architectural criticism or theory, and frequently missing in most writing about architecture: human relationships. The reality is that architecture is the result of interactions that transpire between scores of people involved in bringing a design from its embryonic state to its execution in three dimensions, to live in the fourth dimension — time. For complex projects, thousands of people might be involved. Clients, architects, consultants, and project teams gather around a shared goal of breathing life into a new work of architecture.

The strongest of these human relationships is usually between architects and their clients. Ideally, the architecture they create together should rest on a foundation of collaboration. Such partnerships blossom or wither based on the dozens of professional interactions over the life of the project. Pickard Chilton has found over a span of nearly 25 years of practice (one might describe it as "responsive practice") that relationships between clients and architects (not to mention other project-team members) are best cultivated through seven elements of collaboration: listening, rapport, learning, building consensus, representation, mutual trust, and attention to time and place. The process of defining these elements of collaboration between the architects and their clients is a deliberative one. Once defined and expressed, these elements need to be refined, fostered, nurtured, and protected during the working relationship (sometimes over many years). In such collaborative relationships, the architects and the clients might appear like gardeners working together over the same patch of earth. Their collaboration enriches the architecture, and also helps their relationship to thrive. Beyond trust and understanding, these architects have found that such collaborative relationships help them to create an architecture not only well suited to the clients' functional needs and aspirations. These human relationships also sustain ongoing collaborations across many years and many projects.

This book seeks to redress the dearth of attention paid to understanding architecture as the art of collaboration between clients and architects by describing how Pickard Chilton approaches the design process to allow a nuanced understanding and appreciation of the client's worldview and values that are reflected in the finished architecture. The firm's focus on architecture as the art of collaboration with their clients permeates their practice and is a sustaining portal through which the architects come to know who they are working with, an understanding that serves to validate the architectural solution as a response to the values articulated by the client. An offering to other architectural practitioners and prospective clients of a model of the art of collaboration and the benefits that flow from it, a range of built and in-process works with various clients and at a variety of scales, complexity, and locations are discussed within the context of the art of collaboration that distinguishes the firm's approach to architecture. These are organized into seven chapters, each of which explore one of the seven collaborative elements that are part of the firm's approach, how they are understood by the clients and architects alike, and their expression through architectural design. The seven collaborative elements are as follows:

Listening Both clients and architects listen, but architects strive to be active listeners. They know when to stay quiet in conversation with clients. Architects are not wary of silences in exchanges with the client.

Rapport This allows for the easy and comfortable exchange of information and ideas between clients and architects. Rapport is key in communication and it is part of trust. It facilitates and makes space for candid and sometimes difficult conversations.

Learning Architects always learn from their clients. The experience of creating a project together presents architects with multiple opportunities to learn, to challenge their own and the client's assumptions, and to arrive at new understandings.

Building Consensus Every project potentially results from a give and take of ideas. Ultimately, the architecture reflects the ideas of both parties, with ideas sometimes entwined in ways that make the result greater than their sum. The product is consensus — the outcome of collaboration.

Representation To explore design ideas, a wide range of representation techniques are used by architects, clients, consultants, and others to communicate on many levels over the life of the project and the course of collaboration.

Mutual Trust Clients and architects strive to understand each other's values (even if they are not necessarily shared) as a way to build mutual trust in each other and their work on a project.

Mutual trust is the foundation upon which clients and architects build their relationships and their projects.

Conceptual sketch of the skylit central atrium of the CalPERS Headquarters Complex.

Time and Place Working through the process with client-collaborators, these architects ultimately seek to create architecture that is just the right solution for its time and its place, continuing the tradition of such architects as Eero Saarinen, Kevin Roche, and Cesar Pelli, patriarchs of this approach to creating architecture.

Each key element of the art of collaboration is discussed in the following chapters, which present different projects within the context of the collaborative process. Unlike most architecture books, this one places emphasis on capturing the client's worldview. As such, each chapter presents the art of collaboration in the voice of the client as they recount their experiences of design and construction within this process.

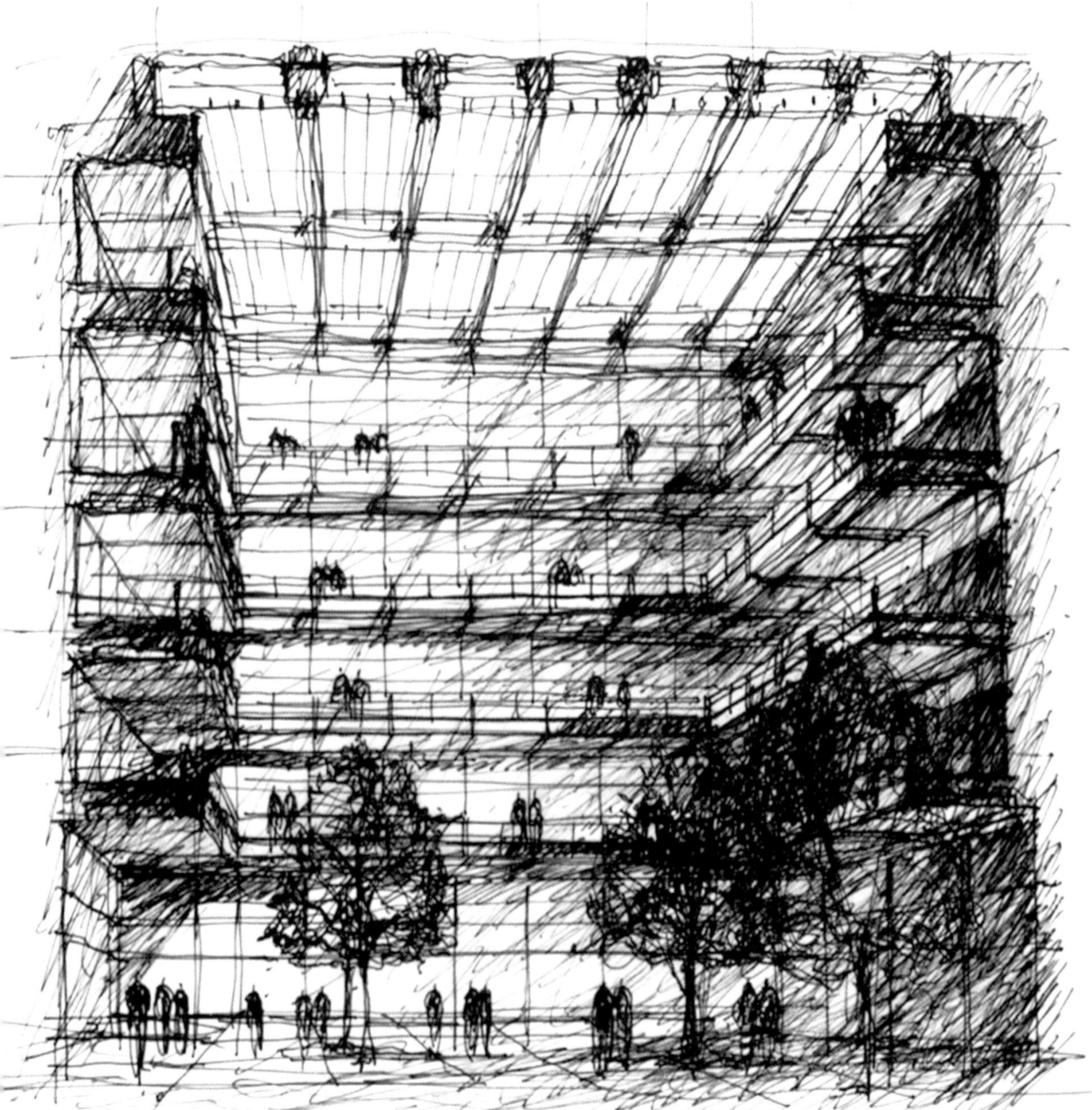

Listening

EATON HOUSE

Eaton
The Richard E. Jacobs Group
Pickard Chilton
MCA Architects
ka Architecture
Barrett Mahony Consulting Engineers
Homan O'Brien Associates
Sisk
Mitchell + Associates
Tom Phillips + Associates
Michael Slattery Associates
AWN Consulting
Pritchard Themis Ltd
Meehan Associates
Integrated Environmental Solutions
J.V. Tierney & Co.
QA Design

Clients and architects listen, but the architect should be an active listener, recognizing that every exchange with a client is an opportunity to learn something new.

How is the architect an active listener?
One technique is to keep asking questions.
If the architect asks lots of them, better insight may be gained into the client as a collaborator and the focus of their work together: to create an environment the design of which reflects the quality of the listening and understanding. The questions asked are often not obvious ones. They might challenge the client to think about one's design needs in new ways: a question that might never have occurred to them. The architect as an active listener not only hears the words, but pays attention to nonverbal cues as well (body language, eye contact, hand and head movements).

The architects verbally and nonverbally reflect back to their interlocutor that they have been heard and understood, which is the start of building rapport, trust, learning, and consensus.

The practice of active listening also keeps the client relationship continuously evolving. What are the hallmarks of an architect who is an active listener? Often, the architects describe it as "leaning in," tracking who they are listening to. If architects do not employ this kind of body language, they might not communicate that they are actively listening to the exchange of information. A client who sees that you are listening actively feels that they are being heard.

How does the architect learn to listen actively — are there "listening habits" that aid one in interactions with clients and in creating architecture? When Pickard Chilton starts working with a new client, they have an idea of what to listen for in a meeting, for instance. This is called "targeted listening," seeking specific information conveyed by clients and consultants that can create a clearer picture with more detail. A "general picture" or a "road map" of a project and a client's agenda is typically

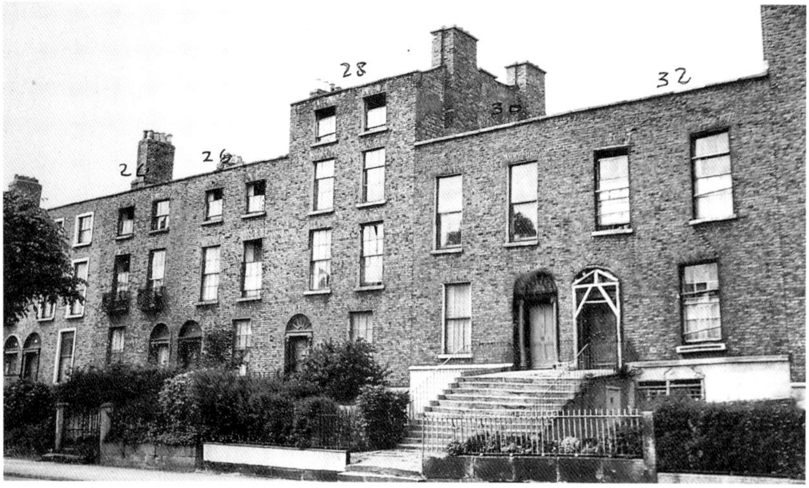

Undated photograph depicting a row of historic Georgian houses in Dublin.

provided to architects. But the long-term goal of client interactions is to fill in the blanks in an effort to achieve a more nuanced vision of a design that meets all the client's wishes.

How is active listening reflected in the architecture? One approach that resonates with many Pickard Chilton clients is a departure from classic architect behavior (inculcated in design school), which takes this tack: "I'm going to show you a solution and this is the only way." Instead, Pickard Chilton starts with a desire to listen and understand what the client wants to accomplish. The result of a design should be: This is what we heard from you.

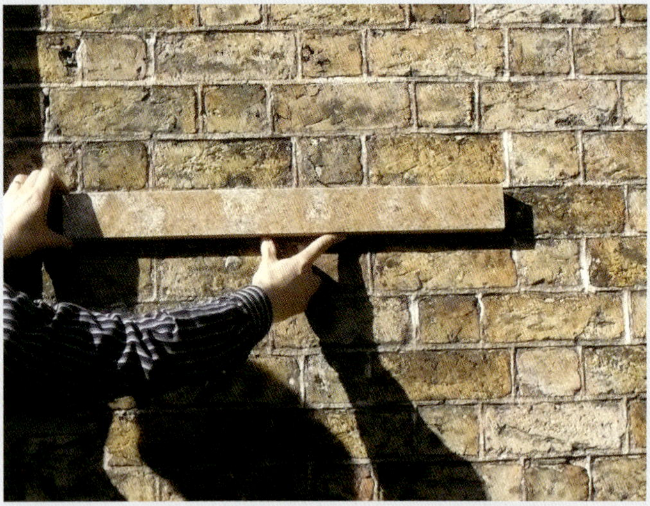
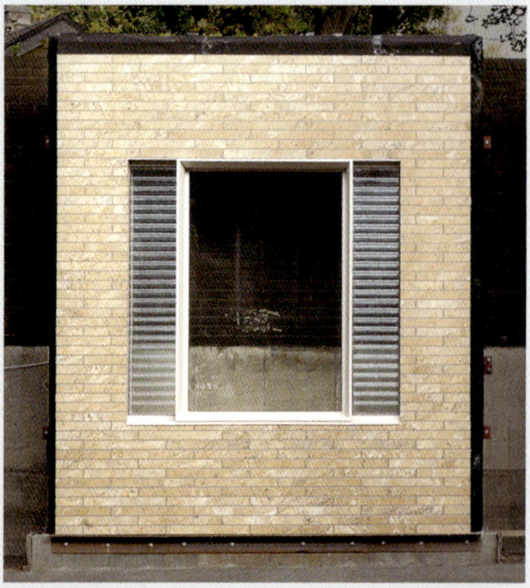
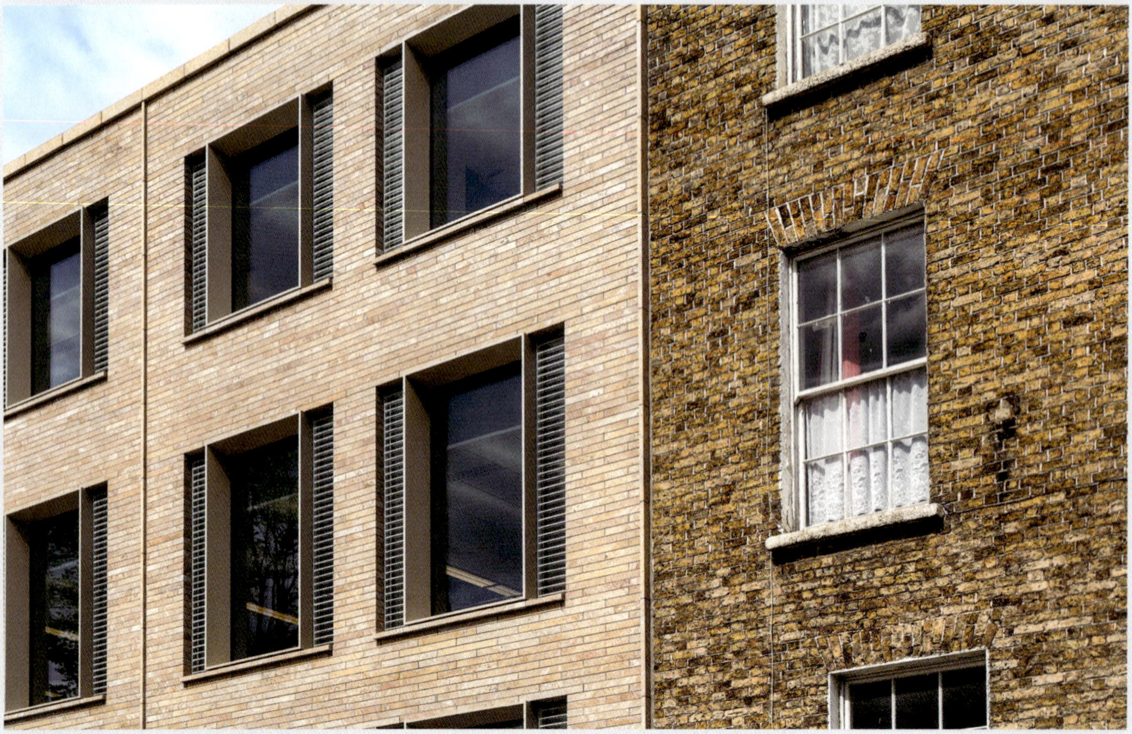

Comparison of stone sample to historical brick façade; mock-up of façade; façade detail.

This provides evidence that the architect has been listening carefully to what the client believes is important, helping to make the design precise and concise.

The studio culture at Pickard Chilton places great value on active listening. The architects then validate what they have learned in listening to the client by integrating a greater breadth and depth of information, ideally picking up on the client's unique character. The architecture becomes far more interesting if it reflects an idiosyncratic quality of the client. In the Eaton House project in Dublin, Ireland, the city's goal was for the building to be of its time and respectful of its historical context. Although the existing early 19th-century terrace housing adjacent to Eaton House was brick, the proposed façade was stone instead of brick as suggested by Eaton's project executive, Sue Cook, who considered stone a more appropriate material for a headquarters.

The reaction of the client and design team was to be sensitive to this feedback, to have empathy with the position of the city and neighborhood, and to further develop the design so that it is a sympathetic yet distinctive design response.

"I don't think we would have received approval for the stone if it hadn't been for Pickard Chilton," says Cook. "The proposed stone is granite. The stone was designed to be cut to the height of a brick, but longer, and the color was complementary with the terrace housing brick next door that's 200 years old." Full-scale mock-ups of portions of the façade were built, one in brick, the other in stone. When reviewed with the city and the neighbors, there was consensus that in this application, stone would be an appropriate material.

The new Eaton headquarters is respectfully integrated with the existing historical architecture of Pembroke Road.

The architect should know when to stay quiet in his or her exchanges with the client. How important are moments of quiet in one's interactions with clients, how do they add value? In active listening, the architects note that silences can be just as important as what is conveyed verbally. Sometimes, what is not said can lead to a deeper understanding of the client's own value system. The lesson of this story about Pickard Chilton quietly listening closely to the clients, review officials, and neighbors in Dublin is that it is often wise to be silent, lest a message not be heard. This is not a quality generally valued in architectural education,

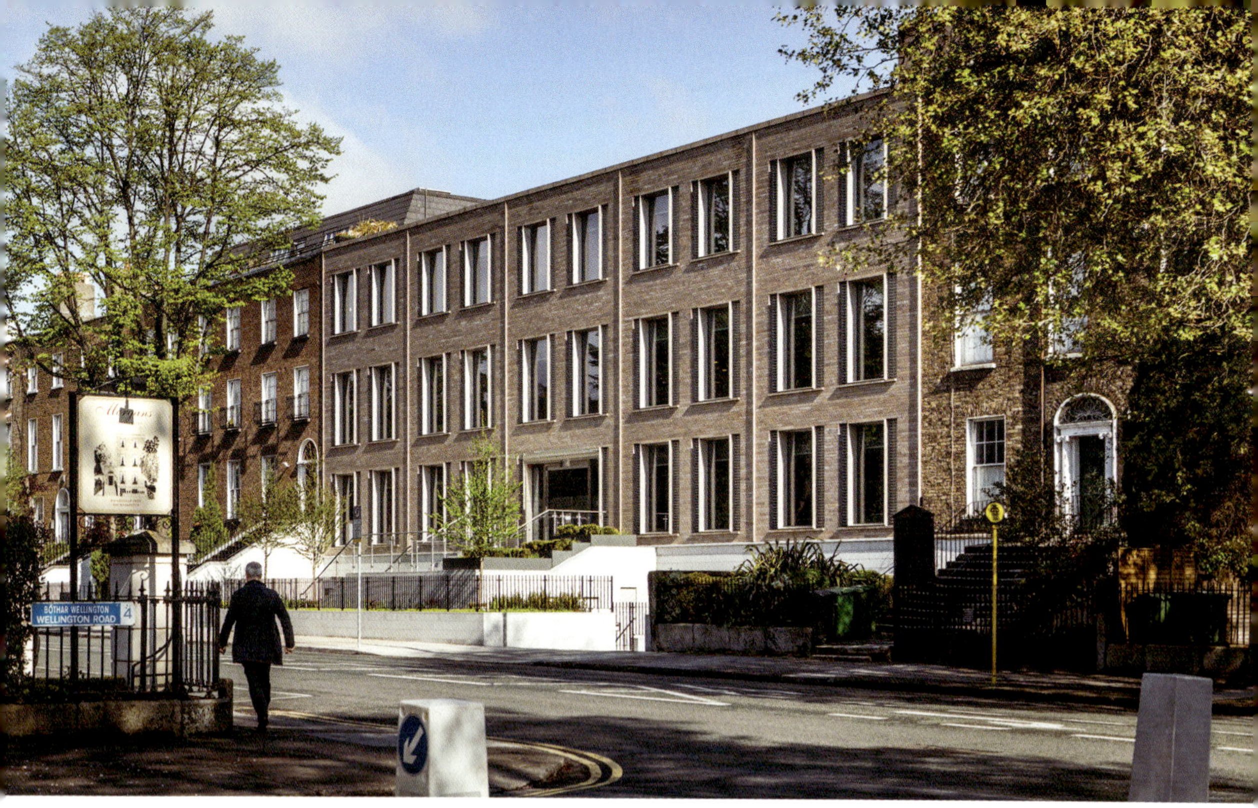

where students and critics often avoid uncomfortable "dead air" in critiques or presentations. The value of silence is often overlooked in the design process.

Sue Cook sums up her experience this way: "For anybody who's going to do a project like this, I think the important thing is to get a good team together. And I really do believe in my heart that if somebody picks Pickard Chilton, that's a pretty good first step on building a good team."

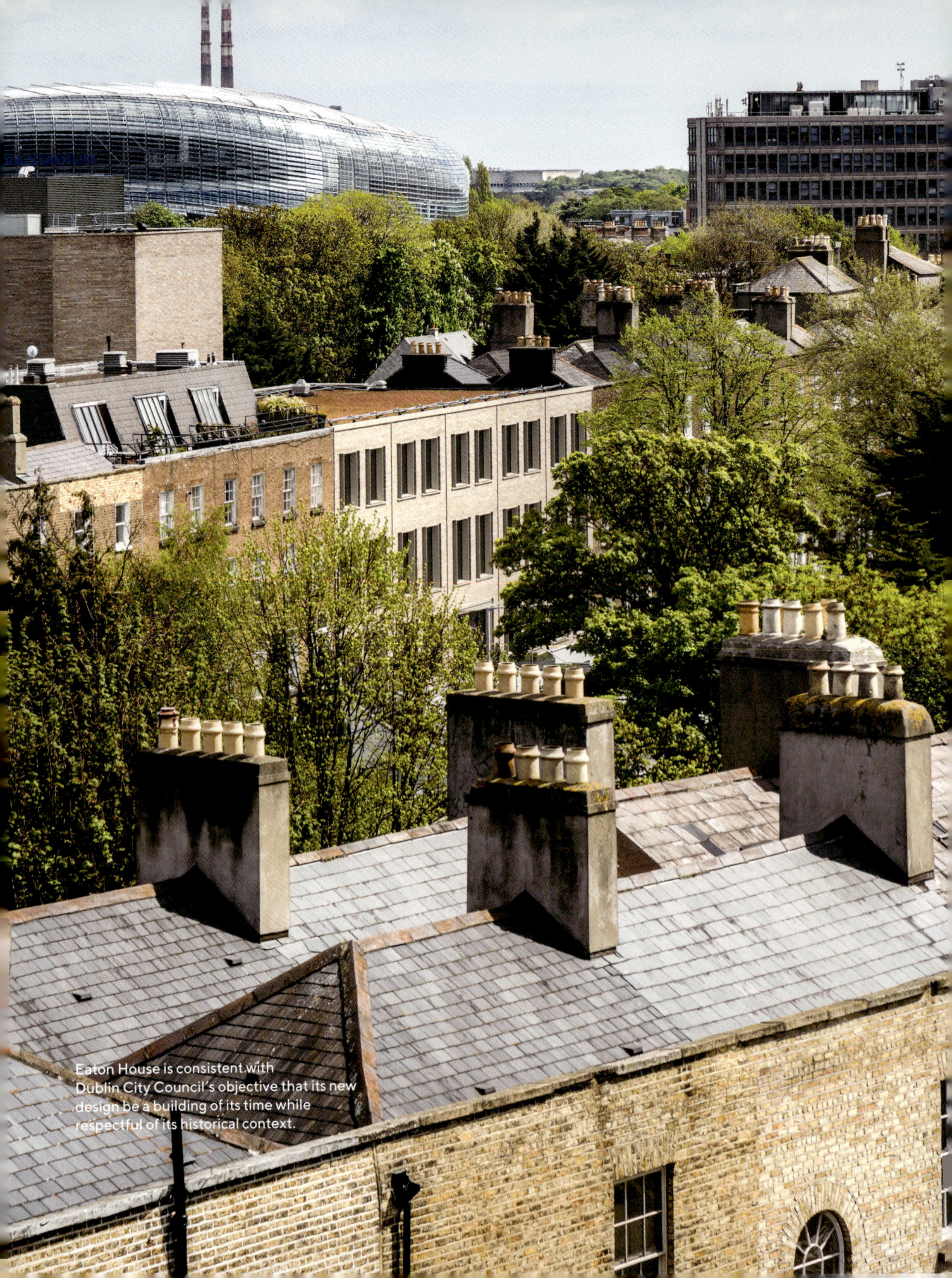

Eaton House is consistent with Dublin City Council's objective that its new design be a building of its time while respectful of its historical context.

In active listening ... silences can be just as important as what is conveyed verbally.

EATON HOUSE
DUBLIN, IRELAND

Completed 2015
33,000 gross square feet / 3,065 gross square meters
LEED for New Construction Gold

Located in Dublin's historic D4 district, Eaton House serves as Eaton's new global headquarters. It is located in an early 19th-century Georgian neighborhood, a rich tapestry of residences, small businesses, parks, and embassies. The site's original five terrace houses from the 1830s were demolished and a new building constructed in 1970.

Reusing much of the 1970 building's concrete frame, Eaton House is designed to be a building of its time while respectful of its historical context, but re-envisions the exterior enclosure in linear coursed stone, clear vision glass, and handmade cast-glass bricks.

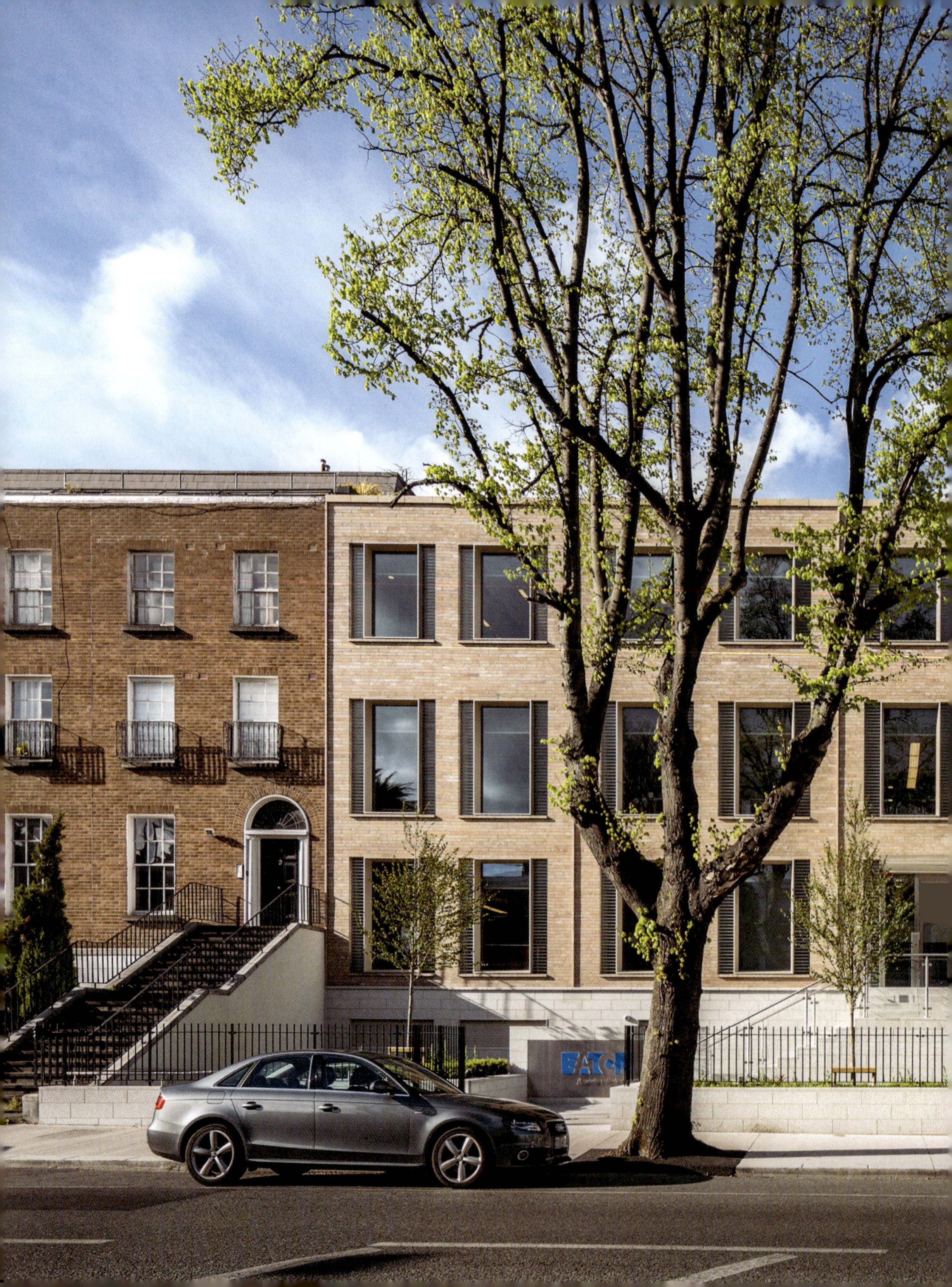

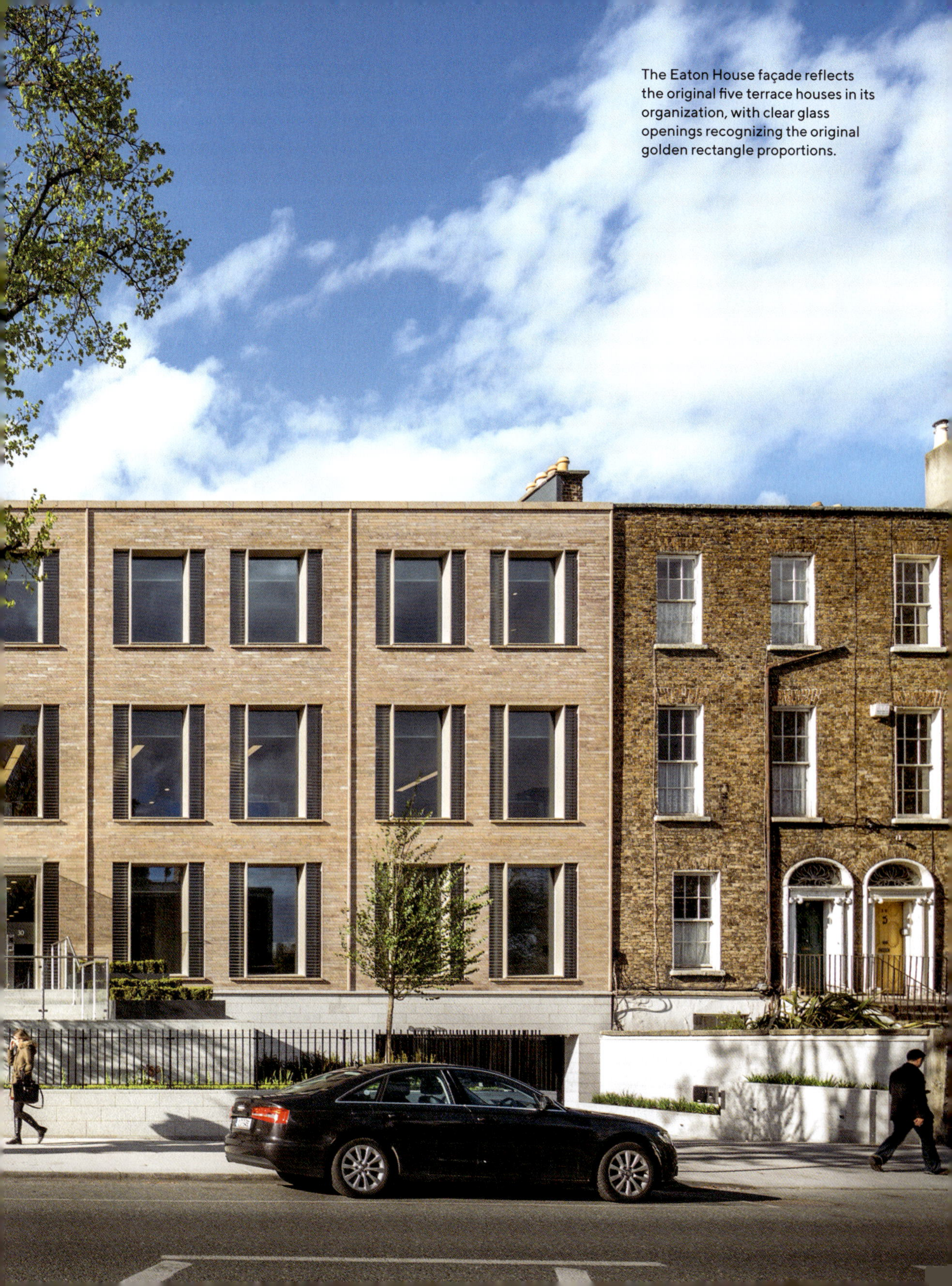

The Eaton House façade reflects the original five terrace houses in its organization, with clear glass openings recognizing the original golden rectangle proportions.

The introduction of cast-glass brick to the sides of the windows resulted in a 38 percent increase in daylight.

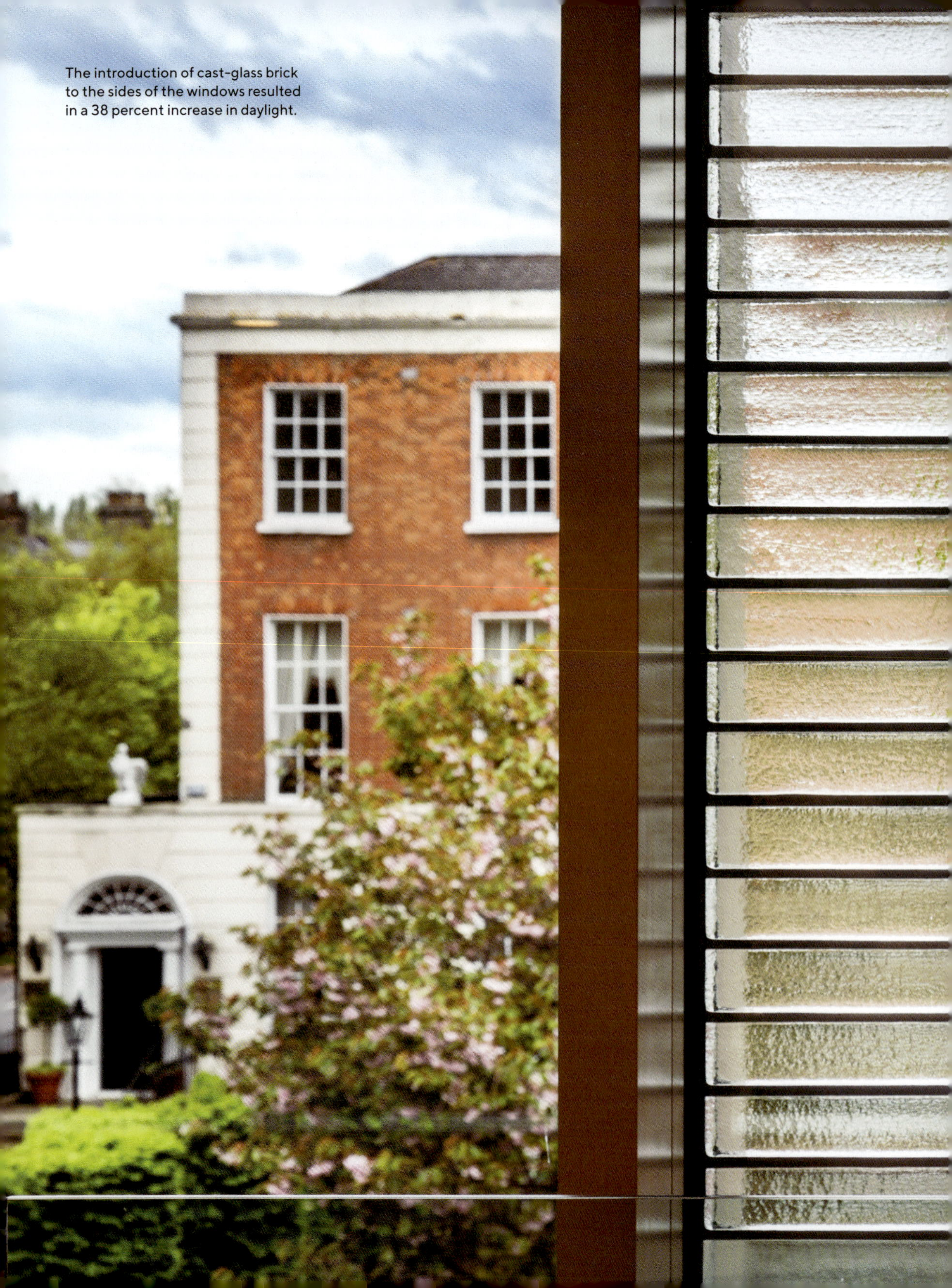

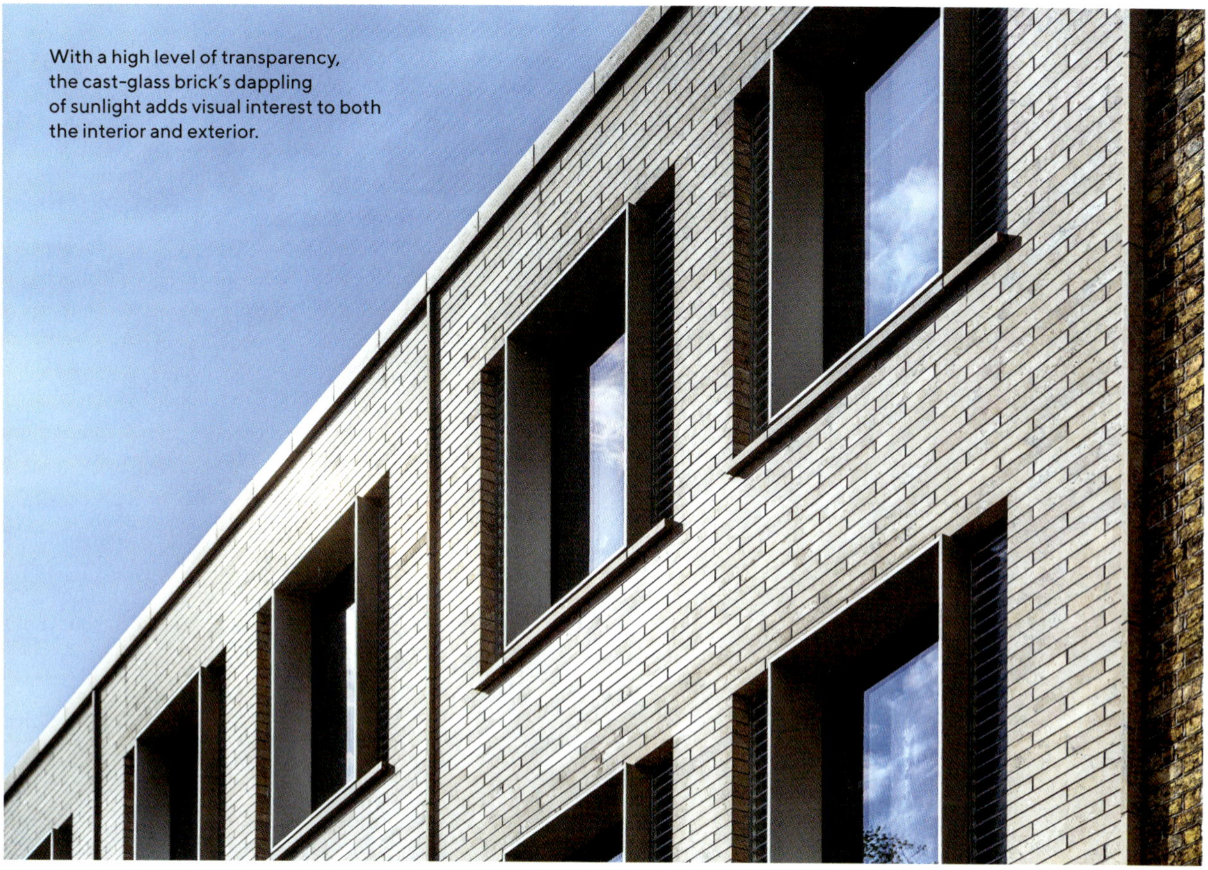

With a high level of transparency, the cast-glass brick's dappling of sunlight adds visual interest to both the interior and exterior.

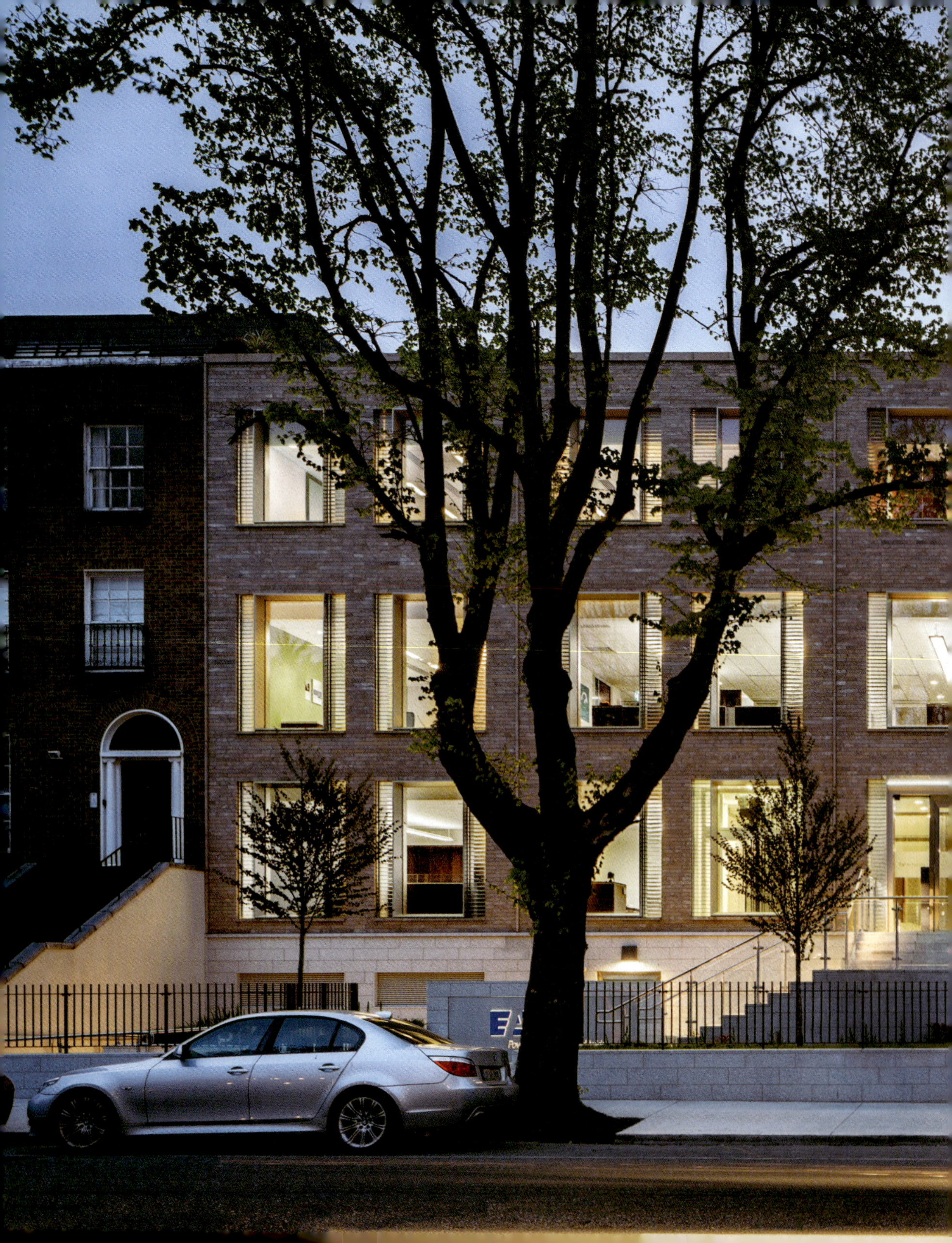

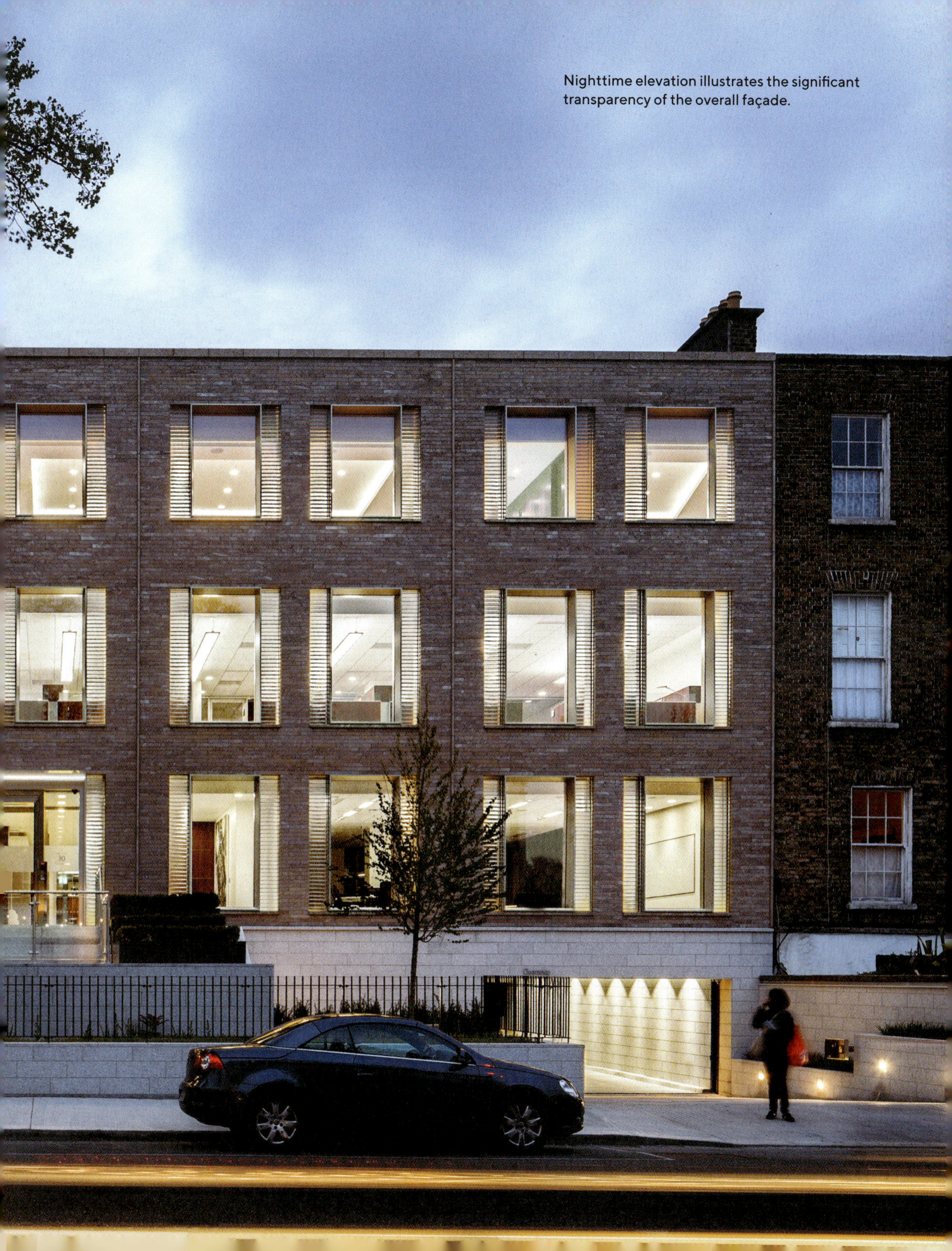

Nighttime elevation illustrates the significant transparency of the overall façade.

Rapport

THE RO

Parcel 1

Transwestern Development Company
Pickard Chilton
The Preston Partnership
Cardno
Jordan & Skala Engineers
Mayfield and Ragni Studio
OJB Landscape Architecture
Lerch Bates

Parcel 2

Transwestern Development Company
Pickard Chilton
Spear Street Capital
Kendall/Heaton Associates
Cardno
I.A. Naman + Associates
Hargreaves Associates
OneLux

2+U

Skanska USA
Pickard Chilton
Kendall/Heaton Associates
Magnusson Klemencic Associates
WSP
Swift Company
Graham Baba Architects
Coughlin Porter Lundeen
HWA Parking

THE EIGHT

Skanska USA
Pickard Chilton
Adamson Associates
Magnusson Klemencic Associates
MacDonald-Miller
Valley
Stantec
Hargreaves Associates
Jensen Hughes
Navix Engineering
Lightswitch
Graham Baba Architects

Establishing rapport between the client and the architect allows for the easy and comfortable exchange of information and ideas. Rapport is key in communication, and it is part of trust. It is also the opportunity for candid conversations. How important is it to establish rapport early in the design process? Is rapport ever discussed between the architect and the client as an important value? With whom on the client team is it most important for the architect to establish rapport? If mutual trust is threatened, is it likely that rapport is also endangered, and vice versa? How is rapport communicated between the client and the architect? How is it guarded and nurtured? How is it used to have "difficult" conversations? How is damage to rapport repaired? How is rapport reflected in the architecture?

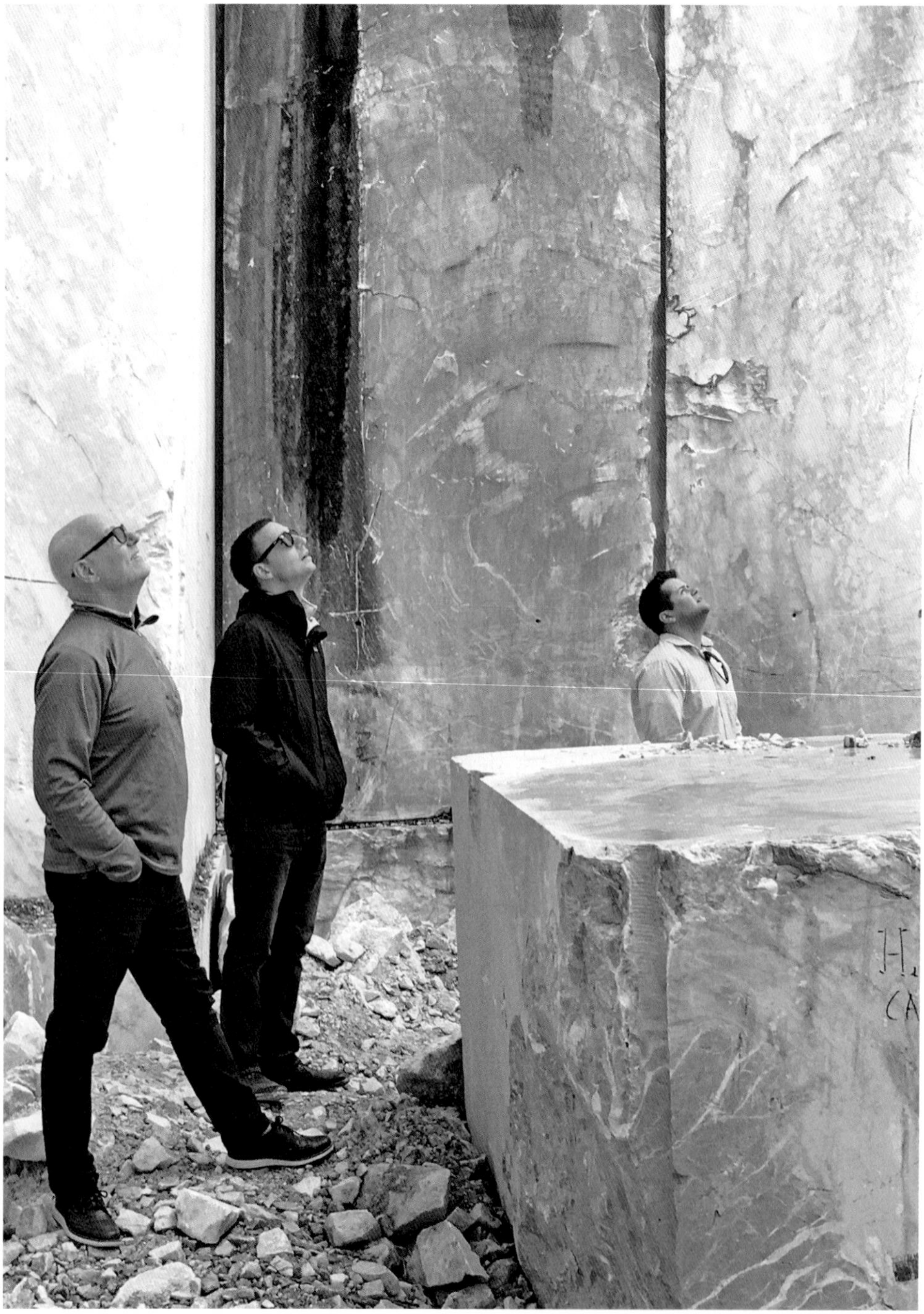

Anthony Markese touring a quarry to select stone.

The fast-paced nature of contemporary architectural practice is not a friend of establishing rapport. Rapport takes time to cultivate, to protect. It rests on trust and respect. Proximity is important. Often, rapport will suffer (or not blossom at all) if the architect and client simply don't spend enough time in each other's company. A revealing example of an opportunity to nurture rapport is the process of selecting stone for a design—something the client and architect might choose together. Rapport might crystalize on a journey with the client, such as a visit to quarries, as it did on a recent trip to Tuscany. Pickard Chilton sees this as a bonding experience, like picking out an engagement ring. Rapport advances to a new level between architect and client. The subsequent mixed-used The RO master plan (2 million square feet / 185,800 square meters in several towers on a 17-acre / 6.9-hectare site) is built upon rapport established over a more than five-year relationship.

Rapport allows for greater honesty between the client and architect, and also room to take architectural risks together. Great rapport results in understanding the limits of what you might do in a design, but it also makes the architect and client aware that there should be nothing they can't talk about, which makes "difficult" conversations less threatening and rarer. For the good of the project, challenging conversations shouldn't be avoided. The rapport built between a client and the architect can support opportunities to have such conversations, and the project will probably be better for it. Lack of rapport often leads to dead-air in a project, where the architect might feel stuck because there is no one on the client side with whom to have a candid conversation.

Hand-drawn sketches and models facilitate further exploration and understanding of The RO master plan.

Pickard Chilton has been challenged in such projects as The RO, 2+U, and The Eight to create rich, active pedestrian environments, places that fit comfortably into the neighborhood, with connections to their arty/funky/industrial contexts. To succeed, candid exchanges between clients and architects, built upon comfortable rapport, are key. Such conversations help provide constructive feedback: You guys are getting there, but you're not there yet.

"It takes a lot of trust to build rapport," says Transwestern Development Company's Managing Director Sean Suffel, who has worked with Pickard Chilton on several projects (including The RO).

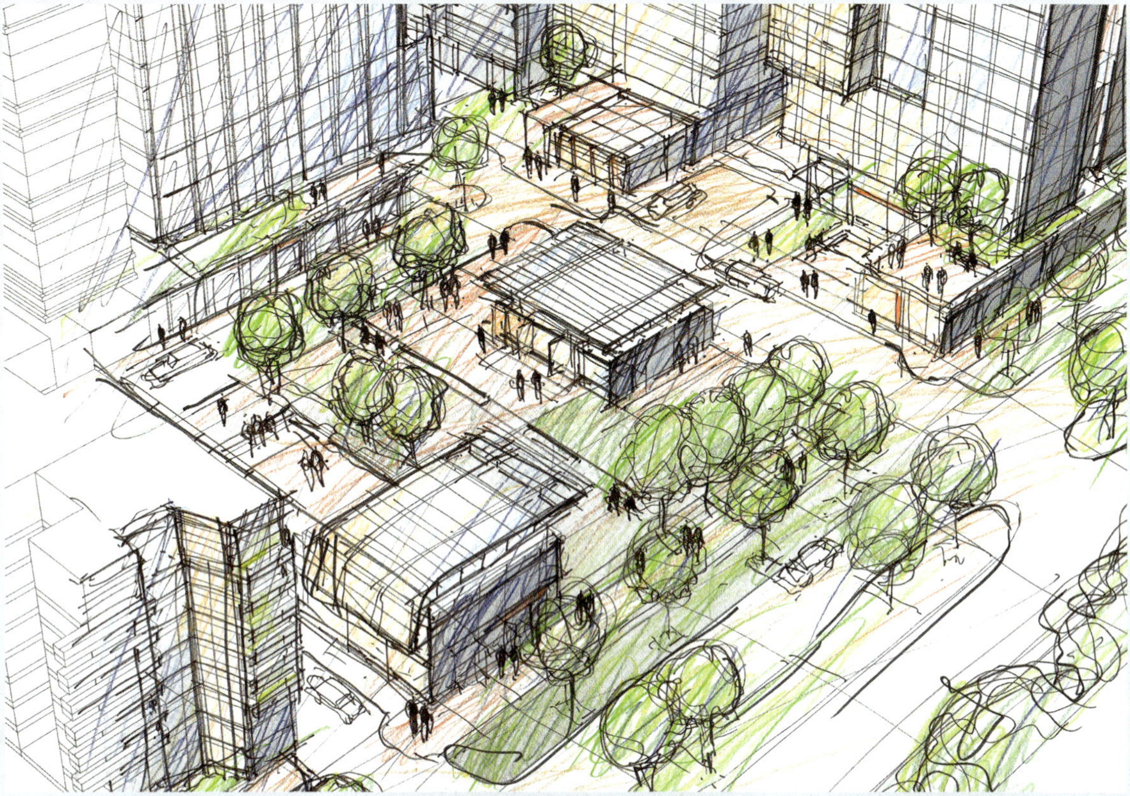

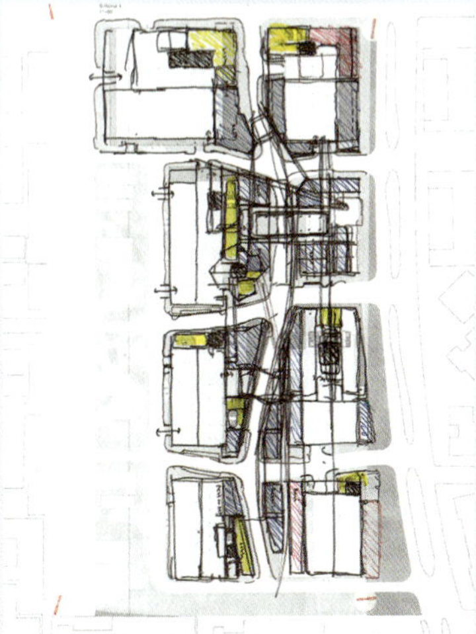

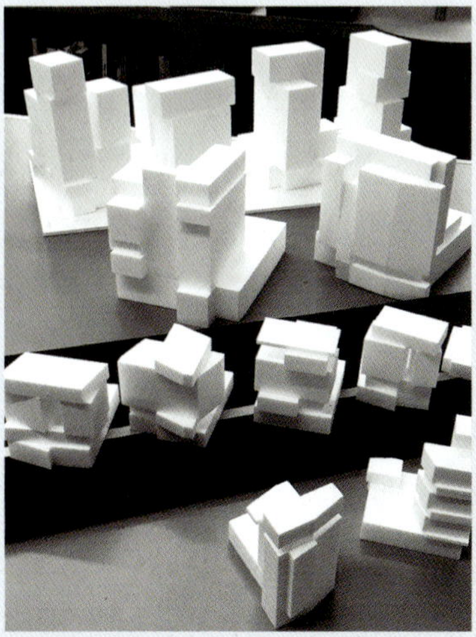

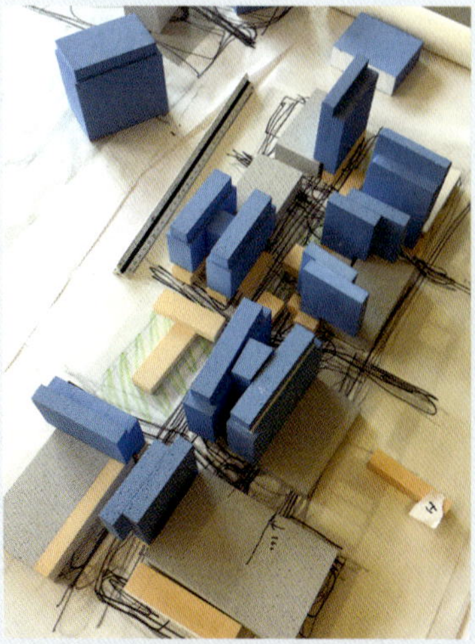

Y columns raise the 2+U tower by 85 feet / 26 meters to create and shelter the Urban Village.

Bi-weekly, protracted project meetings are an environment in which rapport either withers or grows. "That's where rapport, built upon trust and relationships, is established," recalls Suffel. The architects returned with changes to the design that showed they were paying close attention. "It was obvious they were listening, not focused on their own agenda, and took direction well," he says.

Strong rapport can also set the stage for tough questions to be asked. For instance, Transwestern worked with Pickard Chilton to compete for a project also pursued by fellow Houston-based developer Hines. Knowing the architects have history with this developer, Suffel recalls, "I had to ask, 'Is there another team in your shop working on this with Hines?' That question elicited a broader conversation that was honest, transparent, and clear," Suffel says. "Beyond their talent, they are genuine, grounded people who care deeply about their team, clients, and projects. I view them as partners."

Rapport with the client often extends into the pool of those involved in making a project happen—potential tenants, real estate brokers, community

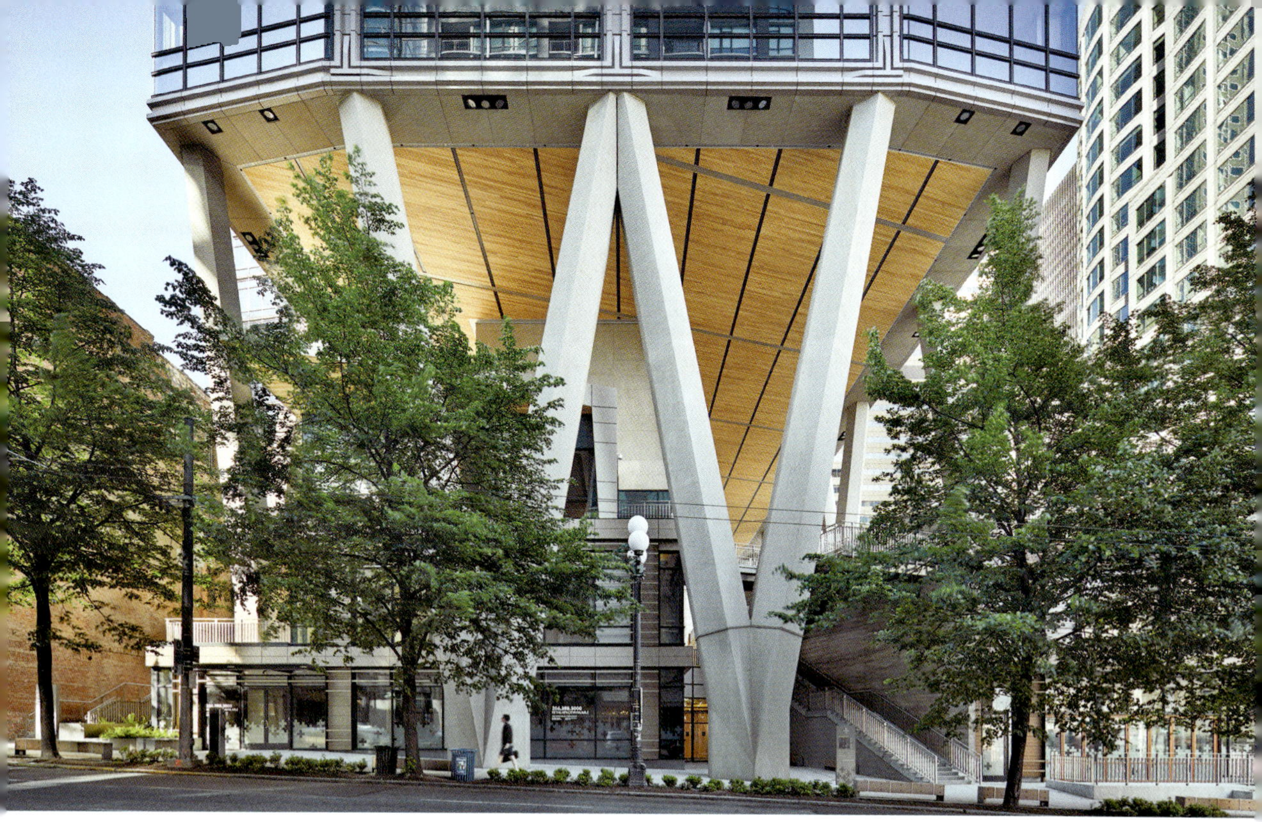

groups, and city government. "Often these people have different ideas about a project, and Pickard Chilton gets that," says Executive Vice President Murphy McCullough with the developer Skanska USA (client for 2+U and The Eight). Moving a project along while hearing and appreciating other voices in the room reflects the goal of creating something "great for the market, and also a great piece of architecture," says McCullough. The downtown Seattle site for the 2+U tower offered an opportunity to create a retail, arts, and cultural

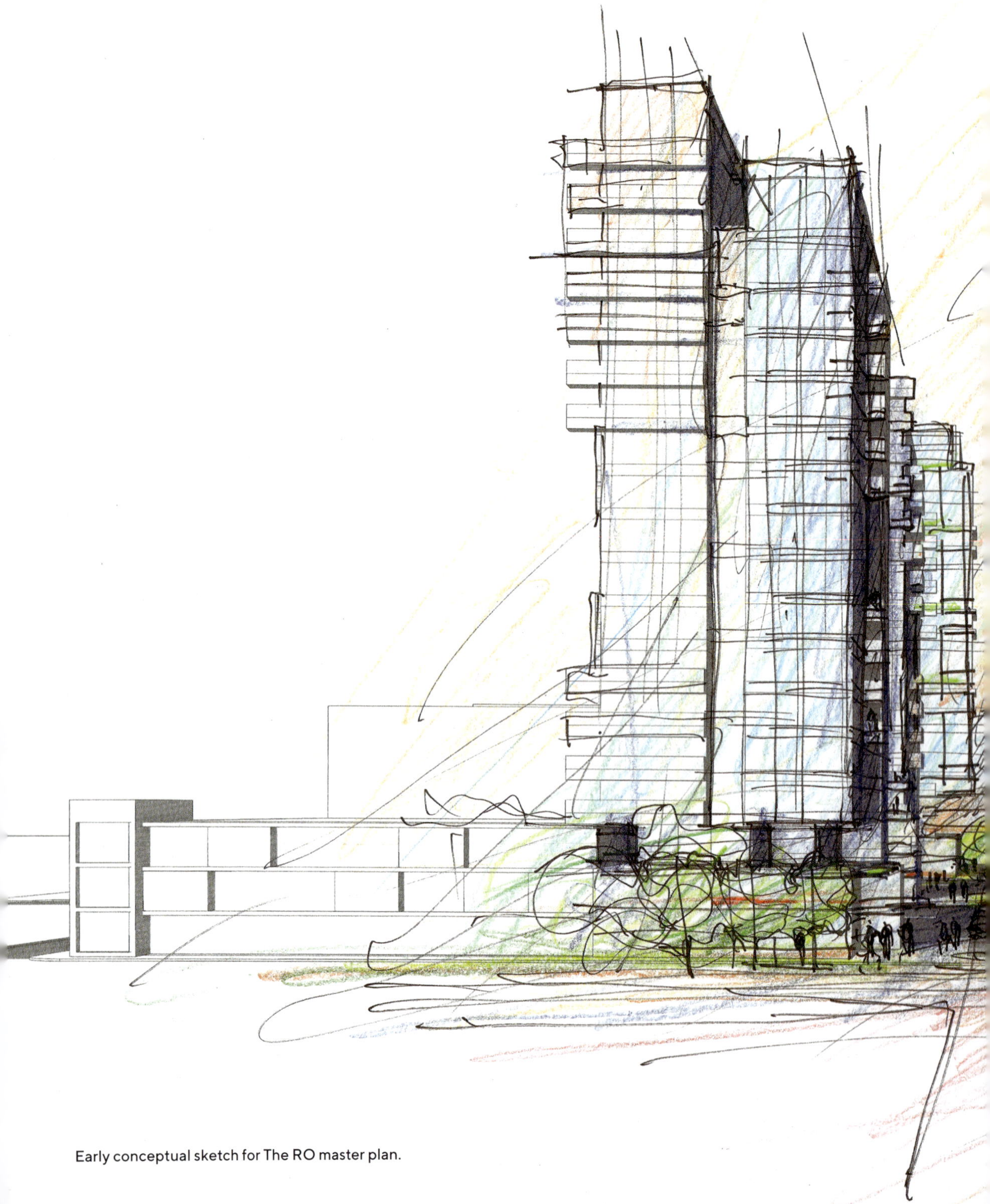

Early conceptual sketch for The RO master plan.

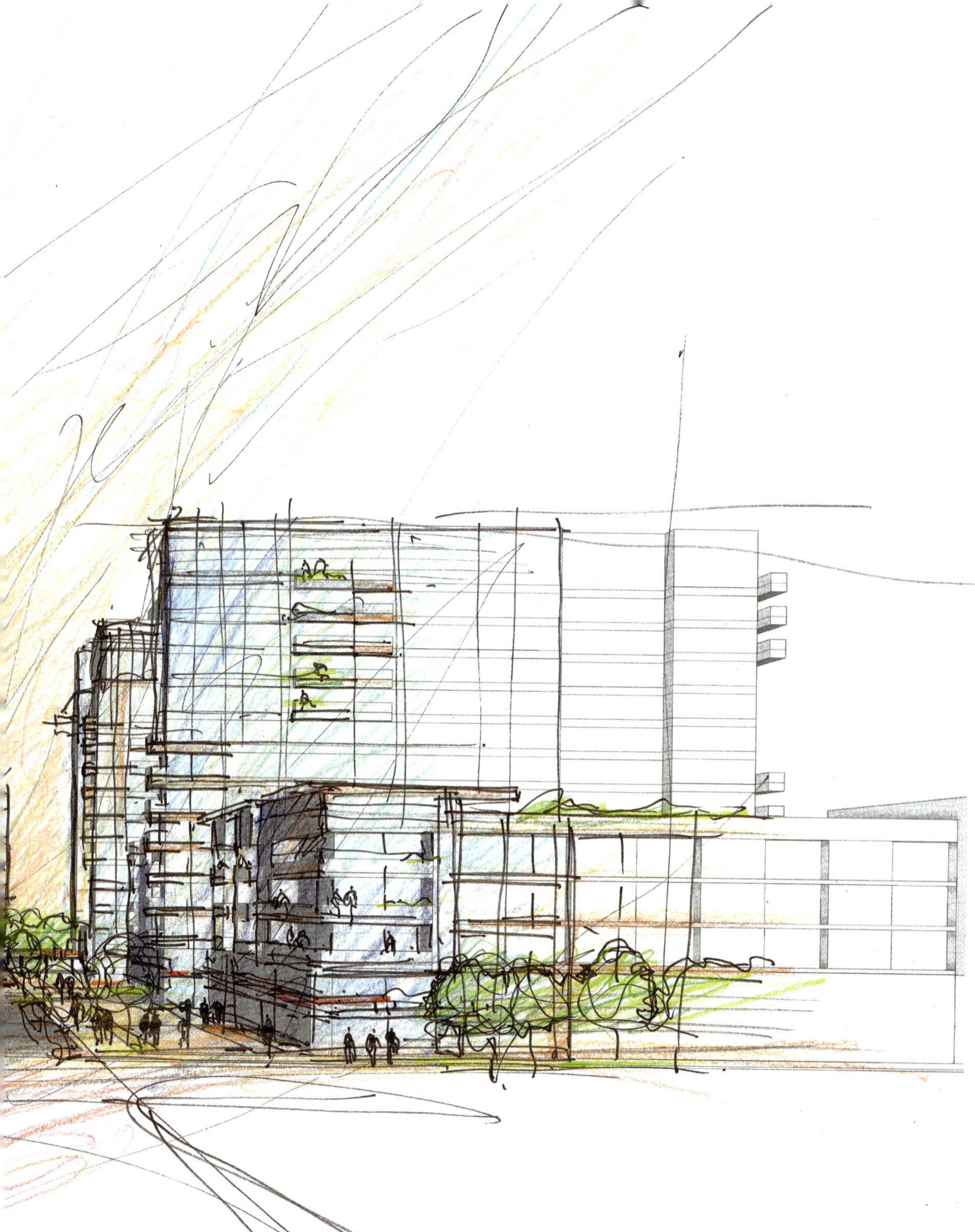

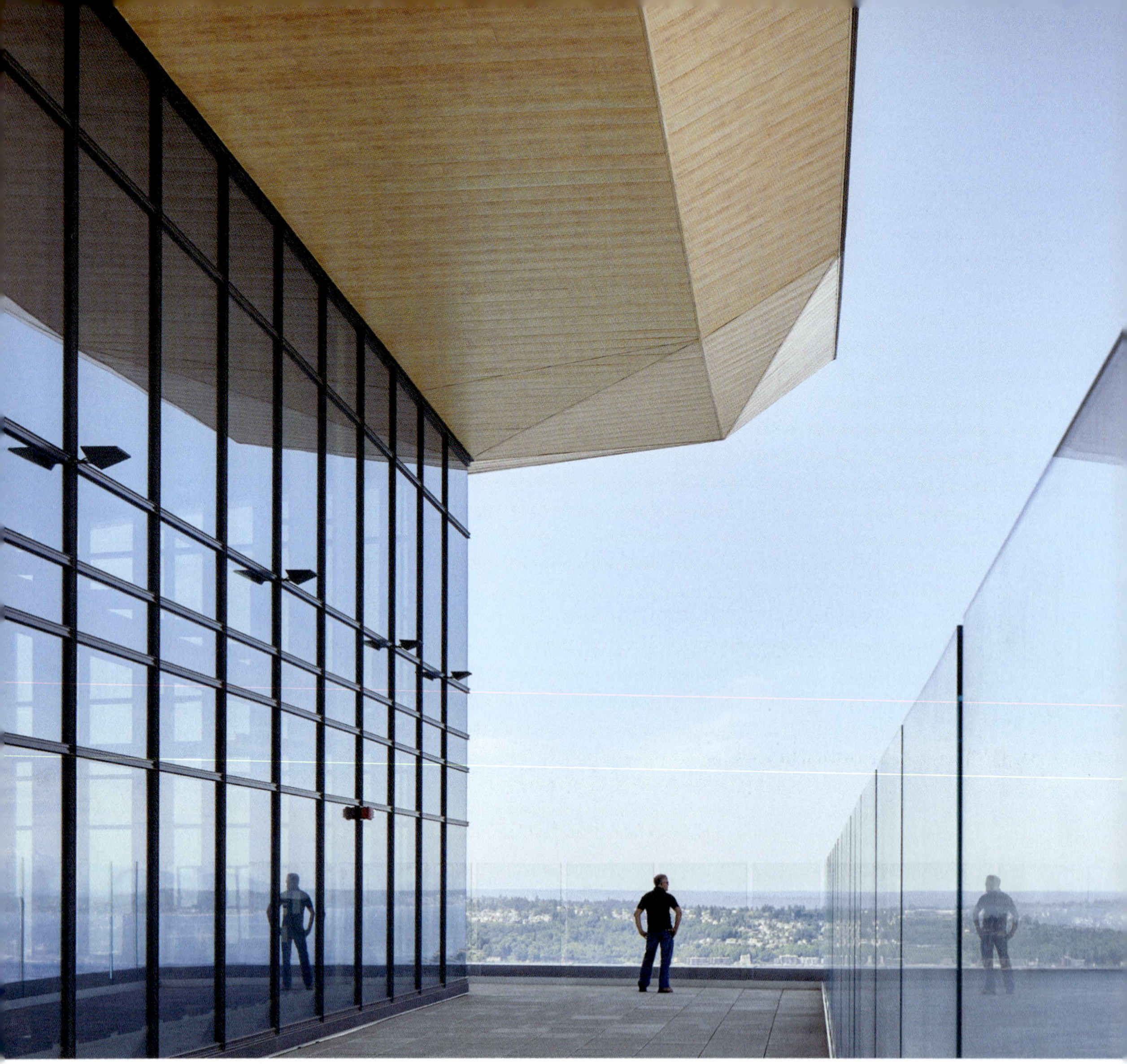

With stunning views of the bay, Mount Rainier, and downtown, the level 38 terrace of the 2+U tower is a popular tenant amenity.

scene at the base, not far from an existing museum and symphony hall. The architects proposed raising the tower 85 feet / 26 meters above the street, lending it grandeur and excitement, but also enhancing views of Elliott Bay from offices. "It shows what can happen with the power of collaboration and rapport," comments McCullough.

When rapport is threatened, rather than closing down, Pickard Chilton opens up. McCullough relates the story of a misunderstanding between Skanska's project team and the architects that cast a pall over the design process. In a phone conversation, a Pickard Chilton principal expressed concern over the role of another project team member, and McCullough explained that they were part of the mix in hopes of creating the best design possible. The principal was on a flight from Connecticut the next morning and in Skanska's Seattle offices that afternoon to ensure the open rapport between them was not damaged. "It's hard to describe what that means to us," says McCullough of the firm's dedication to their client. "To have an architect that committed to preserving the relationship is amazing."

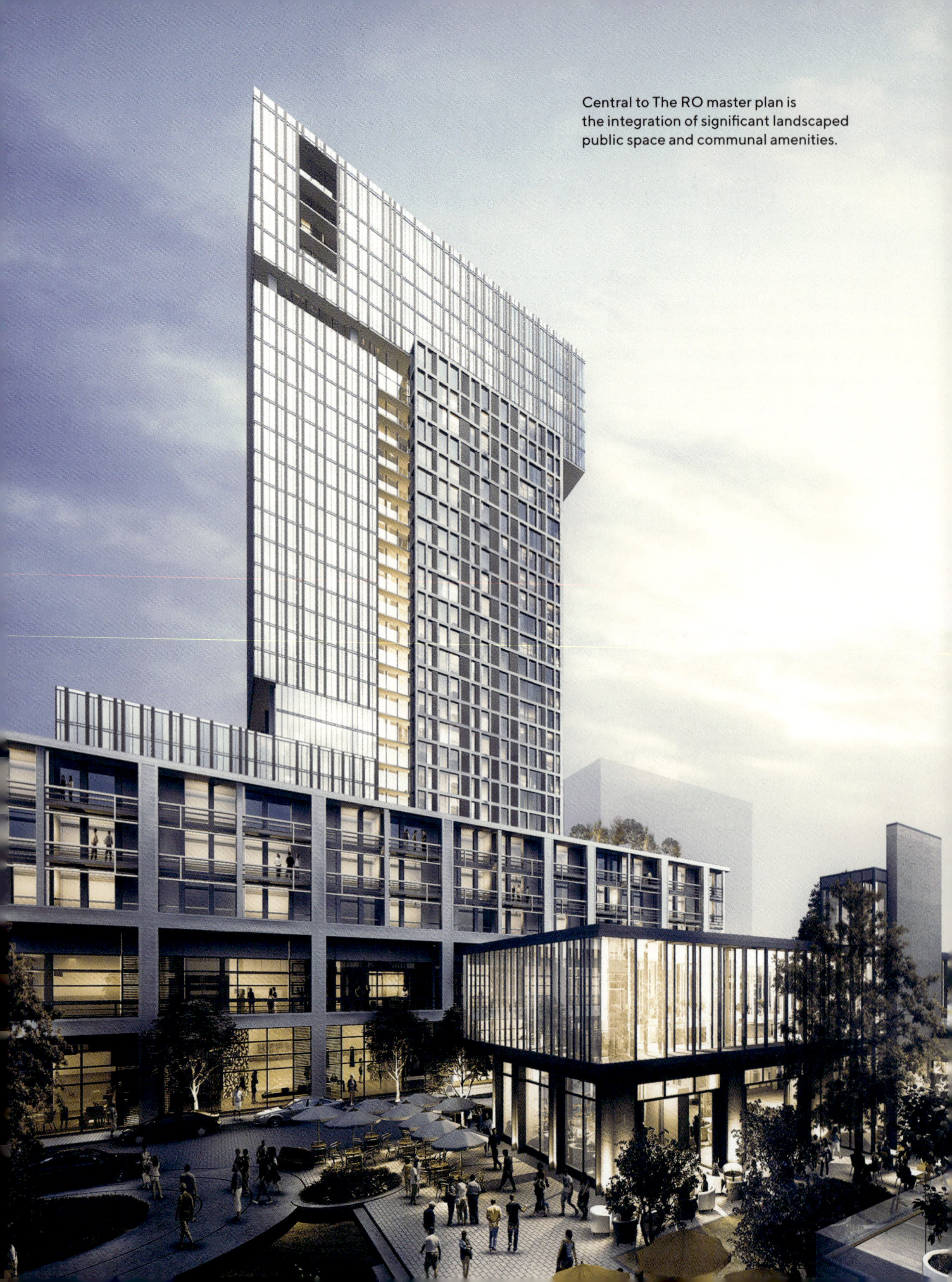

Central to The RO master plan is the integration of significant landscaped public space and communal amenities.

"It became obvious that they were listening."

Sean Suffel
Managing Director, Transwestern Development Company

THE RO
HOUSTON, TEXAS

Master Plan completed 2017
3 million gross square feet / 279,000 gross square meters
80,000 square feet / 7,450 square meters of curated retail

The RO has been master-planned as a best-in-class, urban, multi-use destination on a 17-acre/6.9-hectare site near the affluent Greenway Plaza and River Oaks Districts. Purposefully designed to contrast with a contrived "town center," the vision for this organically phased development is to create a complimentary, high-density environment.

Intended to engage empty nesters and millennials alike, the first phase of the development features a 36-story luxury multifamily high-rise comprising rental units atop a four-story podium and a 300,000-gross-square-foot / 28,000-gross-square-meter office tower offering significant Class AA creative and flexible office space. Maximizing density and flexibility, the design takes advantage of shared access points and shared parking while retaining and enhancing view corridors.

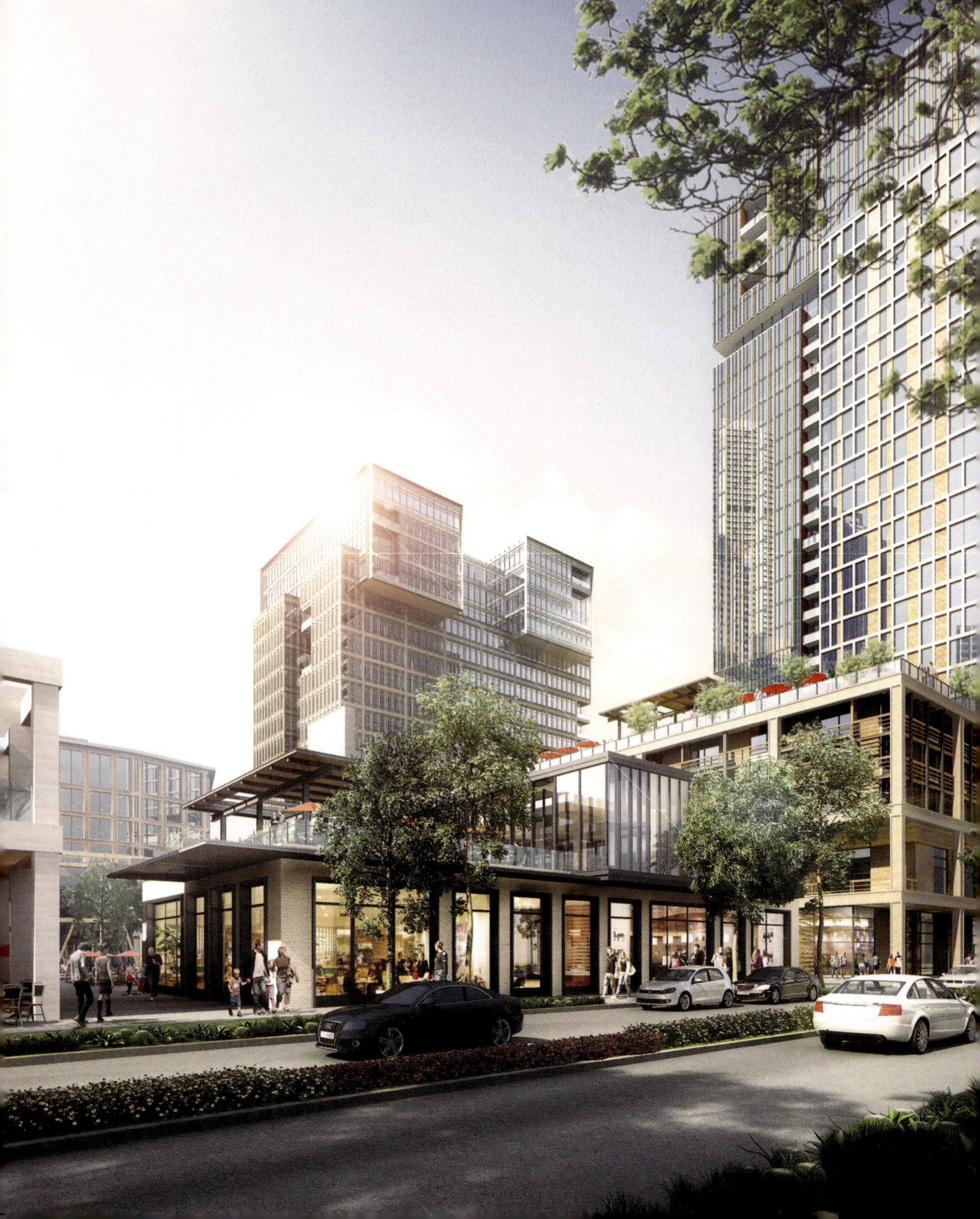

Buildings of varying scale and density enrich the urban experience around The RO.

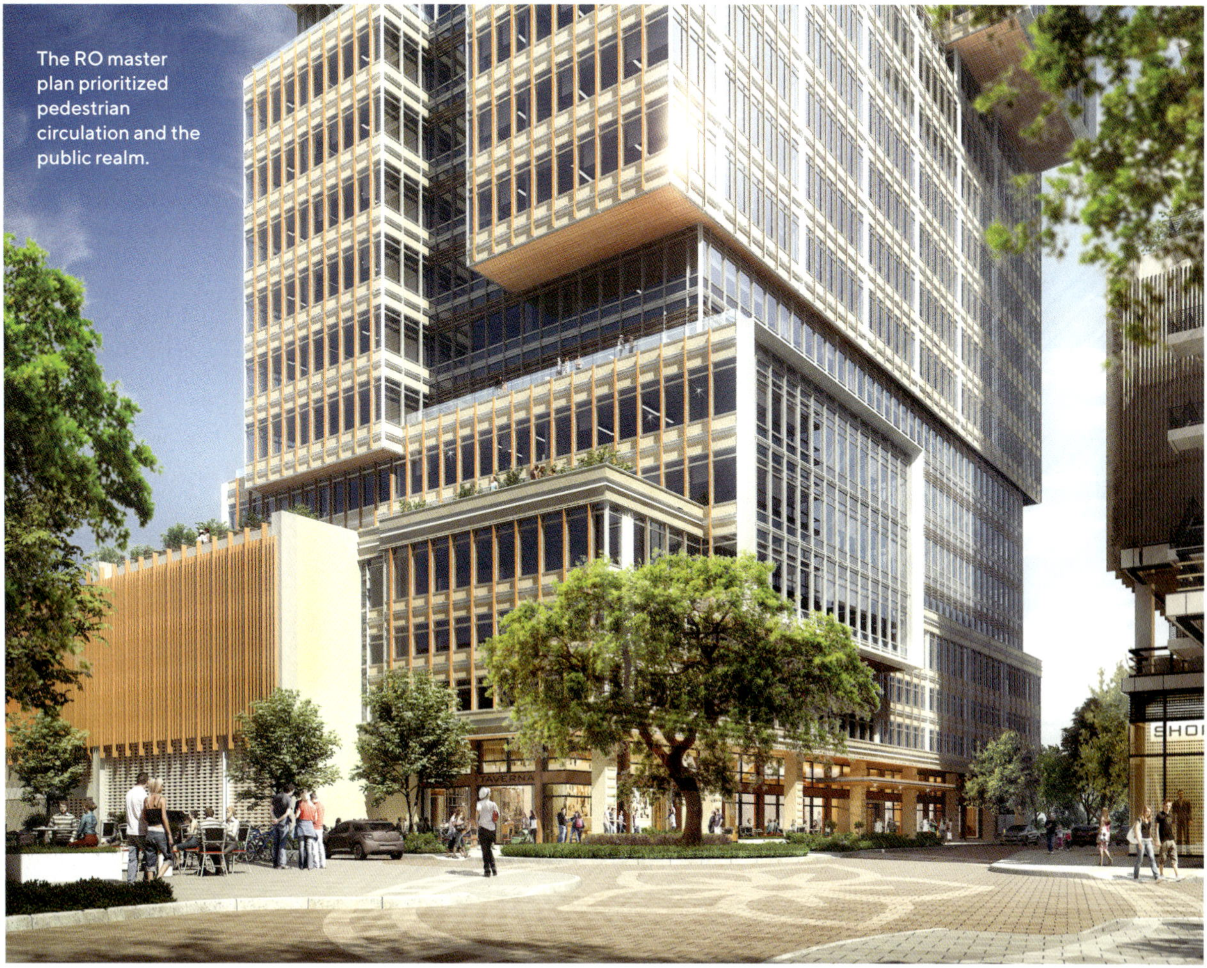

The RO master plan prioritized pedestrian circulation and the public realm.

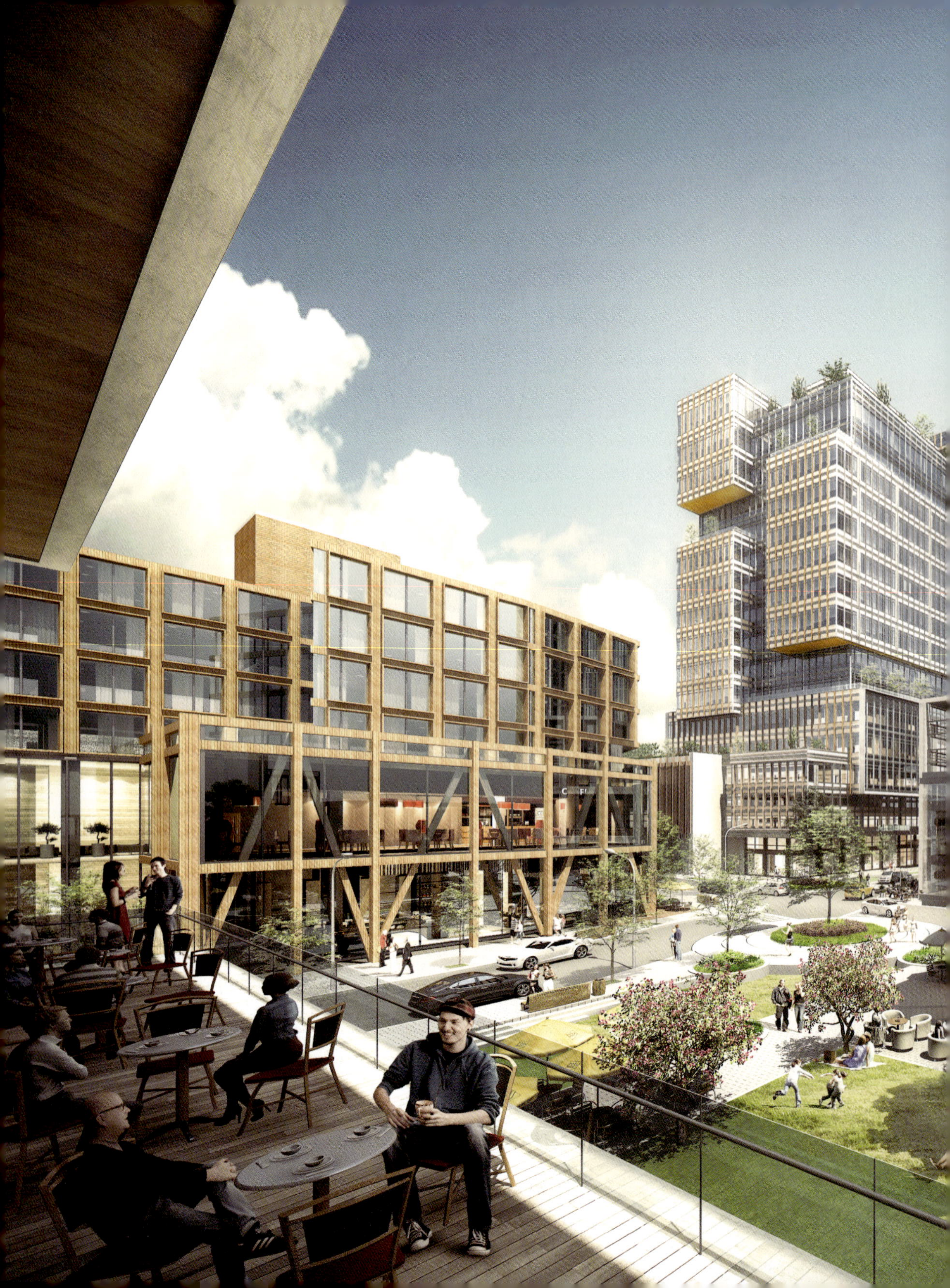

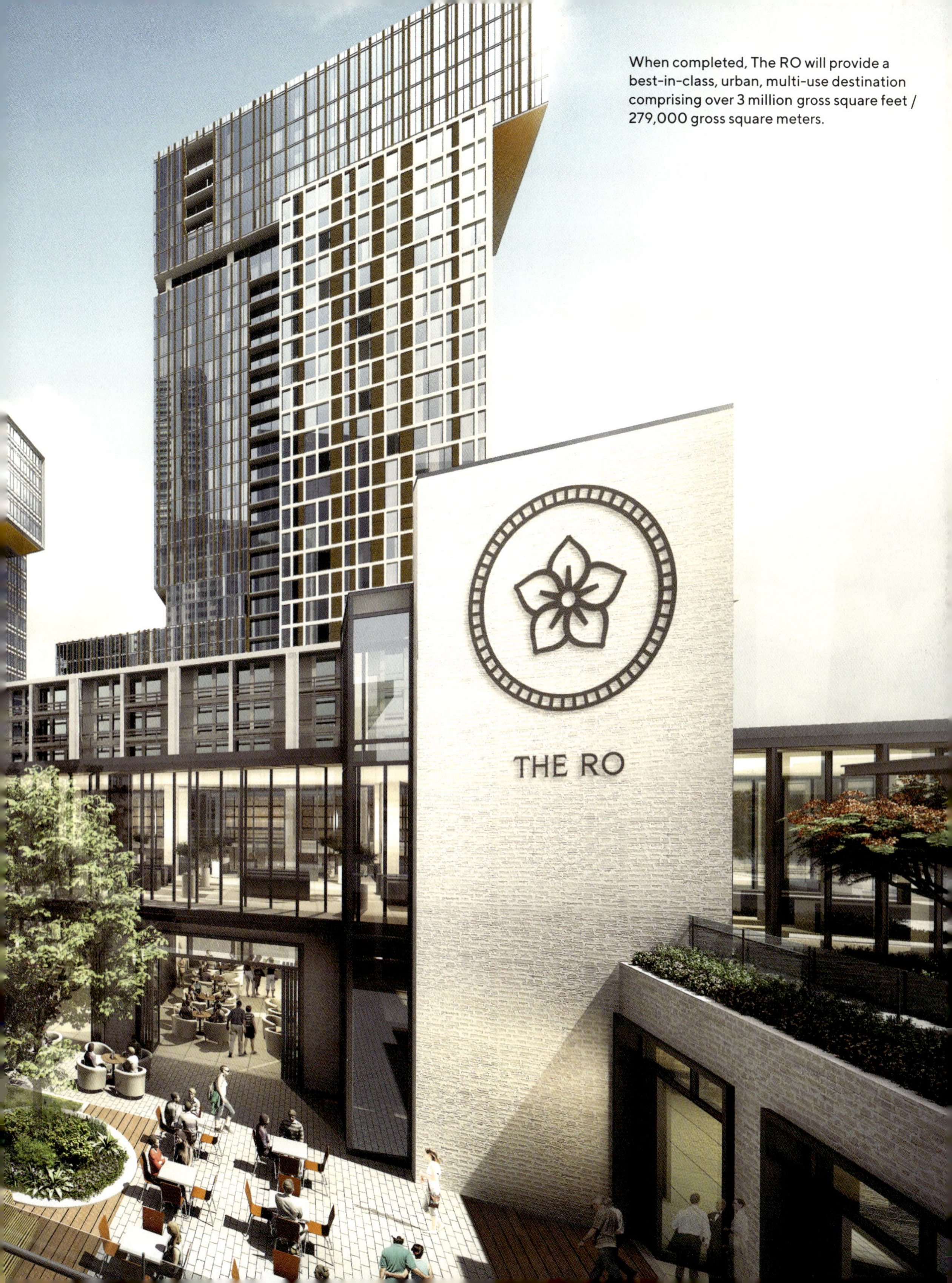

When completed, The RO will provide a best-in-class, urban, multi-use destination comprising over 3 million gross square feet / 279,000 gross square meters.

"It shows what can happen with the power of collaboration and rapport."

Murphy McCullough
Executive Vice President, Skanska USA

2+U
SEATTLE, WASHINGTON

Completed 2019
1 million gross square feet / 92,900 gross square meters
LEED for Core and Shell Gold

Sited at the corner of 2nd Avenue and University Street, 2+U is a Class A office tower in one of the most strategic locations in downtown Seattle. Its compelling connection and access to the waterfront, Pike's Place Market, and the Central Business District offer an invigorating work environment for companies seeking an address in the core. A blend of commerce and culture, 2+U creates a new and welcoming communal destination representative of the region's unique character.

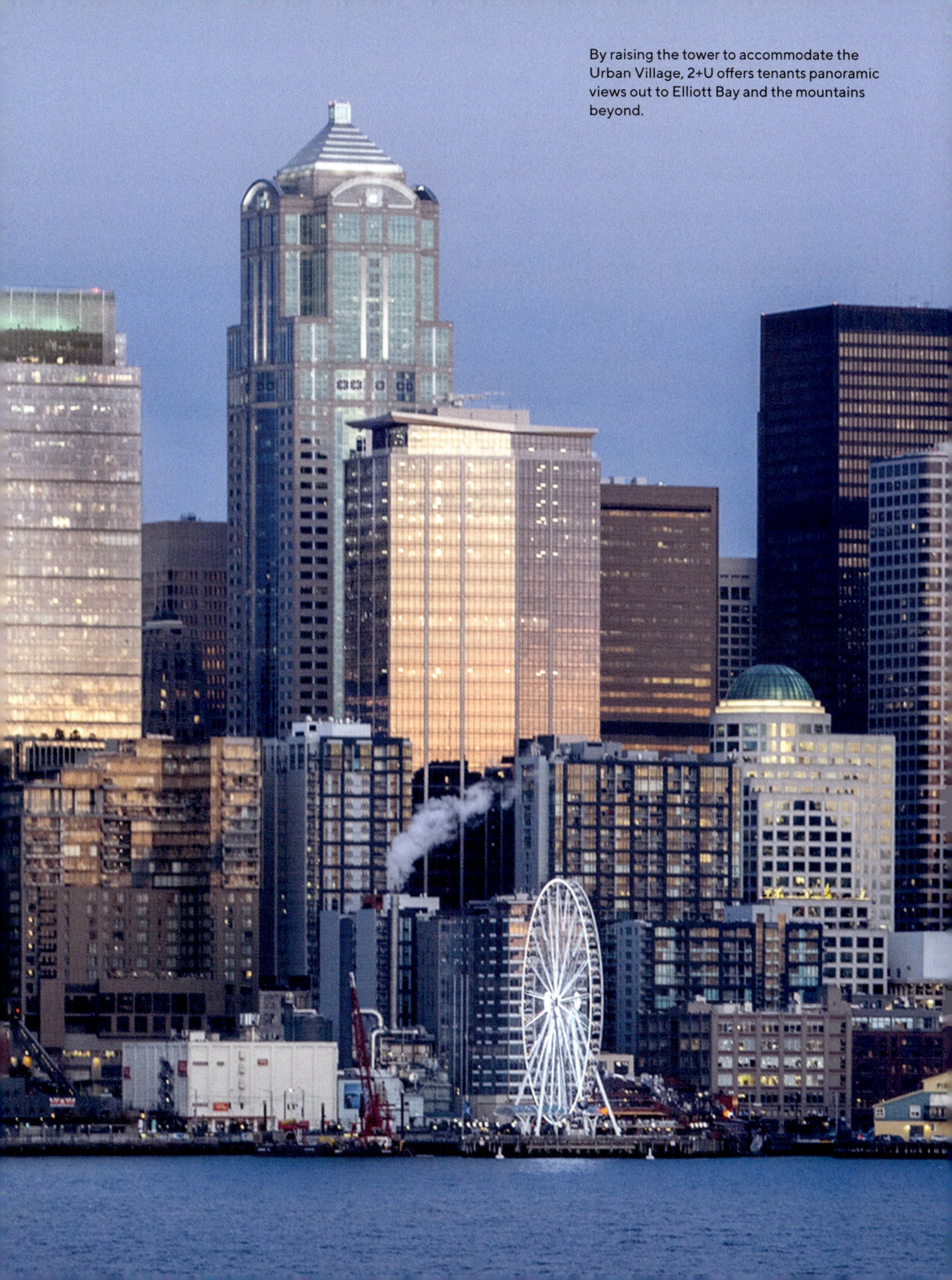

By raising the tower to accommodate the Urban Village, 2+U offers tenants panoramic views out to Elliott Bay and the mountains beyond.

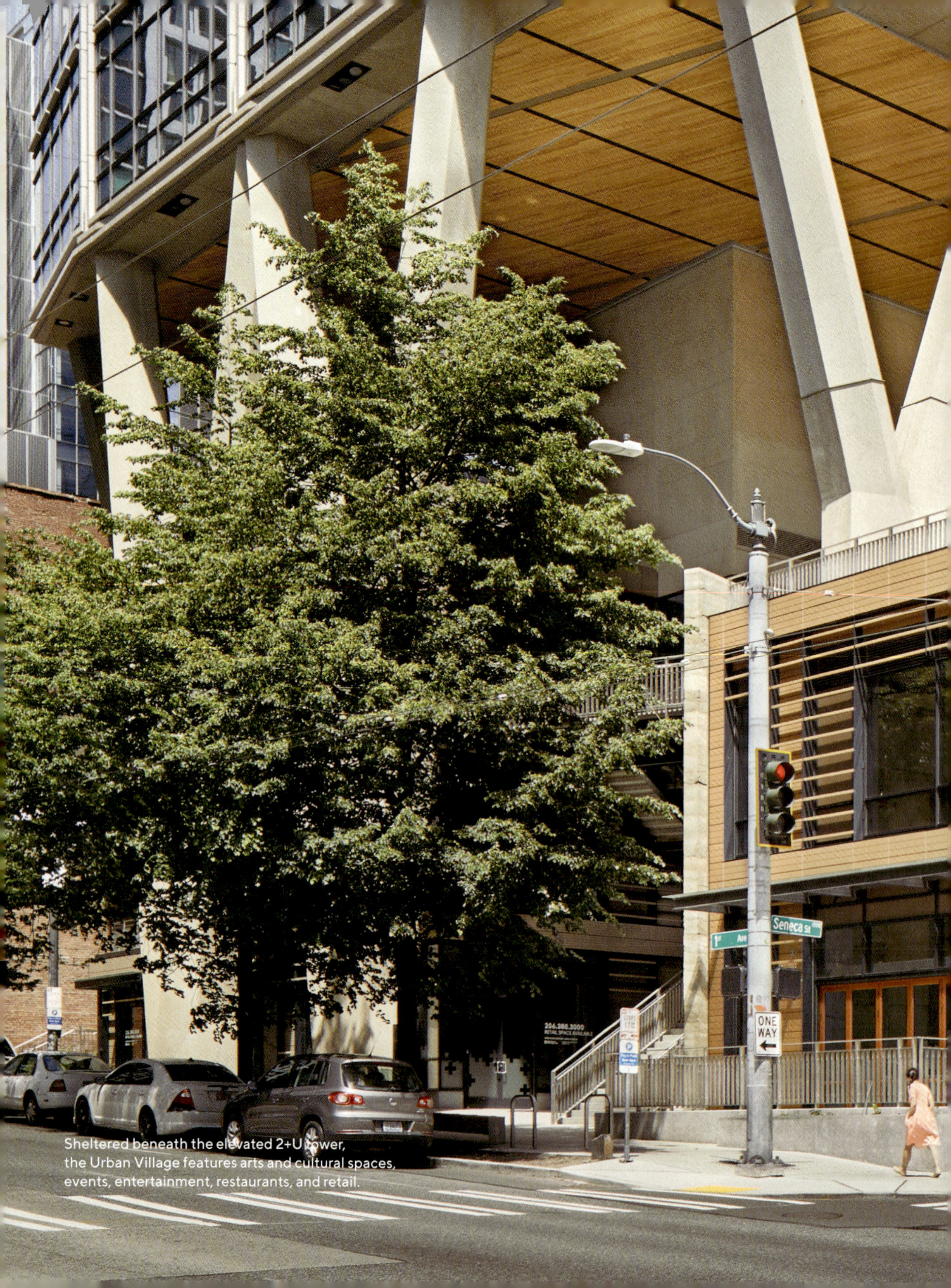

Sheltered beneath the elevated 2+U tower, the Urban Village features arts and cultural spaces, events, entertainment, restaurants, and retail.

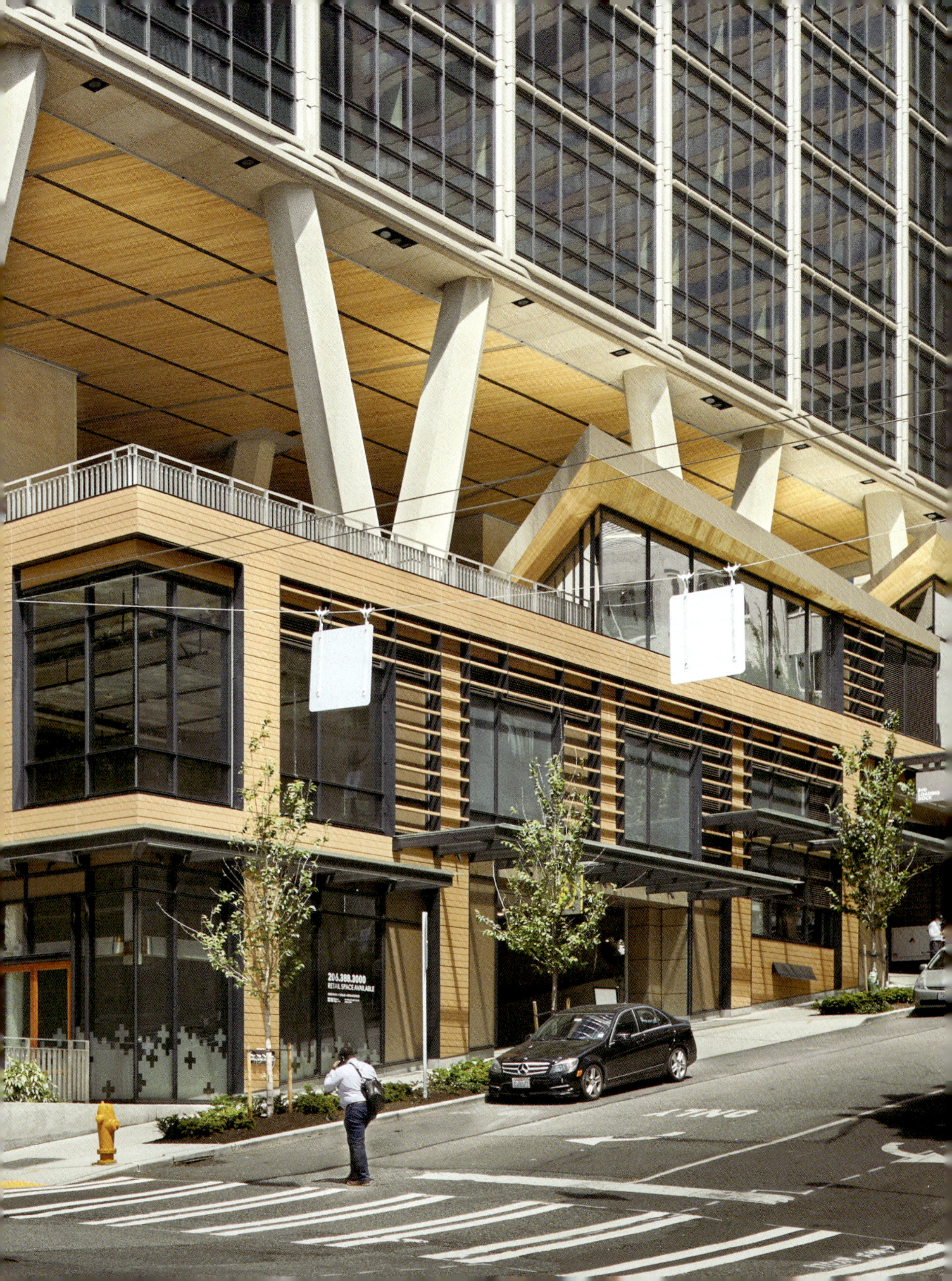
206.388.3000
RETAIL SPACE AVAILABLE
ONLY

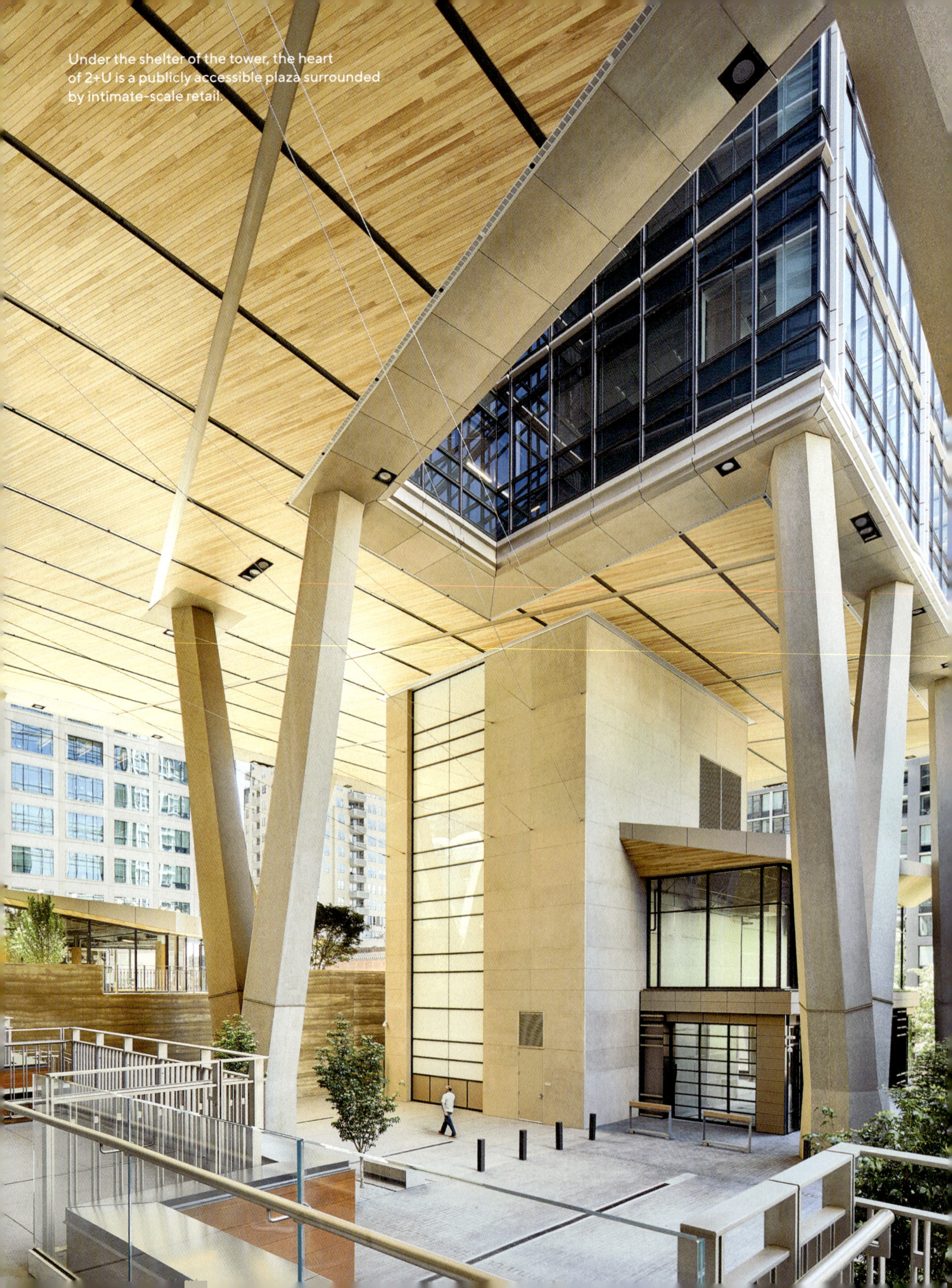

Under the shelter of the tower, the heart of 2+U is a publicly accessible plaza surrounded by intimate-scale retail.

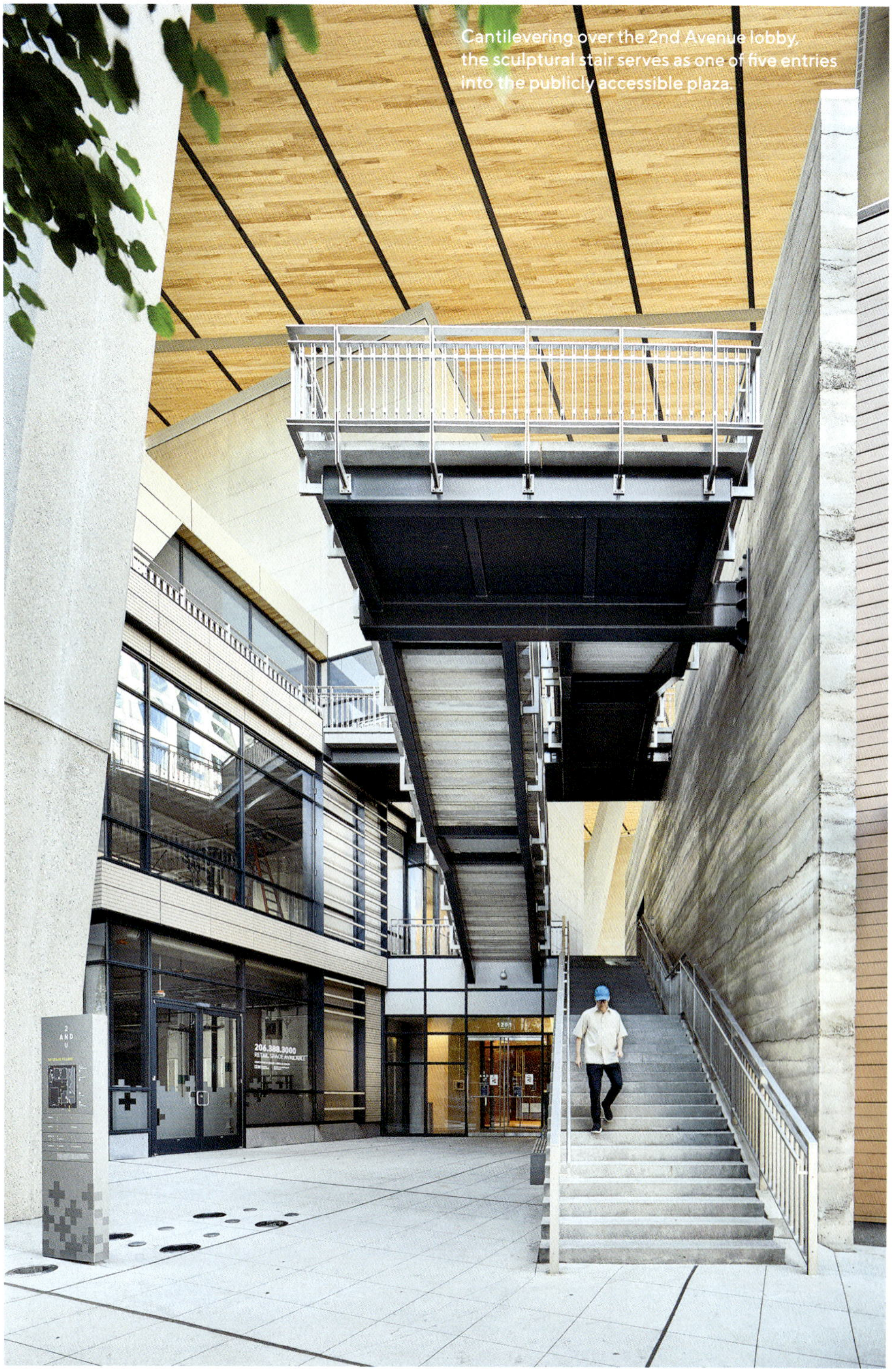

Cantilevering over the 2nd Avenue lobby, the sculptural stair serves as one of five entries into the publicly accessible plaza.

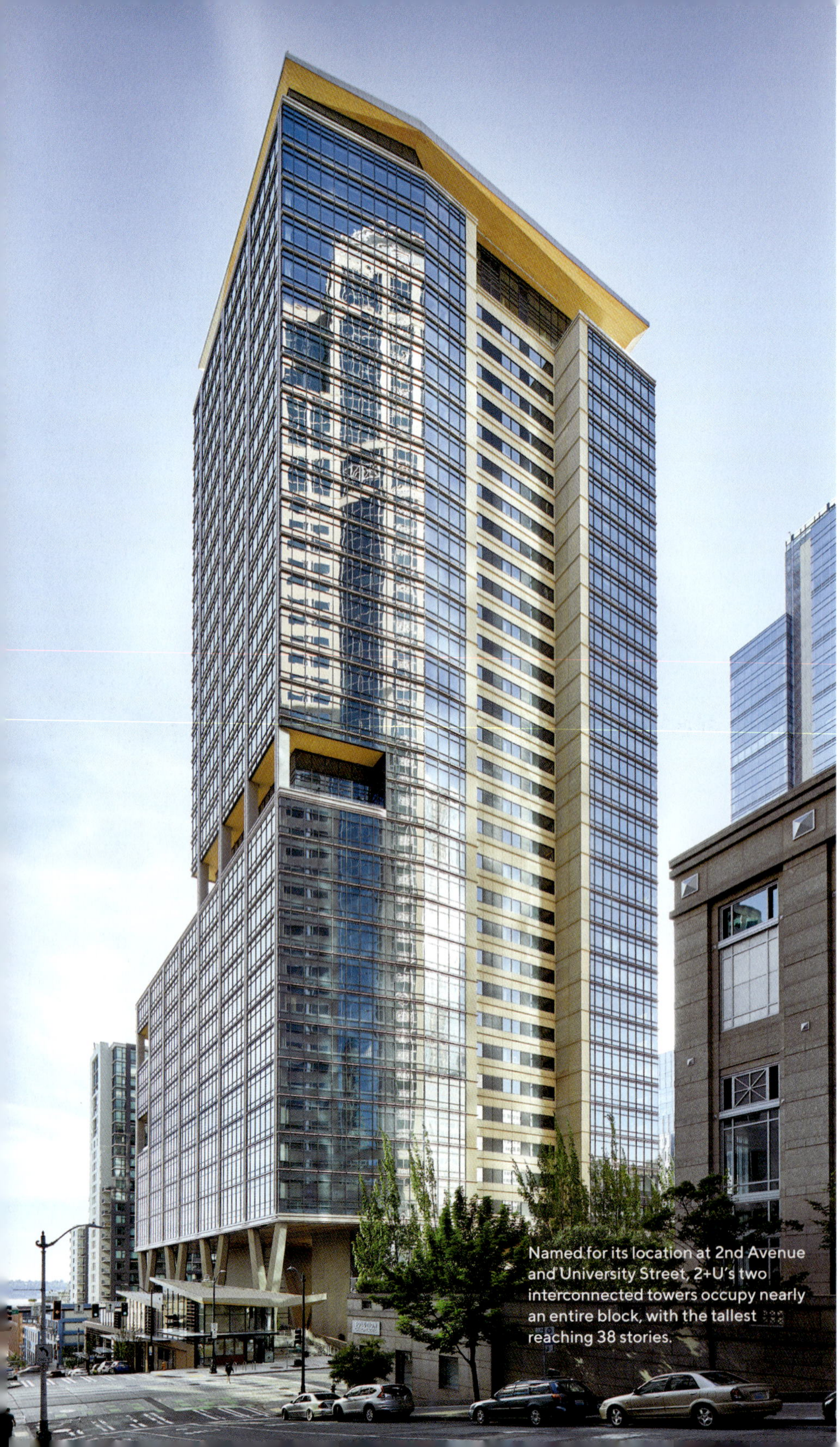

Named for its location at 2nd Avenue and University Street, 2+U's two interconnected towers occupy nearly an entire block, with the tallest reaching 38 stories.

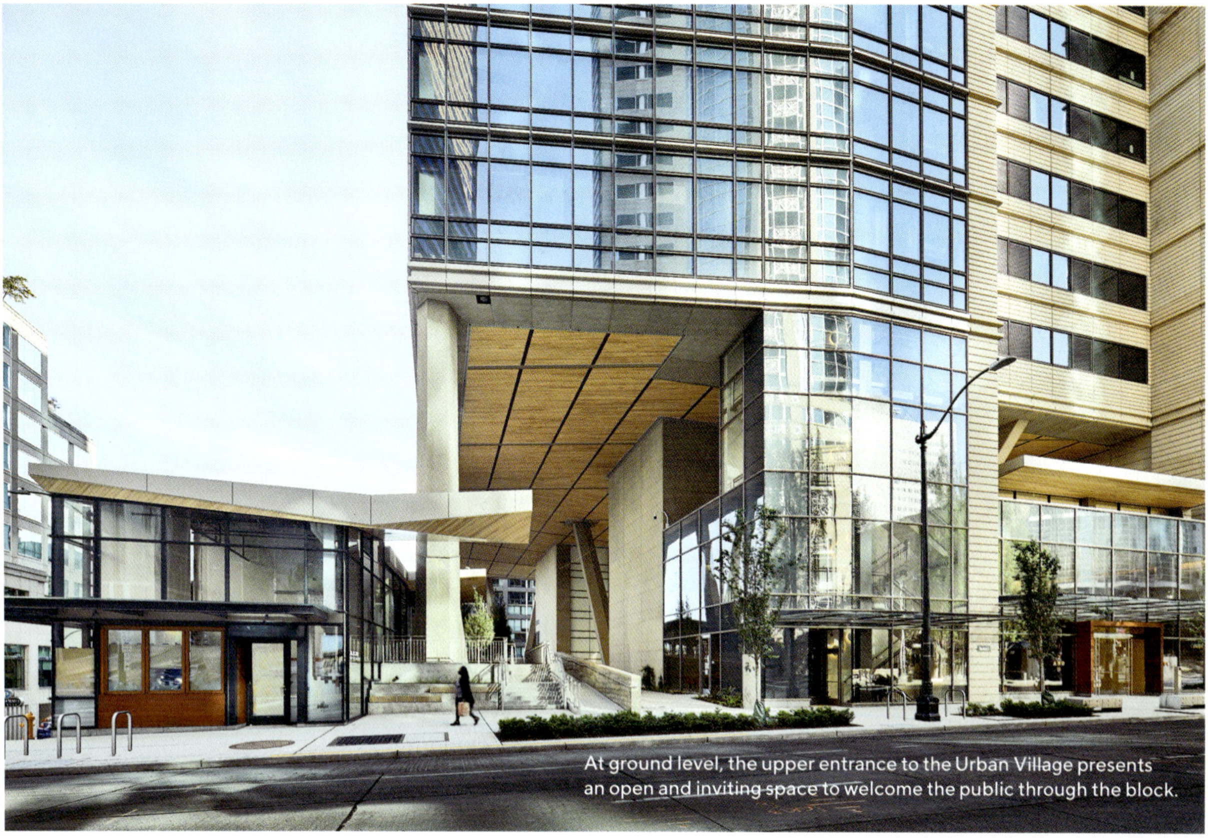

At ground level, the upper entrance to the Urban Village presents an open and inviting space to welcome the public through the block.

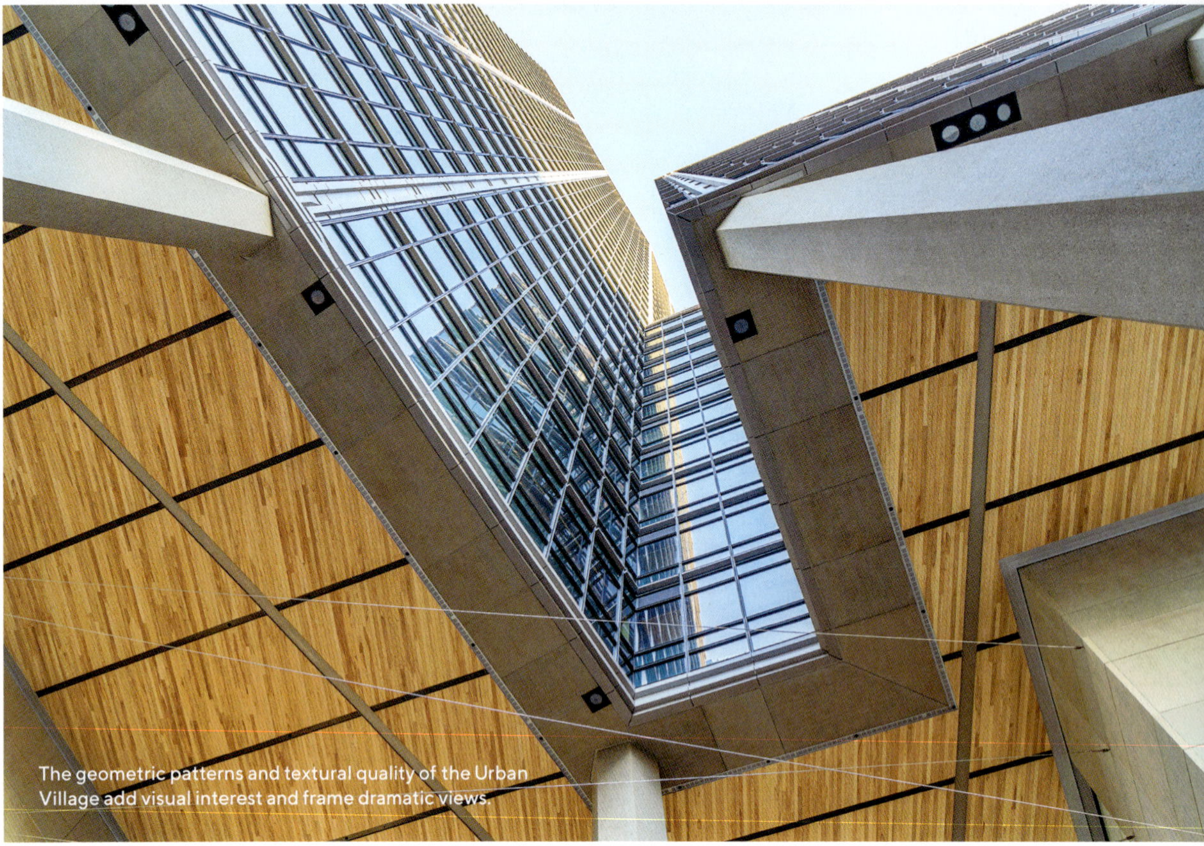

The geometric patterns and textural quality of the Urban Village add visual interest and frame dramatic views.

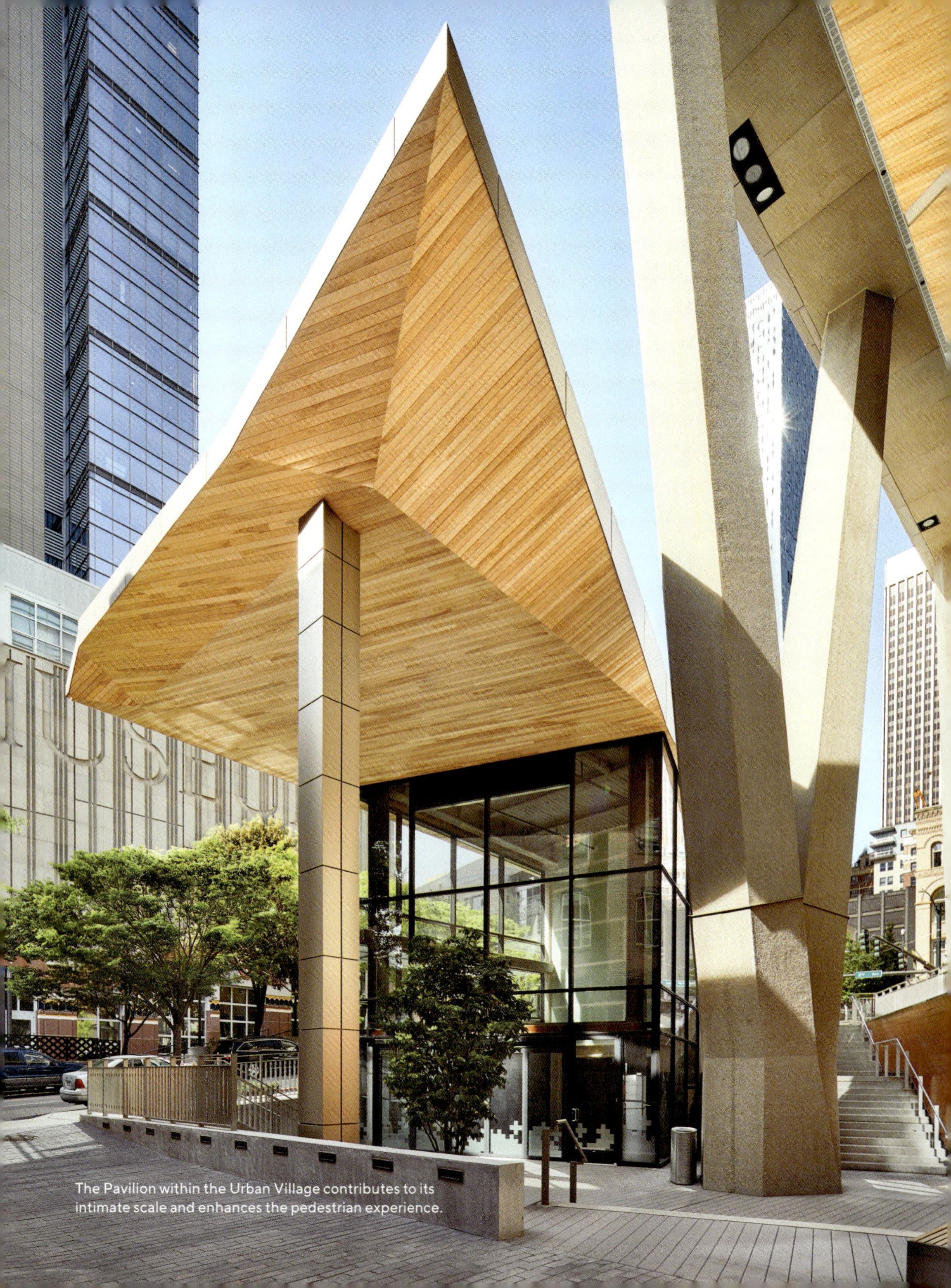

The Pavilion within the Urban Village contributes to its intimate scale and enhances the pedestrian experience.

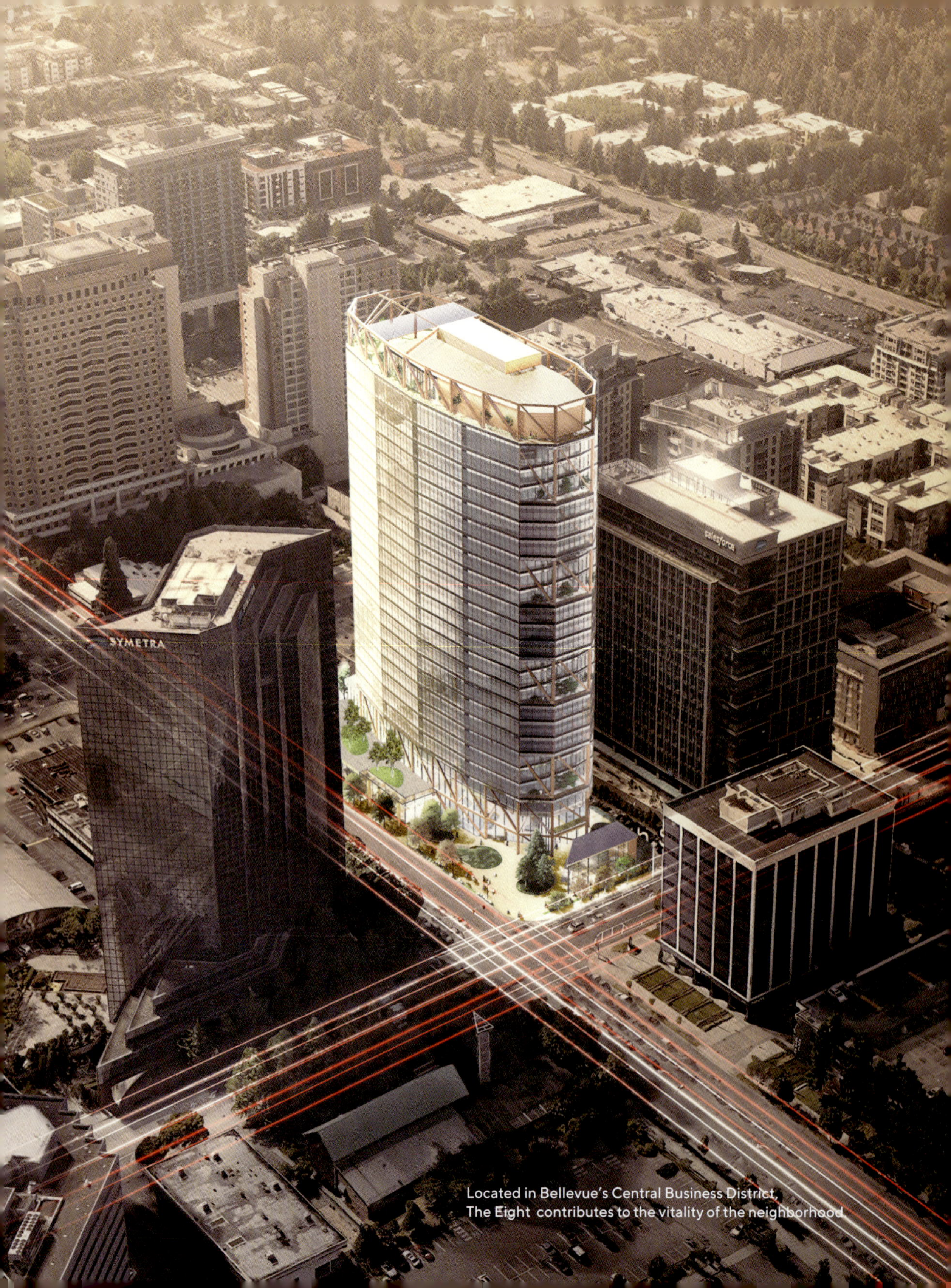

Located in Bellevue's Central Business District, The Eight contributes to the vitality of the neighborhood

"To have an architect that committed to preserving the relationship is amazing."

Murphy McCullough
Executive Vice President, Skanska USA

THE EIGHT
BELLEVUE, WASHINGTON

Completion 2023
800,000 gross square feet / 74,300 gross square meters
LEED for Core and Shell Platinum targeted

The Eight is a next-generation commercial office development in downtown Bellevue. Clad in a high-performance façade, the 25-story tower comprises approximately 500,000 square feet / 46,500 square meters of creative office space with highly efficient floor plates and four levels of below-grade parking. The tower's massing is articulated with exposed structure and balconies that are interwoven with greenery. The development features a wholly unique, activated, and community-focused ground floor with local retail. It is anticipated that The Eight will raise Bellevue's architectural design aesthetic.

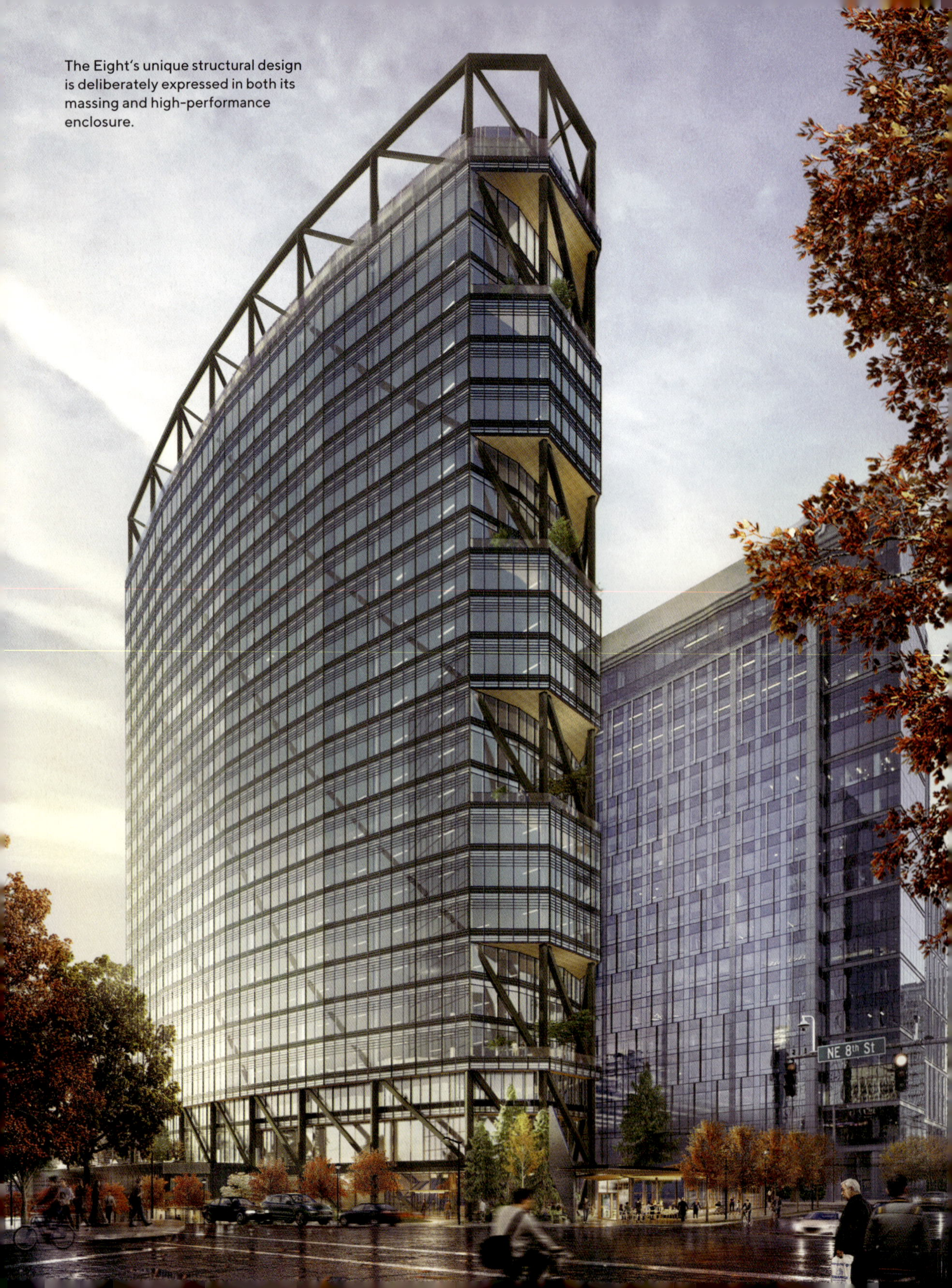

The Eight's unique structural design is deliberately expressed in both its massing and high-performance enclosure.

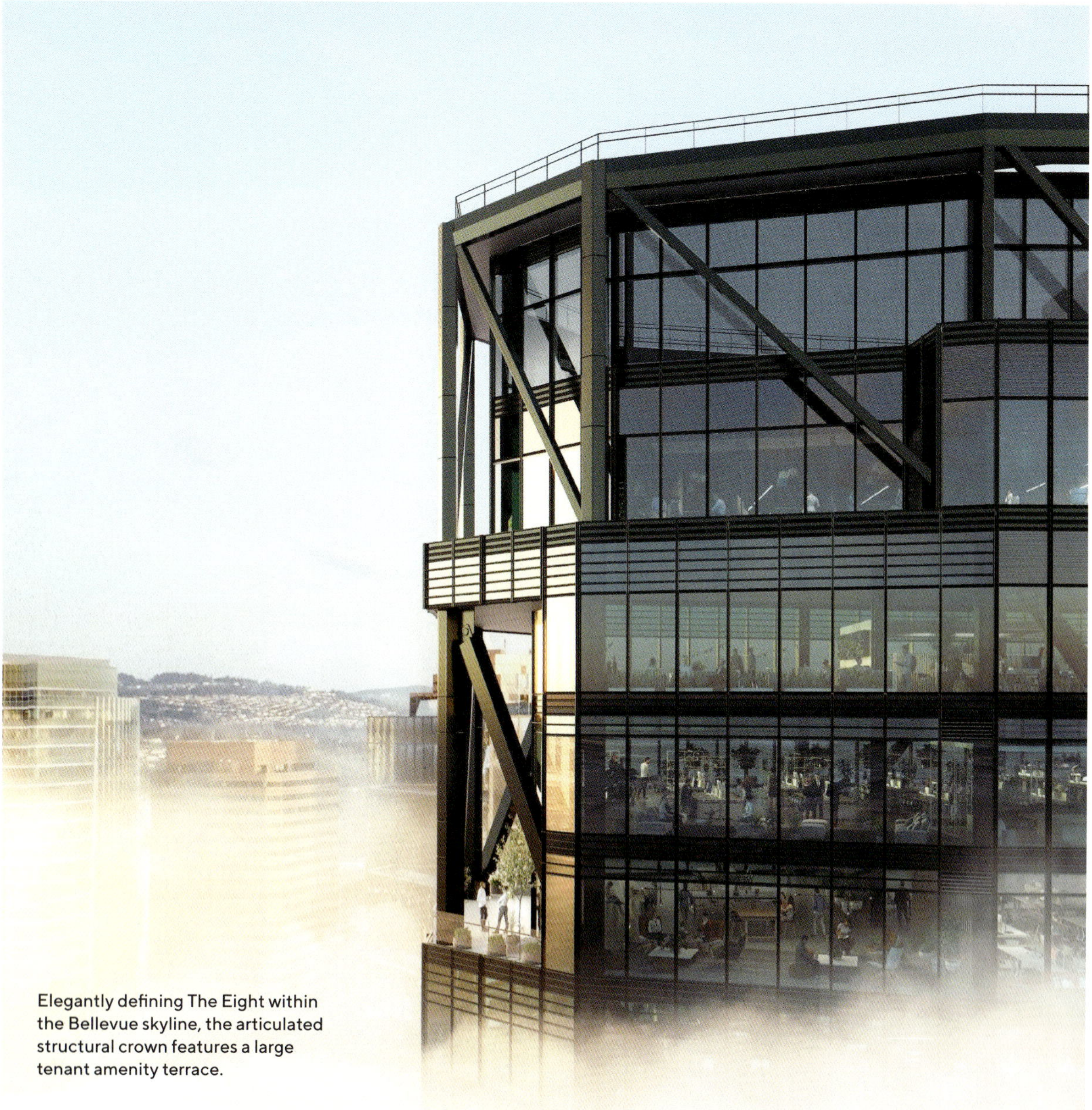

Elegantly defining The Eight within the Bellevue skyline, the articulated structural crown features a large tenant amenity terrace.

The generous landscaped plaza has been designed to serve as a welcoming communal public amenity.

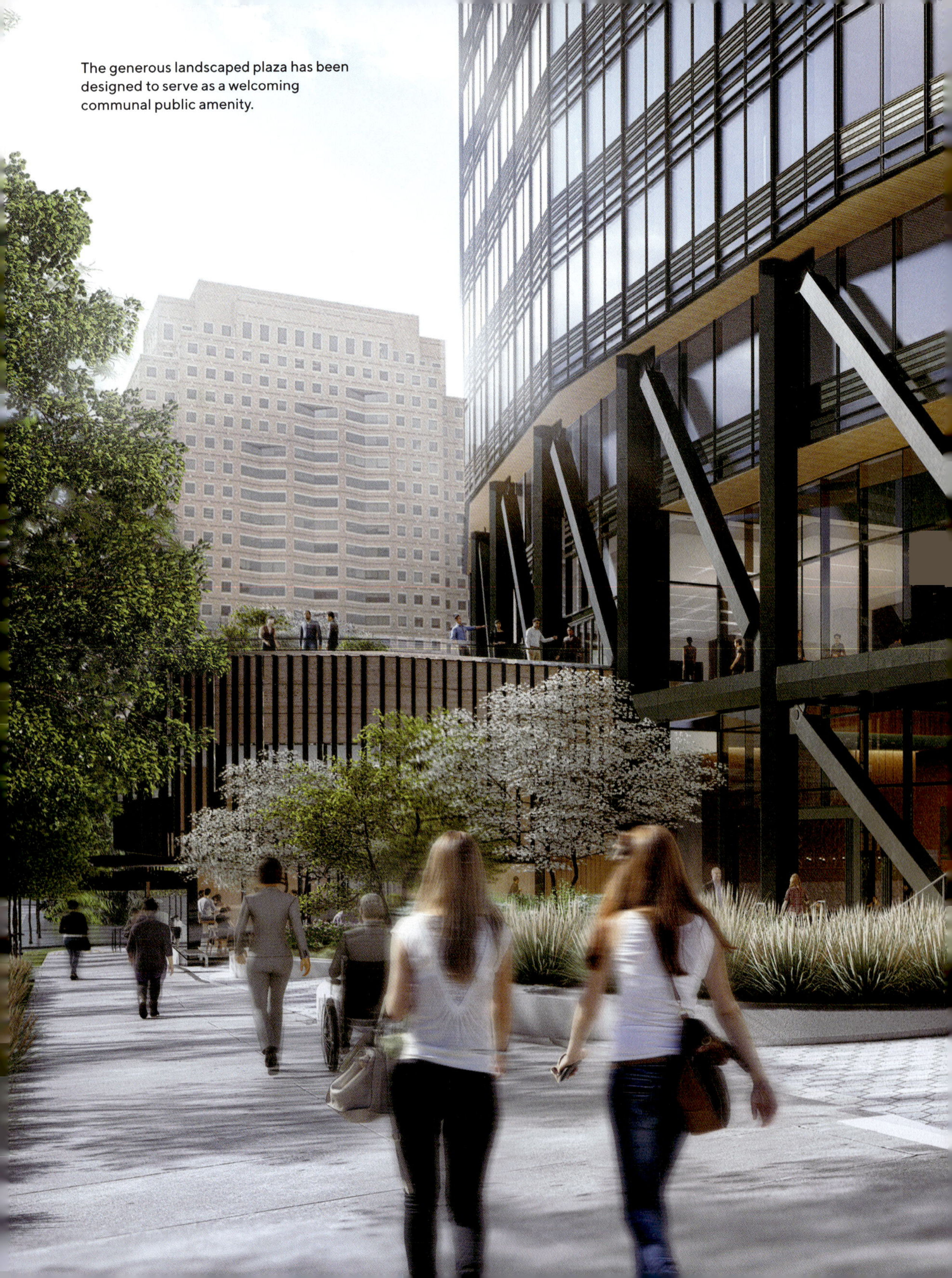

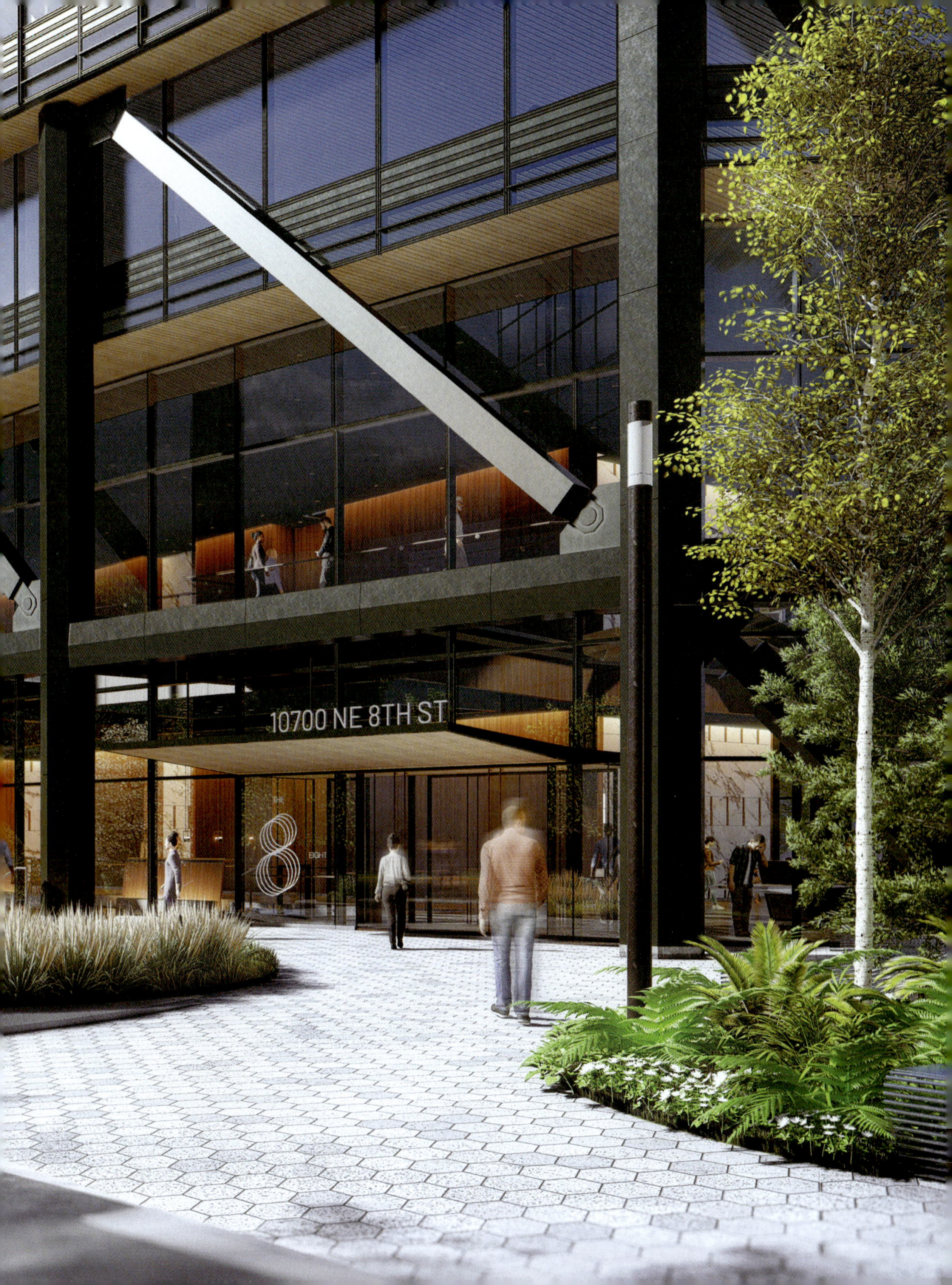
10700 NE 8TH ST

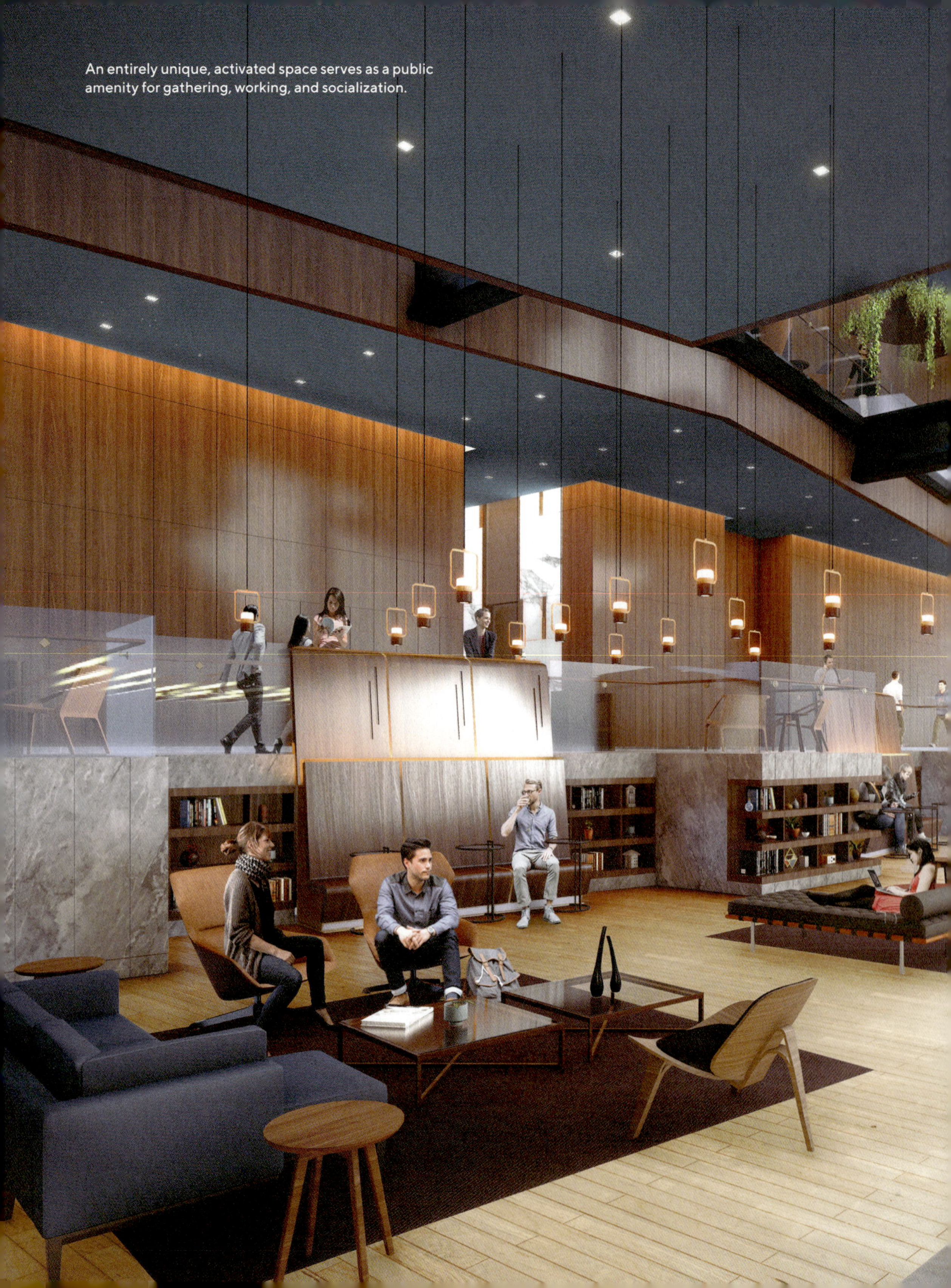
An entirely unique, activated space serves as a public amenity for gathering, working, and socialization.

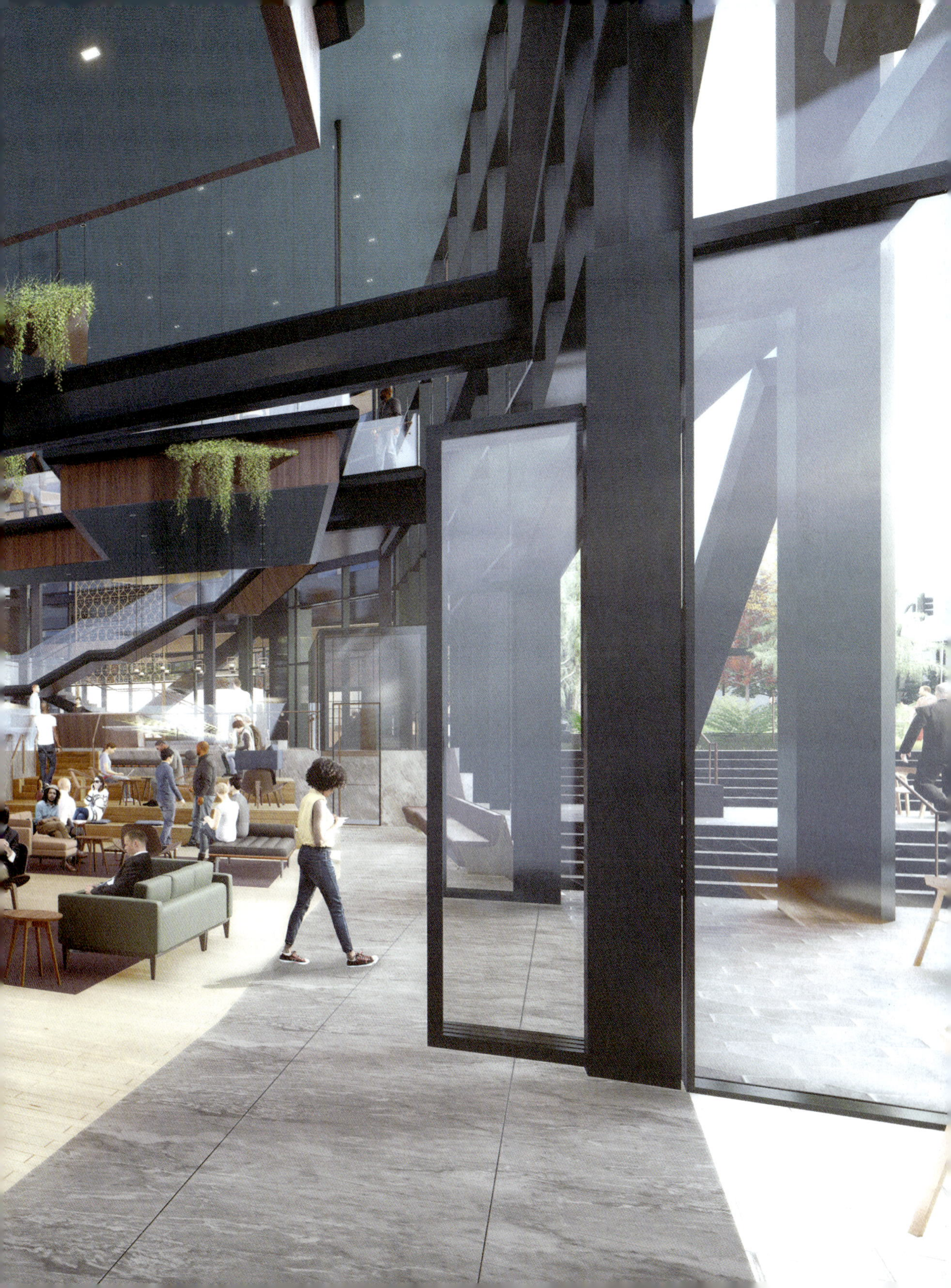

Learning

T3 RiNo

Hines, McCaffery Interests, Ivanhoé Cambridge

Pickard Chilton

DLR Group

Magnusson Klemencic Associates

Alvine Engineering

Whiting-Turner

S.A. Miro

Norris Design

39 North Engineering and Surveying

Quentin Thomas Associates

Noresco

HWA Parking

Morrison Hershfield

Cerami

HMA

1144 FIFTEENTH STREET

Hines

Pickard Chilton

Kendall/Heaton Associates

Design Workshop

Martin/Martin

M-E Engineers

CTL Thompson

Persohn/Hahn Associates

HWA Parking

RWDI

HMA Consulting

Buro Happold

Hensel Phelps

Architects are always learning from their clients, and clients learn from their architects. The experience of creating architecture together presents the designer with multiple opportunities to learn, to challenge assumptions and, in turn, to have one's own conventions challenged, and together arrive at new understandings. What is critical is an openness to the possibility of learning something new from one another. What are some of the most important things architects and clients learn from each other? How does what is learned influence one's practice of architecture? How have assumptions one might have made about architecture been challenged in ways that a new understanding of architecture and design emerges? How is the learning process reflected in the architecture?

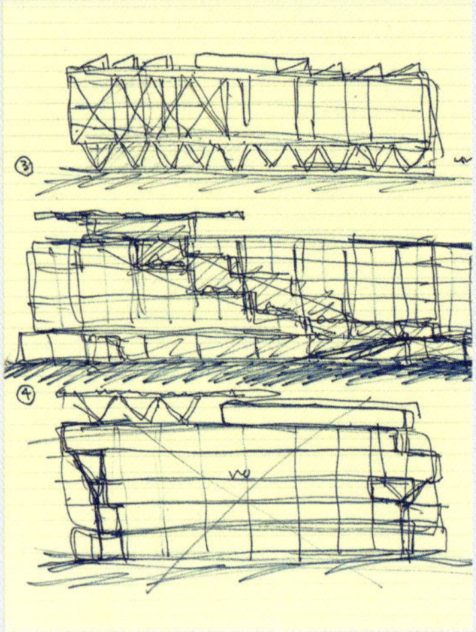

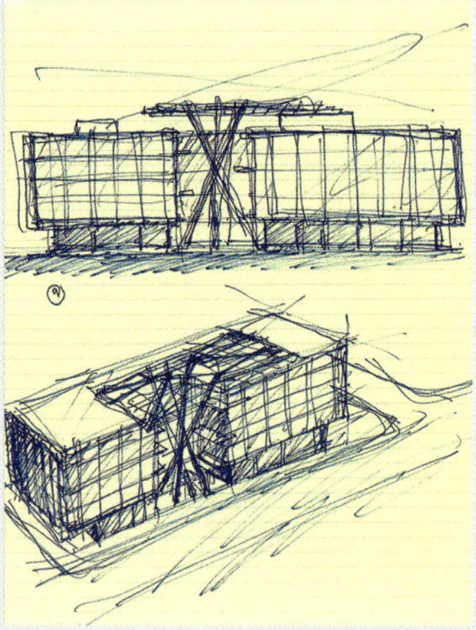

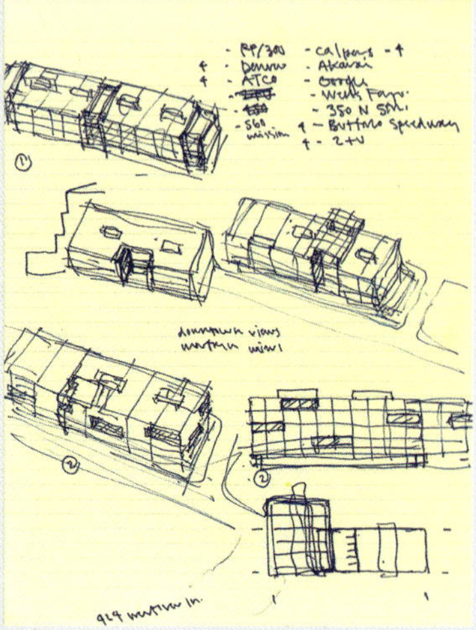

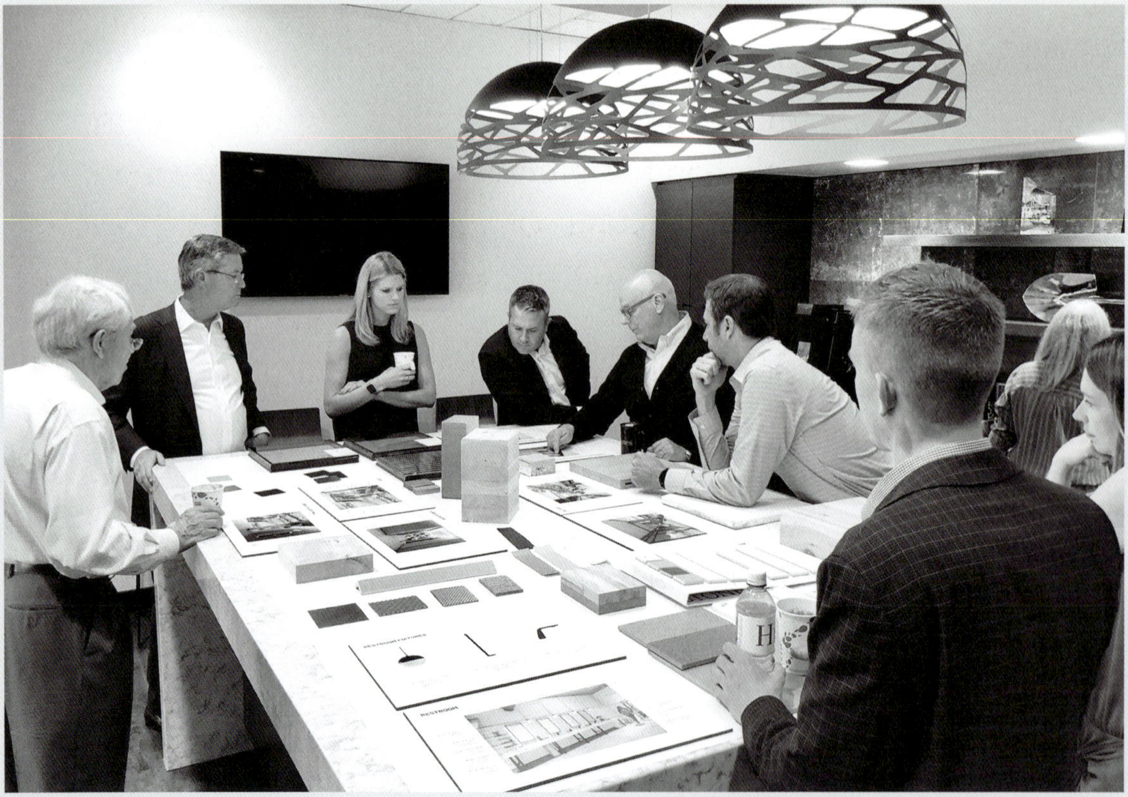

Early concept sketches of T3 RiNo; Anthony Markese and T3 team meet to review potential finishes.

Central to learning is how one chooses to work together — learning is a natural outcome of collaborative work. The architects at Pickard Chilton readily admit that much of what they know about the design and creation of certain kinds of projects has been learned firsthand from their clients. The journey of a project presents a wealth of opportunities for clients to impart to an architect what has been learned in the process of working with other designers — if the architect is listening. The architecture needs to be respectful of the client's spirit and their organization so that the design reflects the client. For the client, the collaborative process is a chance to learn more about the components of the architect's approach: how they think through a design; their underlying principles of problem-solving; the questions they ask in order to accumulate a critical mass of learning to steer the solution in the right direction. Pickard Chilton believes the fingerprints of what the architect and the client learn together in the collaborative process should be all over the building.

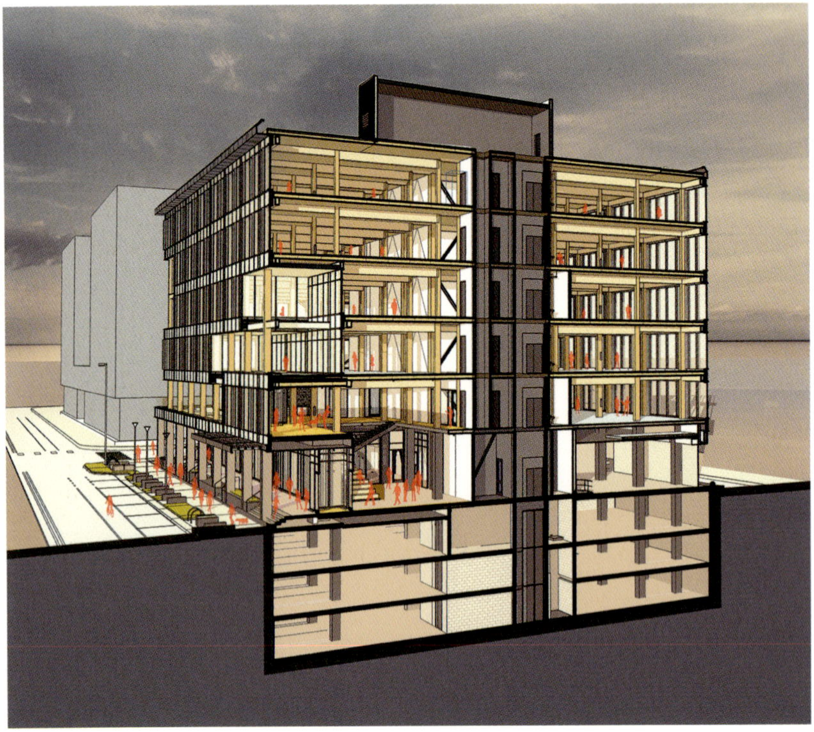

← Sectional diagram of T3's mass-timber composite structure.

→ Interior workspaces feature exposed timber and floor-to-ceiling glass.

The design for T3 RiNo in Denver is such a work that displays the client's and architect's fingerprints. The six-story office building is for a site that overlooks the city, nearby park space, and the Rocky Mountains in the distance. The building reflects prevailing local values — interest in the health of the environment, outdoor activities, nature, and the spectacular natural surroundings. The design incorporates multiple terraces and

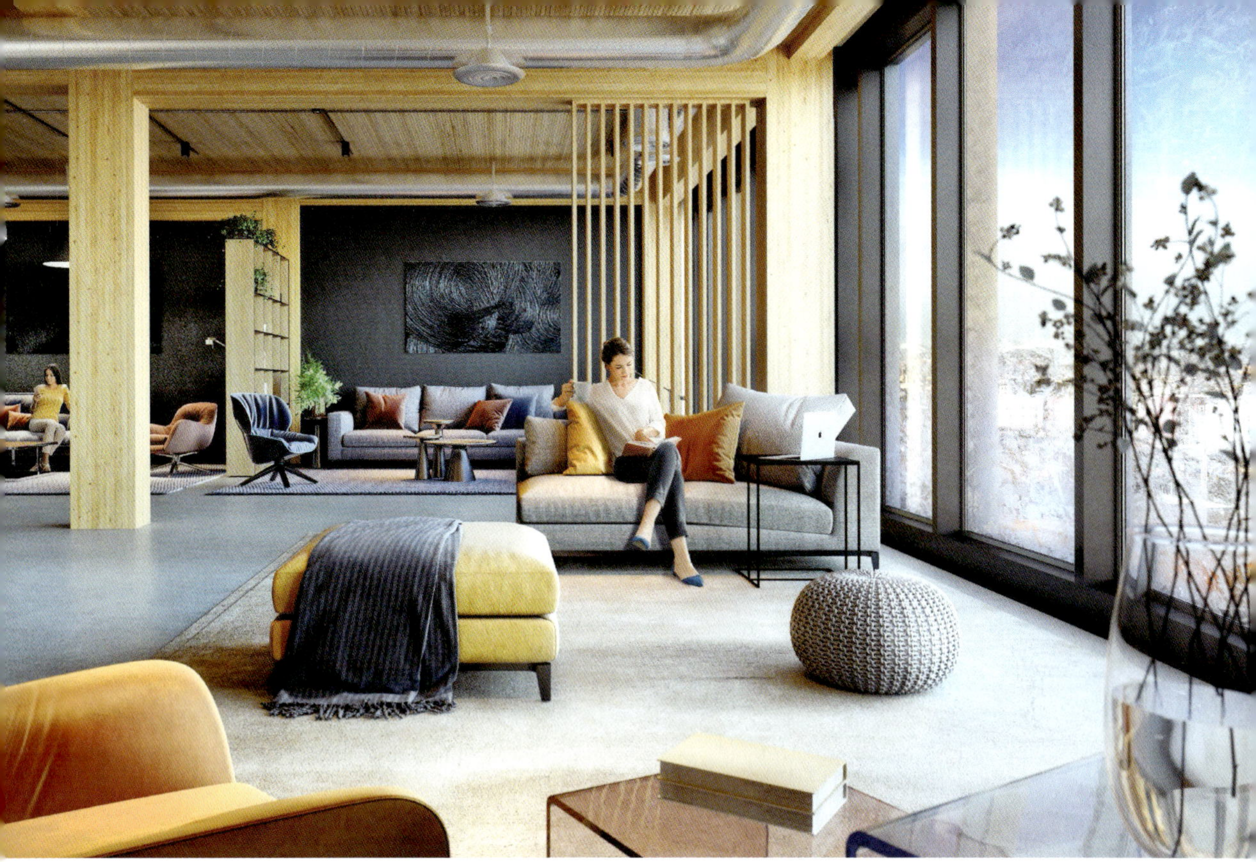

deep balconies throughout the plan, offering 20,000 square feet / 1,858 square meters of outdoor areas that employees can enjoy steps away from their work spaces. The open terraces also provide visual variety and variegate the building's mass. The part of T3 that faces the city's adjacent arts district presents a kinetic artwork animated through the moving cabs of its glass-enclosed elevator banks — an Instagram moment.

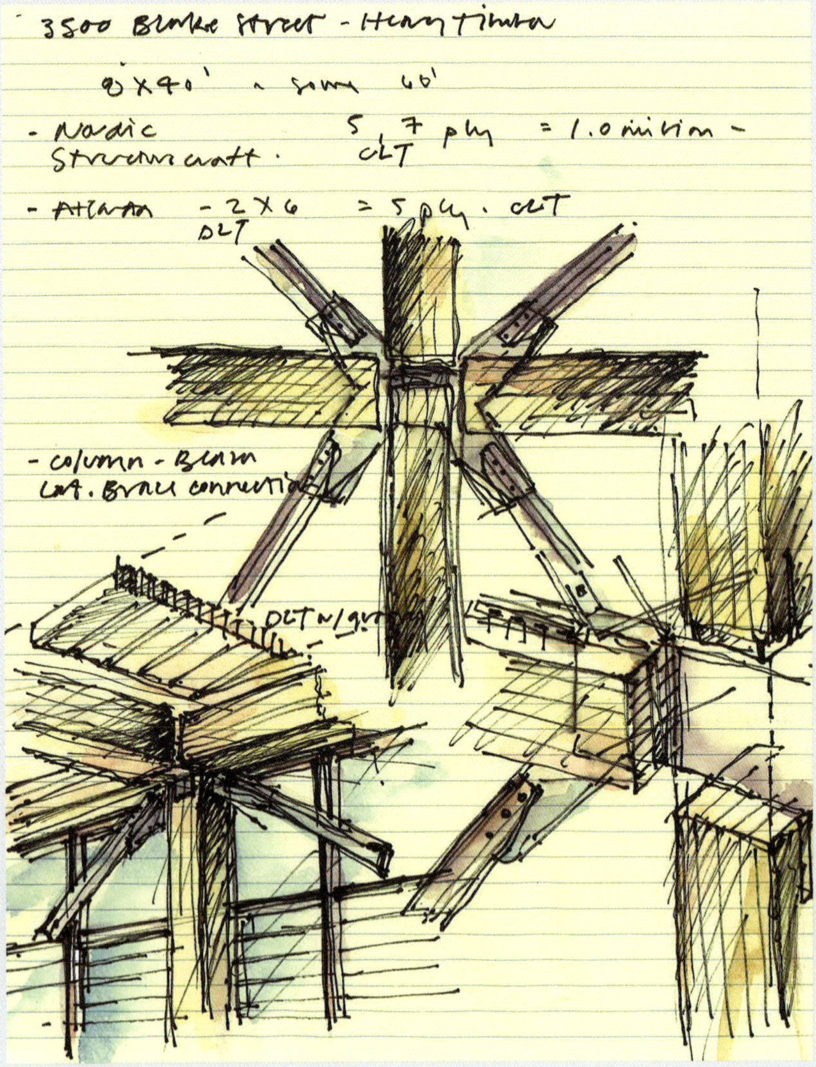

← Sketches of potential timber bracing solutions.

→ T3 RiNo tenant spaces incorporate multiple outdoor terraces at each level.

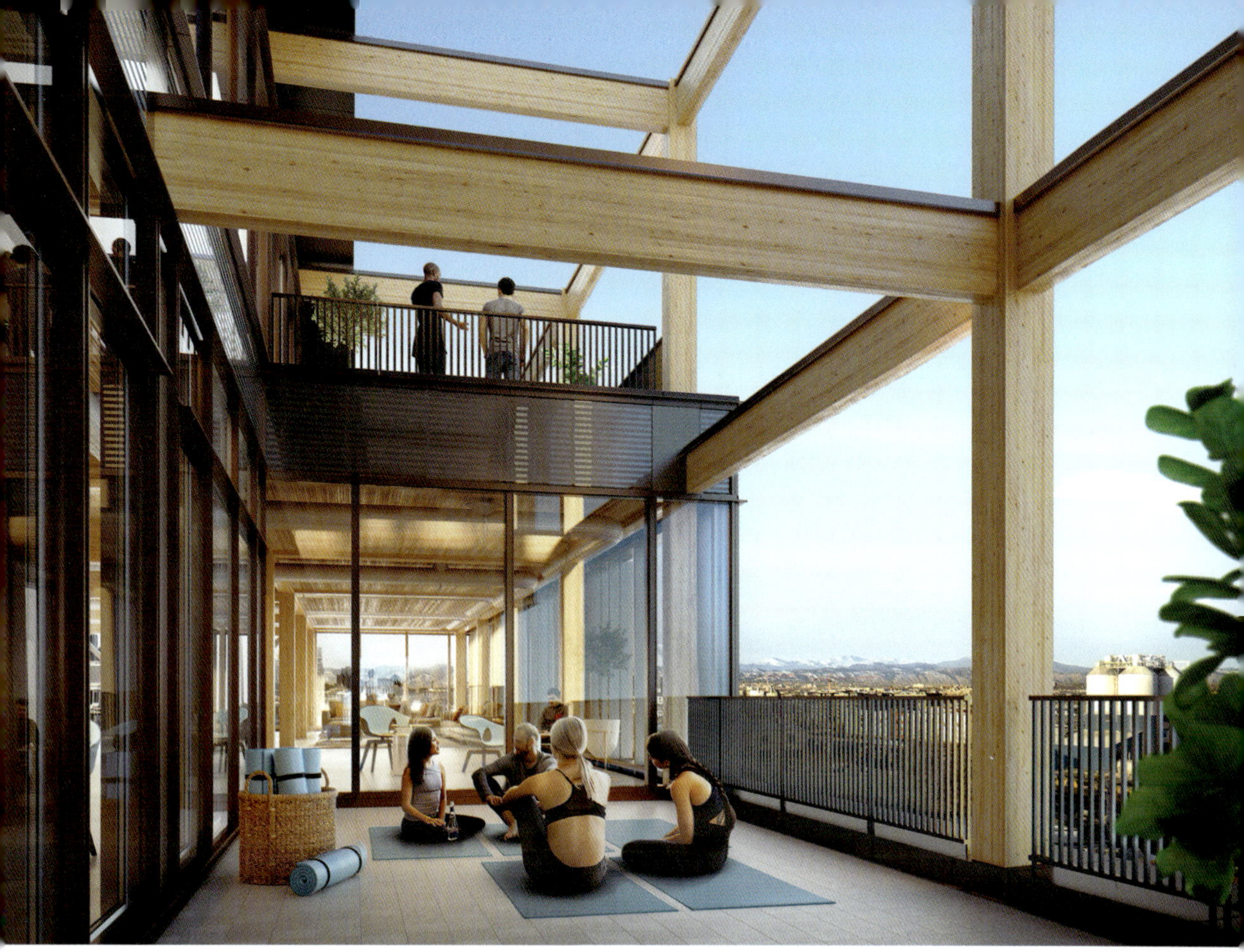

The design's heavy-timber construction is a choice reflective of its place. According to Pickard Chilton, the heavy-timber option presents a new opportunity to learn more about this construction technique, in which interest has been growing in recent years. Sustainability is one of the primary reasons to choose heavy-timber construction, which is manufactured from a readily renewable resource with less embodied energy. The architects found that their extensive research contributed to their experience of working with the material as a generator of the building's design. The choice of heavy timber turned out to have functional, technical, and aesthetic uses that also fulfilled the client's objectives: a mixture of office, entertainment, food, and services in a variety of indoor and outdoor spaces that were attractive to the neighborhood and the local real estate market. The architects describe this process of comprehending the system's potential and creatively using the timber elements as true hands-on learning.

Jay Despard of Hines, one of the project's developers, notes that Pickard Chilton has a track record of understanding the Hines's culture — the value it places on architecture that addresses the market with high-quality design. Despard notes that Pickard Chilton learns to master the issues that are the client's first priority: ground-floor program and layout, egress, and other technical necessities.

"They know more about floor plates than I do," he muses, admitting that Pickard Chilton has taught him some things over the years about highly efficient core-and-shell layouts. "They come into the project early on knowing the ramifications of their design, something operationally efficient while at the same time aesthetically pleasing." Despard sees Pickard Chilton as quick studies, getting up to speed early in a project, while competing firms might present schemes that are formalistically interesting but don't work for the local market. "They set a very high benchmark," says Despard of Pickard Chilton, who finds himself comparing competing architects with what he has learned through his collaboration with the New Haven firm, which he describes as "a lot less work."

The heavy-timber option presents a new opportunity to learn more about this construction technique.

T3 RiNo
DENVER, COLORADO

Under construction
383,000 gross square feet / 35,600 gross square meters
LEED for New Construction Gold targeted

T3 RiNo is a six-story, heavy-timber office building featuring numerous open terraces, a variety of amenity spaces, and three levels of below-grade parking. Ideally centered in the heart of the RiNo neighborhood, T3 RiNo's location offers immediate connectivity and accessibility. The project offers prime opportunities for retailers, tenants, and community residents alike. Office floors offer panoramic views of the Denver skyline and the Rocky Mountains while outdoor terraces thoughtfully break down the building's mass to provide tenants with multiple private outdoor experiences. Coalescing natural light and sculpture, the design emphasizes occupants' connection to nature through both form and materiality.

T3 RiNo entrance and ground-floor amenities.

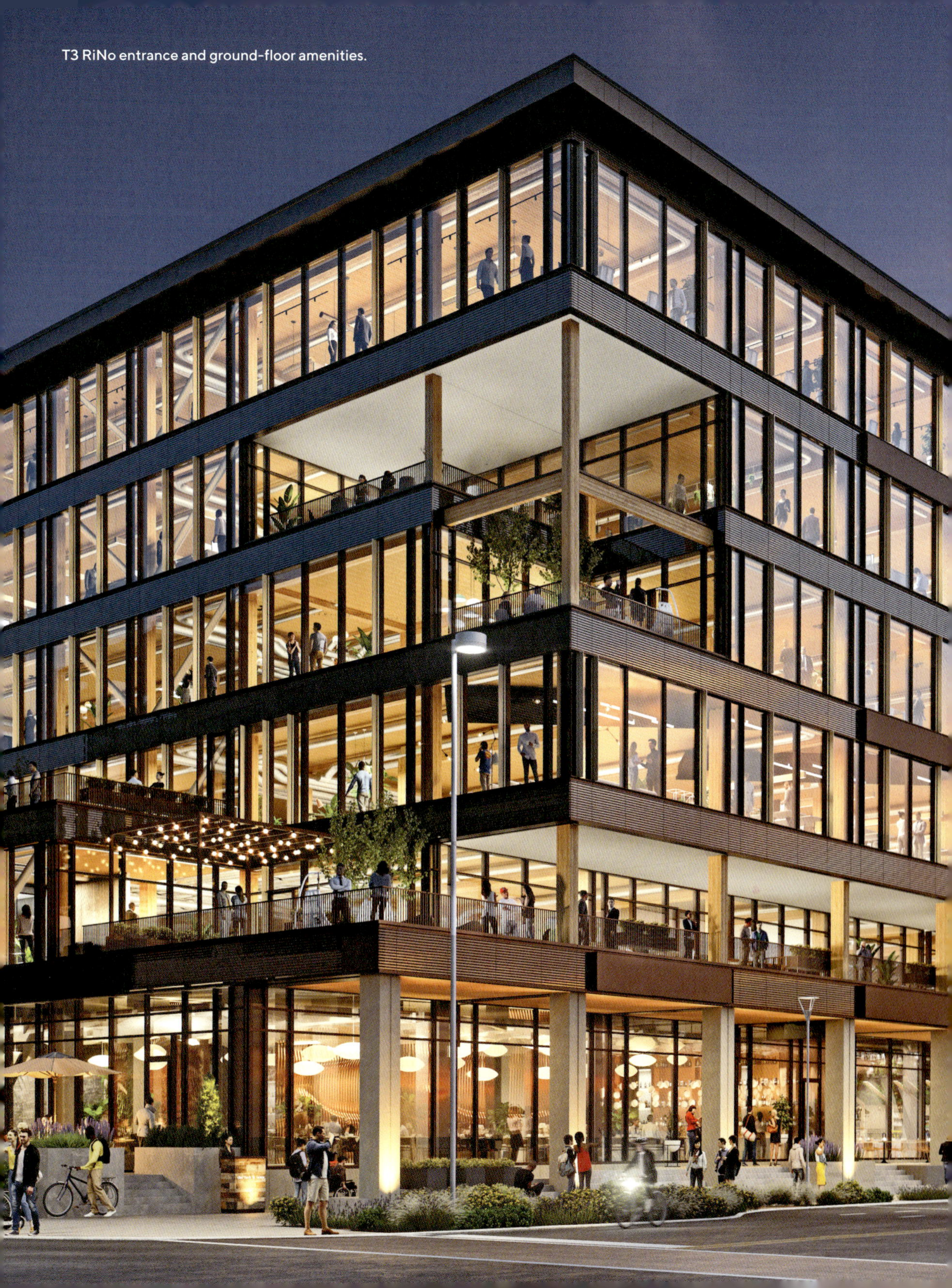

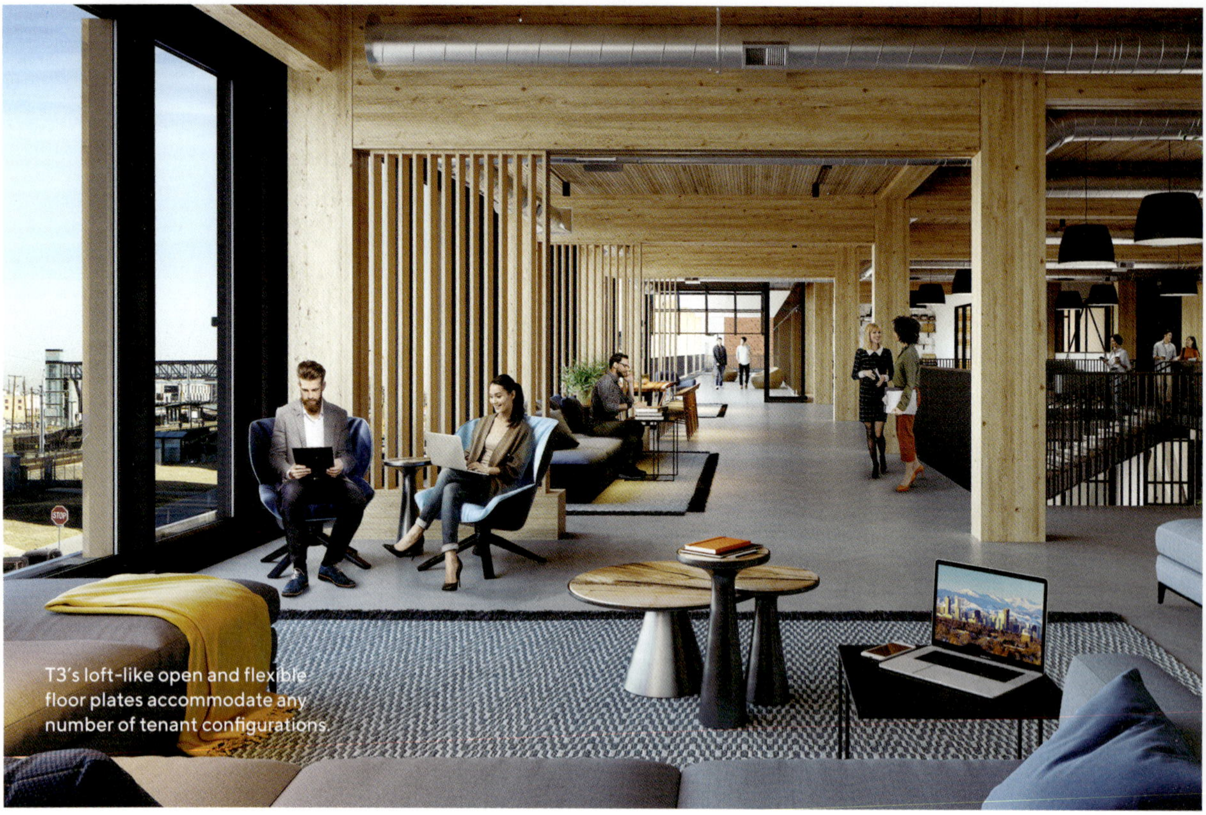

T3's loft-like open and flexible floor plates accommodate any number of tenant configurations.

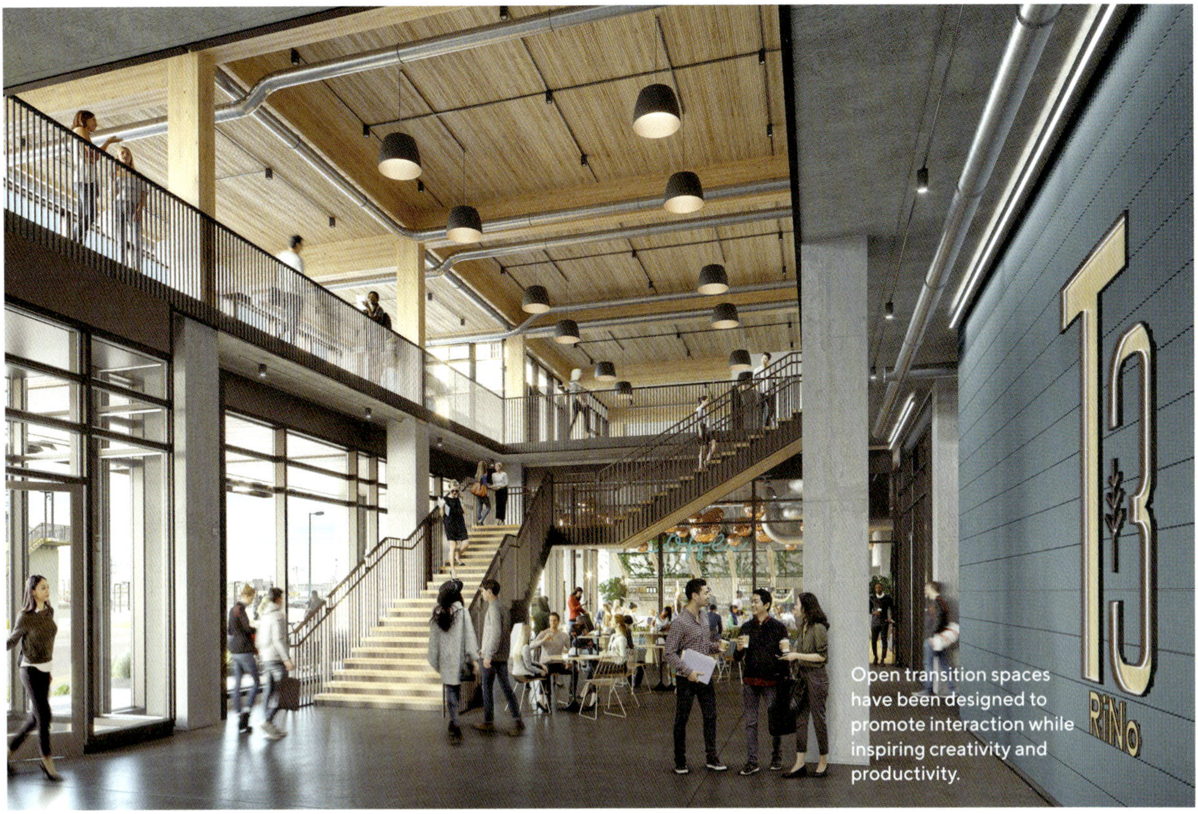

Open transition spaces have been designed to promote interaction while inspiring creativity and productivity.

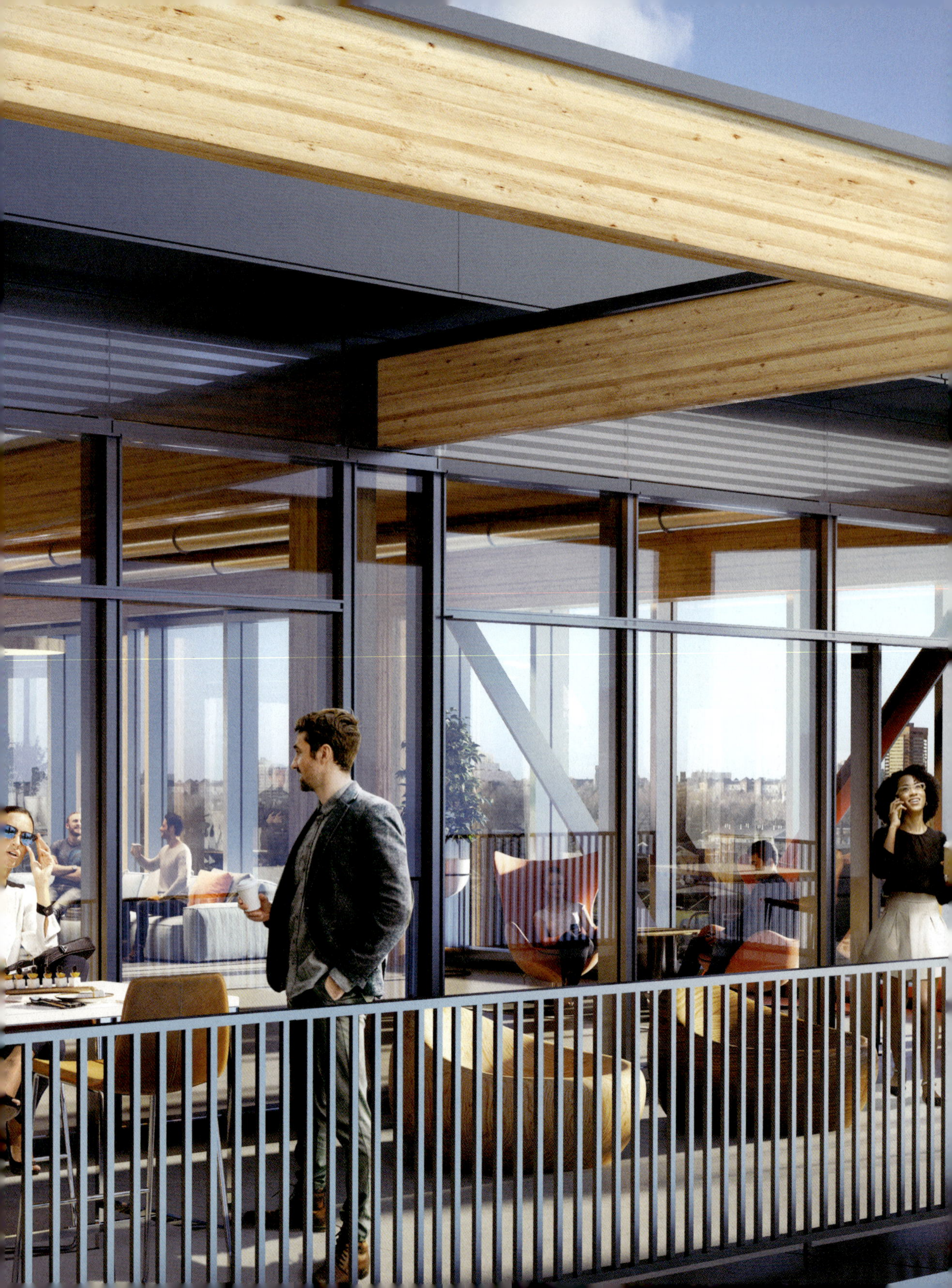

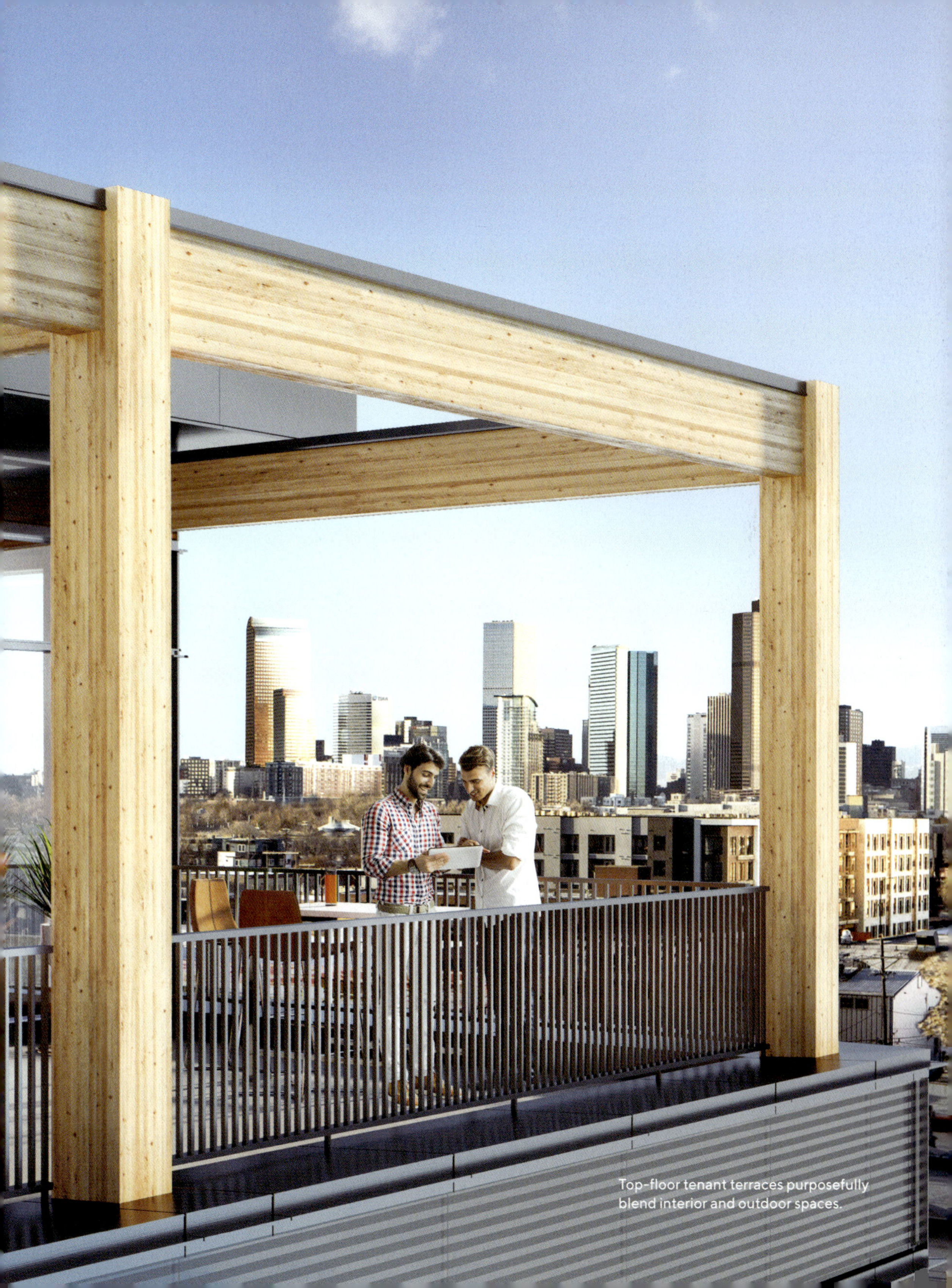

Top-floor tenant terraces purposefully blend interior and outdoor spaces.

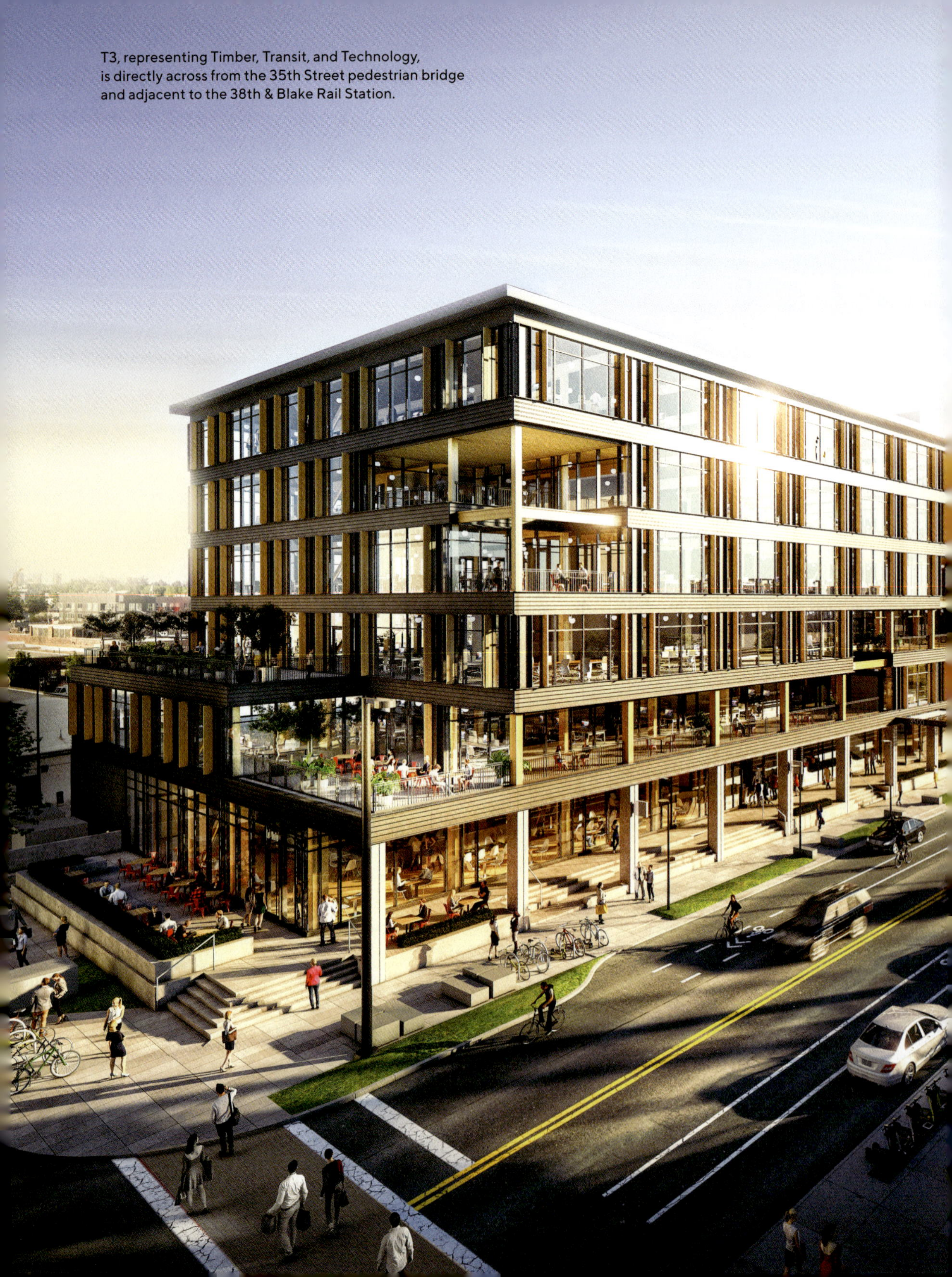

T3, representing Timber, Transit, and Technology, is directly across from the 35th Street pedestrian bridge and adjacent to the 38th & Blake Rail Station.

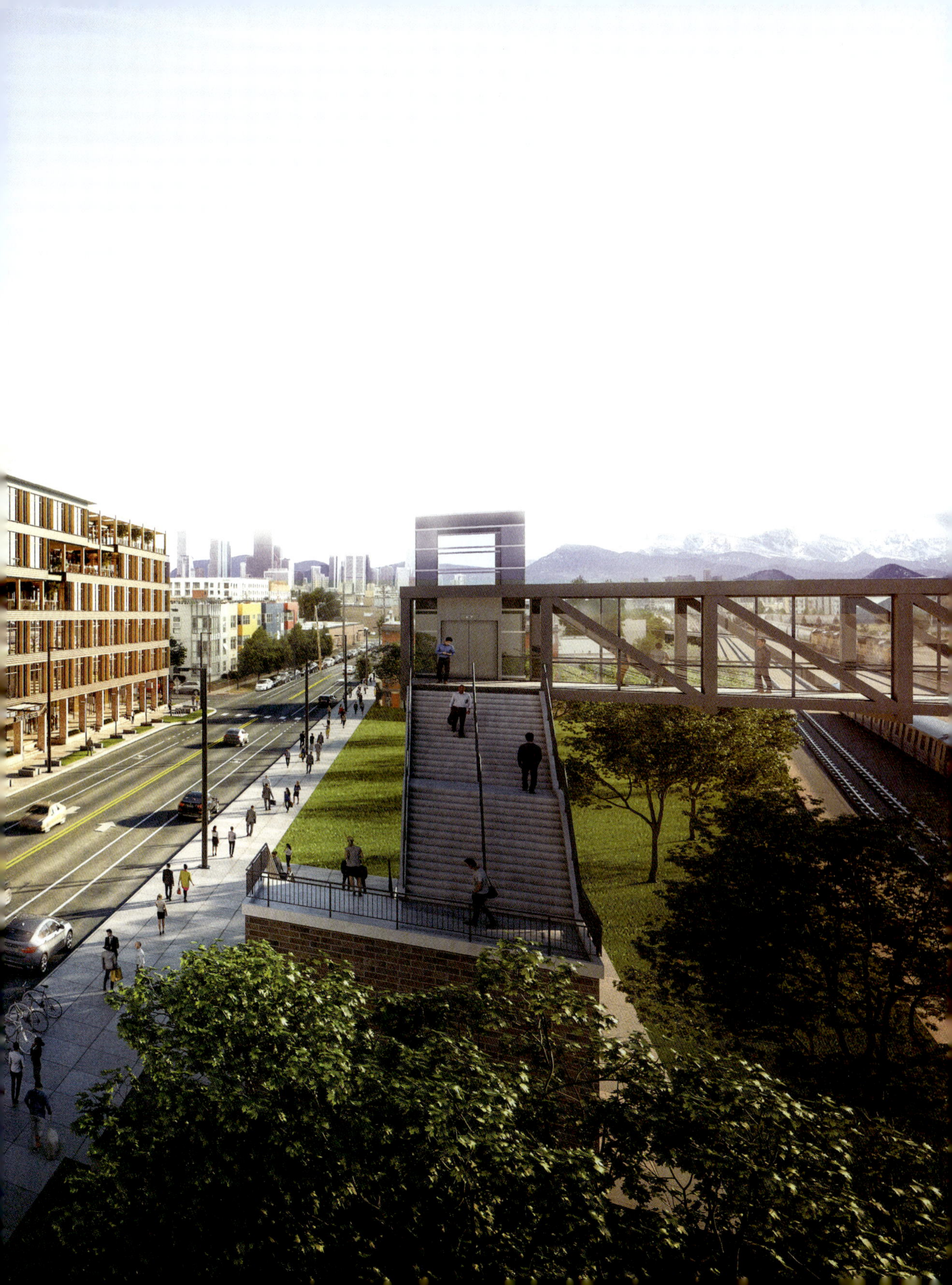

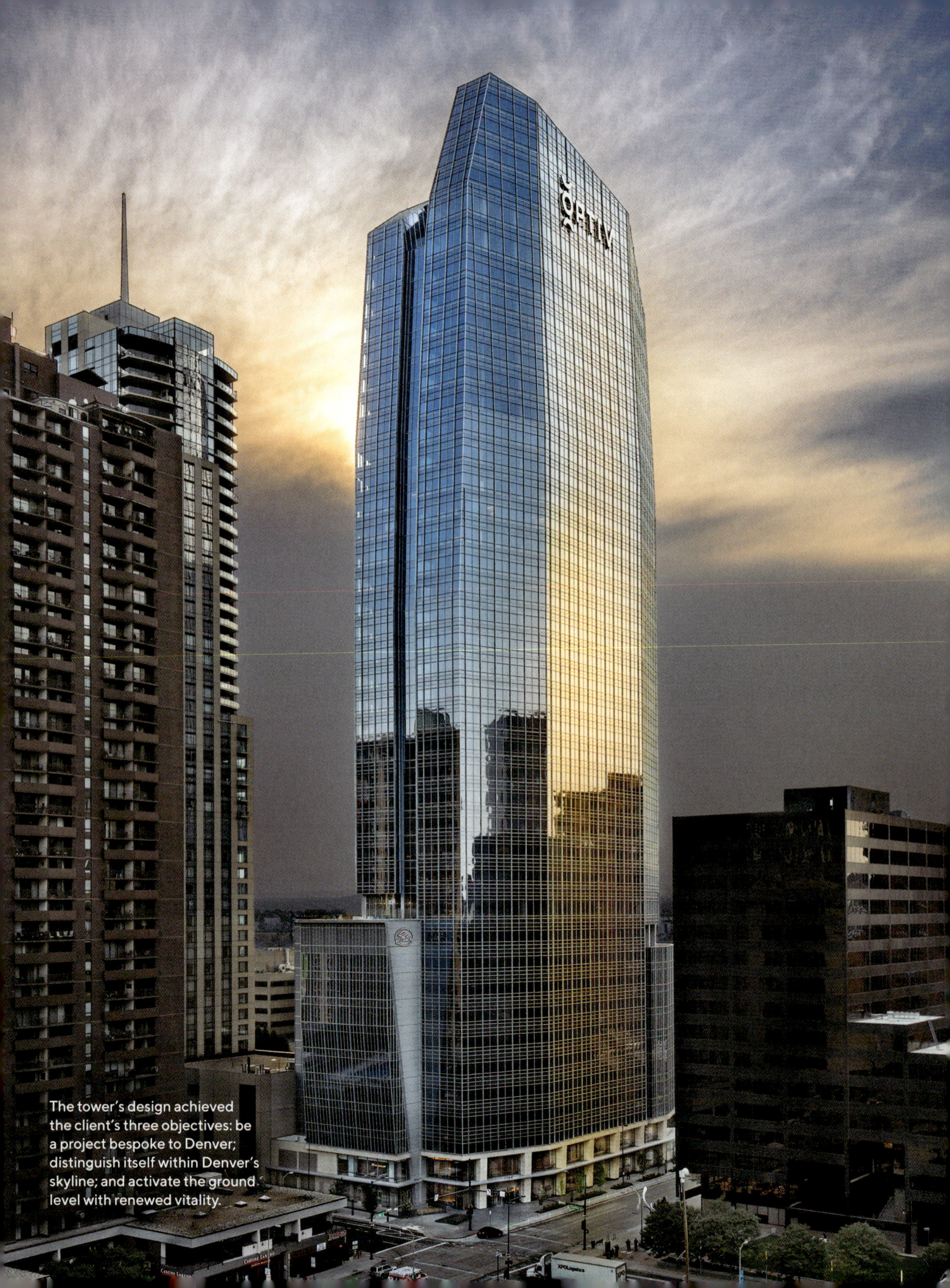

The tower's design achieved the client's three objectives: be a project bespoke to Denver; distinguish itself within Denver's skyline; and activate the ground level with renewed vitality.

The collaborative process allows one to learn about the architect's design approach.

1144 FIFTEENTH STREET
DENVER, COLORADO

Completed 2018
1.2 million gross square feet / 111,500 gross square meters
LEED for Core and Shell Gold

Forty-story-tall 1144 Fifteenth Street is a high-performance, office tower incorporating twenty-seven floors of Class A office space atop a thirteen-story podium comprising retail, restaurants, a fitness center, and an 880-space parking garage. The elegant tower and its massing have been designed to be evocative of the surrounding Rocky Mountains and to establish a geological metaphor within its urban context.

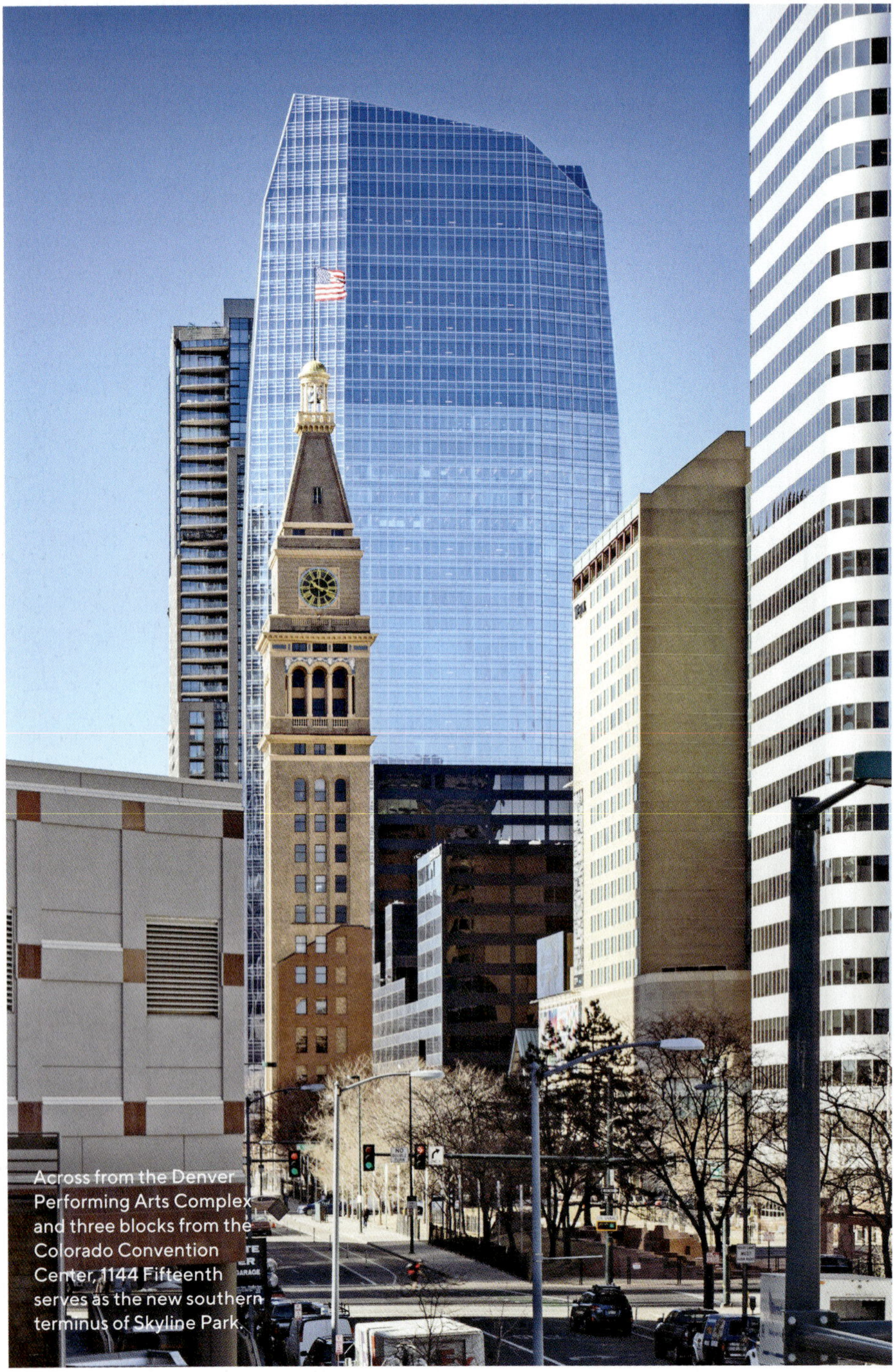

Across from the Denver Performing Arts Complex and three blocks from the Colorado Convention Center, 1144 Fifteenth serves as the new southern terminus of Skyline Park.

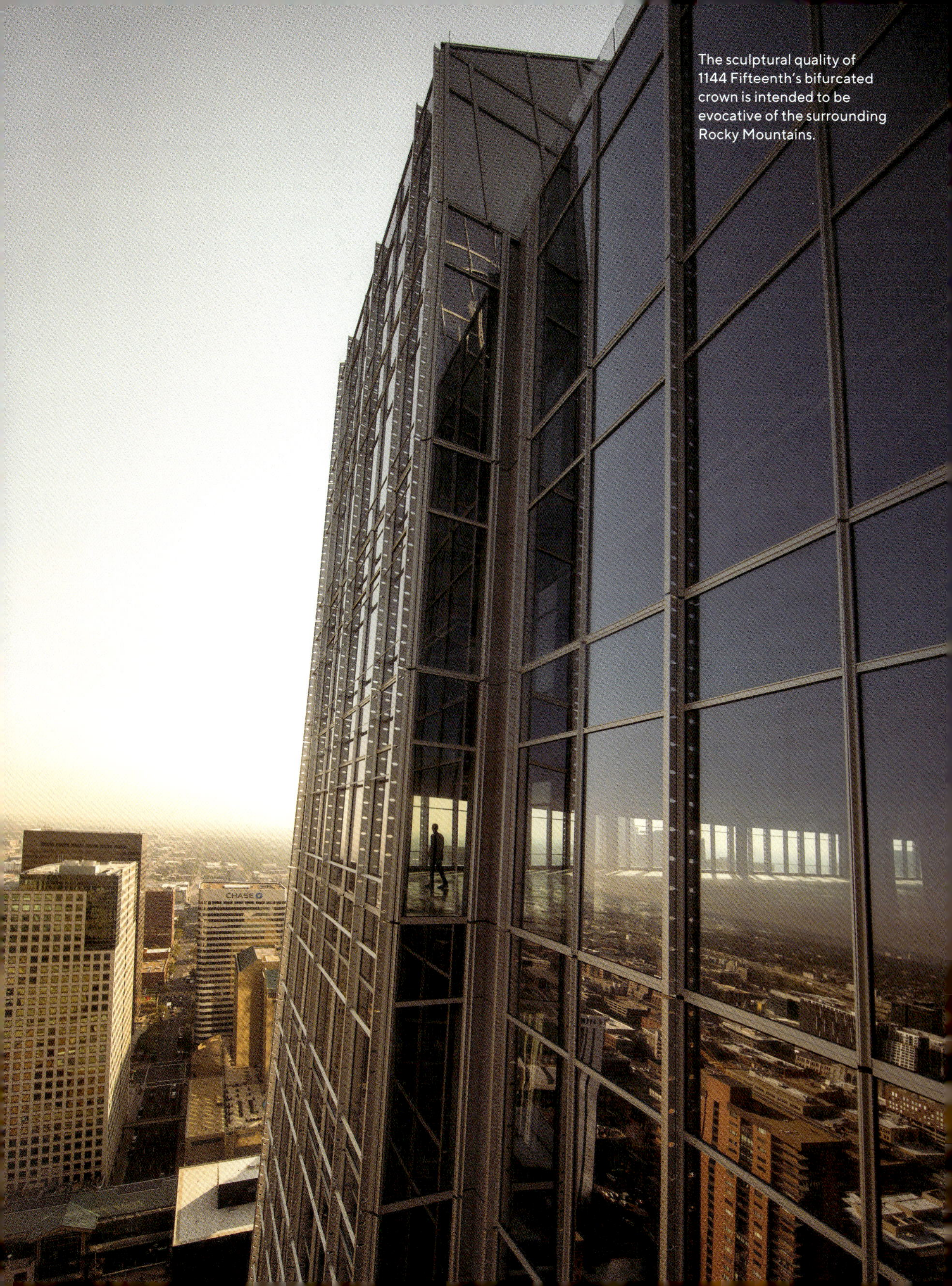

The sculptural quality of 1144 Fifteenth's bifurcated crown is intended to be evocative of the surrounding Rocky Mountains.

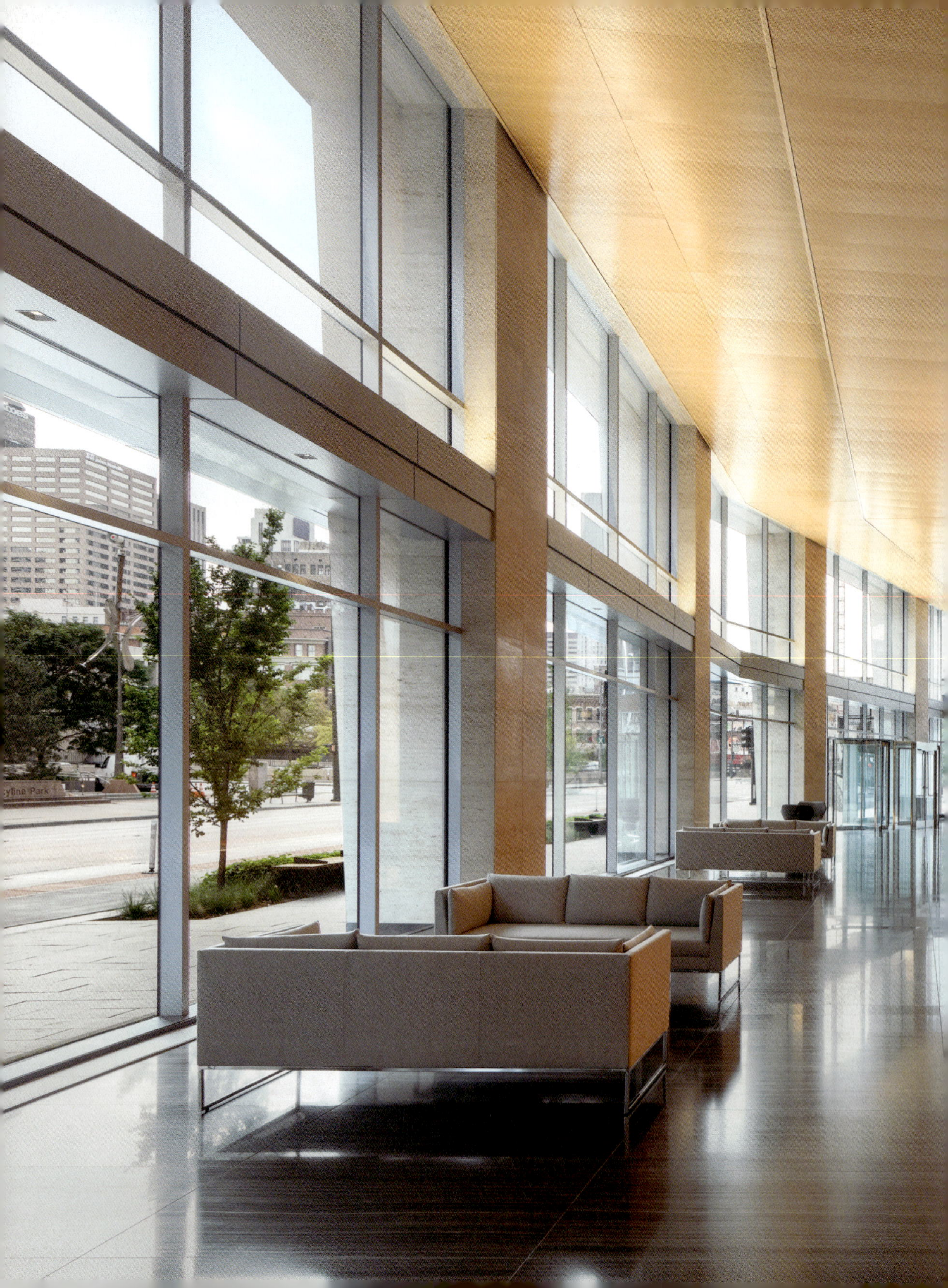

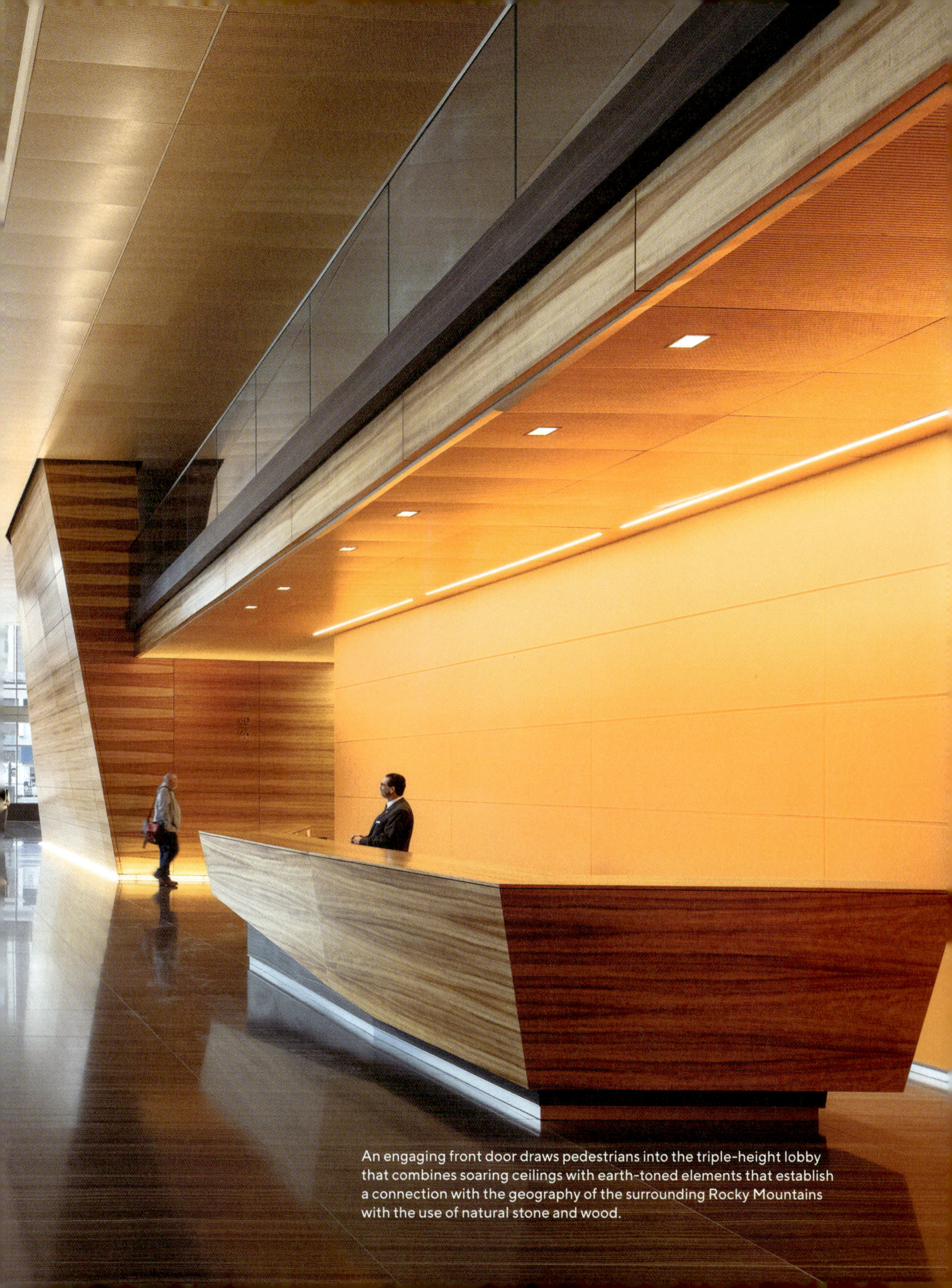

An engaging front door draws pedestrians into the triple-height lobby that combines soaring ceilings with earth-toned elements that establish a connection with the geography of the surrounding Rocky Mountains with the use of natural stone and wood.

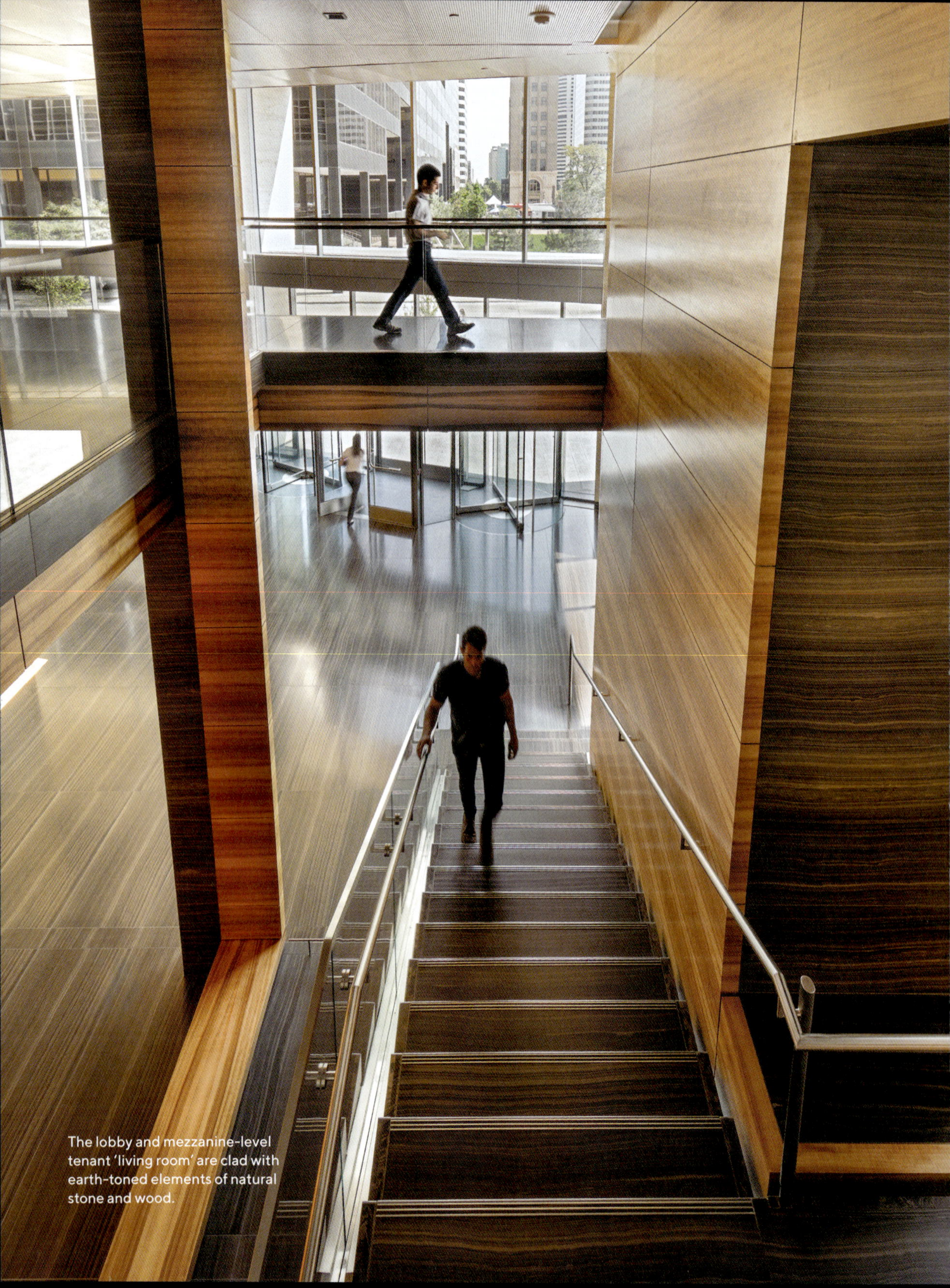

The lobby and mezzanine-level tenant 'living room' are clad with earth-toned elements of natural stone and wood.

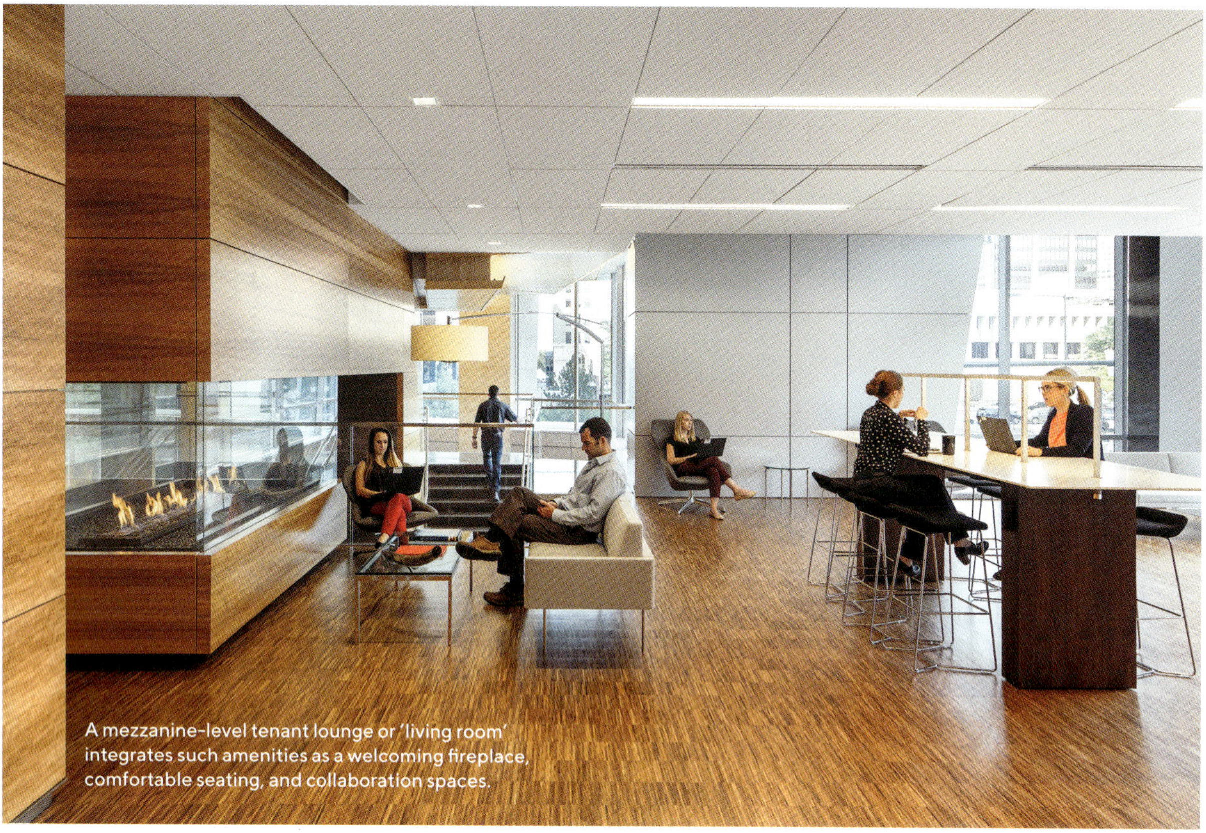

A mezzanine-level tenant lounge or 'living room' integrates such amenities as a welcoming fireplace, comfortable seating, and collaboration spaces.

The bifurcated crown of 1144 Fifteenth draws upon the Rocky Mountains and its sculptural quality creates a spectacular jewel-like shape, catching light to be continuously visible and recognizable from across Denver.

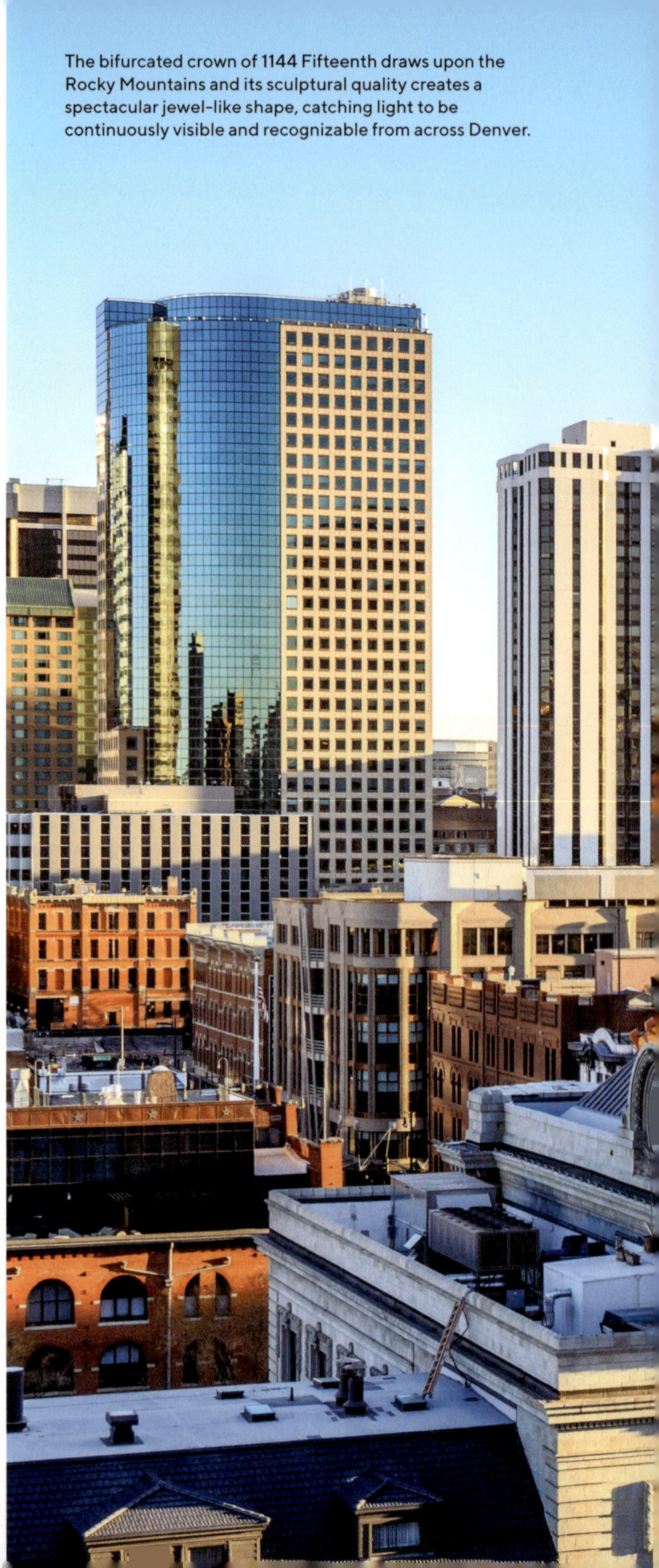

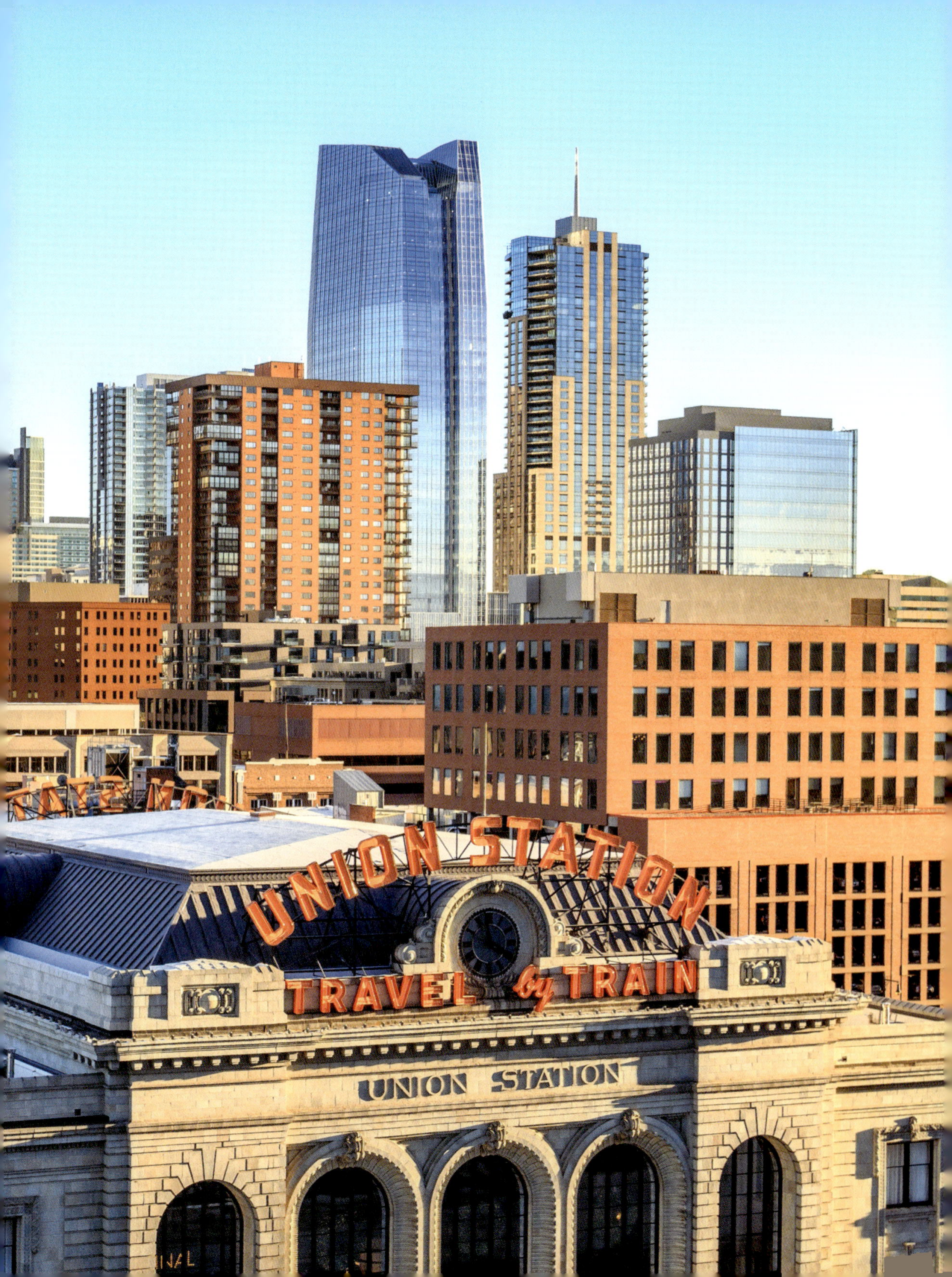
UNION STATION
TRAVEL by TRAIN
UNION STATION

Building Consensus

MINNESOTA
SENATE BUILDING

Minnesota Department of Administration

Pickard Chilton

BWBR

CPMI

Ericksen Roed & Associates

Dunham Associates

Coen+Partners

EVS

M. A. Mortenson Company

CALPERS HEADQUARTERS
COMPLEX

California Public Employees Retirement System

Pickard Chilton

Kendall/Heaton Associates

Magnusson Klemencic Associates

CYS Structural Engineers, Inc

Arup

Hart Howerton

Interior Architects

Hensel Phelps

Every design project results from the give-and-take of ideas. Ultimately, the architecture reflects the ideas of the many individuals involved in its creation, with ideas often entwined in ways that make the result greater than their sum. The product is consensus — the outcome of collaboration. When do you know that you have a good collaborator in a client? How does architecture become greater than the sum of the architect, the client, and others whose lives will be affected by this work of architecture? How is the goal of consensus reflected in the architecture, how does it express itself in the finished design?

In the design of civic architecture — the environments that frame our role as citizens — the goal of consensus as an outcome of collaboration is key. For example, the majestic Minnesota State Capitol is the centerpiece of an ensemble of government

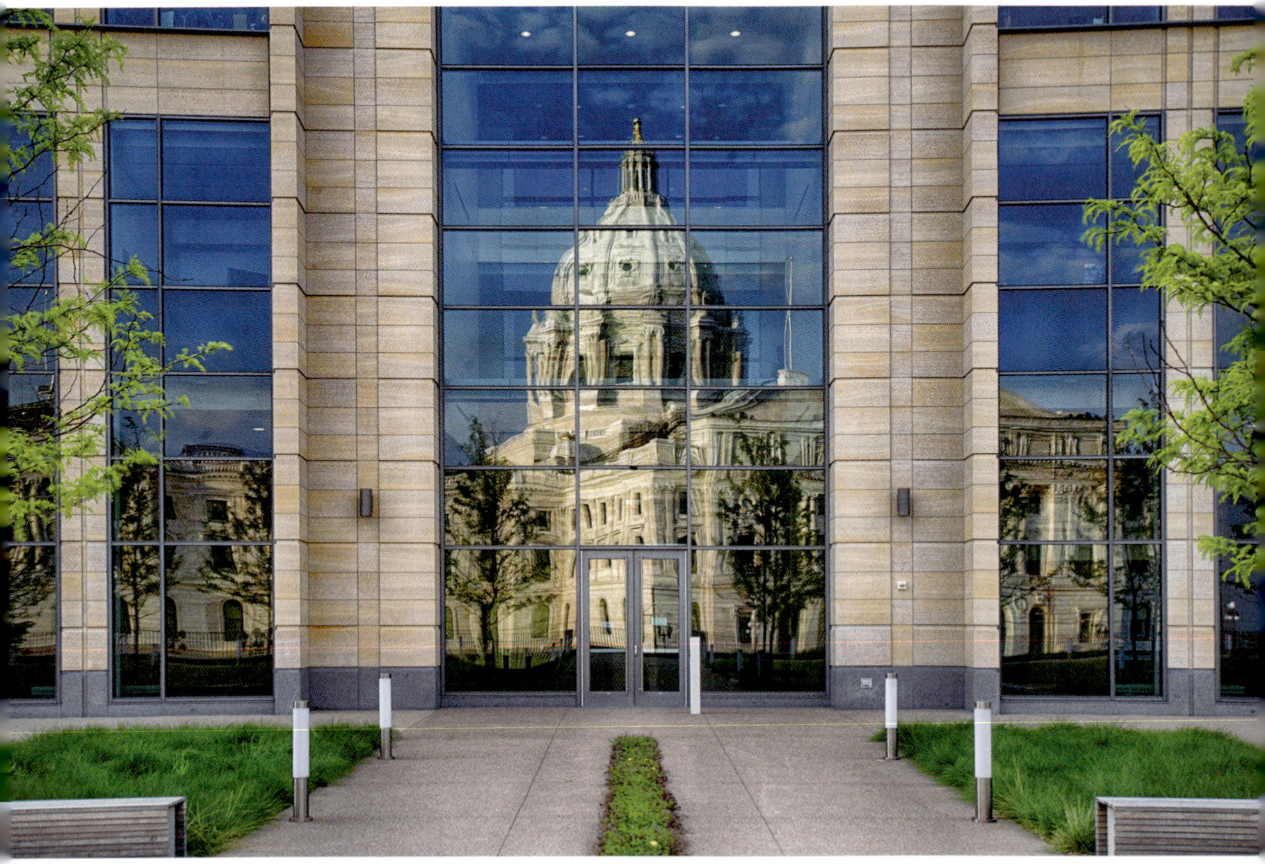

Senate Building façade reflects the majesty of the Minnesota State Capitol Building.

buildings that defer to it, as they radiate from Cass Gilbert's 1905 statehouse that surmounts Capitol Hill. The deference of the surrounding architecture to the capitol is an expression of consensus — often adhered to, other times ignored — that has shaped the siting and design of the state's civic buildings constructed around the capitol. State Senator Ann Rest, who was involved on the client side with the design of the new Minnesota Senate Building, notes that a key expression of Pickard Chilton's understanding of this deference to the existing design consensus is a conceptual sketch (it now hangs in her office) that shows how the new senate building in its siting and architectural form might reflect the importance of the capitol — the focus of the attention of all whose senate offices face the capitol across the street. The Minnesota Senate Building's curved south wall allows each senate office to have a slightly different orientation toward the capitol dome, framing views of it. For Senator Rest, the design reflects the consensus in this capital city that the dome is the preeminent symbol of the government. All — people and architecture — should defer to the "people's house."

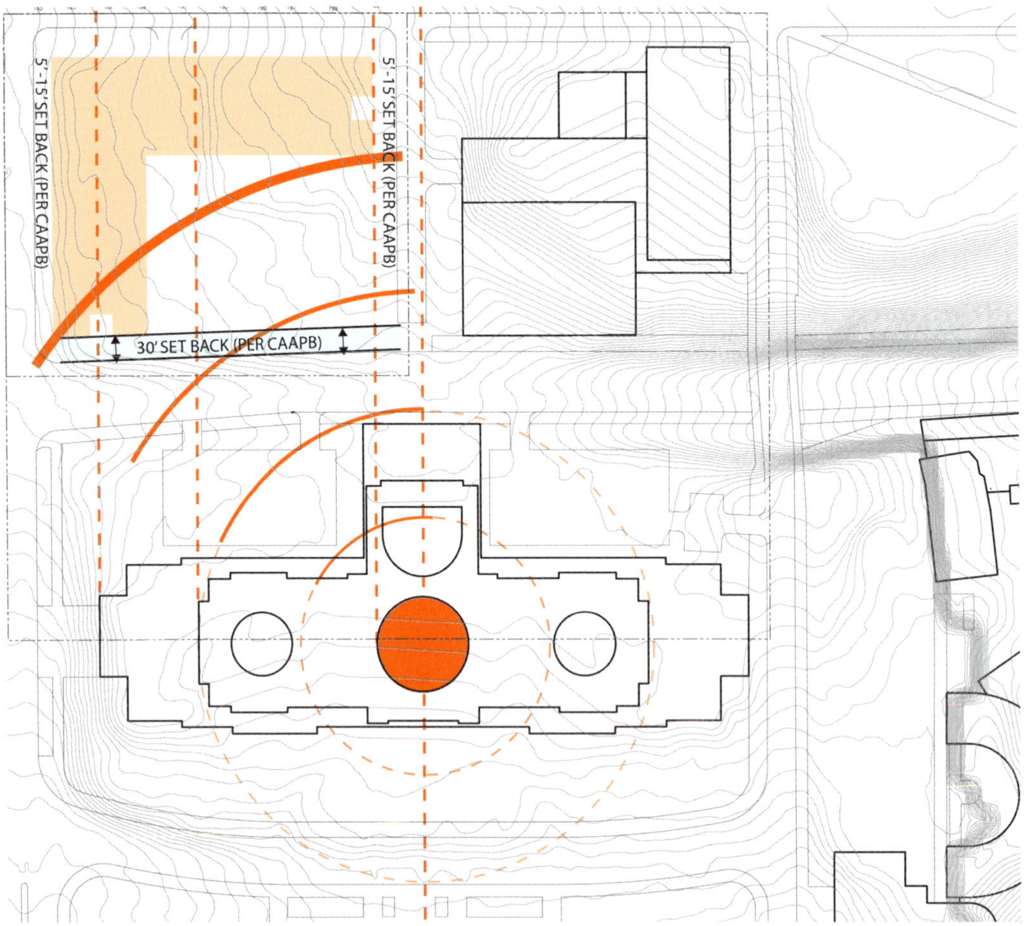
5'-15' SET BACK (PER CAAPB)
5'-15' SET BACK (PER CAAPB)
30' SET BACK (PER CAAPB)

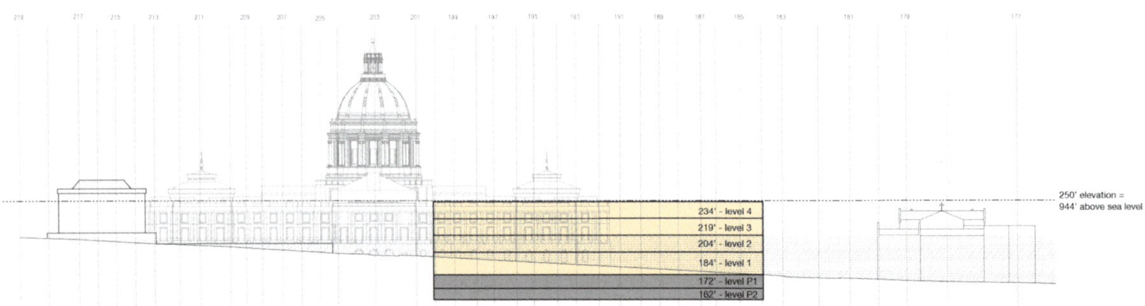
234' - level 4
219' - level 3
204' - level 2
184' - level 1
172' - level P1
162' - level P2
250' elevation =
944' above sea level

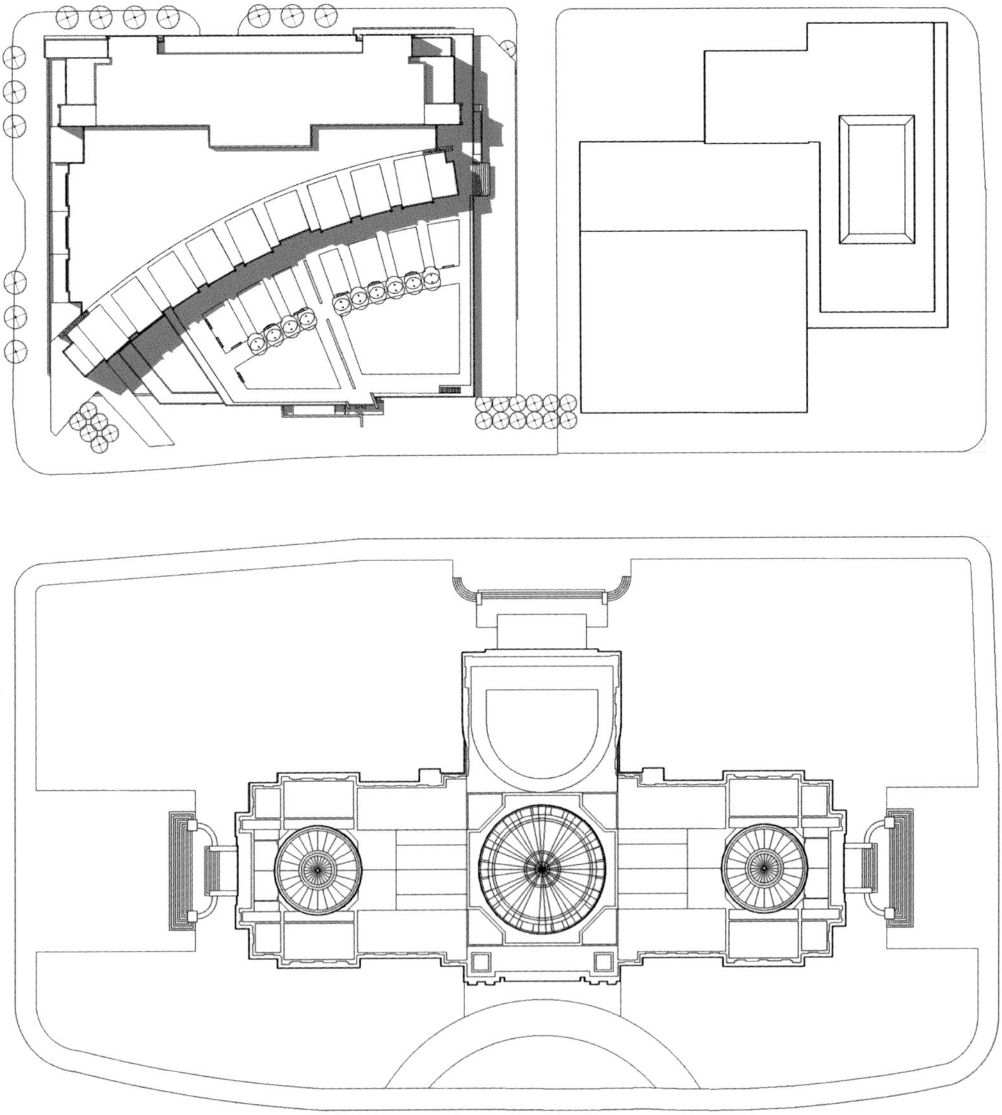

Illustrations of the Minnesota Senate Building's radial form in homage to the State Capitol Building.

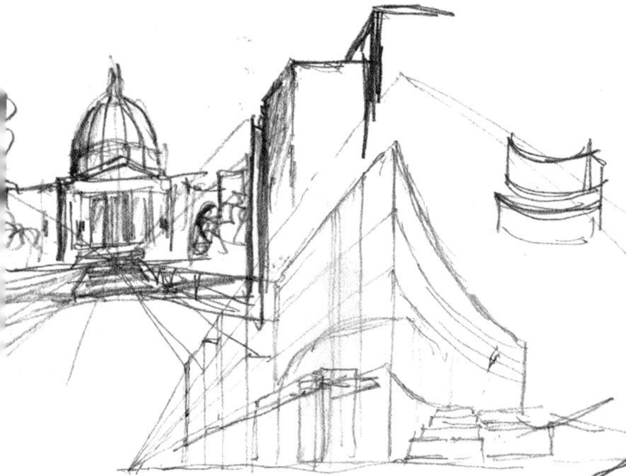

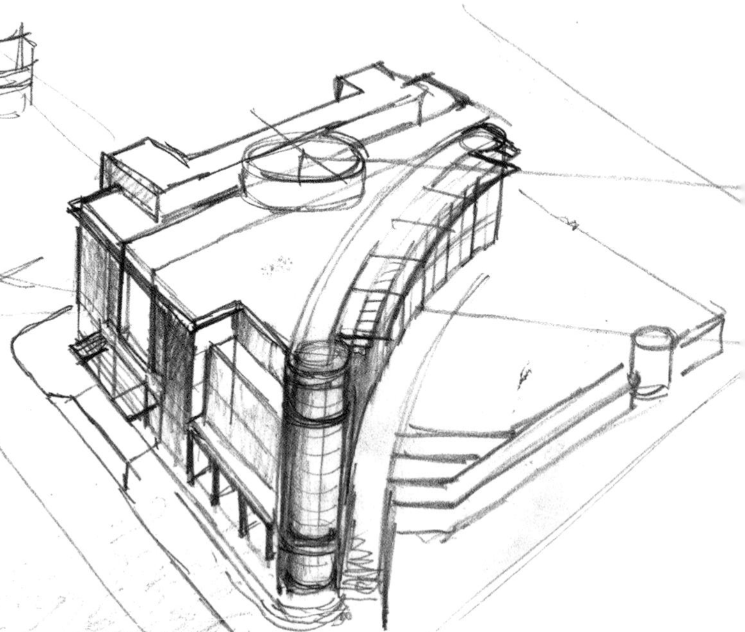

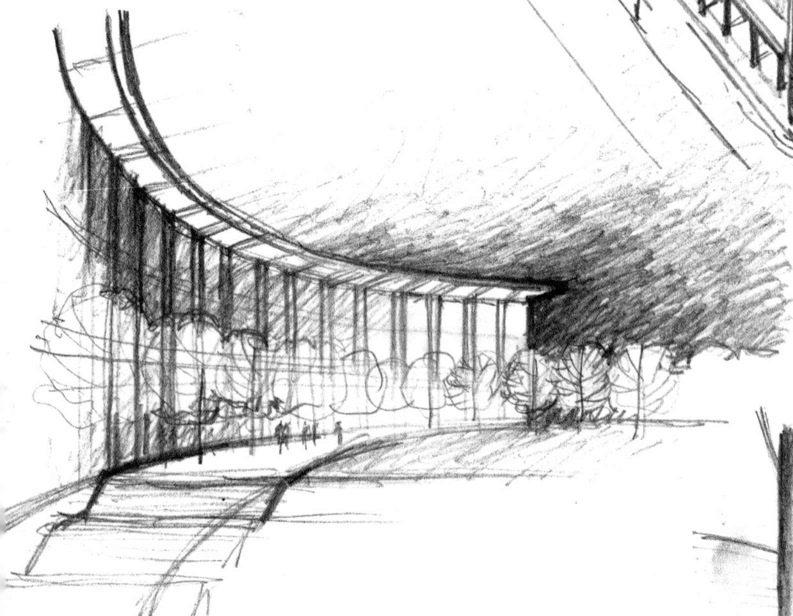

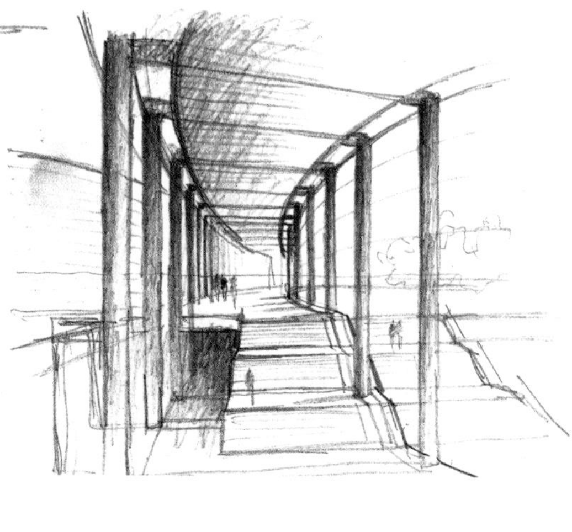

Sketches by Jon Pickard demonstrating architectural response to the capitol building.

The architectural language of the Minnesota Senate Building is appropriate in its relation to Cass Gilbert's landmark. "When you walk into the capitol, there is an overwhelming sense of grandeur," explains Senator Rest. The Senate Building is in marked contrast to this landmark. She describes the new building as warm, collegial, comforting, even accepting. That the design of the new buildings needed to defer to the capitol was a strong message that Senator Rest and her colleagues communicated early in the design process. The series of conceptual design drawings that resulted clearly reflect that the client was heard. There was consensus among both the client and architect that this would be the most appropriate design response.

Building consensus about the design of a new headquarters for the California Public Employees Retirement System (CalPERS) involved a carefully considered, disciplined, and directed effort on the part of the architects working closely with the CalPERS board committee overseeing the project to enfranchise those in the neighborhood who would be affected by the architecture. The process was very open, with all the meetings of the

CalPERS's board committee being public. The client and the architects engaged local citizens through dozens of public sessions where consensus building was transparent. According to Diana Proctor, CalPERS's project director, "Each meeting with the public was followed immediately by a meeting with the board. The board was deeply engaged in the early design, and they were provided with input from the community. Likewise, at each public meeting the public was told what the board's perspectives were." Proctor adds that the architects "did an outstanding job of communicating between these groups, building the relationship with each one through their honesty, integrity, and ethics."

CalPERS's massing was oriented to maximize access to natural light while minimizing solar heat gain.

The goal was to design a project that not only satisfied CalPERS's needs, but also enhanced the urban experience of this part of Sacramento, which was subdued after work hours. The architects and client purposely didn't have preconceived ideas about a design—consensus became the objective. According to Proctor, the architects "listened and engaged people on the street with their openness. We held public meetings, and the architects had nothing on paper. Sometimes a designer begins to formulate a scheme before the public process,

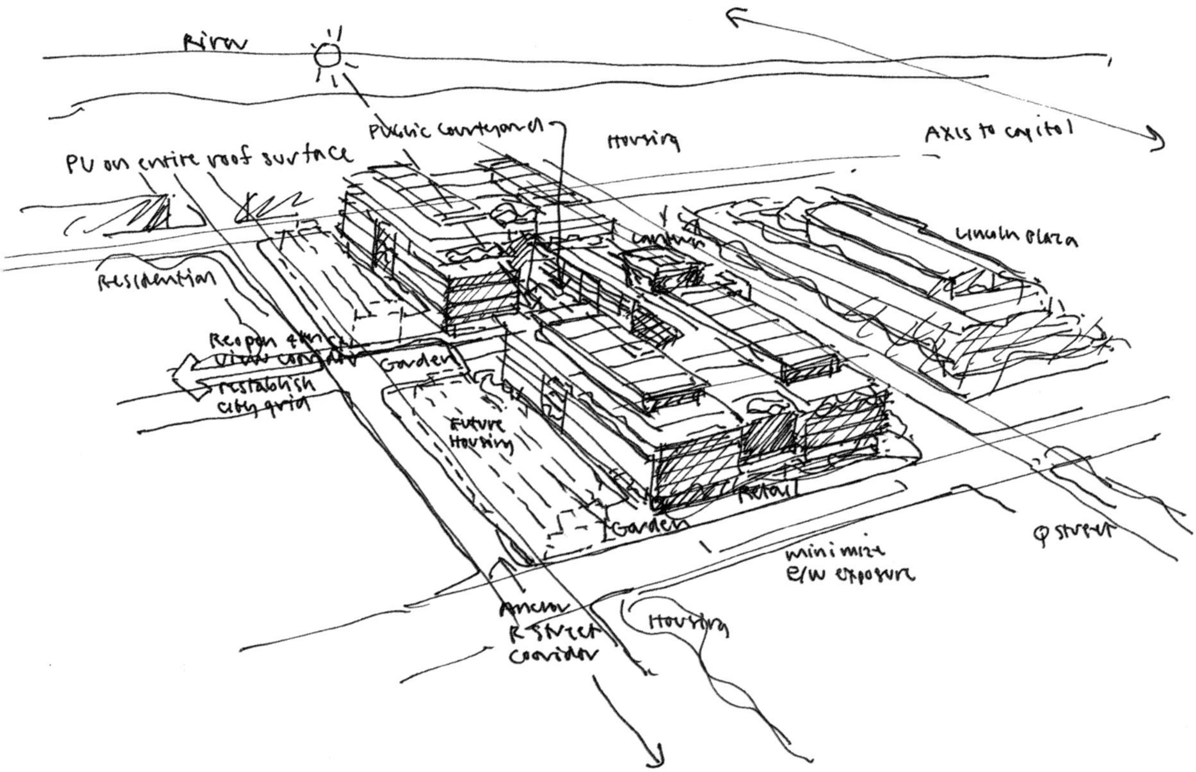

but Pickard Chilton had blank sheets. When we started a programming design charette with the community, it was hostile. But the process lasted for six months and was critical to building a successful relationship as well as trust with the community." Proctor recalls of this consensus-building process: "By the time we did the environmental impact report, which is often contentious, we ended up with no litigation, no opposition to the project."

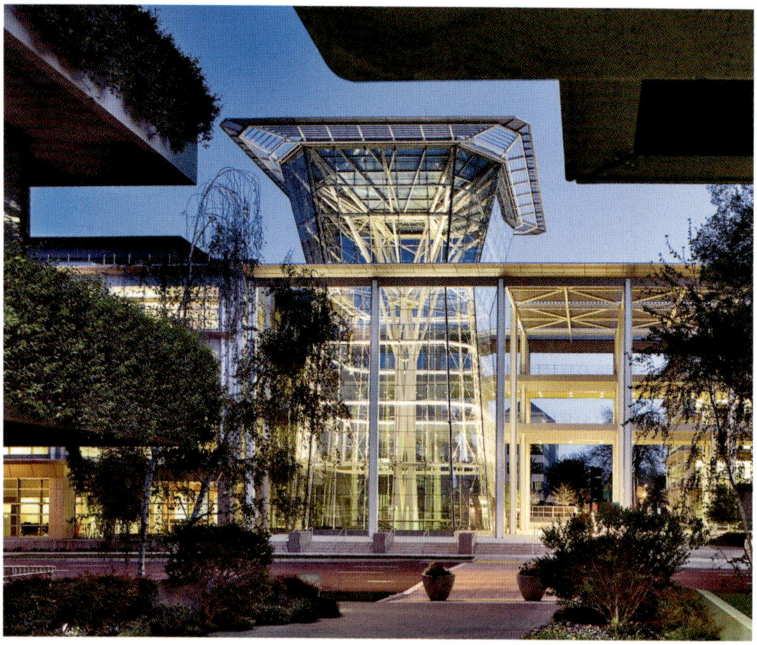

← The six-story lantern's visible prominence clearly identifies the entrance to the headquarters complex.

→ Sectional sketch illustrates pedestrian and vehicular circulation at the entrance.

Local interest that the project generate urban liveliness resulted in a design that allowed an existing street to pass through the building, encouraging street life, and keeping the headquarters from feeling like an impenetrable fortress (a criticism about the existing building). Comments about not being able to find the front door to CalPERS's existing headquarters, which was set back from the street, resulted in the new building's entrance being a light-filled lantern of an atrium, with a tree-like structure right up front, uplifting the entire neighborhood.

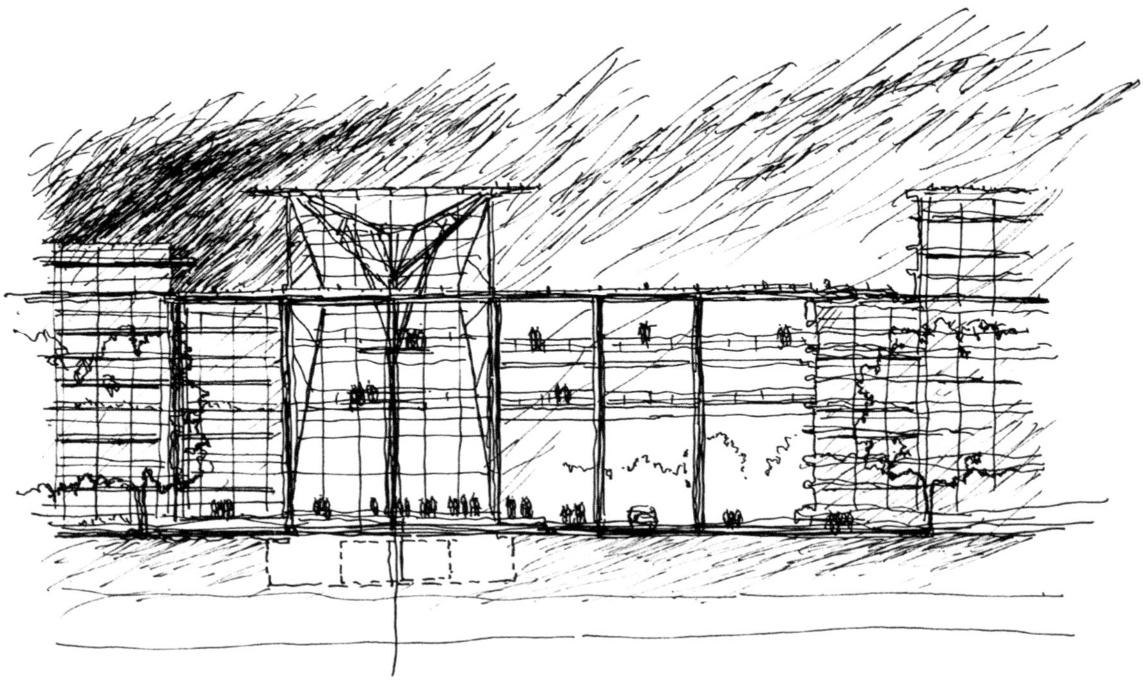

The design's glassy nature also helps to put the art selected for the interior on public display as an amenity for the local community, which is also welcome to enjoy the park-like spaces around the new building.

"The community feels enfranchised in this design," explains Proctor. Involvement in the process by community members validated the design for those in the neighborhood. "If we didn't truly engage them, we would have lost the opportunity for collaboration and building consensus."

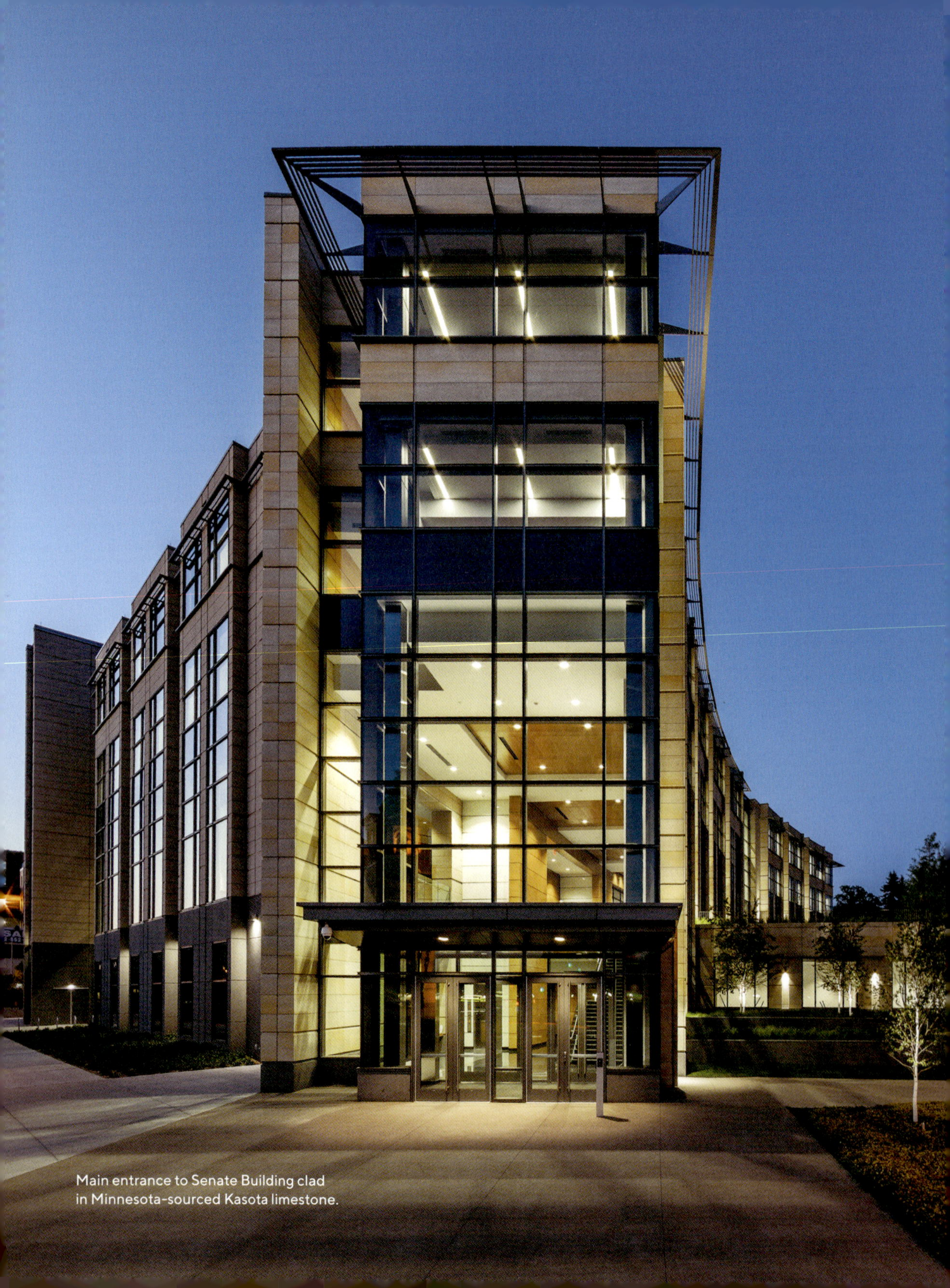

Main entrance to Senate Building clad in Minnesota-sourced Kasota limestone.

The product is consensus – the outcome of collaboration.

MINNESOTA SENATE BUILDING
ST. PAUL, MINNESOTA

Completed 2017
293,000 gross square feet / 27,220 gross square meters
B3 Certified

Sited directly northwest of Cass Gilbert's historic 1905 State Capitol Building, the new Minnesota Senate Building has been designed to respond to Senate majority leader Tom Bakk's vision for "a landmark in its own right, architecturally distinctive and worthy of the 21st century." Its design purposefully facilitates greater interaction and communication with the citizens of Minnesota.

Arcing along the radius of the capitol's dome, the building's massing gently curves to maximize views back to the capitol.

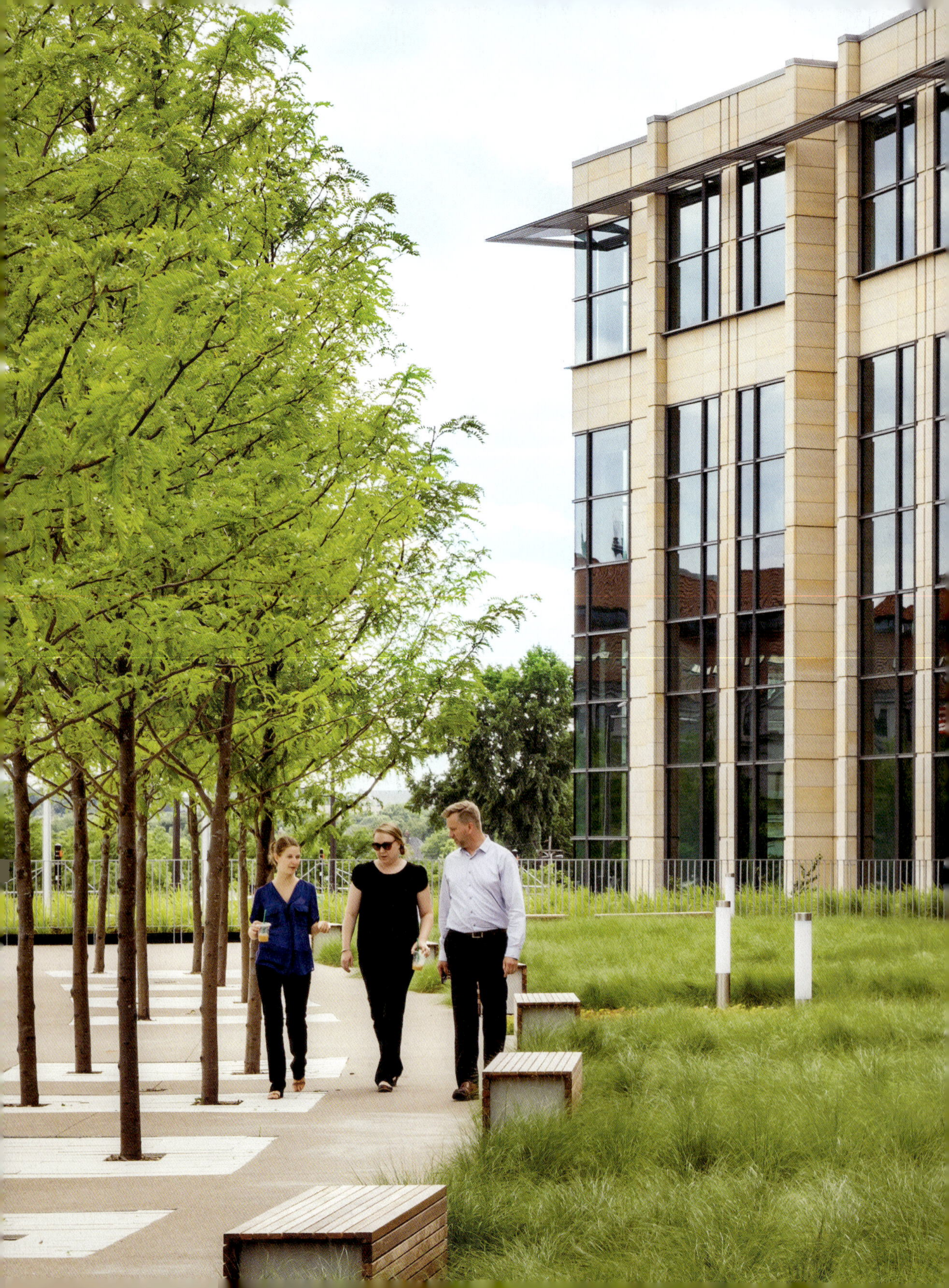

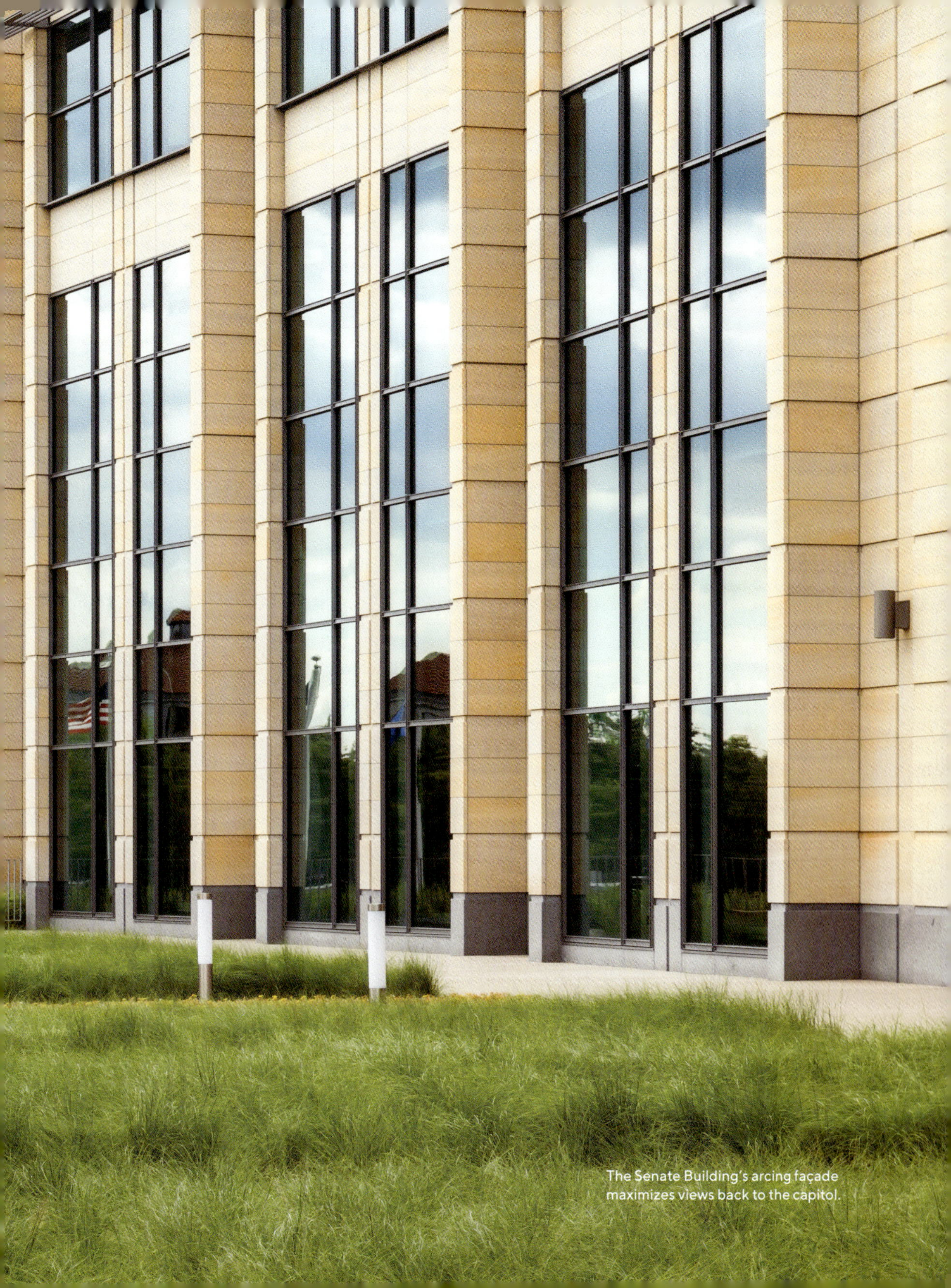

The Senate Building's arcing façade maximizes views back to the capitol.

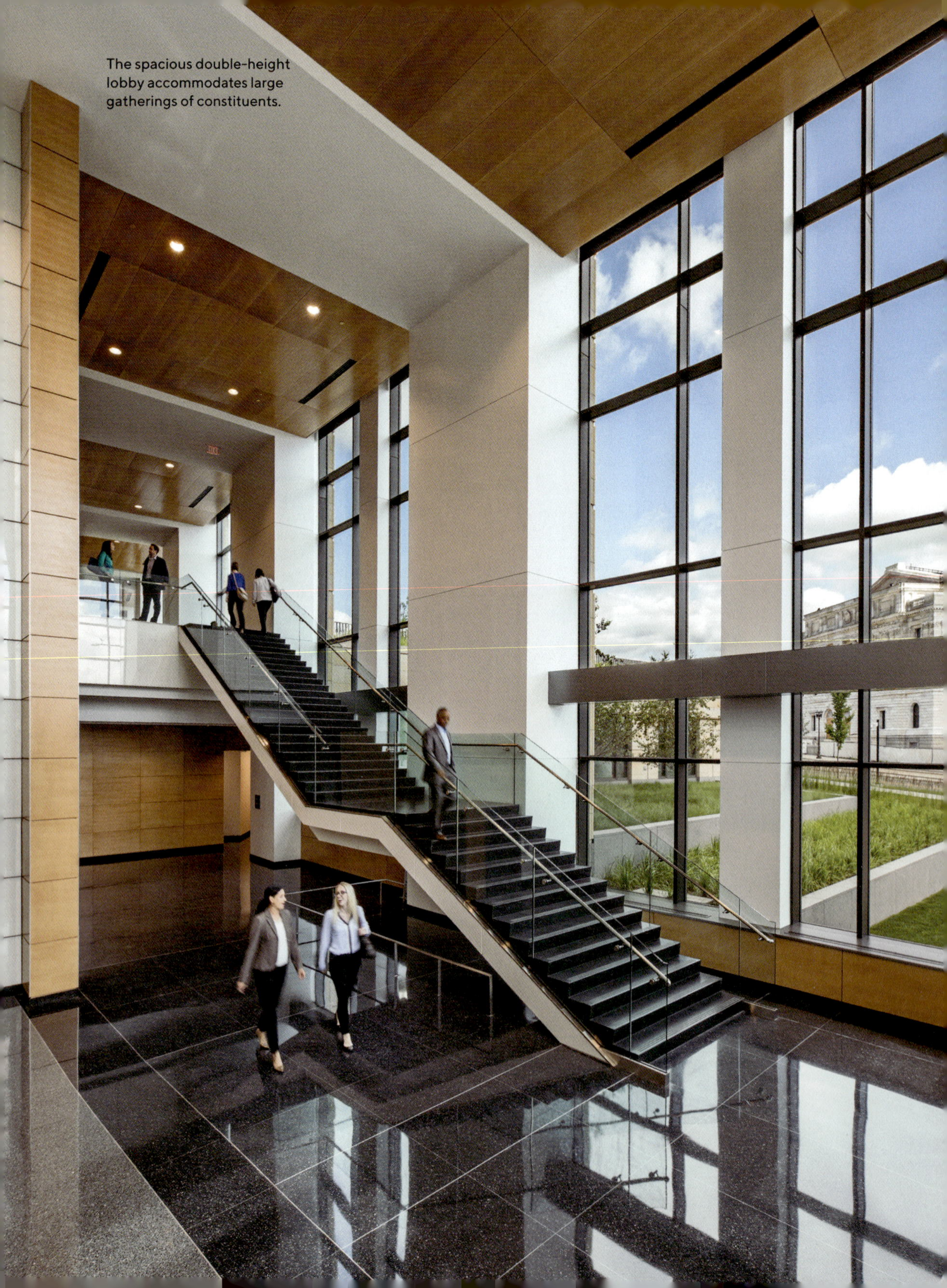

The spacious double-height lobby accommodates large gatherings of constituents.

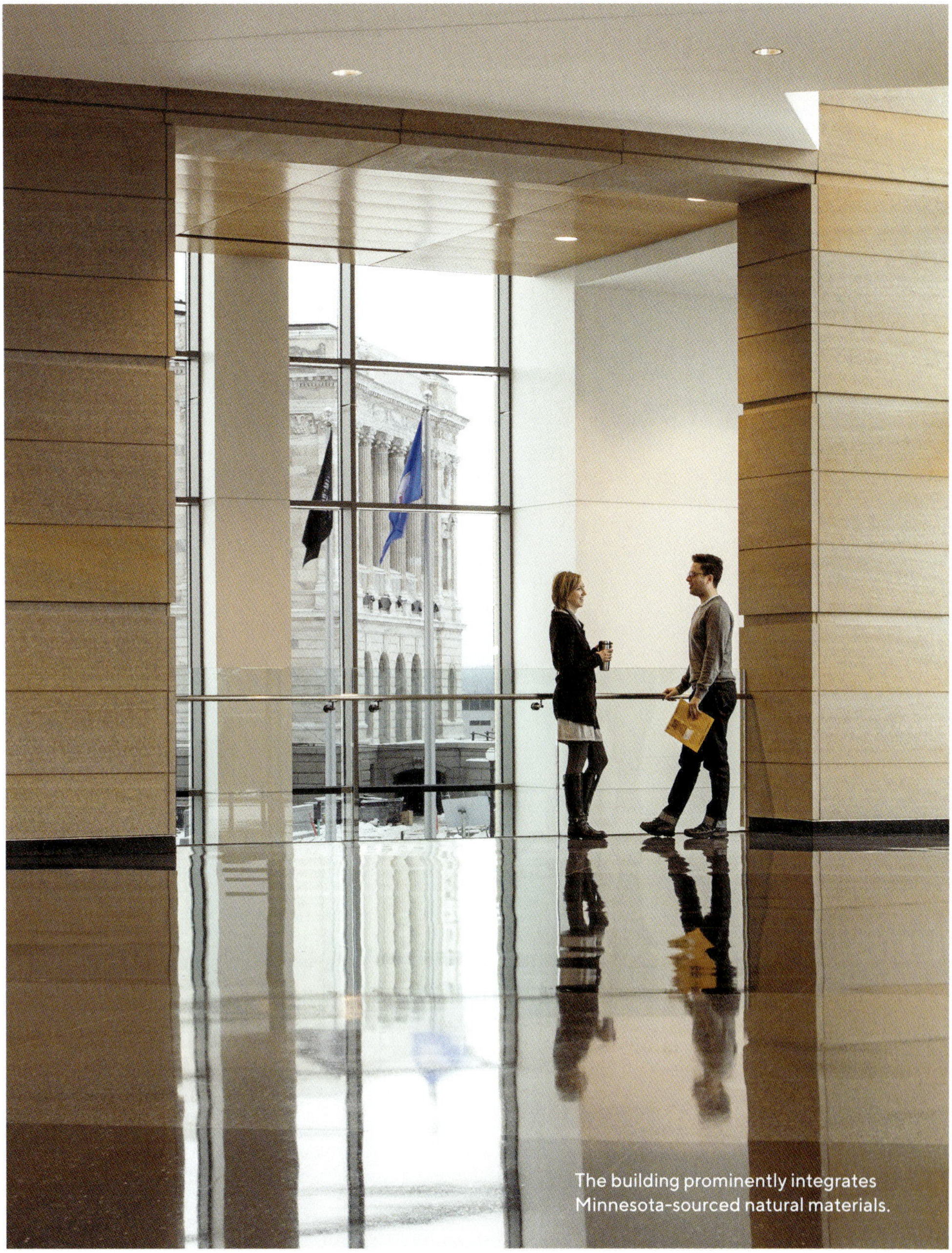

The building prominently integrates Minnesota-sourced natural materials.

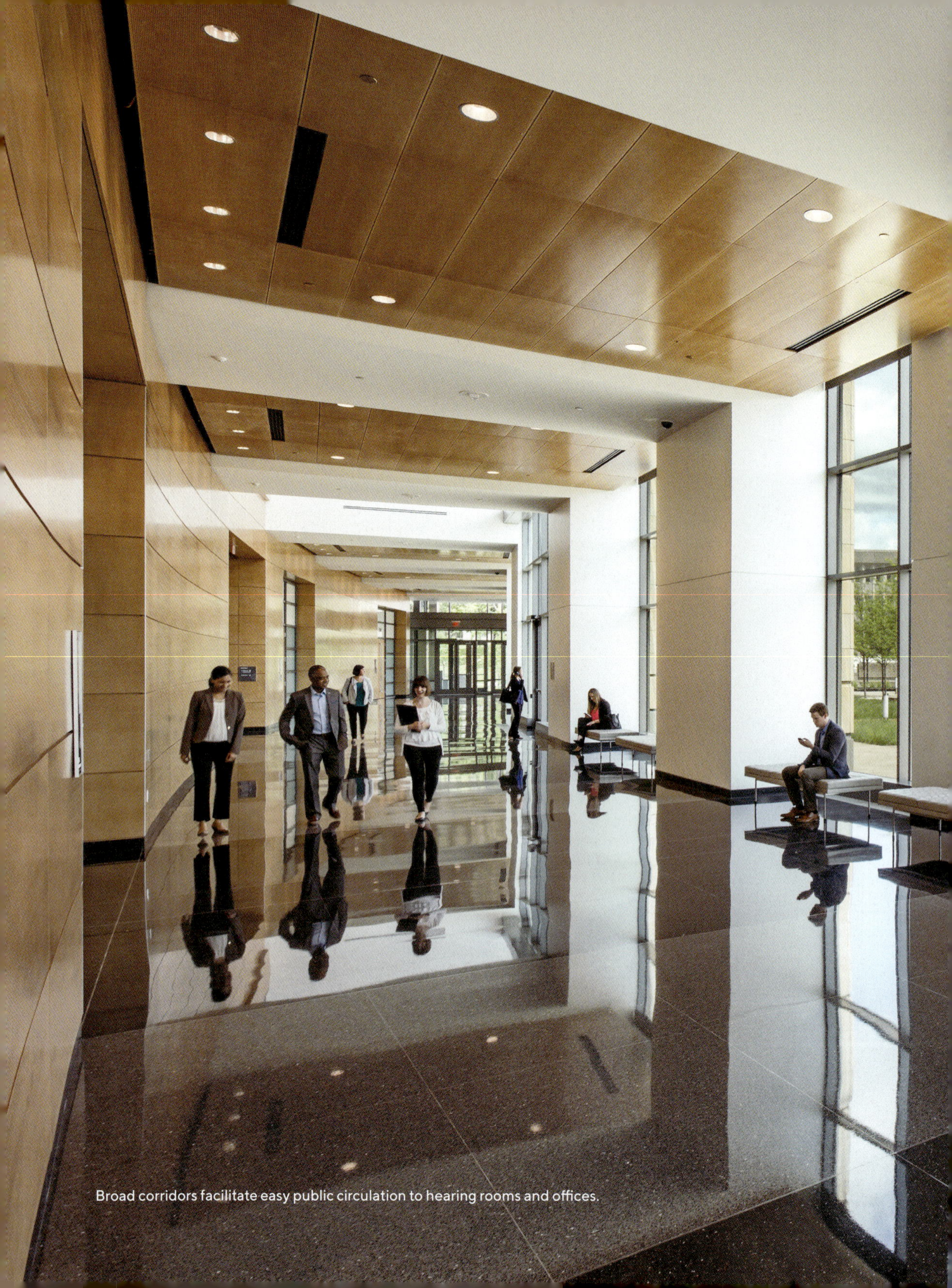

Broad corridors facilitate easy public circulation to hearing rooms and offices.

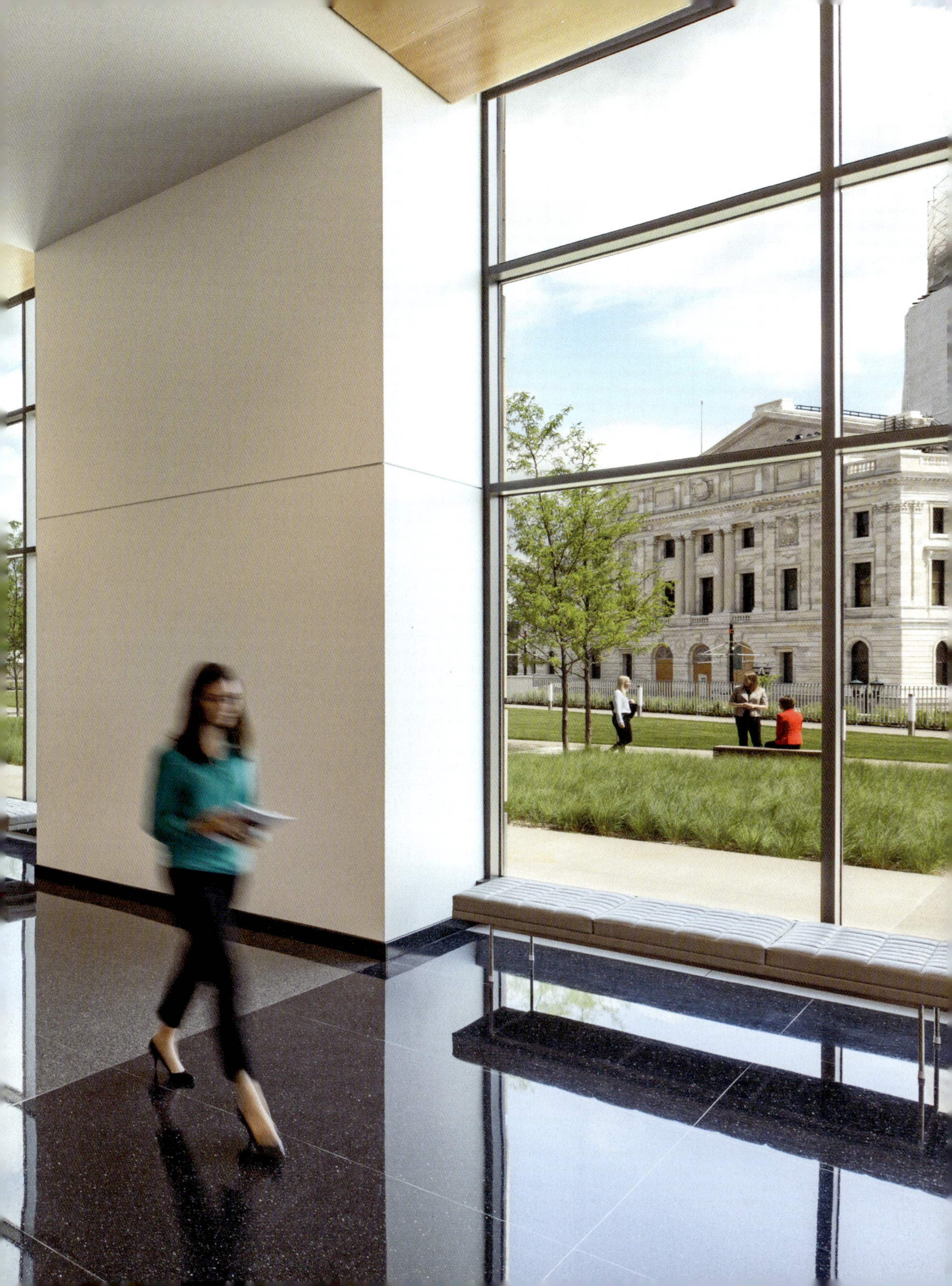

“The community feels enfranchised in this design.”

Diana Proctor
Project Manager, CalPERS

CALPERS HEADQUARTERS COMPLEX
SACRAMENTO, CALIFORNIA

Completed 2006
1.1 million gross square feet / 102,200 gross square meters
LEED for New Construction Gold

The California Public Employees Retirement System (CalPERS) Headquarters Complex is a mixed-use development integrating 550,000 square feet / 51,100 square meters of commercial office space, 25,000 square feet / 2,322 square meters of retail space, 180,000 square feet / 16,722 square meters of housing, and below-grade parking for 1,000 cars. The site comprises two contiguous blocks located in Sacramento’s downtown.

An iconic six-story glass pavilion announces the entrance to the headquarters.

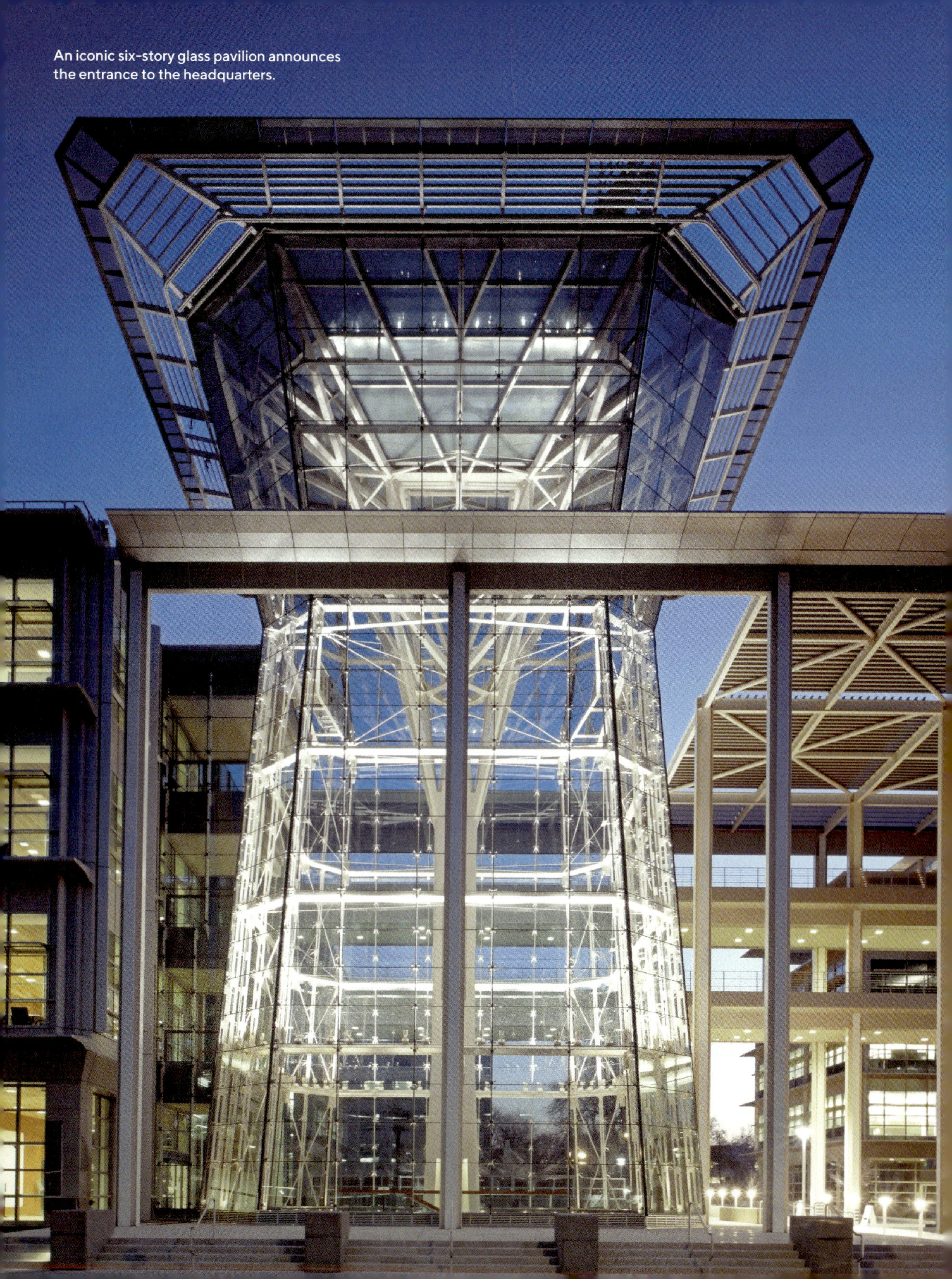

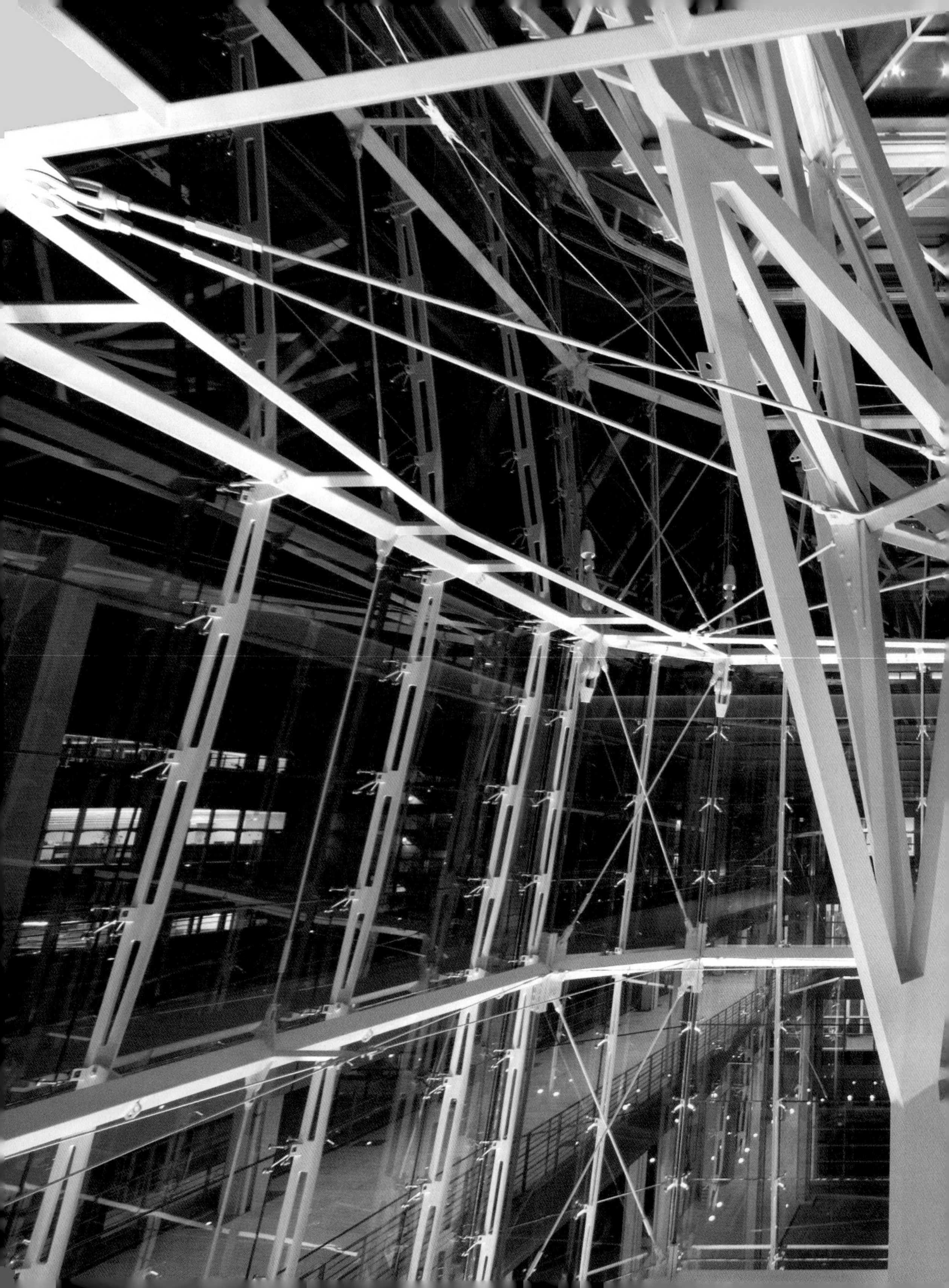

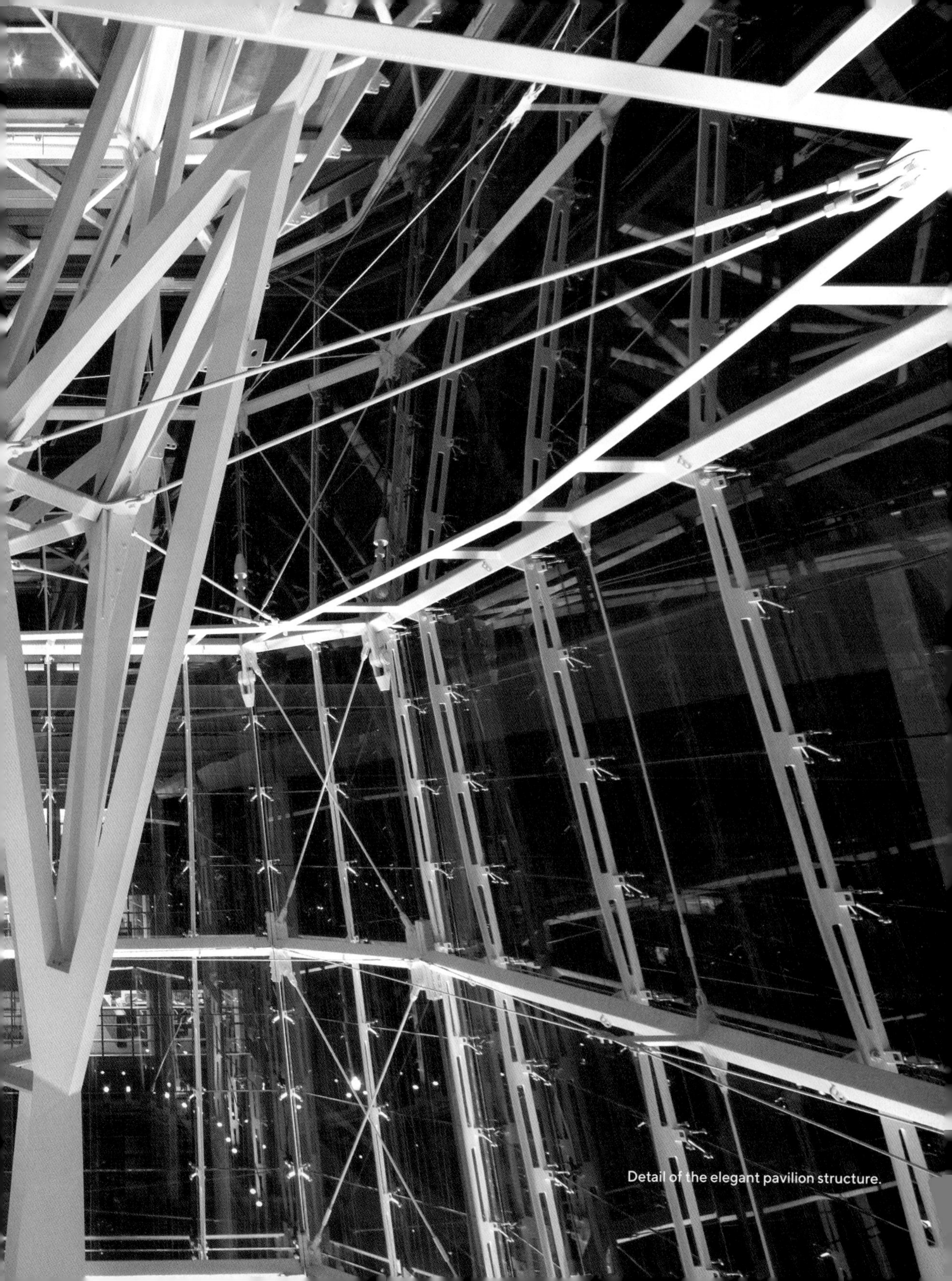

Detail of the elegant pavilion structure.

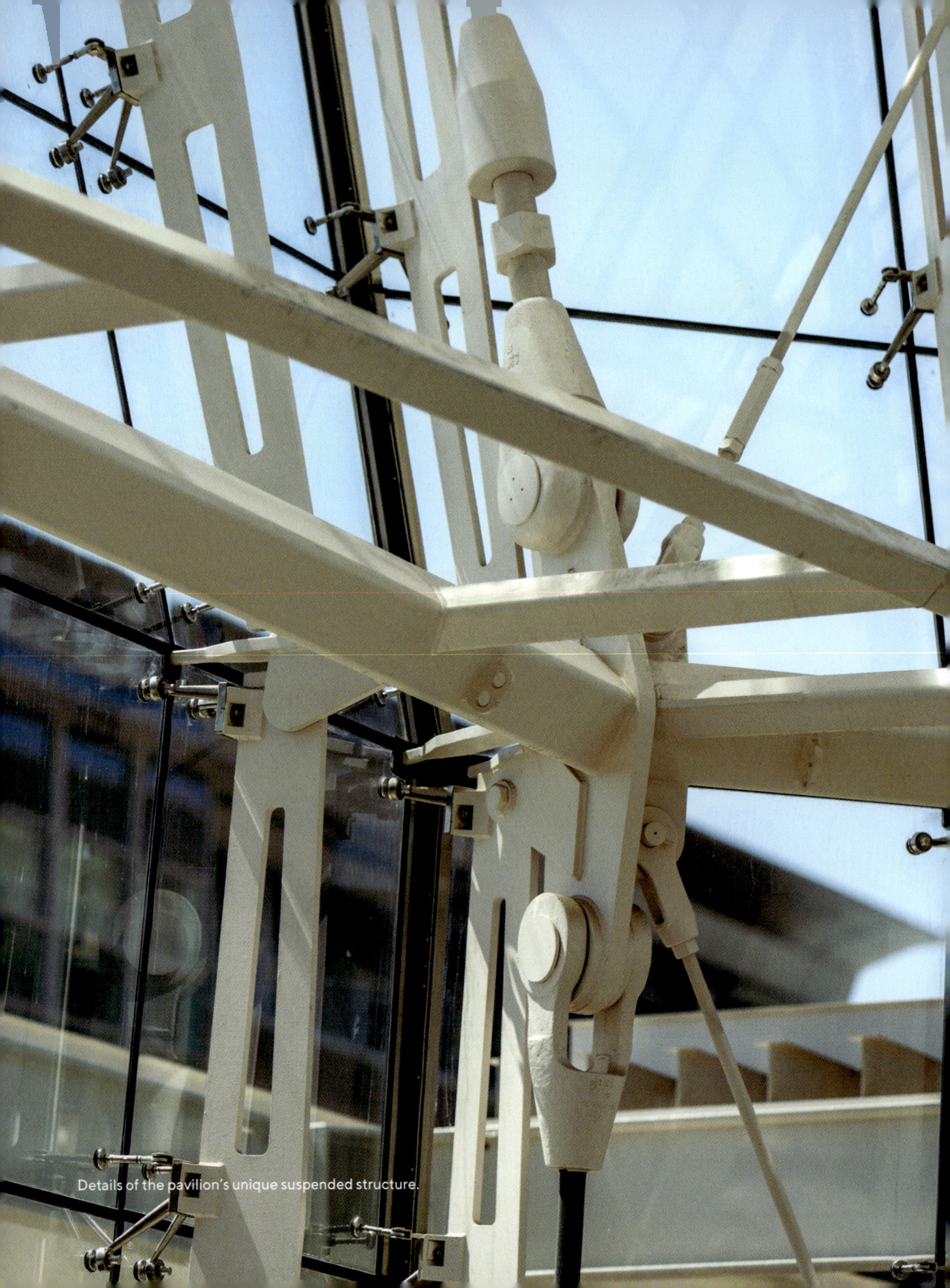

Details of the pavilion's unique suspended structure.

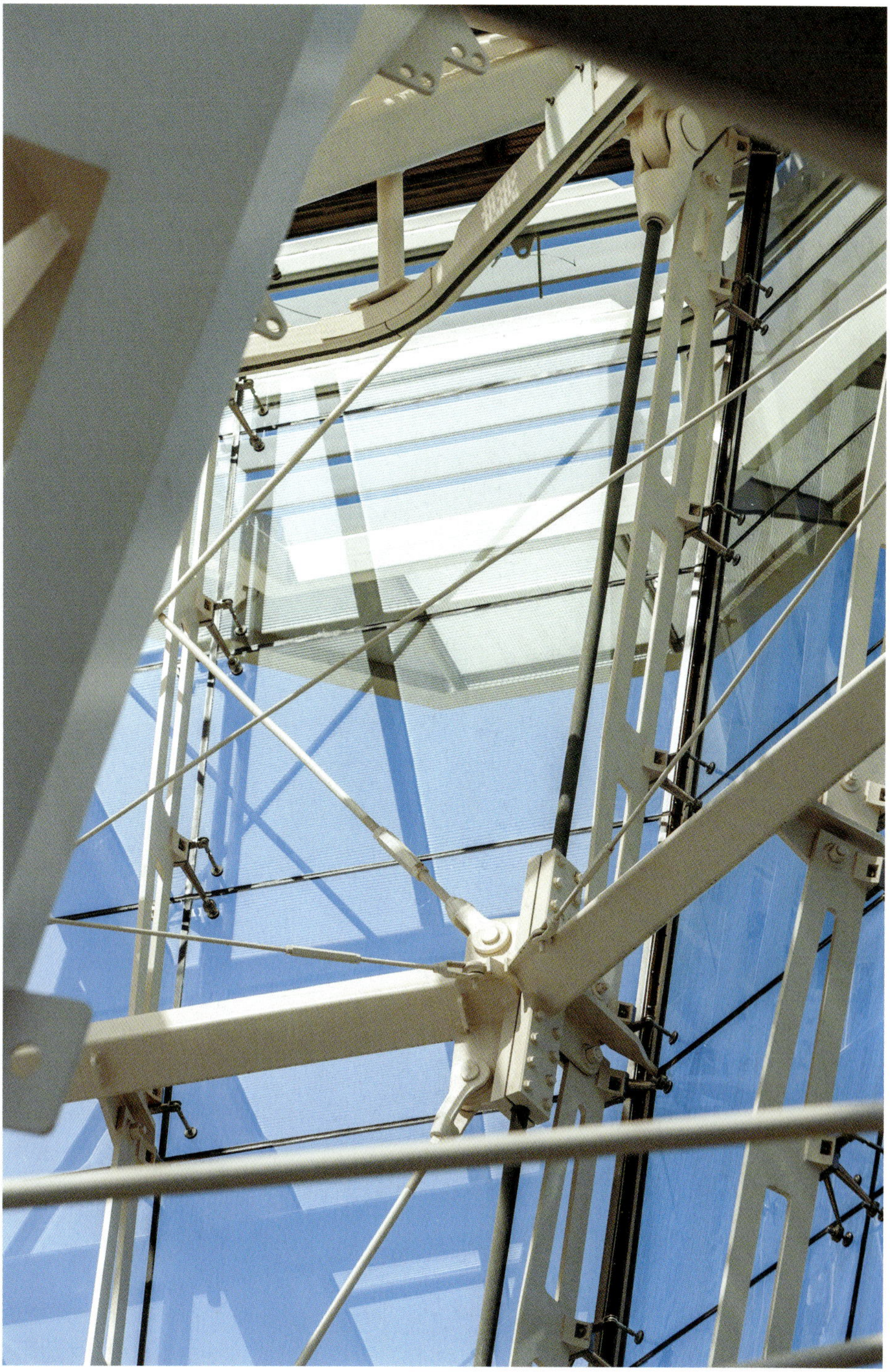

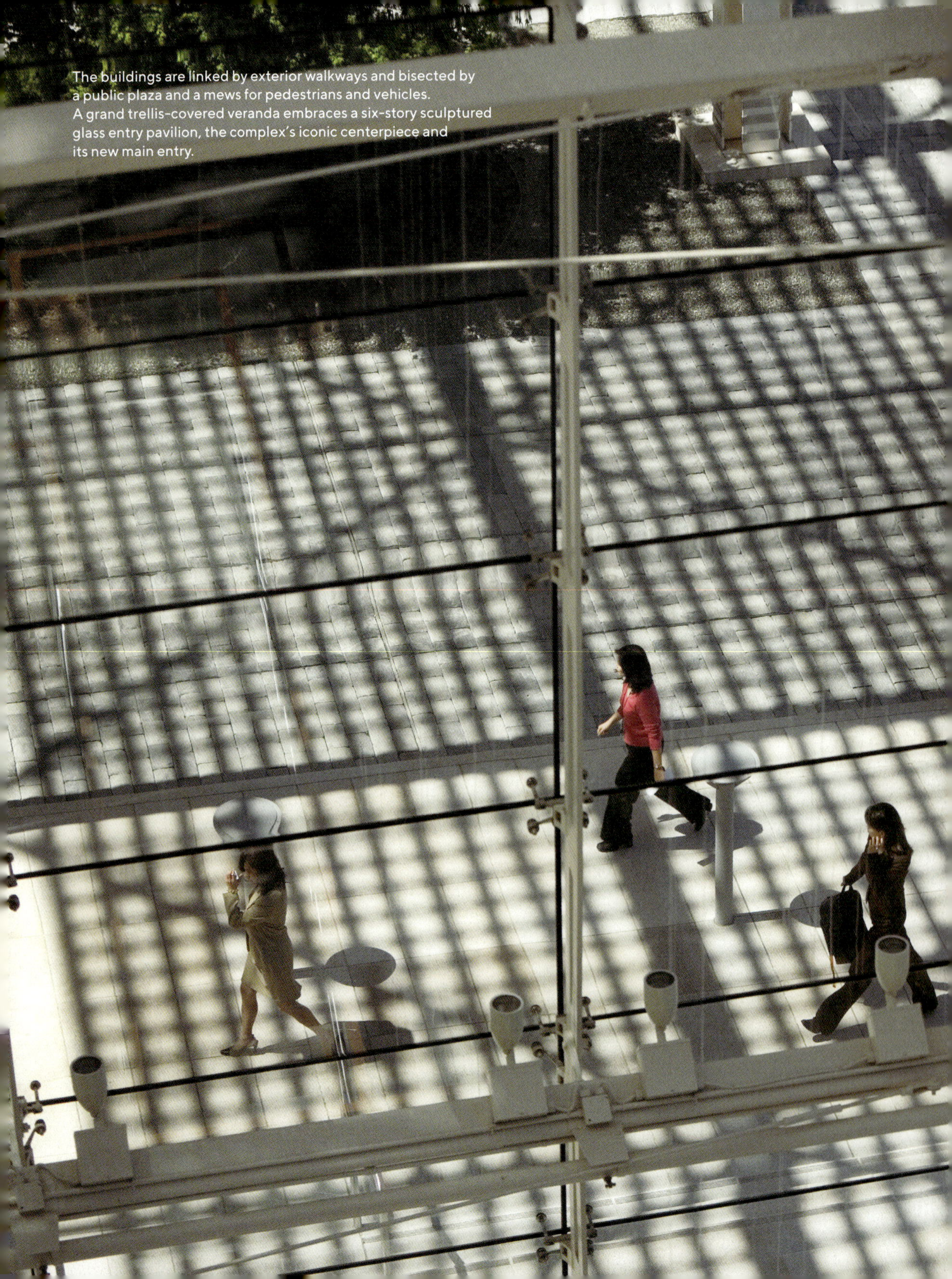

The buildings are linked by exterior walkways and bisected by a public plaza and a mews for pedestrians and vehicles. A grand trellis-covered veranda embraces a six-story sculptured glass entry pavilion, the complex's iconic centerpiece and its new main entry.

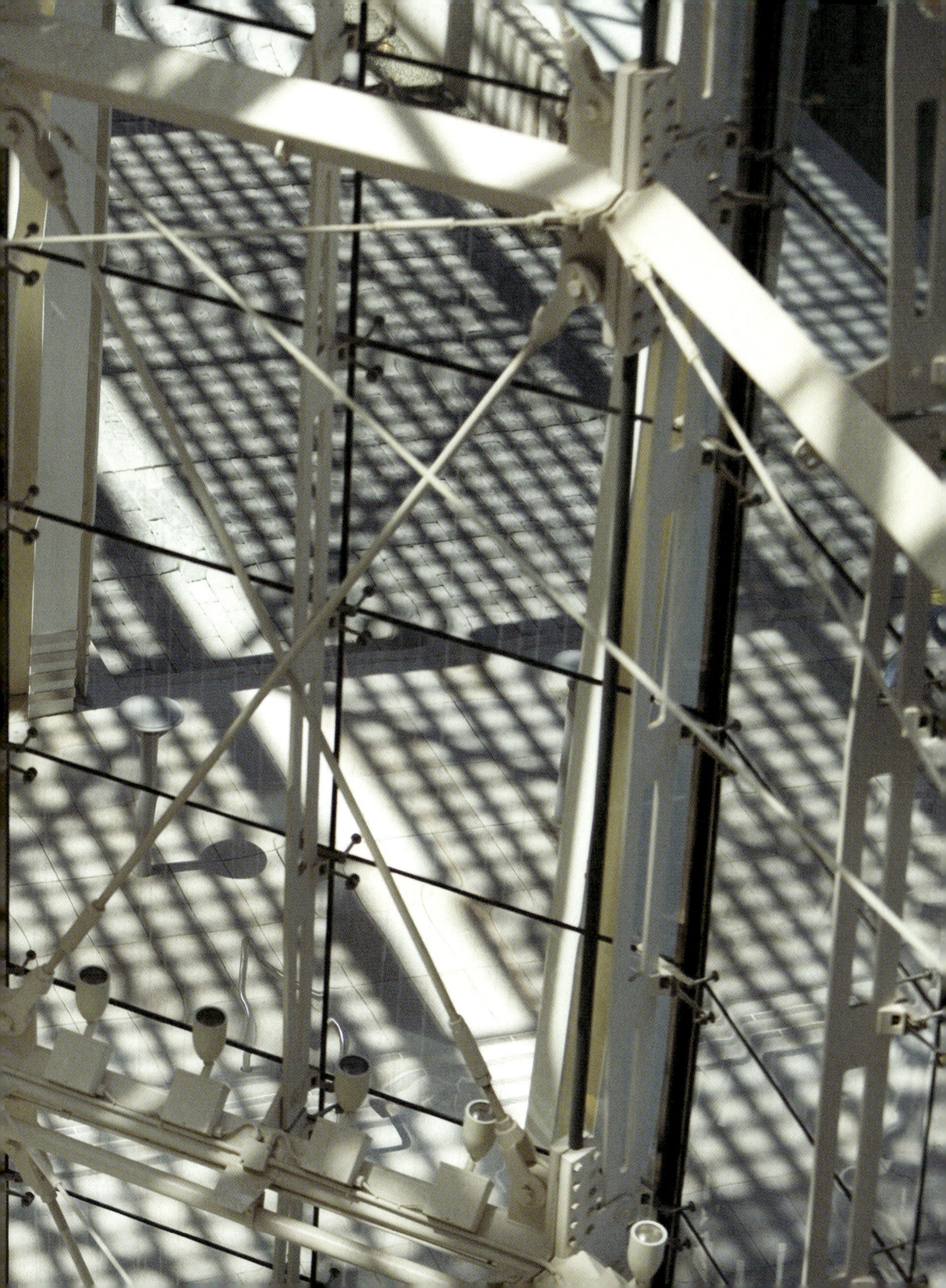

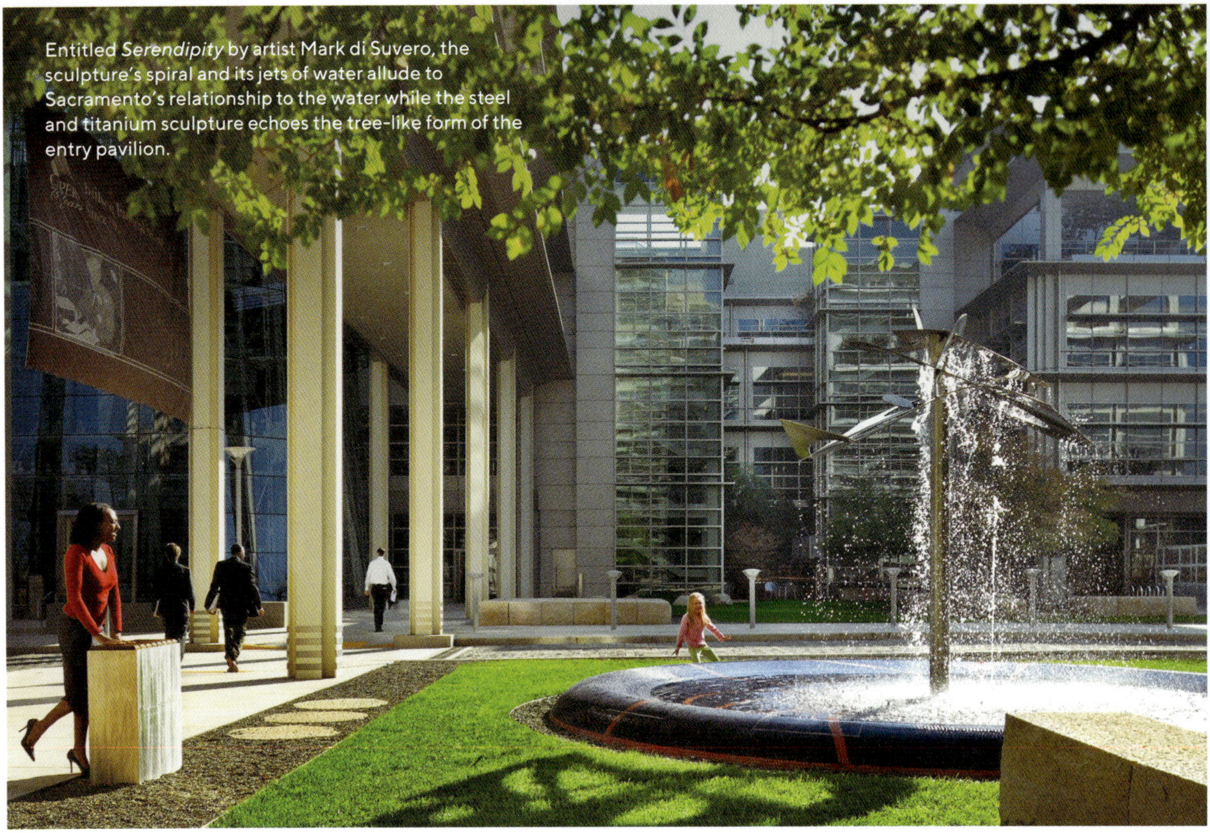

Entitled *Serendipity* by artist Mark di Suvero, the sculpture's spiral and its jets of water allude to Sacramento's relationship to the water while the steel and titanium sculpture echoes the tree-like form of the entry pavilion.

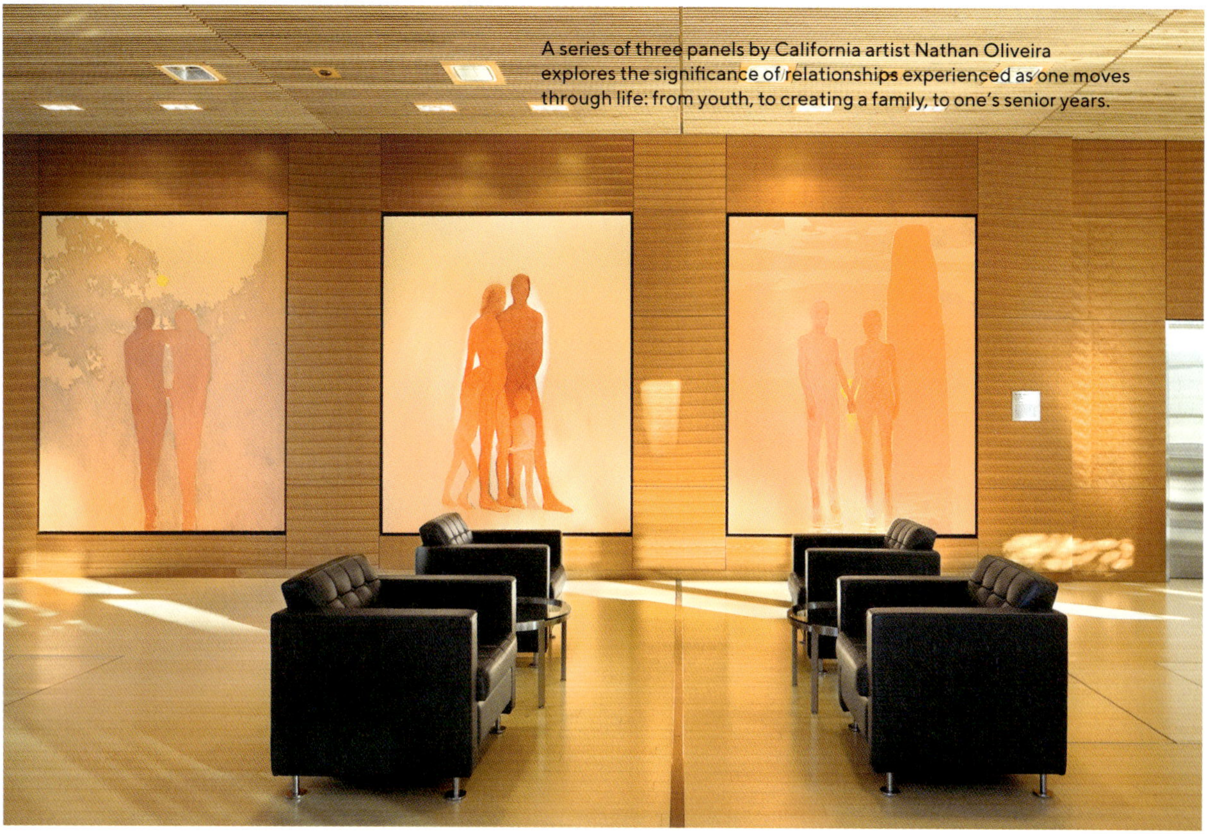

A series of three panels by California artist Nathan Oliveira explores the significance of relationships experienced as one moves through life: from youth, to creating a family, to one's senior years.

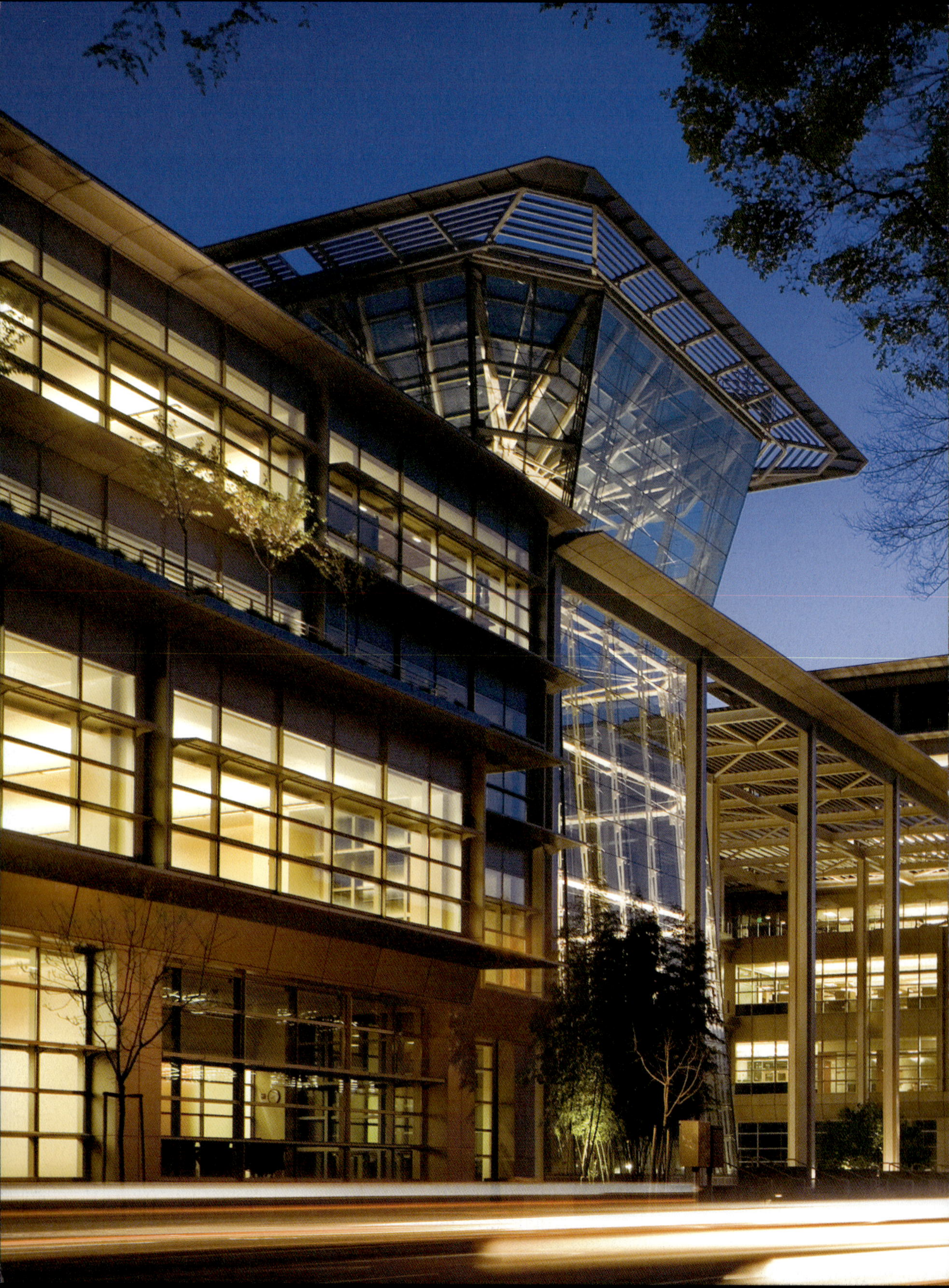

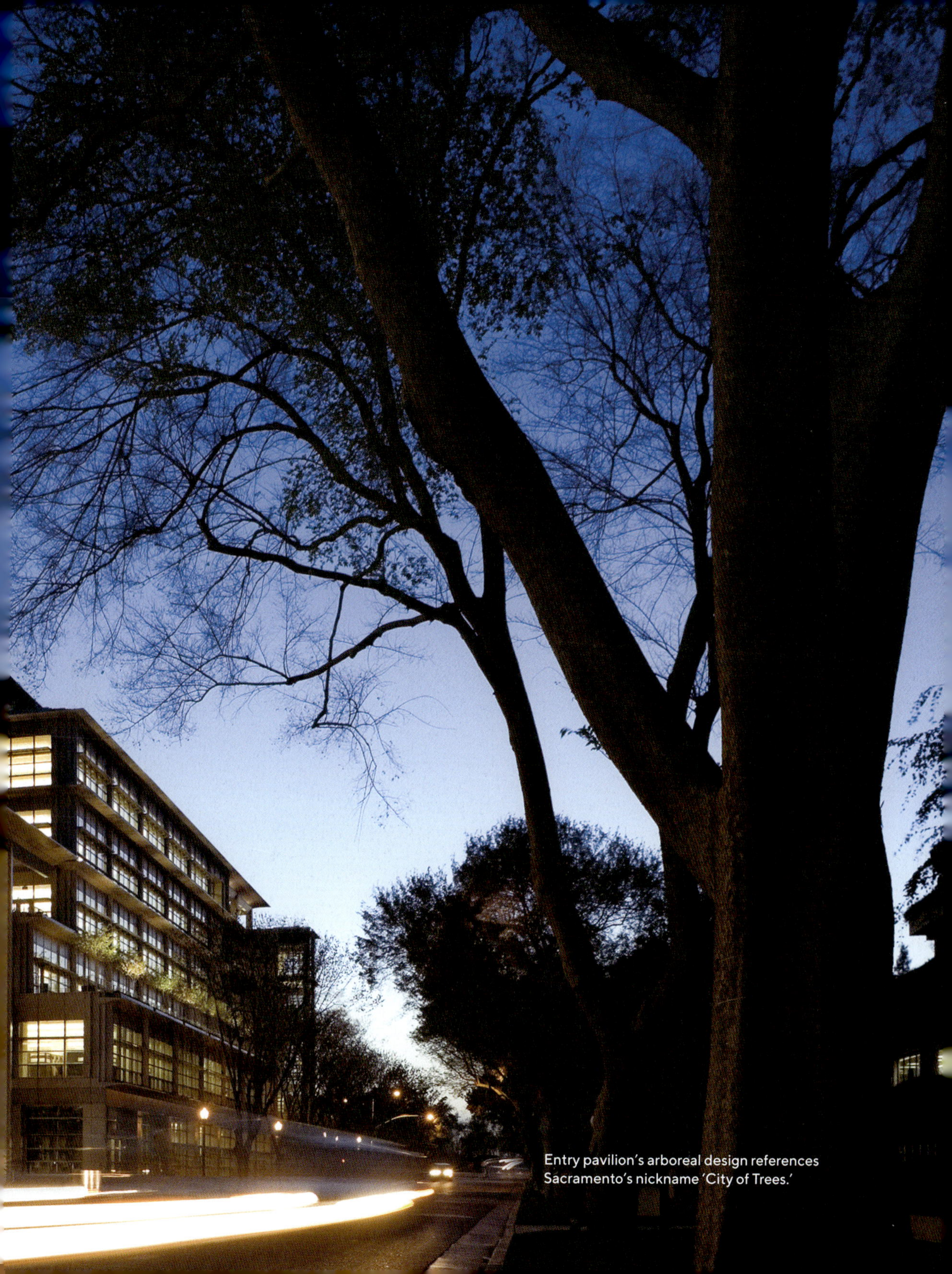

Entry pavilion's arboreal design references Sacramento's nickname 'City of Trees.'

Representation

GLOBAL GATEWAY SHINAGAWA

East Japan Railway Company

Pickard Chilton

Design Joint Venture:
JR East Design Corporation
JR East Consultants Company
Nihon Sekkei, Inc.
Nikken Sekkei, Ltd

Kengo Kuma & Associates

325 MAIN—GOOGLE CAMBRIDGE HEADQUARTERS

Boston Properties

Pickard Chilton

Stantec

Turner Construction

Magnusson Klemencic Associates

Bala

Lemon Brooke

Lerch Bates

VHB

Vidaris

Jensen Hughes

Lam Partners

The Green Engineer

Haley & Aldrich

Building Envelope Technologies

An essential element in the practice of architecture is exploring ideas through representation. Values expressed by the client and architect alike form the groundwork to study approaches, concepts, and further development of the design through material expression and details. To do so, a wide range of representation techniques (like tools in a toolbox) are used by the architect, client, and others on the project team to communicate on many different levels over the life of a project and the course of collaboration. Representation that communicates a design approach can demonstrate the architect's understanding of a client's values to arrive at an appropriate solution. Diagrams, sketches, detailed drawings, scale models, simulations, and videos are just some of the ways that architects and client collaborators share their visions with each other, study alternatives, spark dialogue, and navigate the creative process. How does the architect capture the client's worldview in such representations?

How do they demonstrate the architect's consideration of the client's values? How is representation expressed in the final design?

There is a wide array of visualization and communication tools that can be employed in the service of defining the design and furthering it. A bedrock value of Pickard Chilton in the selection of representation is to tune it to the character of the client. This requires the architect to be attentive to that character in order to communicate ideas, concepts, and details in a way that client collaborators and others on the project team can absorb, depending on their frame of reference. Representation is part of architectural design itself.

For example, a two-stage competition was organized by East Japan Railway Company (EJRC) for the mile-long (1.6-kilometer-long) Global Gateway Shinagawa master plan and tower design in Tokyo. Pickard Chilton's approach, as revealed through representation, was rooted in the unique character of the site and its history. This was an invitation to the client to understand the architecture as a narrative — one that tells the story of the project.

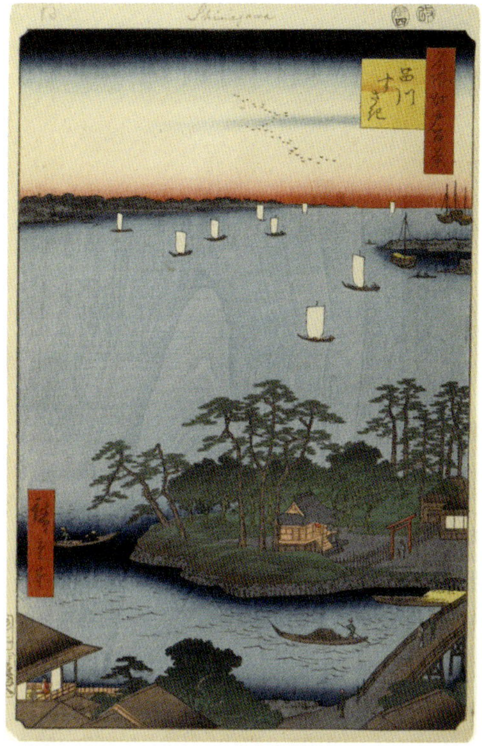

Shinagawa Susaki, No. 83 from One Hundred Famous Views of Edo (1857) by Utagawa Hiroshige.

EJRC's Yoshihiko Ito notes that the architects' sensitivity to the site's location, history, and cultural significance was wonderfully expressed in representations of the design in Japanese-style woodcut prints that portrayed the master plan. This gesture of honoring the culture in which they were working was a memorable moment for the client. "The architects used the technique of historical carvings to express through their representation their understanding of the history," explains Ito-san. "It tied into the cultural history of the site and the people who would use it." He adds, "they created the architectural concept, which reflected our vision of the project — the history of the site, the memory of the shoreline. They captured the past and offered a vision of the future, which is what we wanted."

Selection of images representative of the Global Gateway Shinagawa team and client meetings during competition and design phases.

The firm never uses a prototype presentation template; each presentation to the client is tailored to the design challenge. Being able to "read the room"— body language, facial expressions, verbal and nonverbal responses — allows the architects to make subtle shifts in delivery. In the case of Global Gateway Shinagawa, the result was that EJRC dispensed with the second stage of the competition. As the architects see it, along with representation, quickly creating a human connection with the client is what makes the difference.

Three-dimensional models as representations are typically preferred to drawings, because they allow clients to enter into the project, to physically

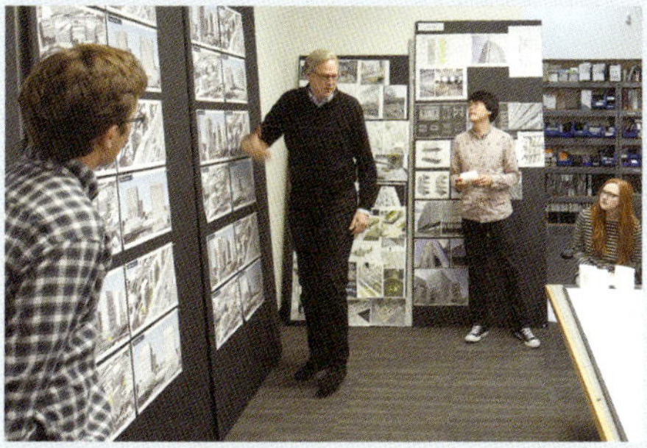

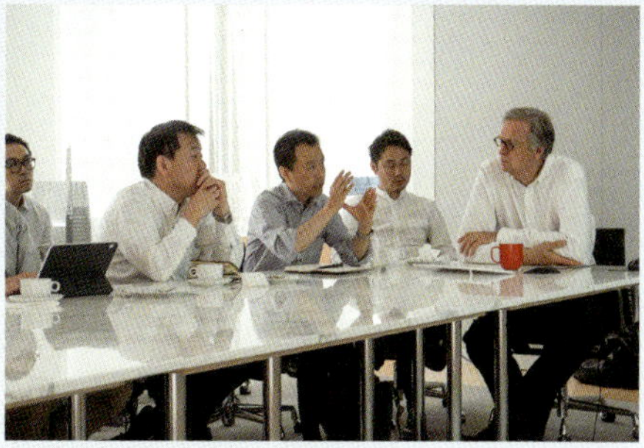

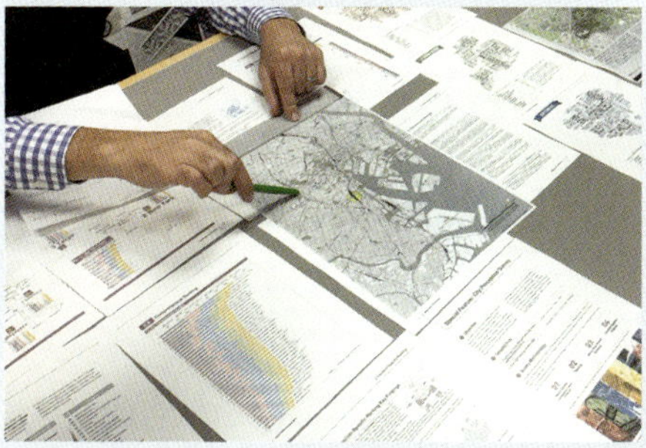

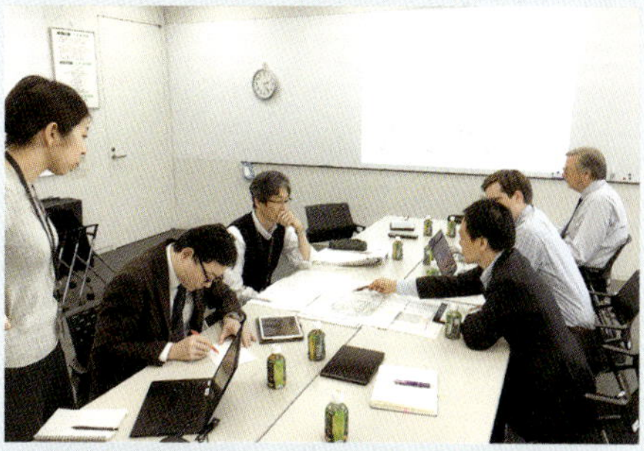

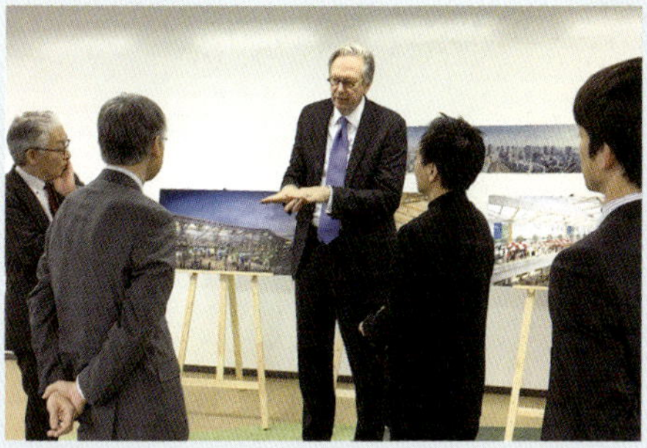

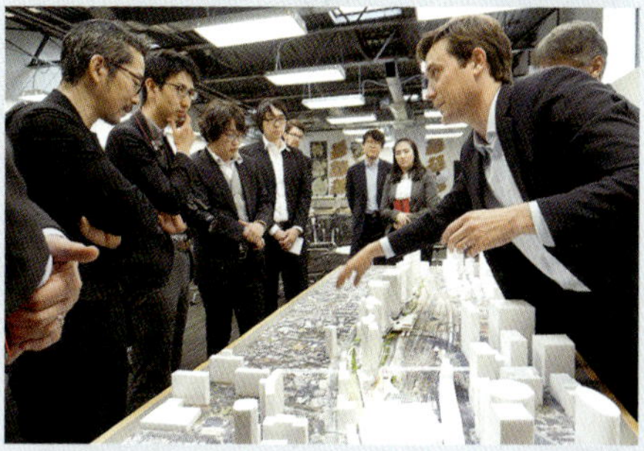

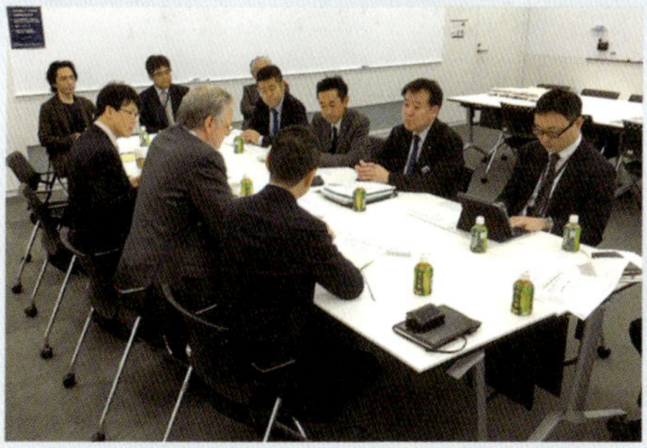

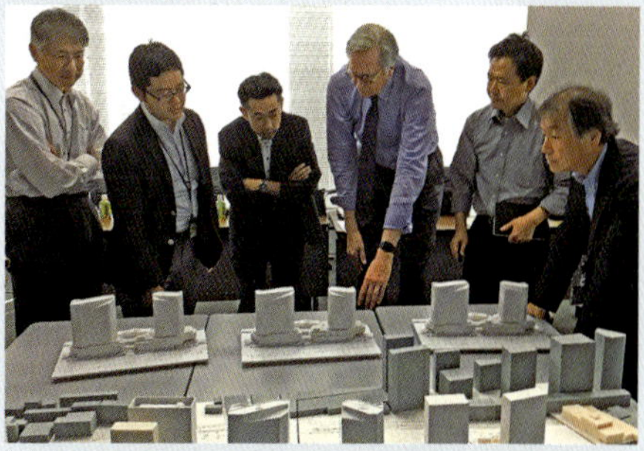

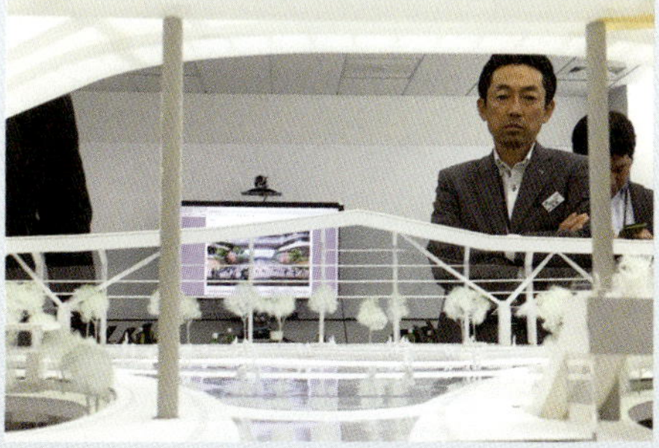

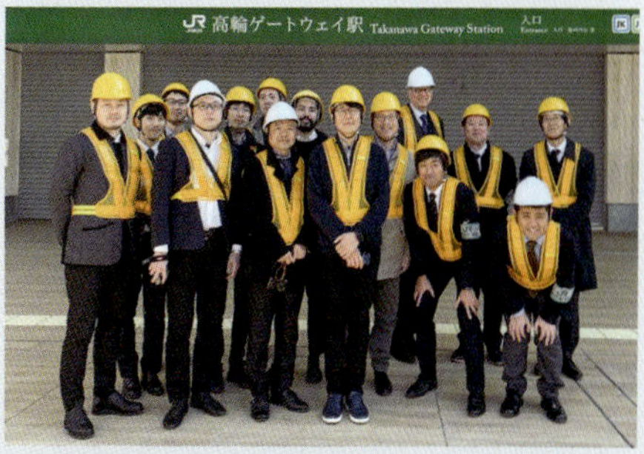
JR 高輪ゲートウェイ駅 Takanawa Gateway Station
入口
Entrance

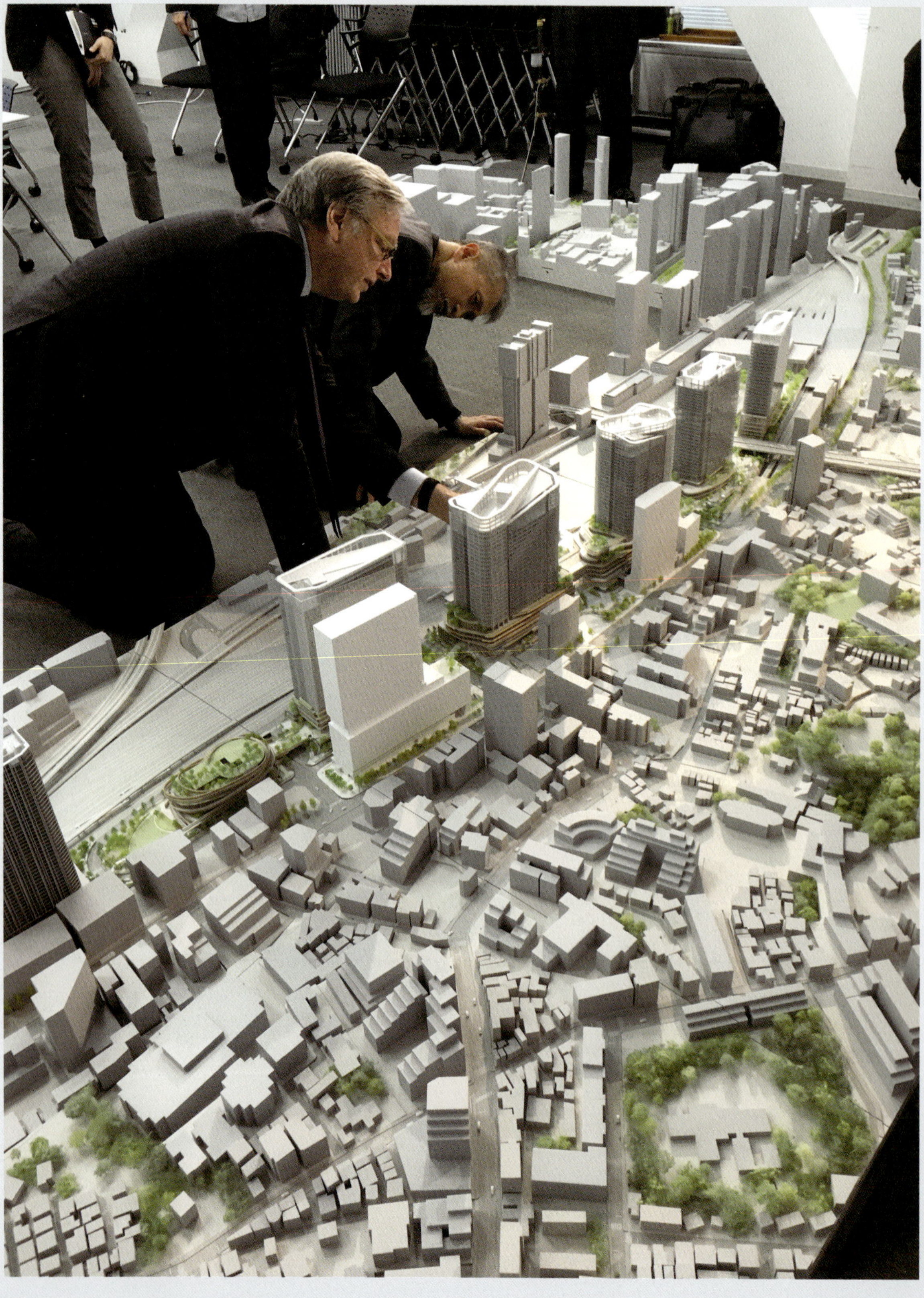

← William Chilton discussing details of the model of Global Gateway Shinagawa in the office of the client.

→ Illustration showing streams of movement that define the form and organization of the master plan.

↘ Series of competition models generated for Block 4 design.

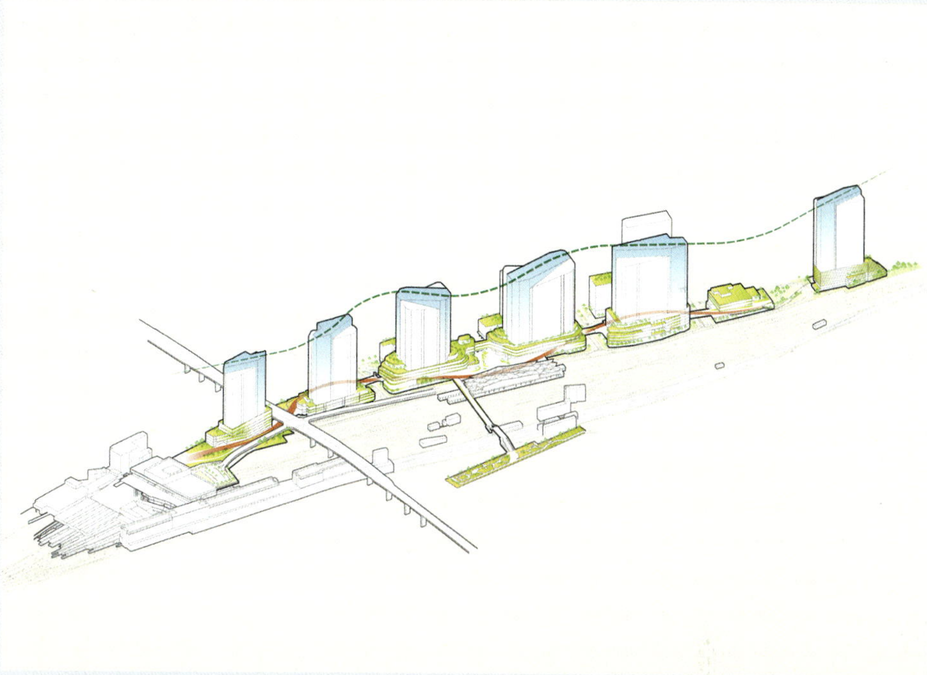

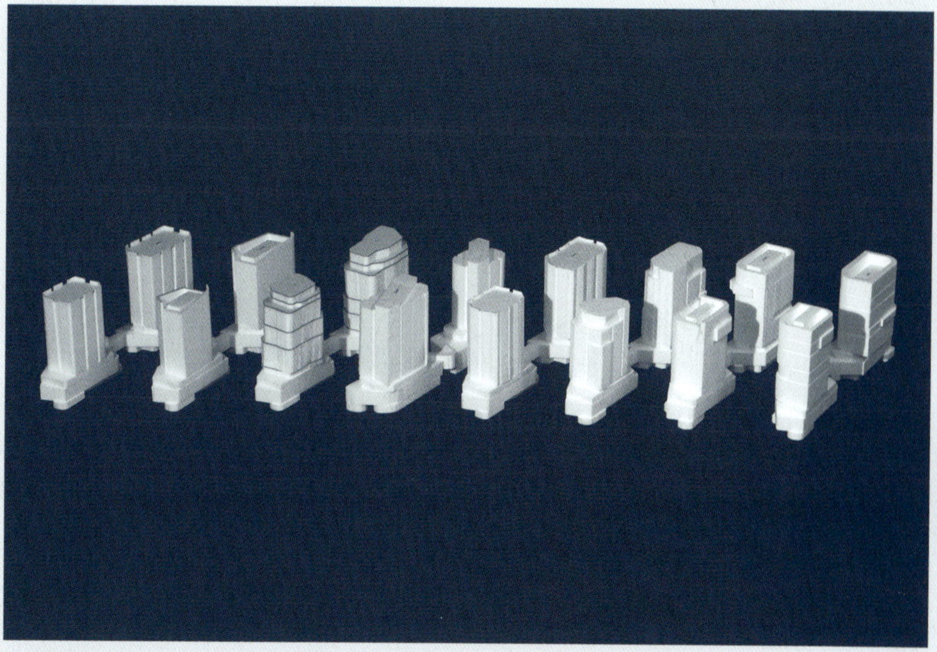

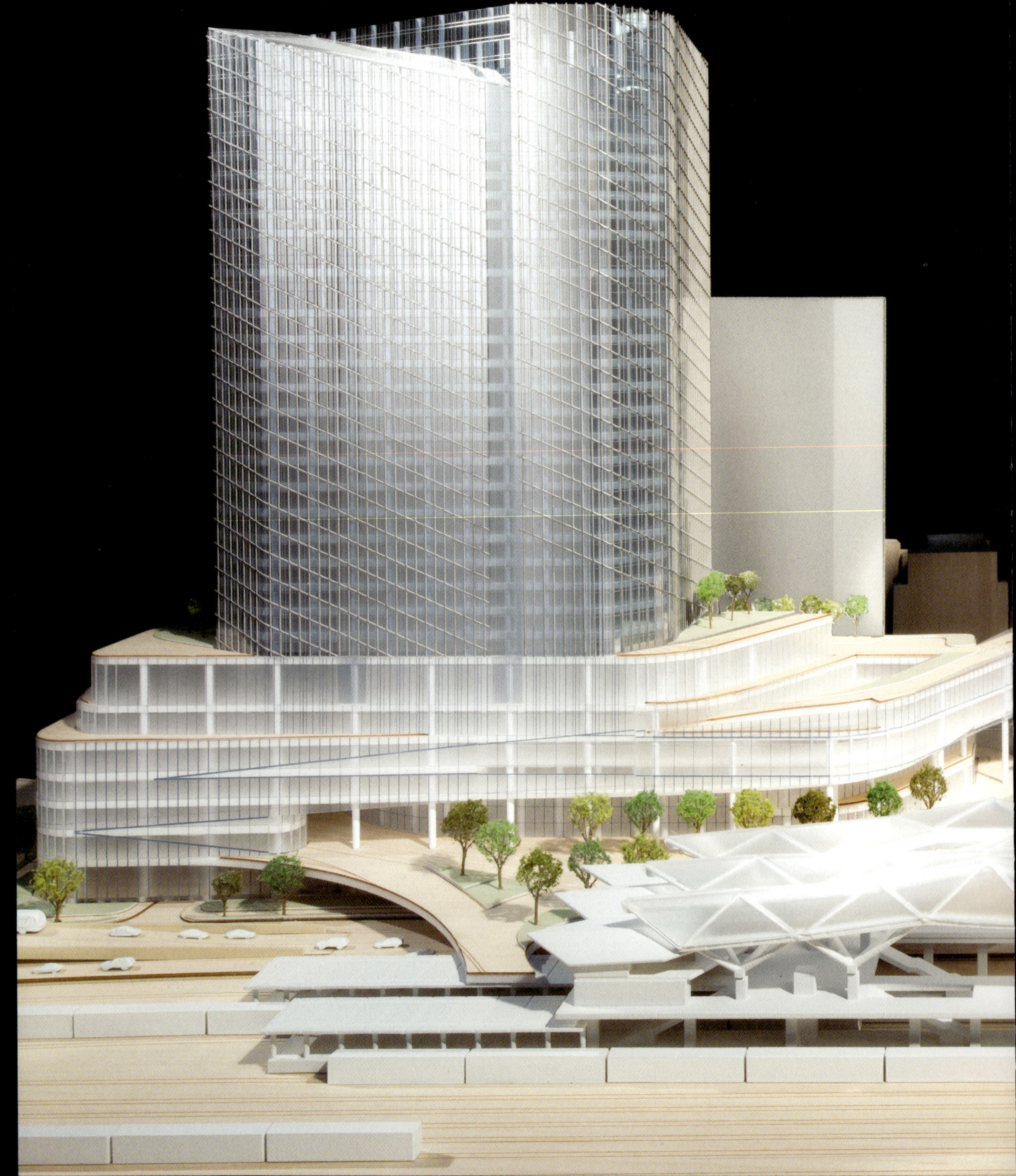

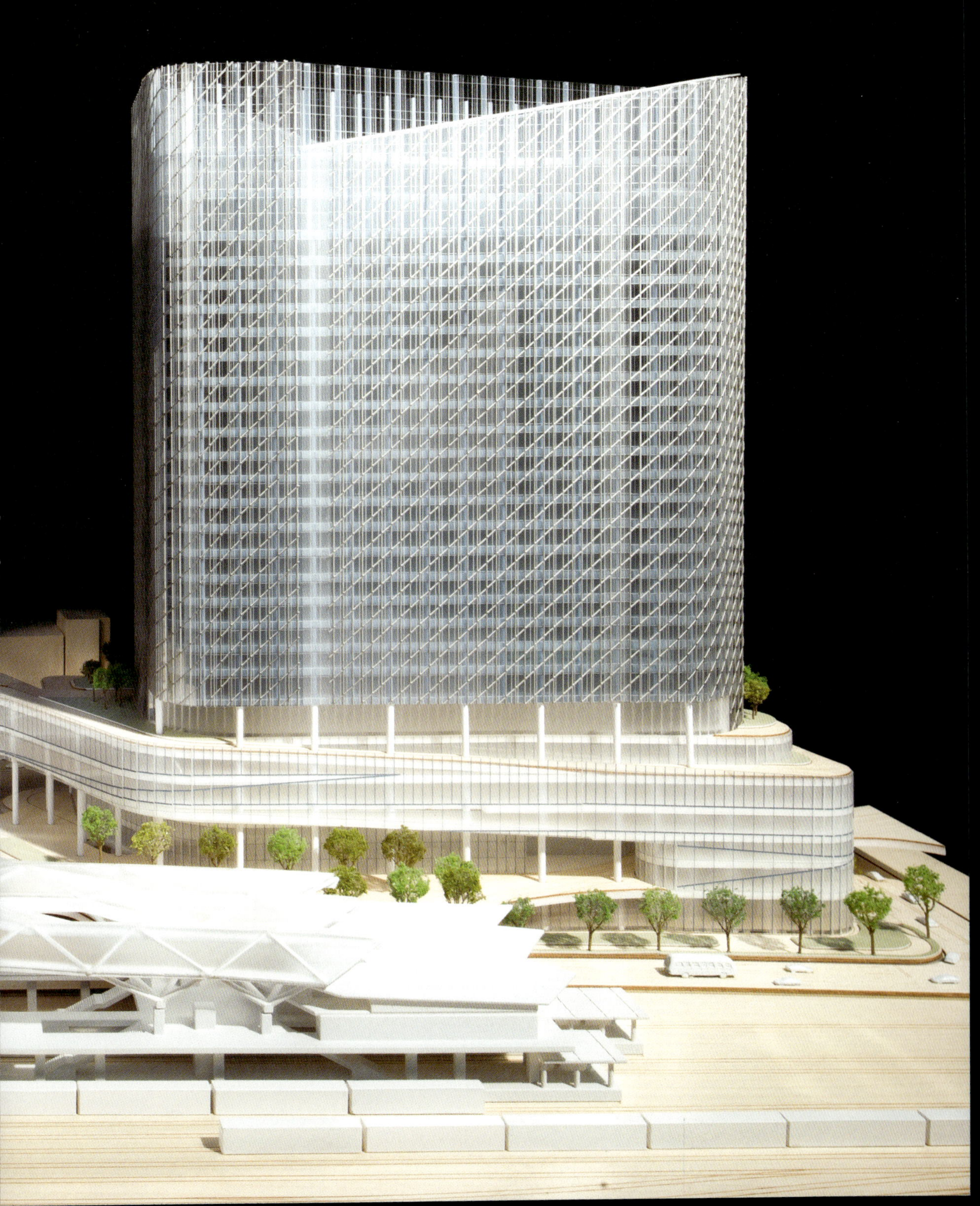

Block 4 competition model illustrating the podium's seamless connection to Kengo Kuma's Takanawa Gateway Station.

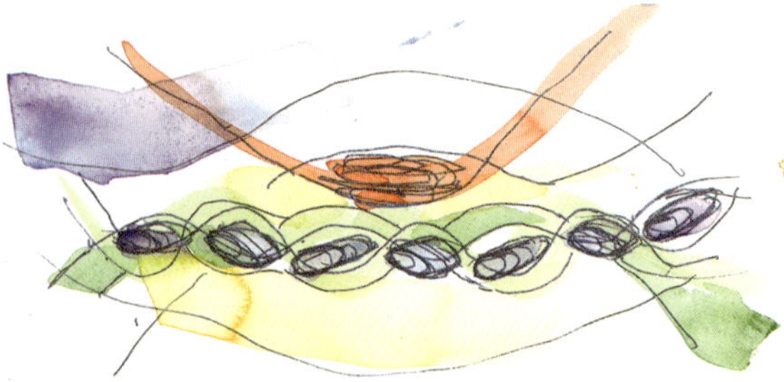

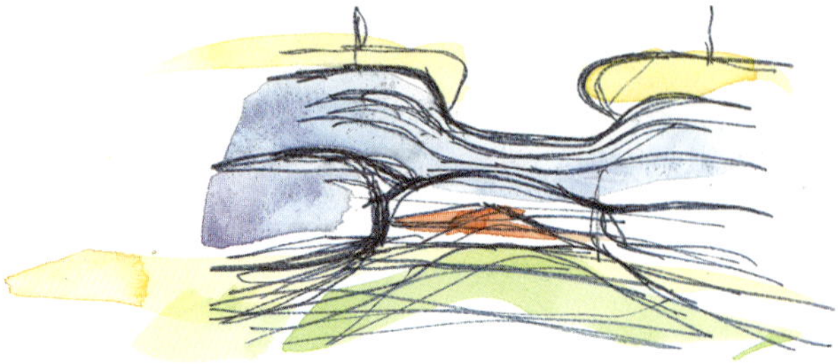

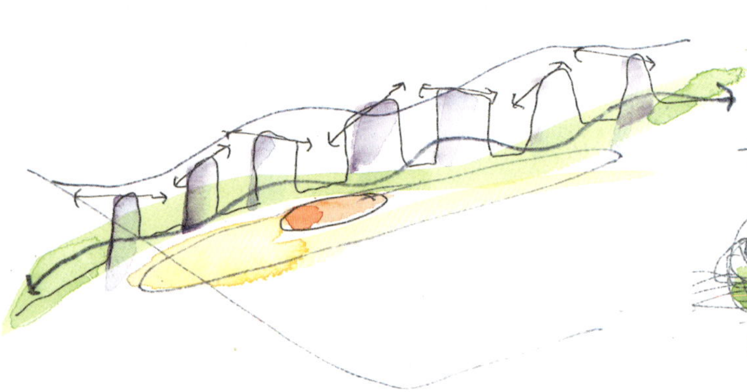

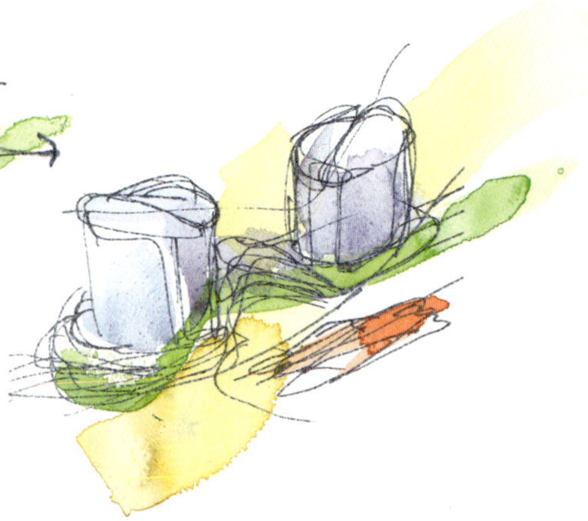

engage with it, move it around, see it from different perspectives. According to Michael Tilford of Boston Properties, which developed more than 400,000 square feet / 37,160 square meters of new headquarters for Google on a Kendall Square site in Cambridge, Massachusetts, Pickard Chilton's representations at various phases of the project helped them to thoroughly understand the implications and think through various design

Watercolor vignettes of Global Gateway Shinagawa competition submission.

decisions. Tilford relates that the architects represented their approach to the design using six-foot-tall boards that immersed the client into the architect's design process. "It was very dramatic," recalls Tilford of the effectiveness of these large board representations. But design concepts were also explored in small, hand-drawn sketches with soft watercolors. "You get this sense of the design happening before your eyes," says Tilford, as if the client is designing with the architects.

As the design progressed, new media were employed to bring the client into greater details of the project. Tilford notes that, in his experience, many architects rely exclusively on digital renderings. In this case, Pickard Chilton balanced their design-communication techniques with highly detailed models "that brought the project to life," says Tilford. The design was represented with a large-scale, 3D model that rotated with the slightest touch of the presenter's hand so that different elements could be seen in more detail. "As he explained it and moved it around," says Tilford, "it wasn't a static presentation." The model became a conversation piece in Boston Properties's offices, where it is still on display. Tilford adds that one of

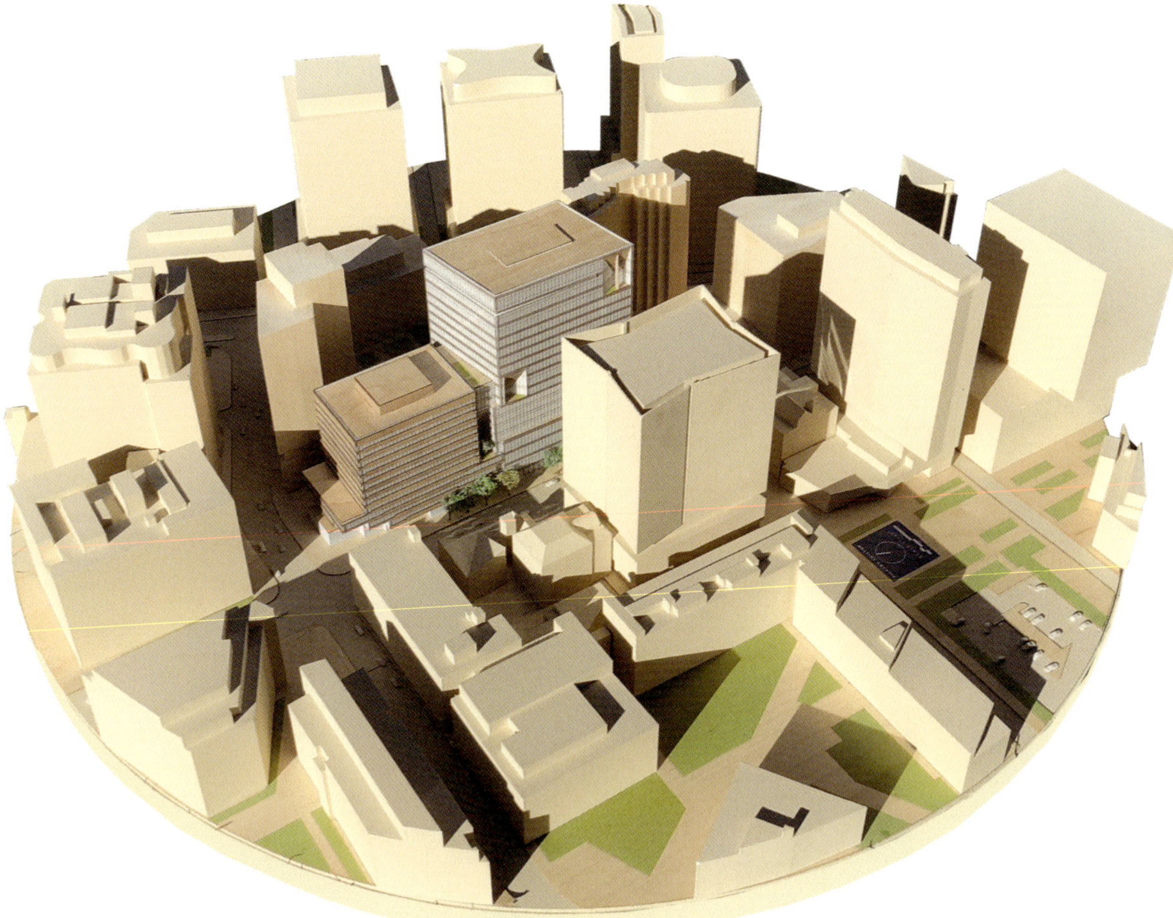

Schematic Design site models of 325 Main,
Google's new headquarters in Cambridge, Massachusetts.

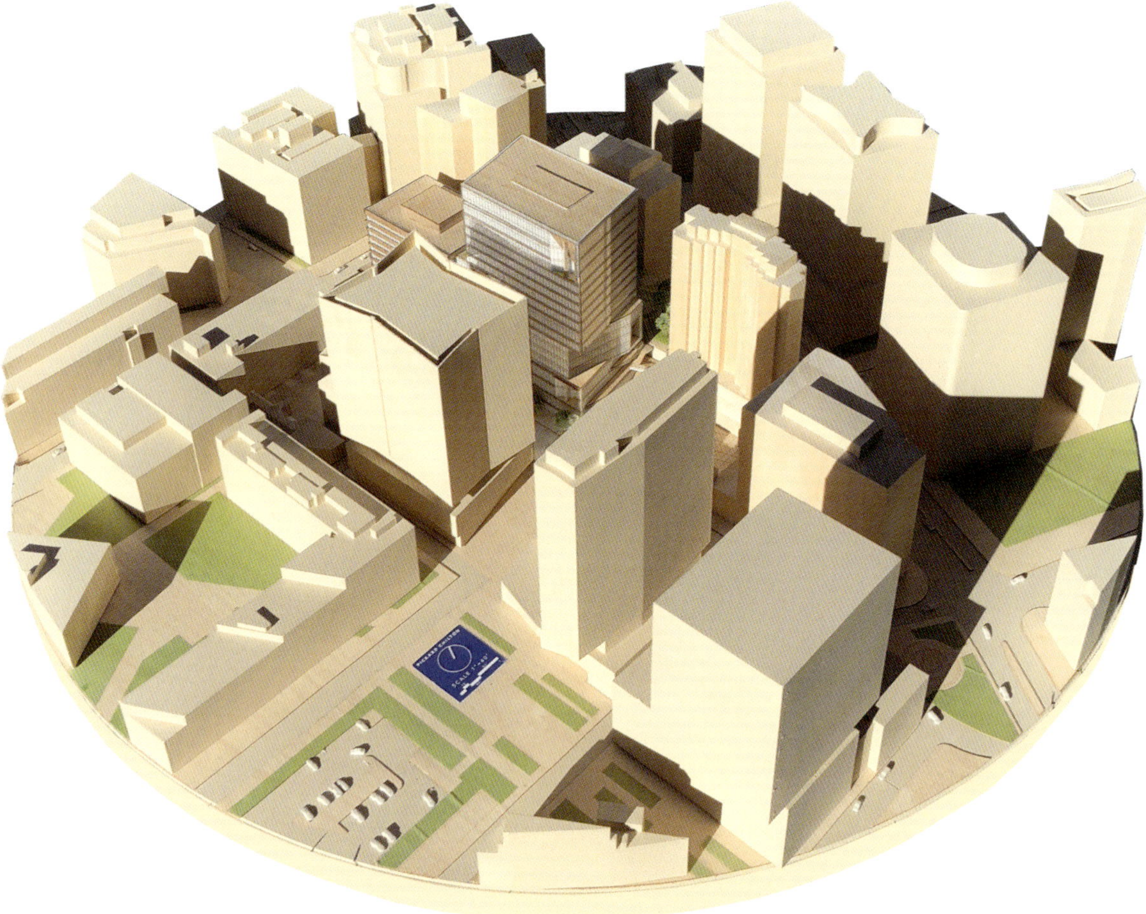

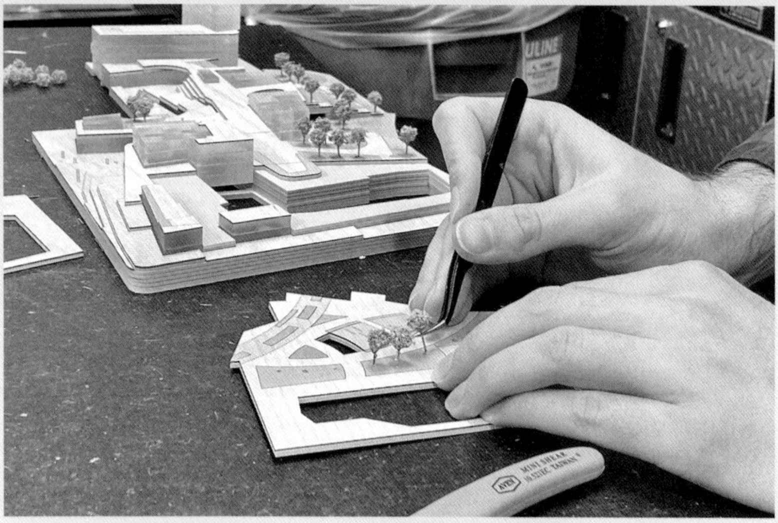

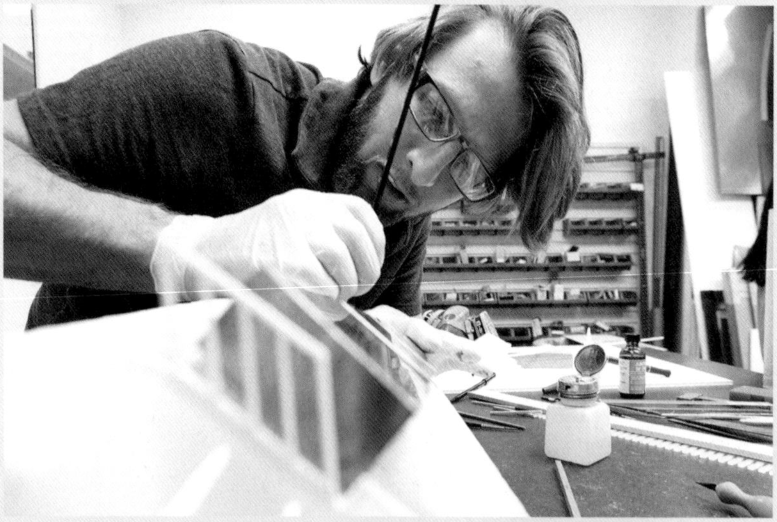

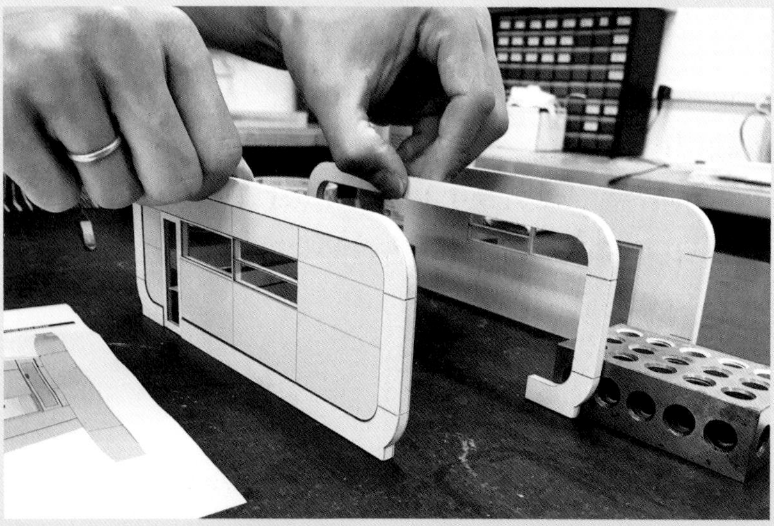

← From small-scale models to full-scale mock-ups, to final built projects, a great deal of energy is committed to the process of making physical objects utilizing a full spectrum of methods, from the latest technology in 3D printing to the most basic and tactile in hand-built models of wood, foam, and plastic.

→ Multimedia diagrams illustrating public circulation through the new pedestrian connection from Kendall Plaza up to the Kendall Square Rooftop Garden.

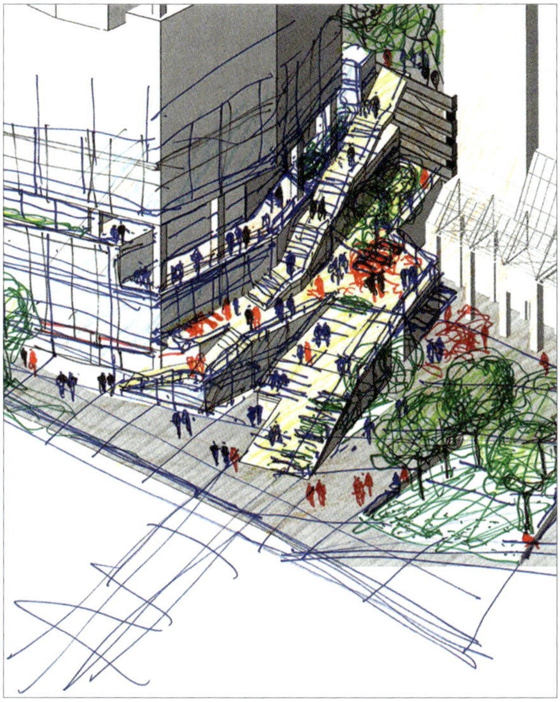

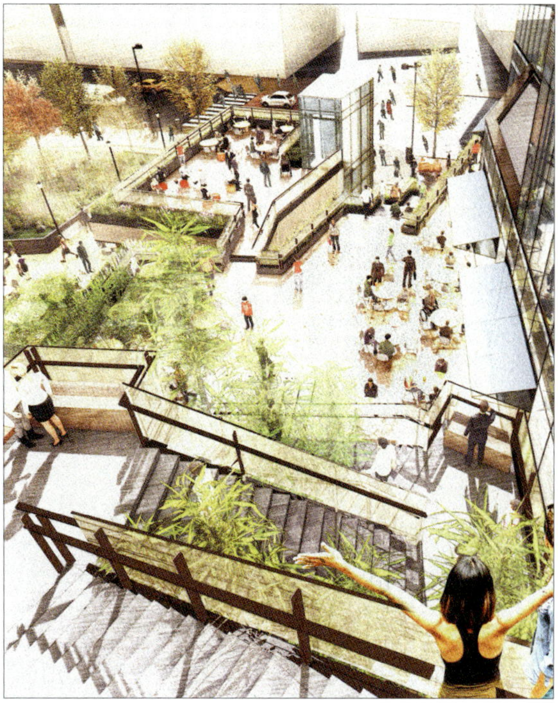

the highlights of a trip to Pickard Chilton's offices in New Haven was a tour of their model shop, which helped explain their design process.

Representations change as the project moves into finer detail. One example is seen in the design of Google's curtain wall, which Tilford says was approached by the architects like a hand-crafted object.

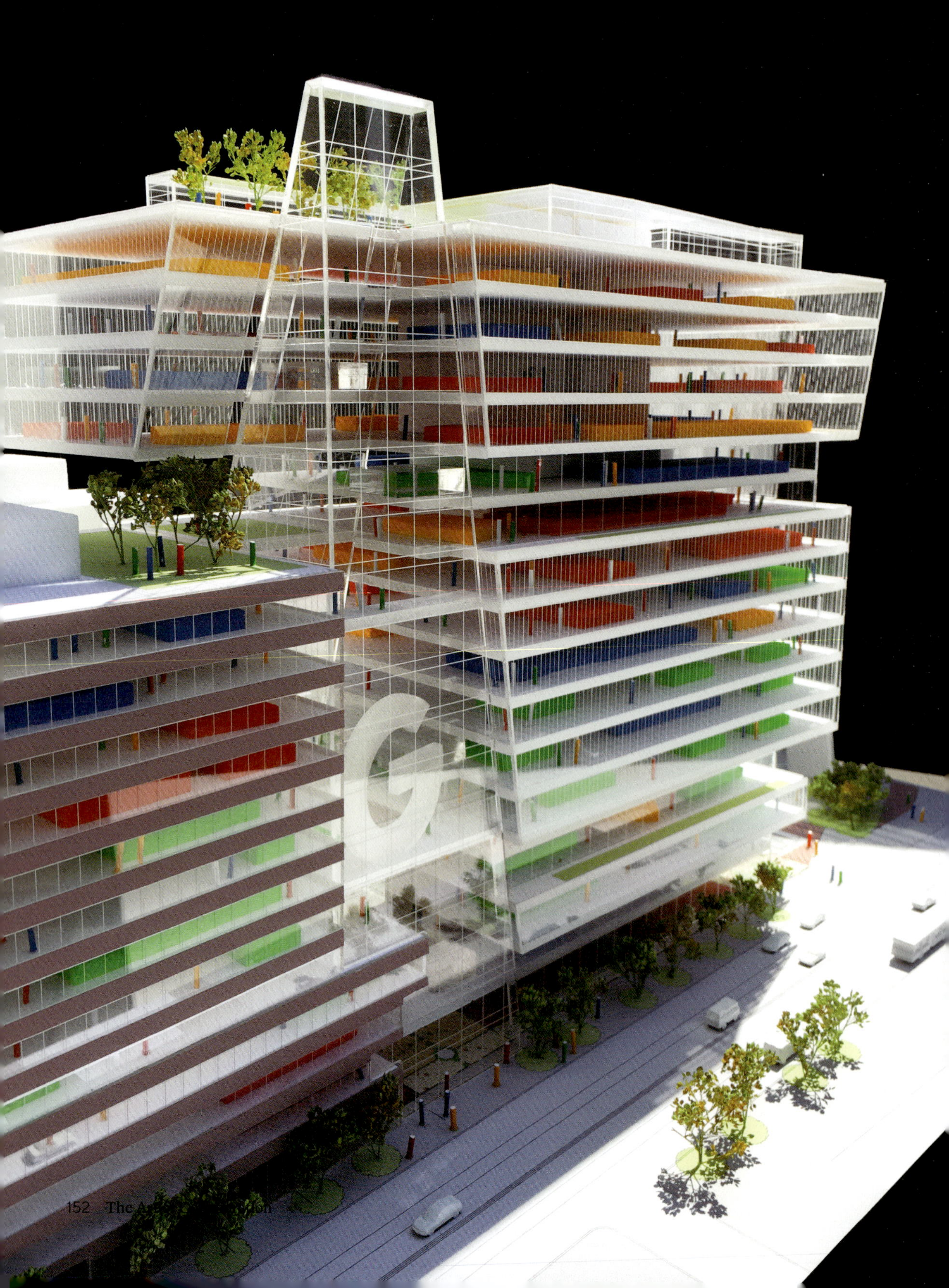

Early concept design model for Google's new headquarters at 325 Main.

Full-scale curtain-wall models represented the look, feel, warm colors, light-scattering surface textures, even the luminance of the materials in the way they were lit and displayed. Tilford says that the architect used a variety of representations: models, virtual reality, compositional features, even a shadow box where elements such as the glass could be moved to study its reflective effects. Physical curtain wall models were studied on site. "They nailed it," says Tilford of the way the curtain-wall design was represented and studied. The design resonated with those on the client team, says Tilford, "and they wanted to take ownership."

Representation is part of architectural design itself.

GLOBAL GATEWAY SHINAGAWA
TOKYO, JAPAN

Under construction
13.6 million gross square feet / 1.25 million gross square meters
32 acres / 13 hectares

Envisioned as a new global hub connecting Tokyo to the world, Global Gateway Shinagawa has been designed as a next-generation urban environment that symbolizes Japan's openness and is a catalyst for innovative, international companies to create new businesses and cultures.

Nighttime view from competition phase of Block 4 tower within the context of the overall development.

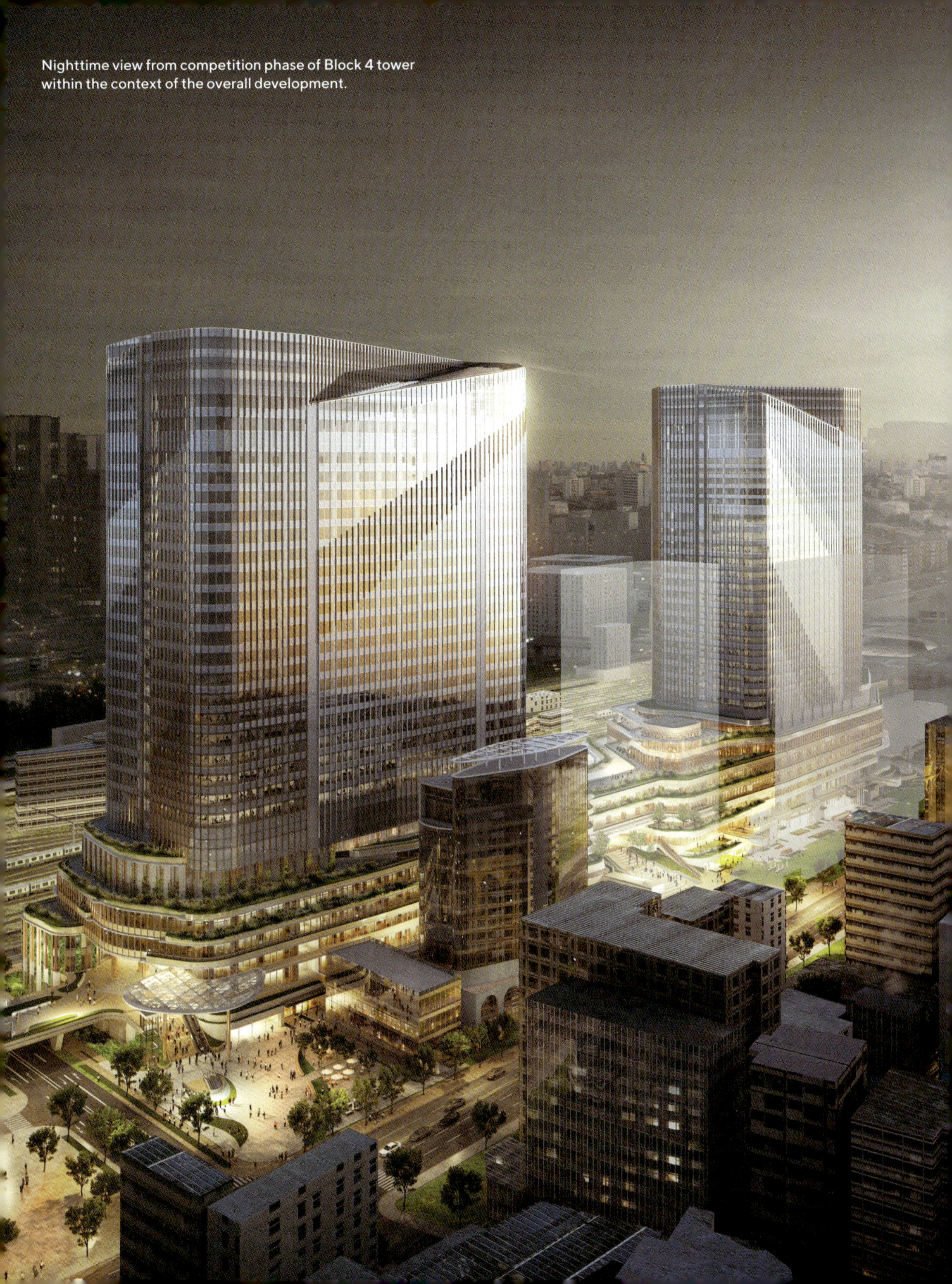

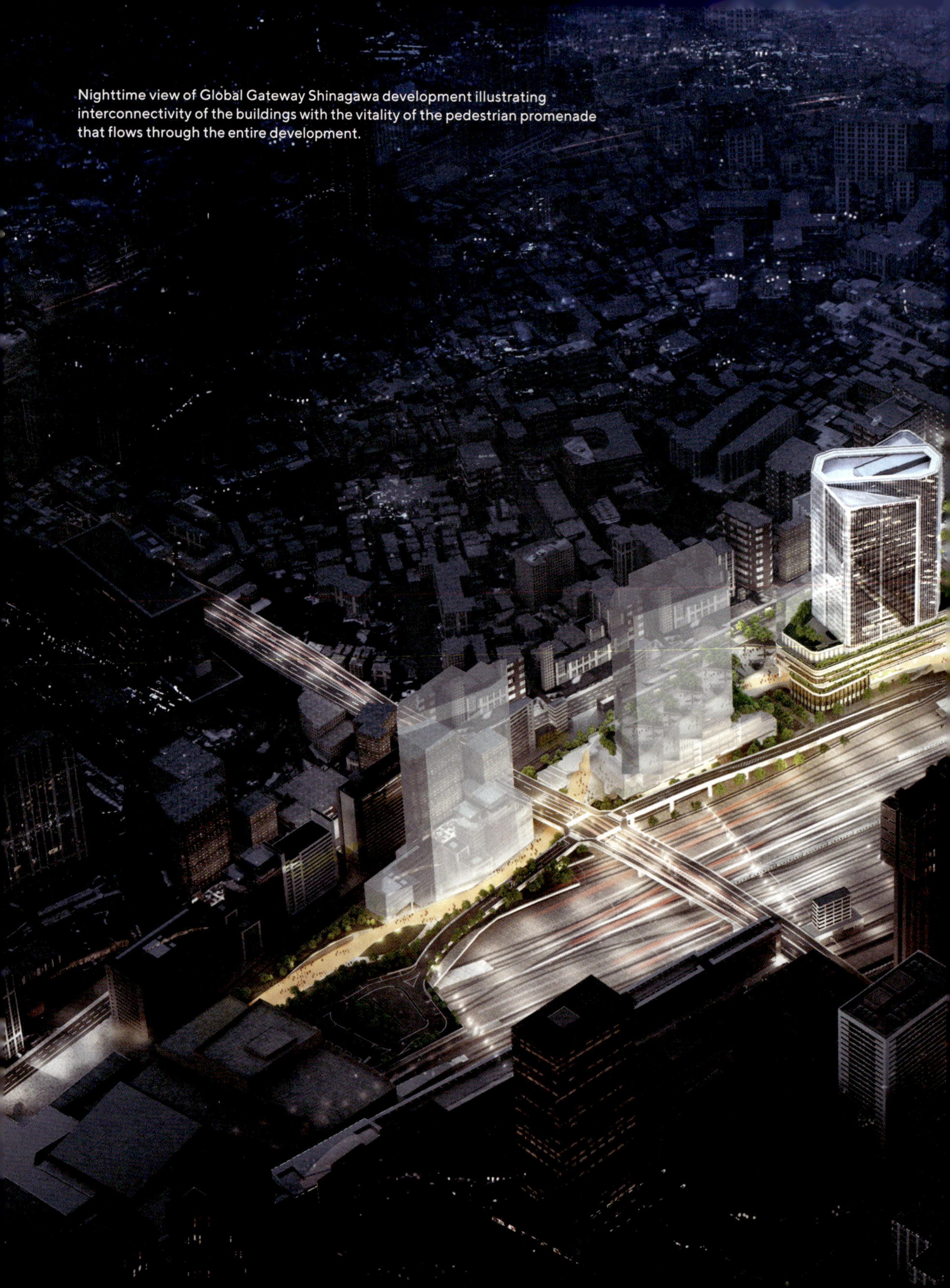

Nighttime view of Global Gateway Shinagawa development illustrating interconnectivity of the buildings with the vitality of the pedestrian promenade that flows through the entire development.

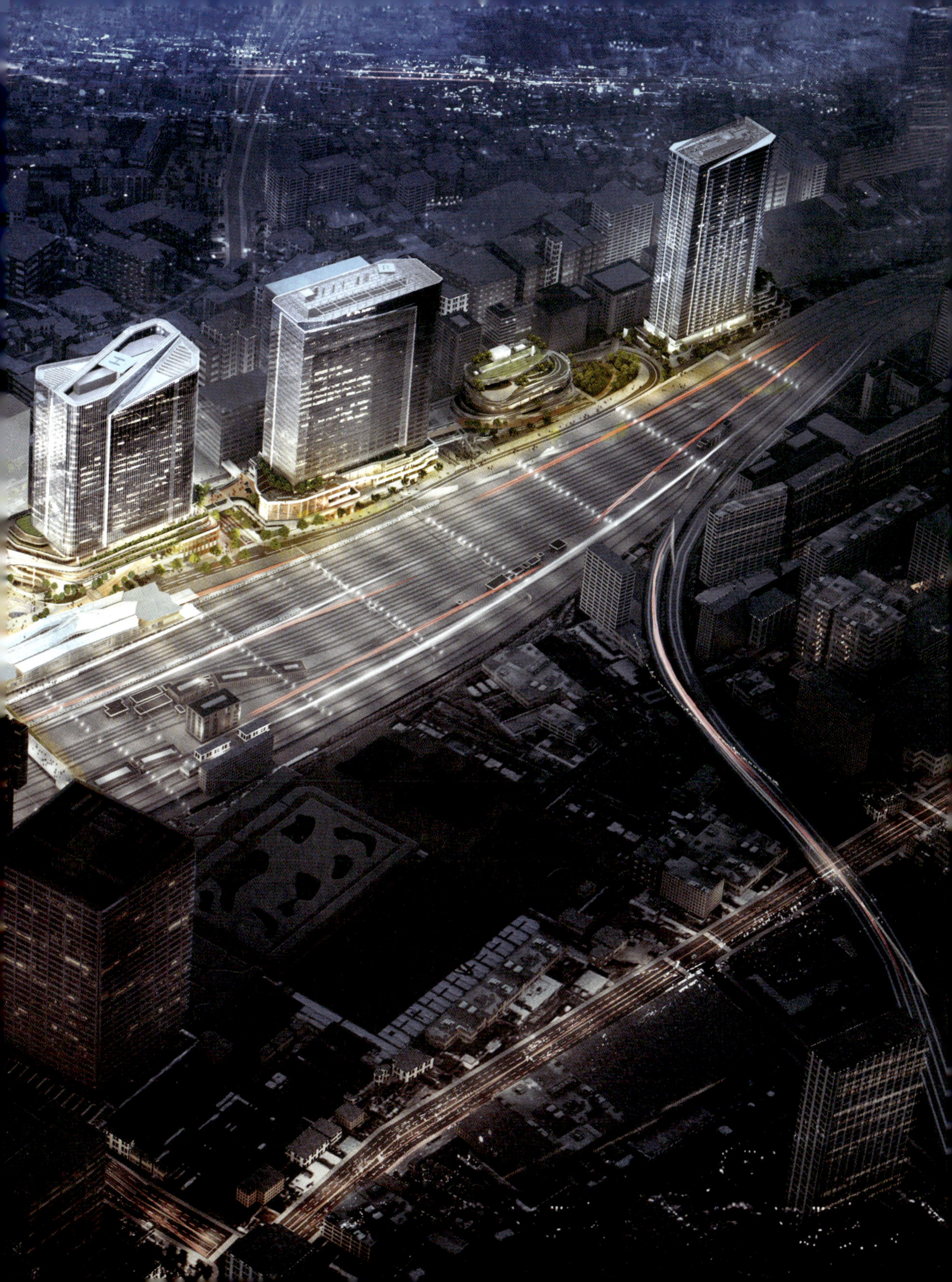

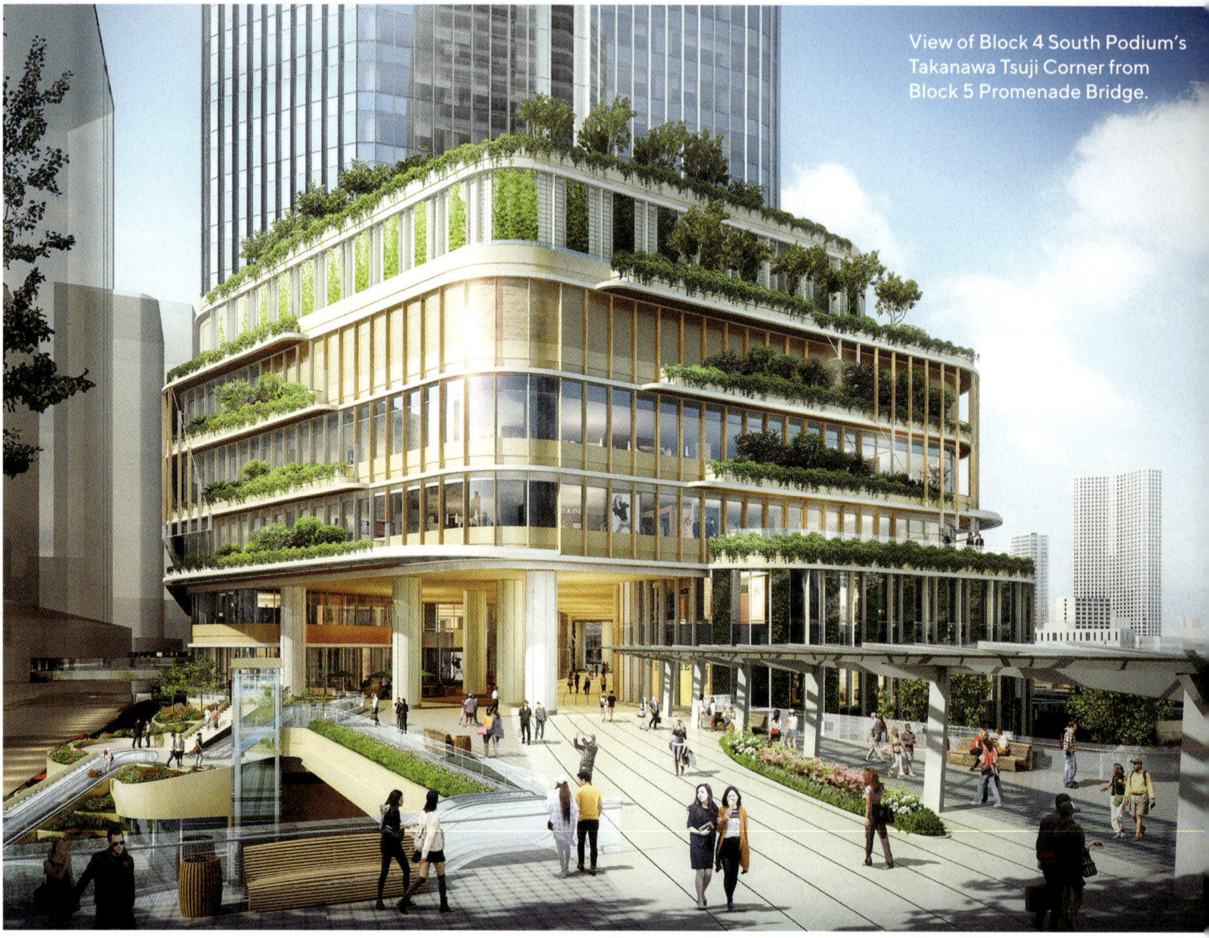

View of Block 4 South Podium's Takanawa Tsuji Corner from Block 5 Promenade Bridge.

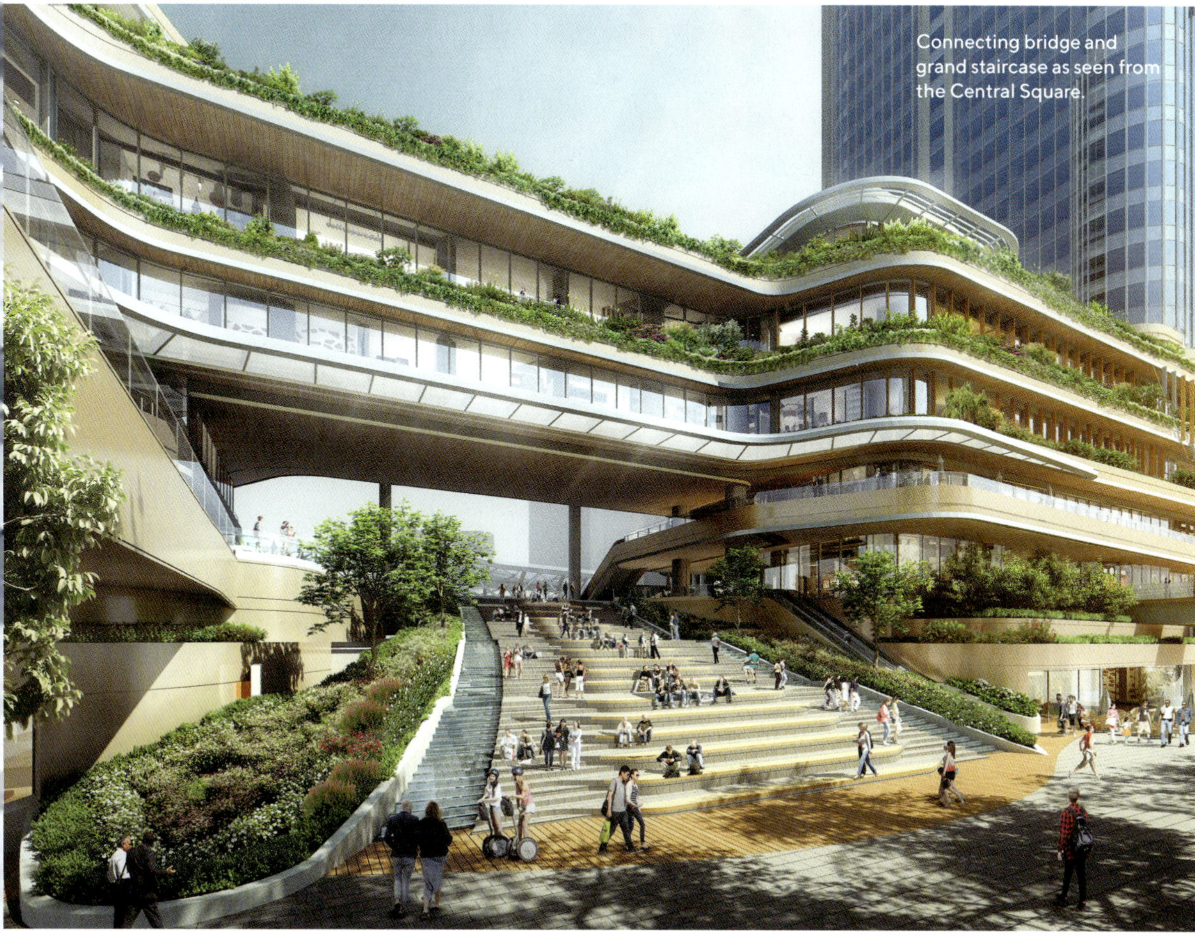

Connecting bridge and grand staircase as seen from the Central Square.

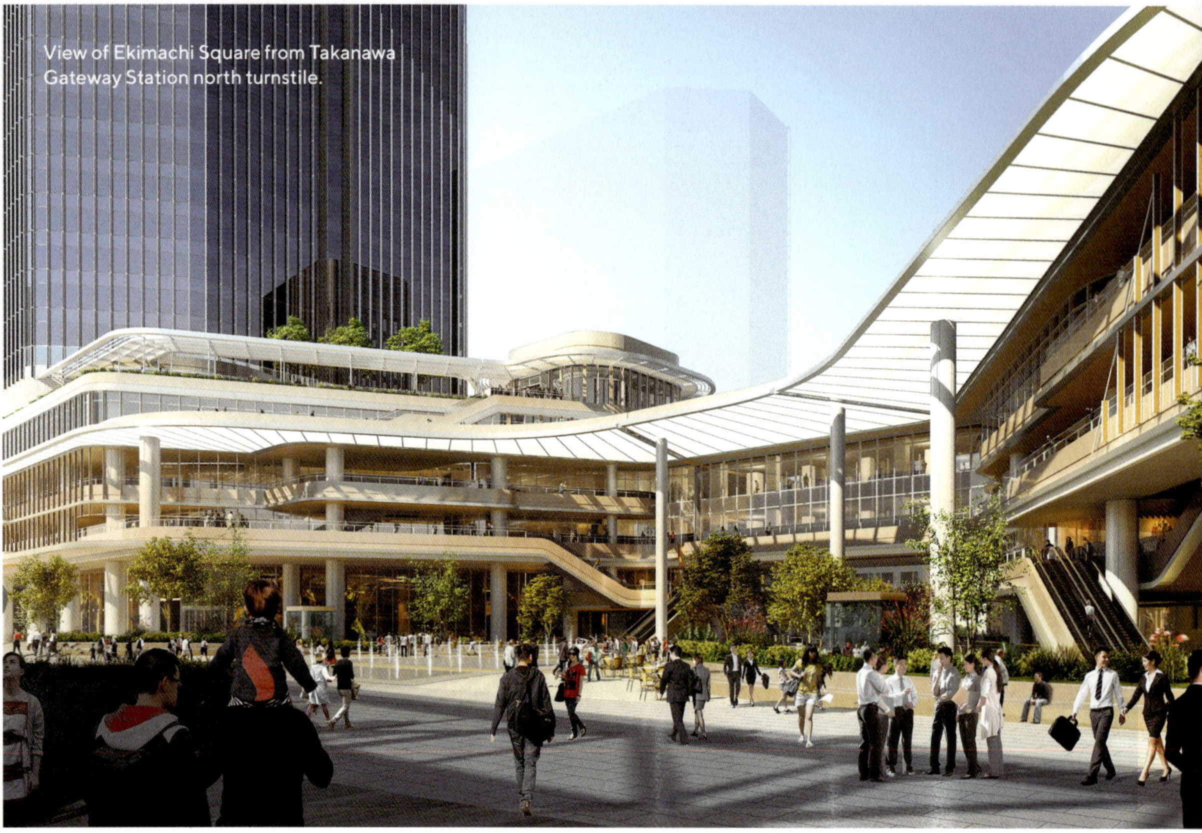

View of Ekimachi Square from Takanawa Gateway Station north turnstile.

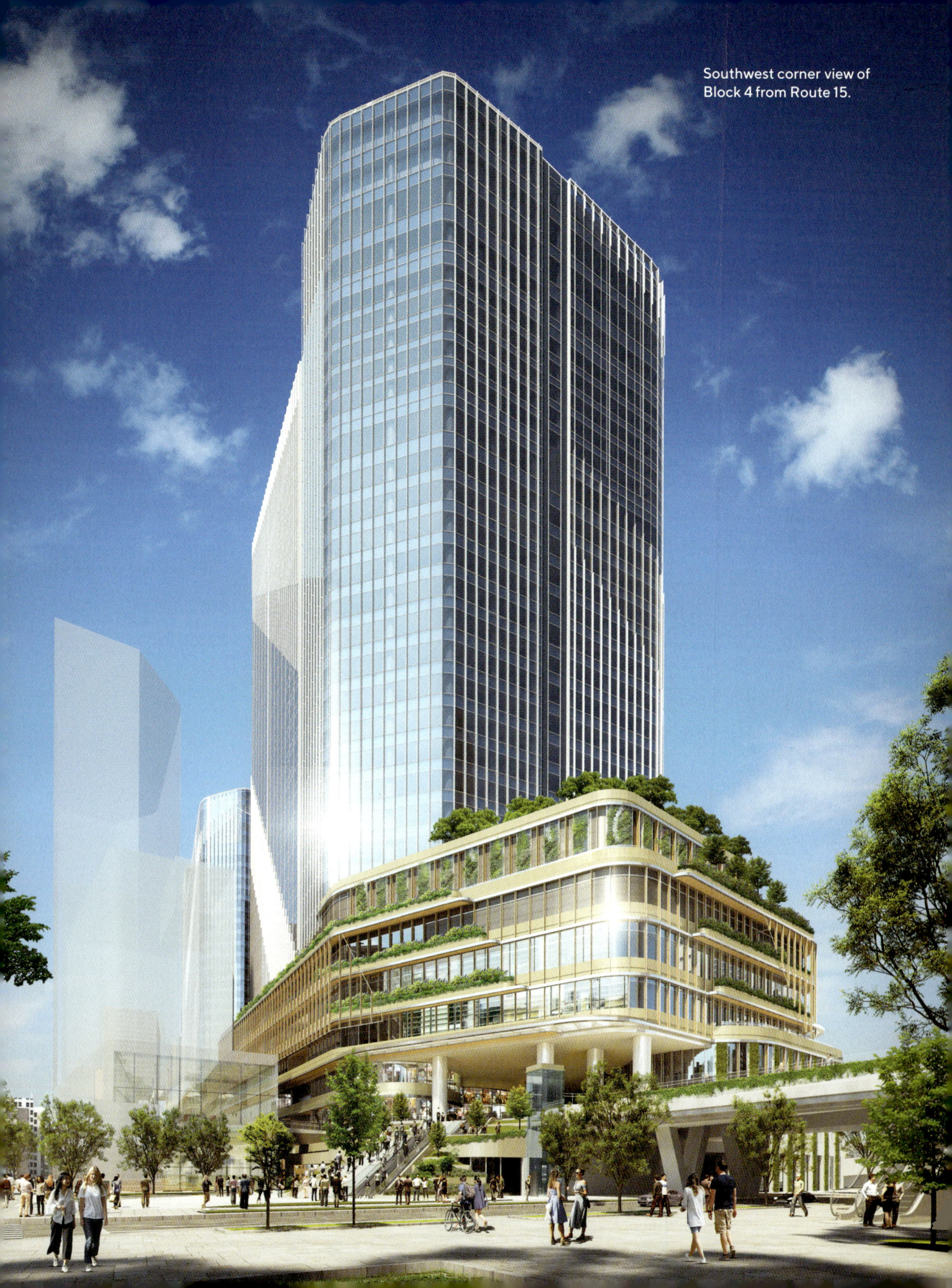

Southwest corner view of Block 4 from Route 15.

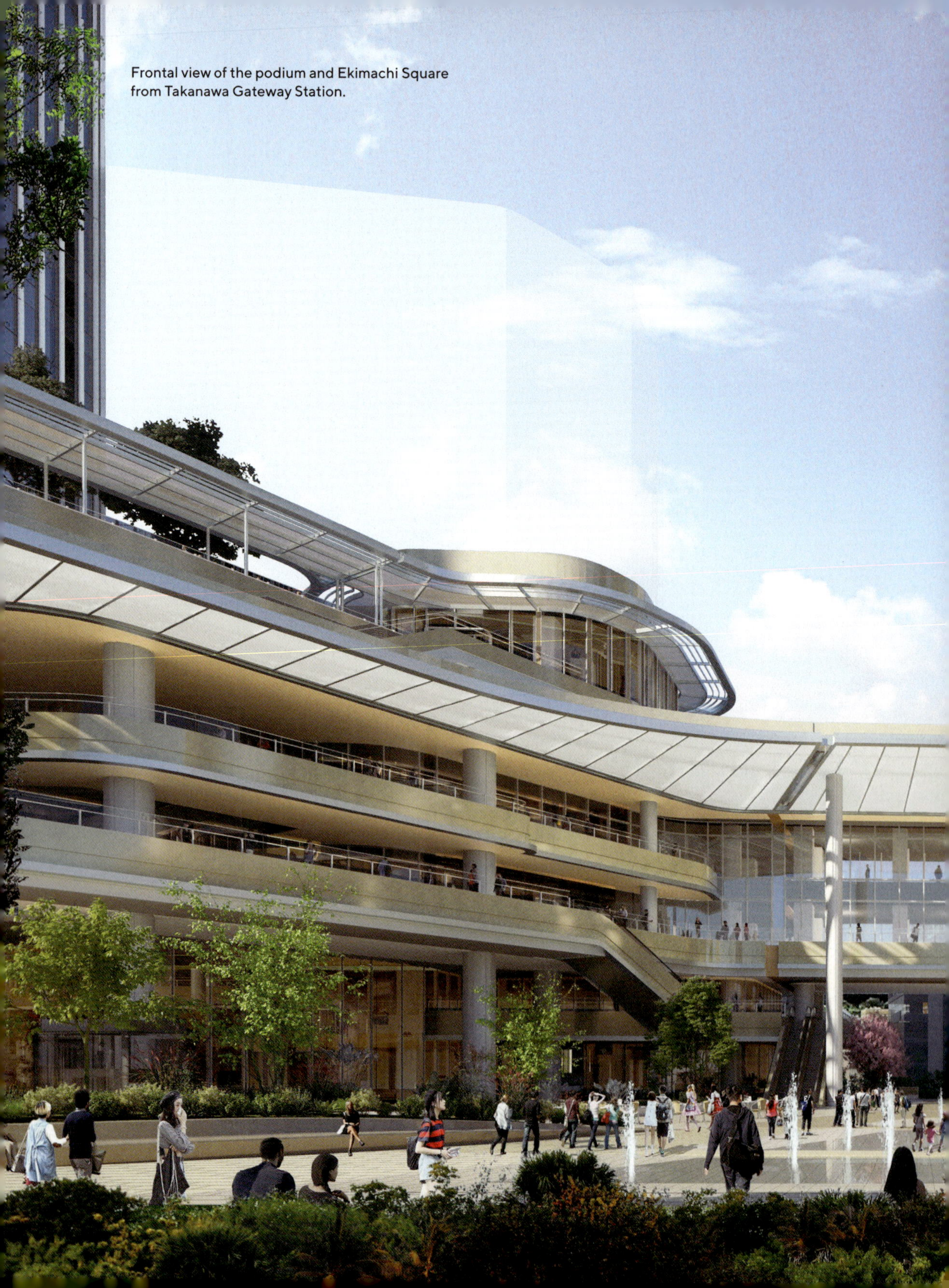

Frontal view of the podium and Ekimachi Square from Takanawa Gateway Station.

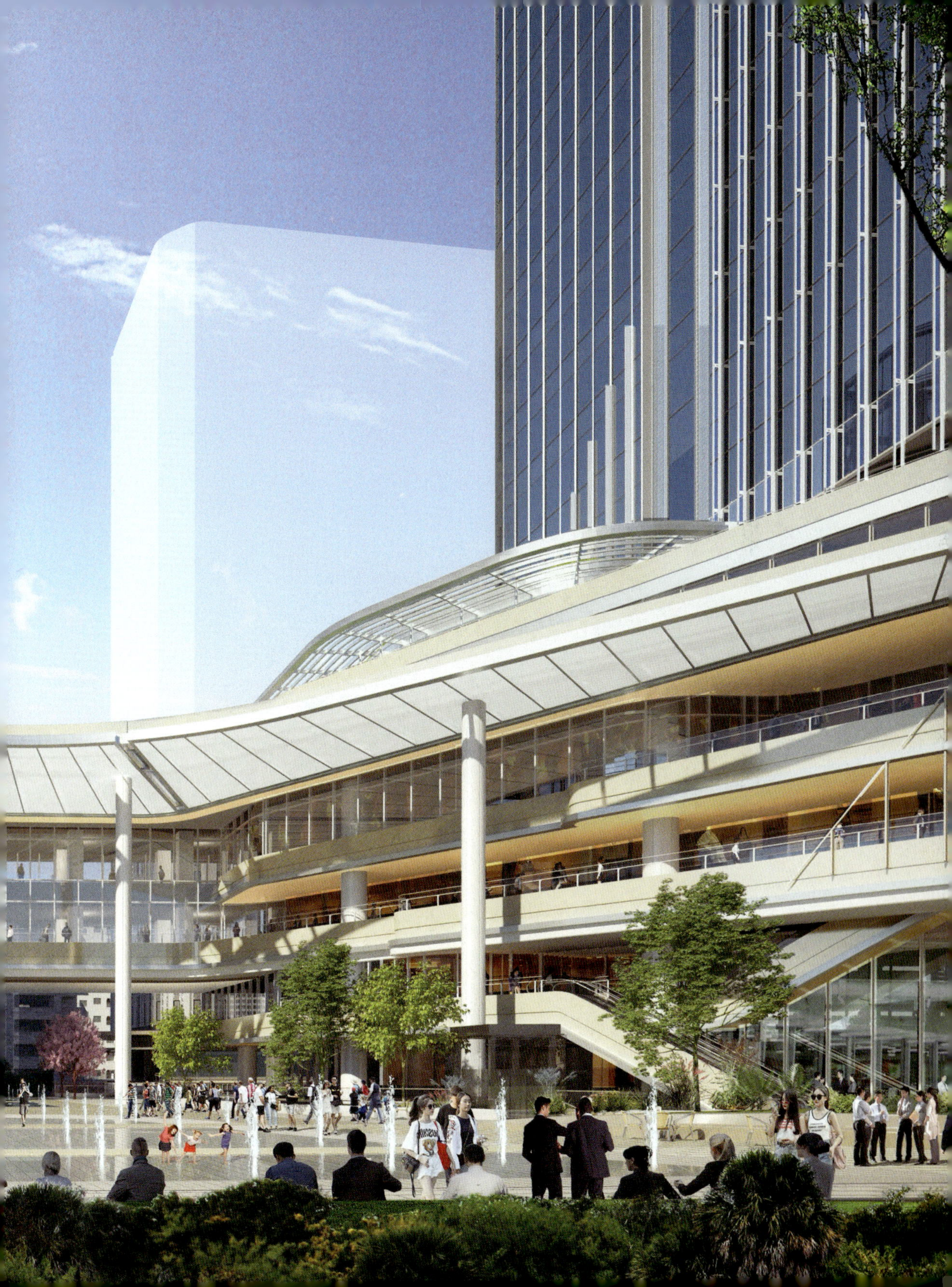

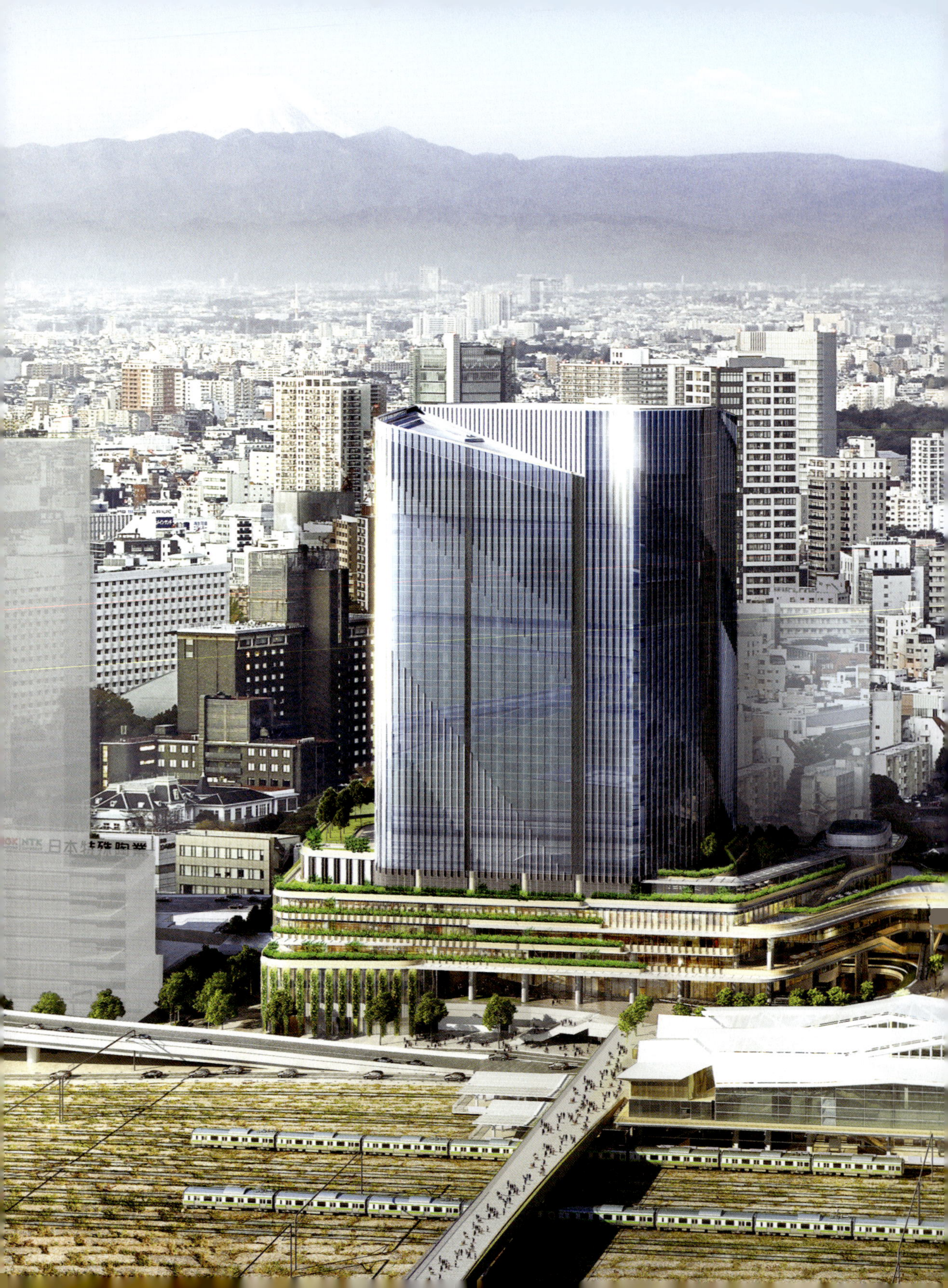

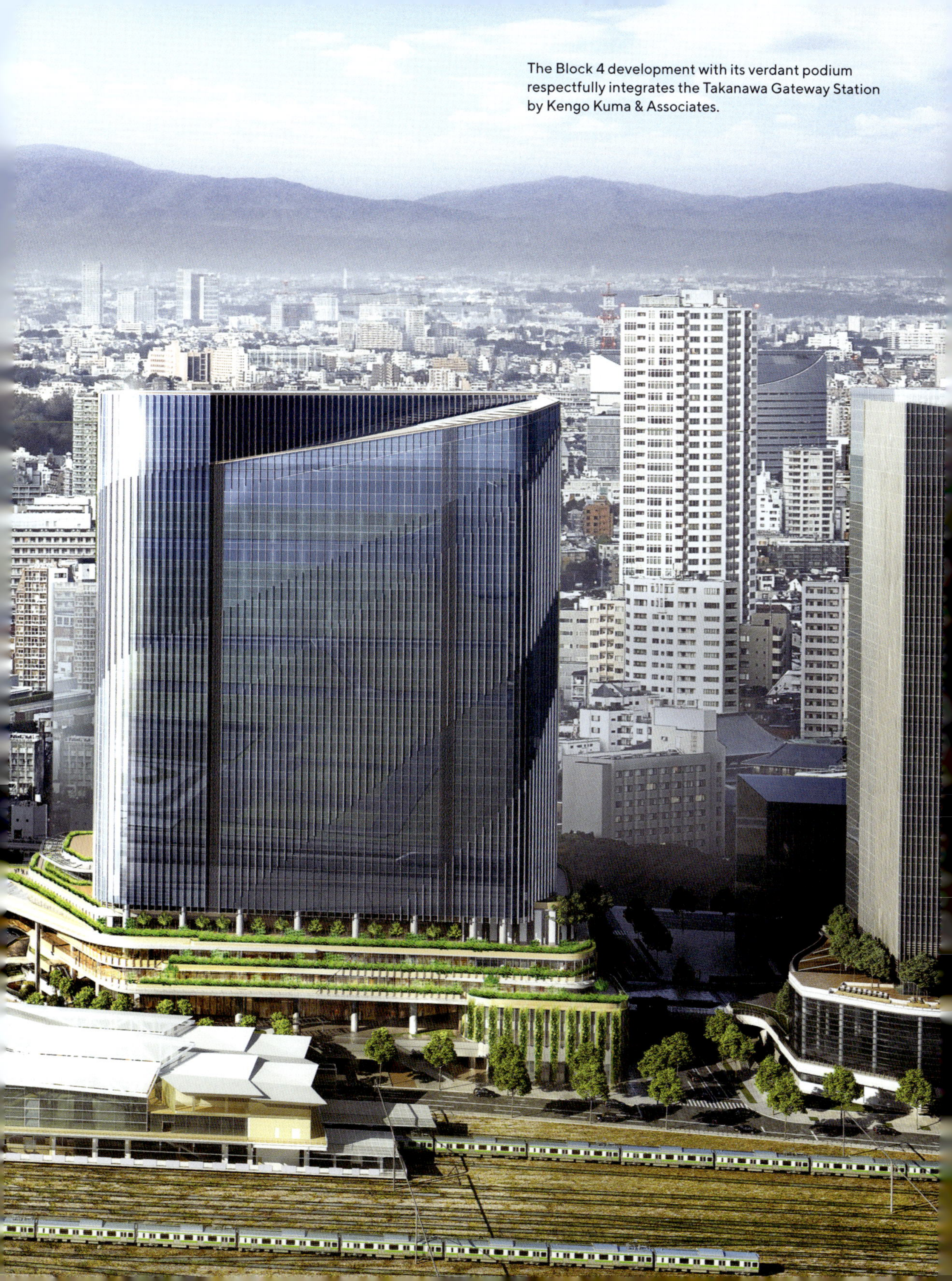

The Block 4 development with its verdant podium respectfully integrates the Takanawa Gateway Station by Kengo Kuma & Associates.

"You get this sense of the design happening before your eyes."

Michael Tilford
Vice President, Development, Boston Properties

---

325 MAIN
GOOGLE CAMBRIDGE HEADQUARTERS
BOSTON, MASSACHUSETTS

Completion 2022
417,000 gross square feet / 38,740 gross square meters
LEED for Core and Shell Gold targeted

With an activated ground- and second-floor retail edge along Main Street and the façade abutting Kendall Plaza, 325 Main will significantly enhance the pedestrian experience and enliven the public realm. A new pedestrian connection from Kendall Plaza up to the Kendall Square Rooftop Garden creates a multilevel public terrace overlooking Main Street and Kendall Plaza with potential for programming.

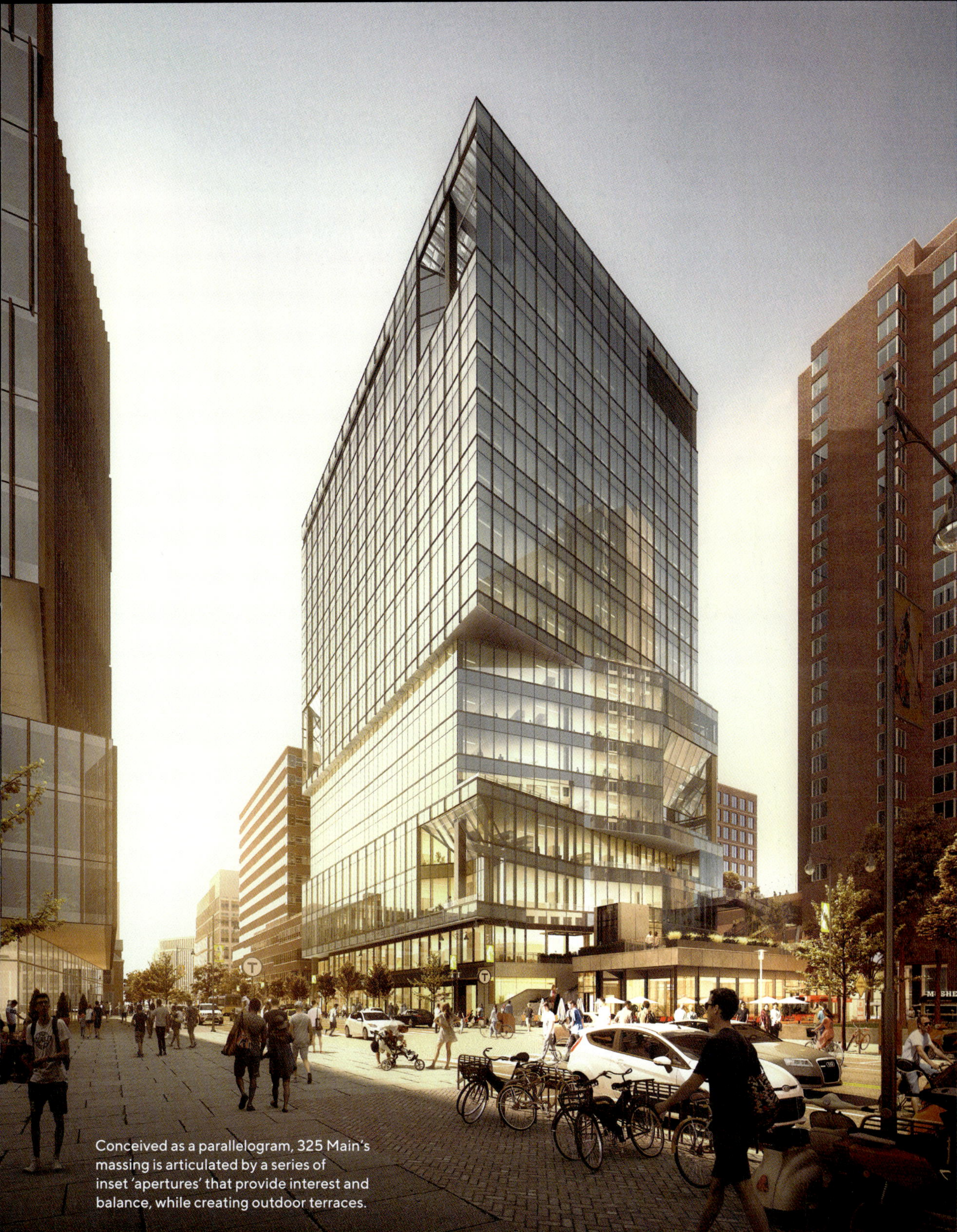

Conceived as a parallelogram, 325 Main's massing is articulated by a series of inset 'apertures' that provide interest and balance, while creating outdoor terraces.

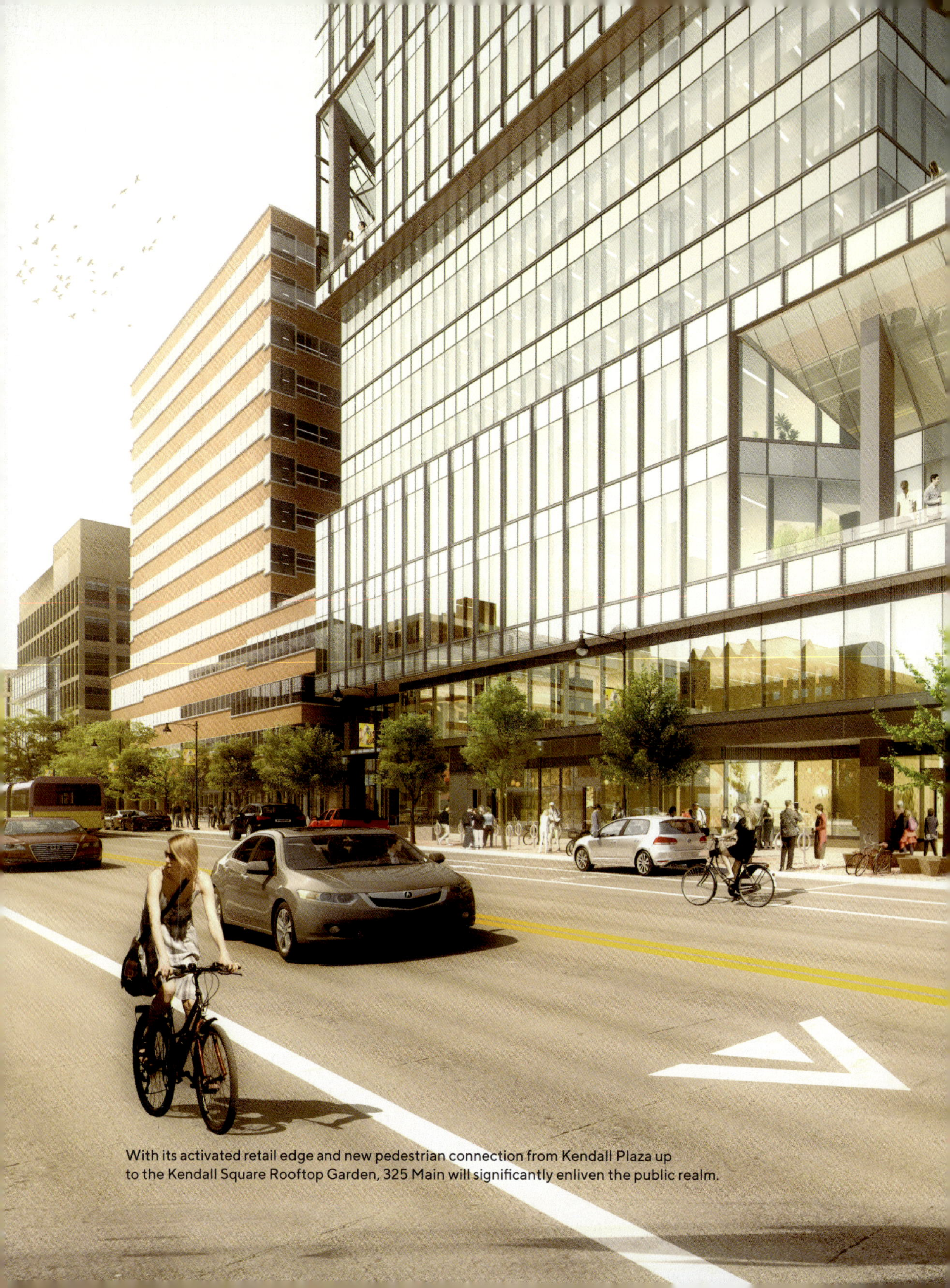

With its activated retail edge and new pedestrian connection from Kendall Plaza up to the Kendall Square Rooftop Garden, 325 Main will significantly enliven the public realm.

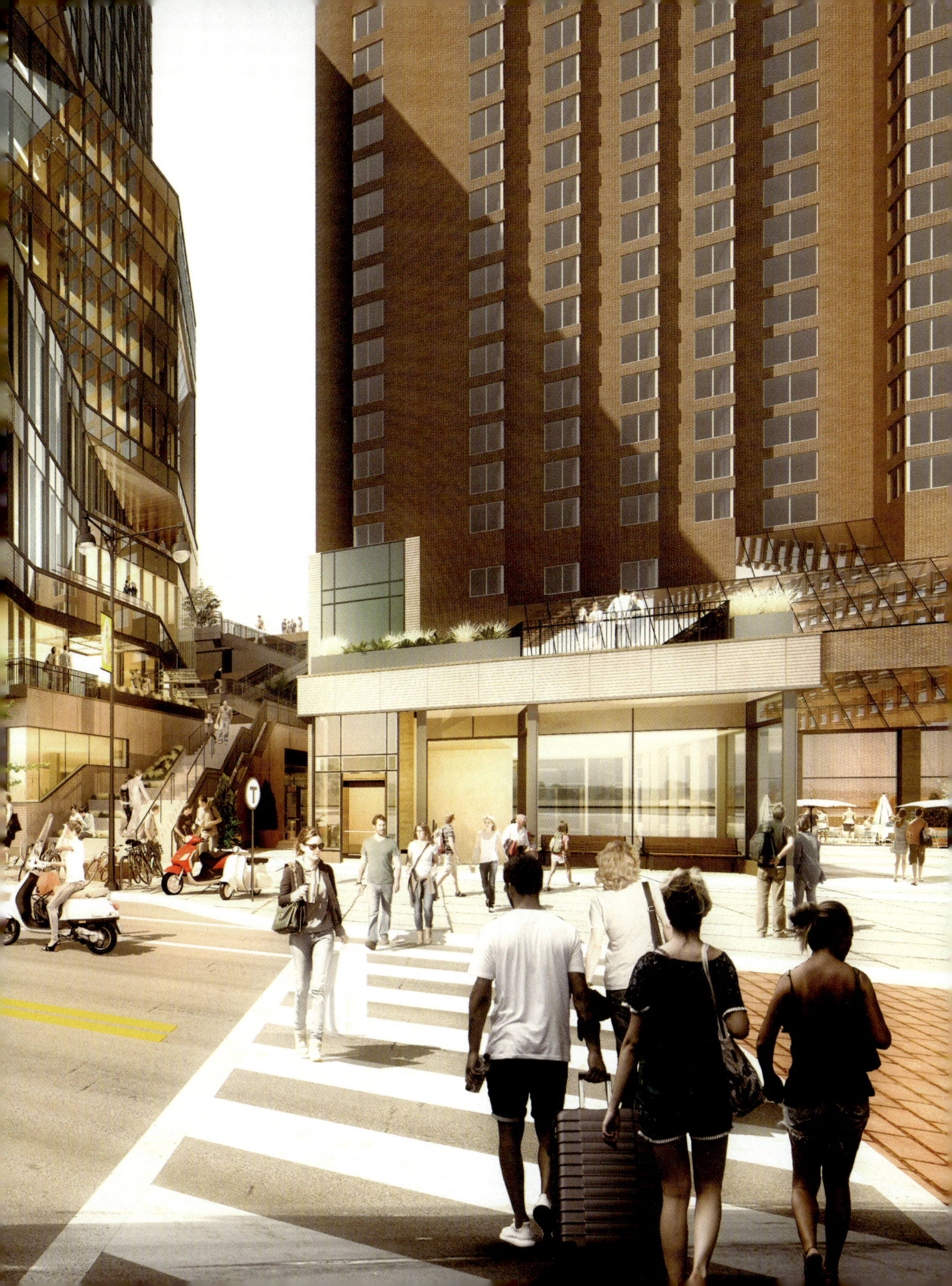

T

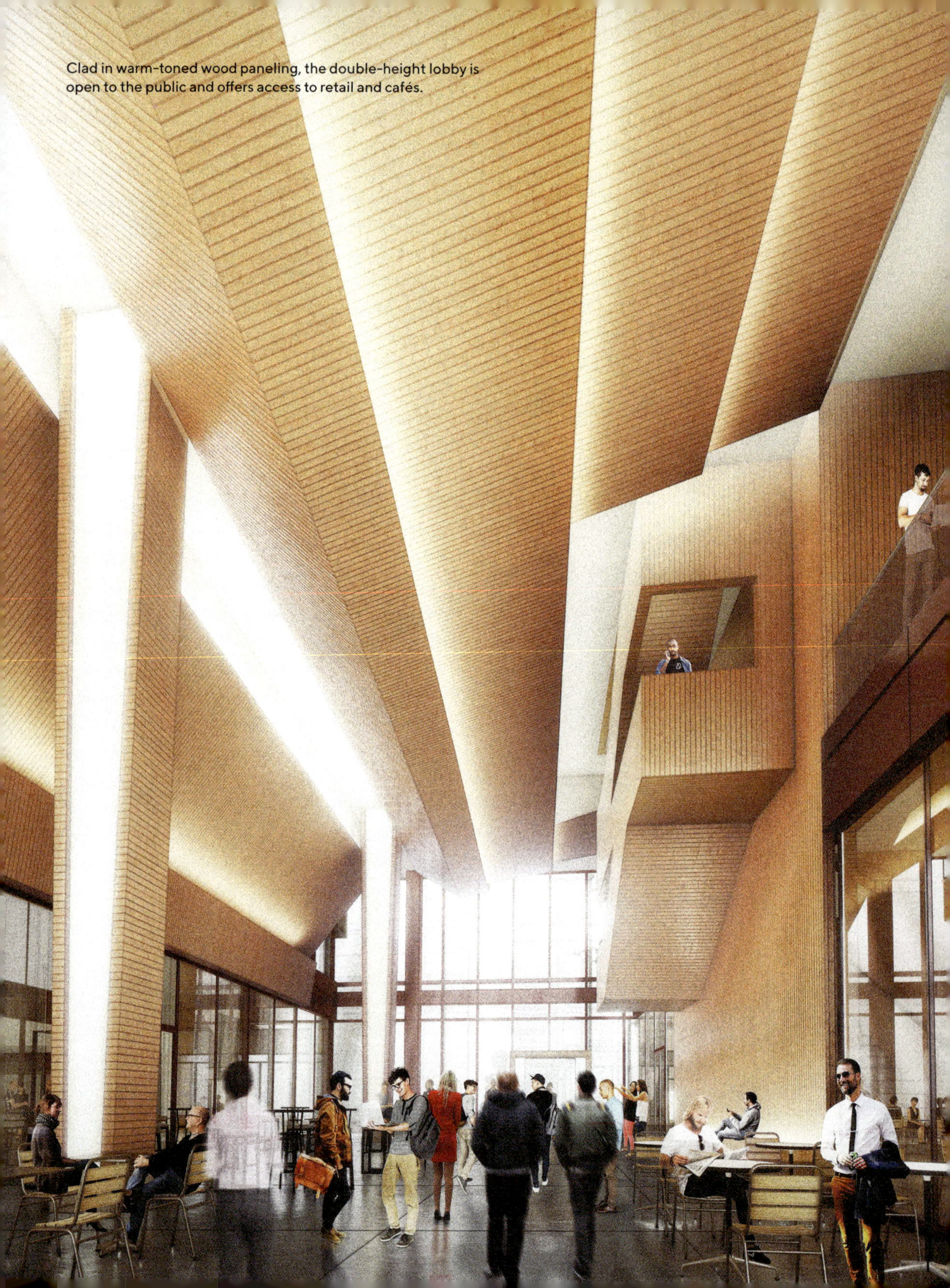

Clad in warm-toned wood paneling, the double-height lobby is open to the public and offers access to retail and cafés.

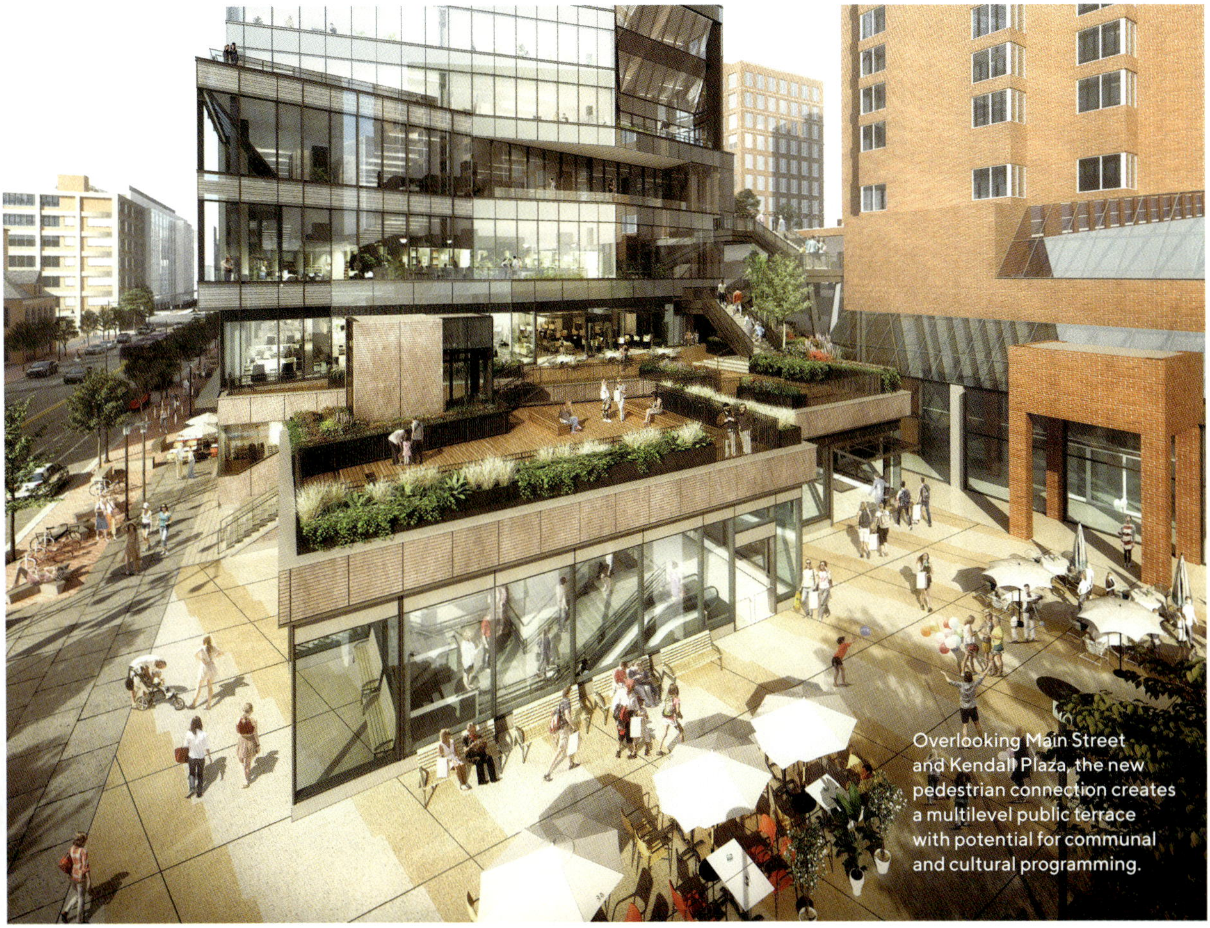

Overlooking Main Street and Kendall Plaza, the new pedestrian connection creates a multilevel public terrace with potential for communal and cultural programming.

A sloped 'gasket' connects the 325 and 355 Main Street buildings, creating a visual distinction between them while upper floors along Main Street have been pulled away from 355 Main to further enhance the visual separation.

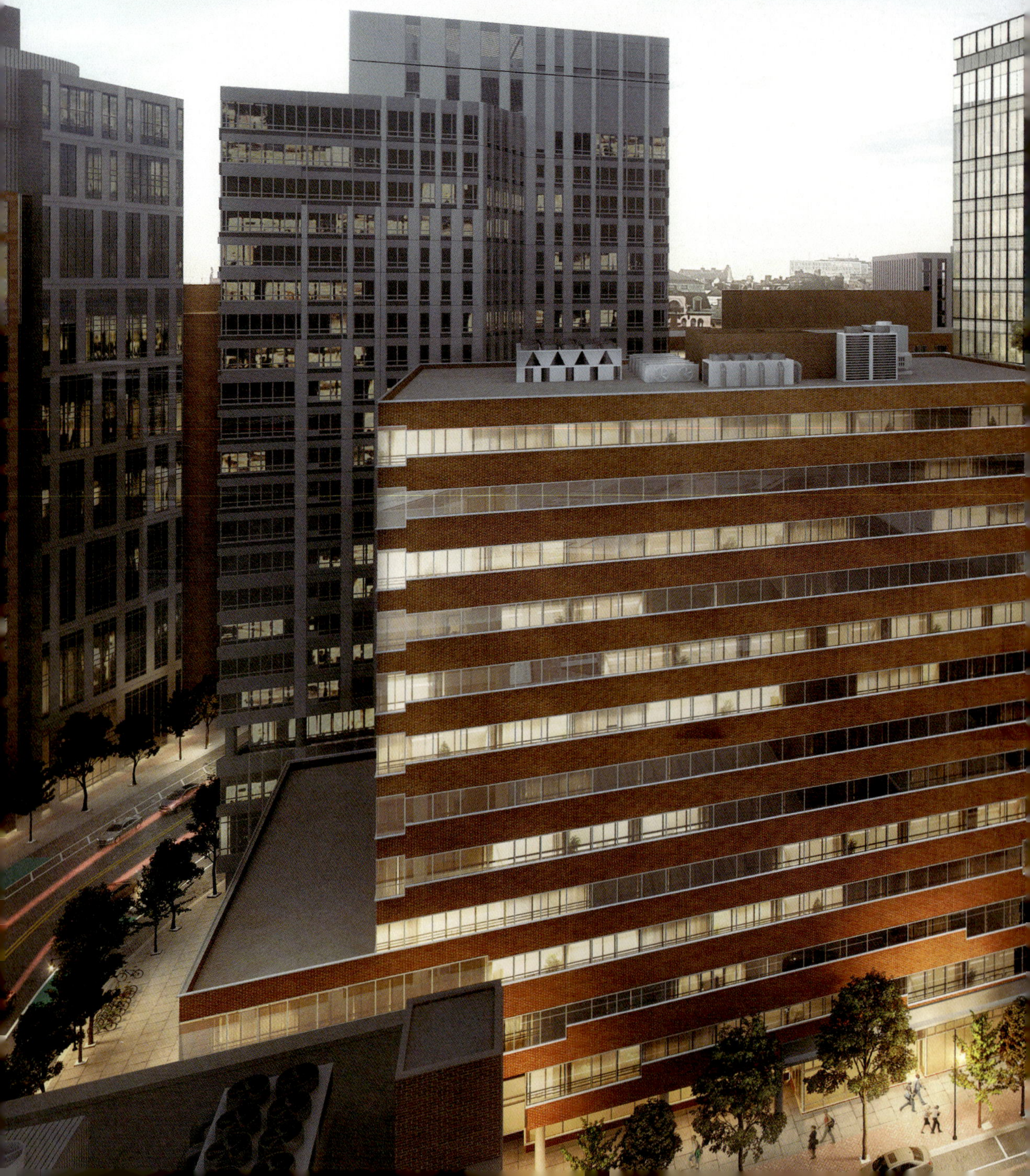

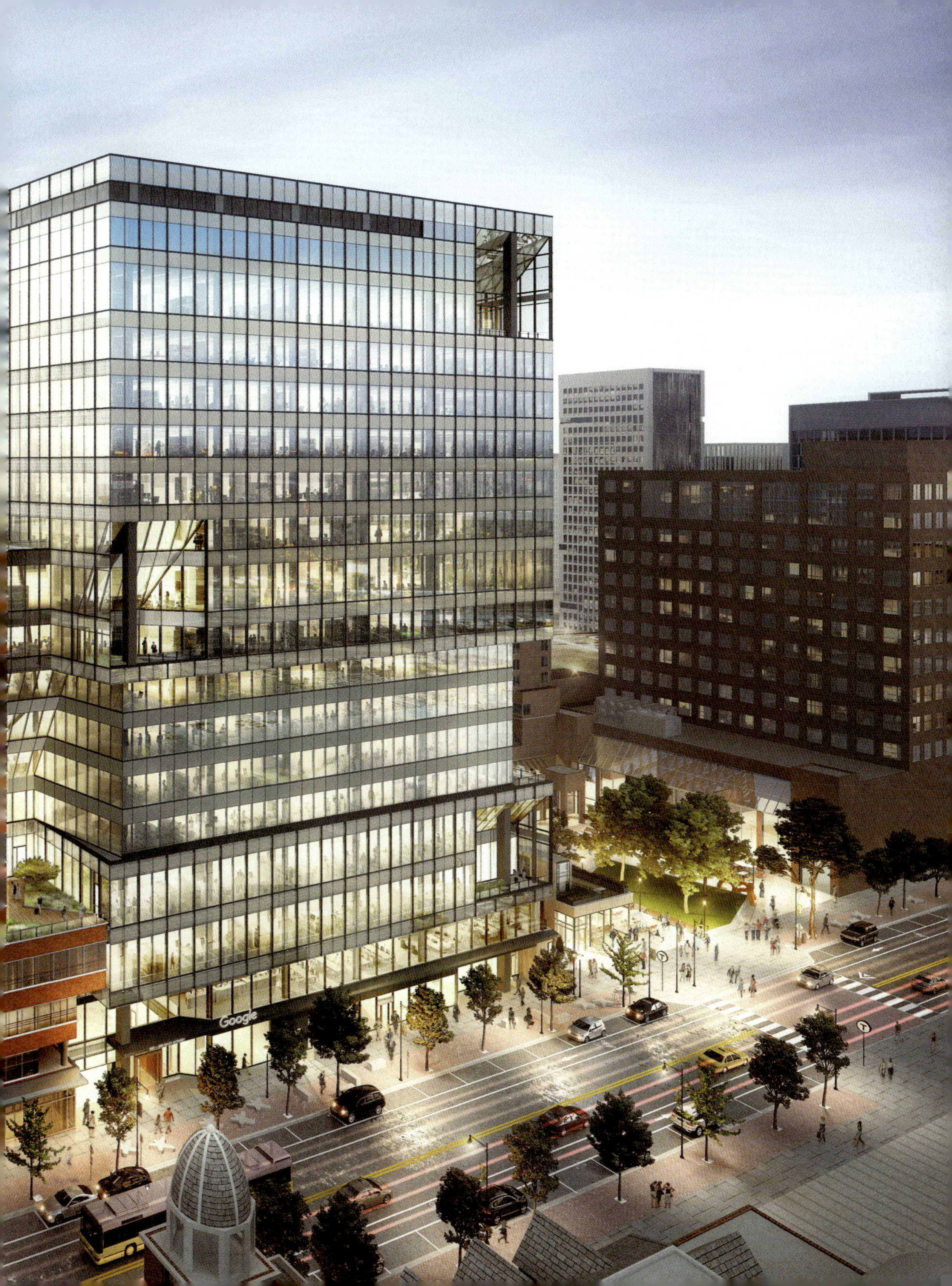
Google

Mutual Trust

DEVON ENERGY CENTER

Devon Energy
Hines
Pickard Chilton
Kendall/Heaton Associates
Gensler
Thornton Tomasetti
Cosentini Associates
OJB Landscape Architecture
Murase Associates
Quentin Thomas Associates
Persohn/Hahn Associates

It is important for the architect and the client to understand each other's values (even if they are not necessarily shared) as a way to build mutual trust in each other and in the project. Mutual trust is the foundation upon which clients and architects build their relationships and (subsequently) their projects. How is mutual trust cultivated between the architect and the client? What is the evolution of the development of this trust? How might mutual trust be challenged? Is there a point where mutual trust is articulated between the architect and the client? How is mutual trust expressed in the design process? How is mutual trust reflected in the completed design and construction? Does mutual trust developed in working with one client inform the design of future projects, perhaps with future clients?

One of the keys to building mutual trust is to spend time with each other. Conversations in relaxed settings — over dinner, for instance — between the architect and key decision makers can allow mutual trust to blossom naturally. Trust is earned, and it is a two-way street: the trust of the client matching that of the architect. The context of mutual trust permits the exploration of design ideas that the client and the architect might not initially see eye-to-eye on. Mutual trust allows a candid conversation to happen, ideas to be shared and challenged, and a design to develop in a direction that neither the architect nor the client might have expected.

A good example is Devon Energy Center in Oklahoma City. The client—particularly Devon chairman Larry Nichols — had a vision about embracing the city. Oklahoma City competes for talent against places like Houston, Dallas, Denver, even London. Devon's vision was to make its new headquarters a special place where employees would feel welcome and proud. Along with improving the surrounding site, infrastructure, and public parks, a design strategy for the building's

Devon Energy's Klay Kimker with Jon Pickard at a Design Development presentation.

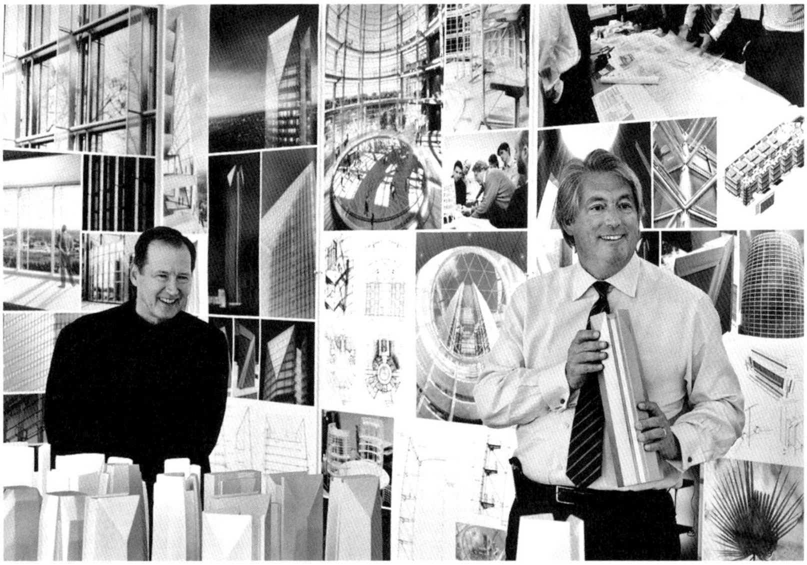

lobby challenged the prevailing idea of the office building as fortress. The idea was to make the tower's lobby a truly public space, one in which the public could pass through and even stop by for lunch. The result is one of the great public spaces in a contemporary office tower, akin to that in Cesar Pelli's World Financial Center in New York. Devon's vice president of administration and president of the company's real estate advisory subsidiary during the project, Klay Kimker, credits

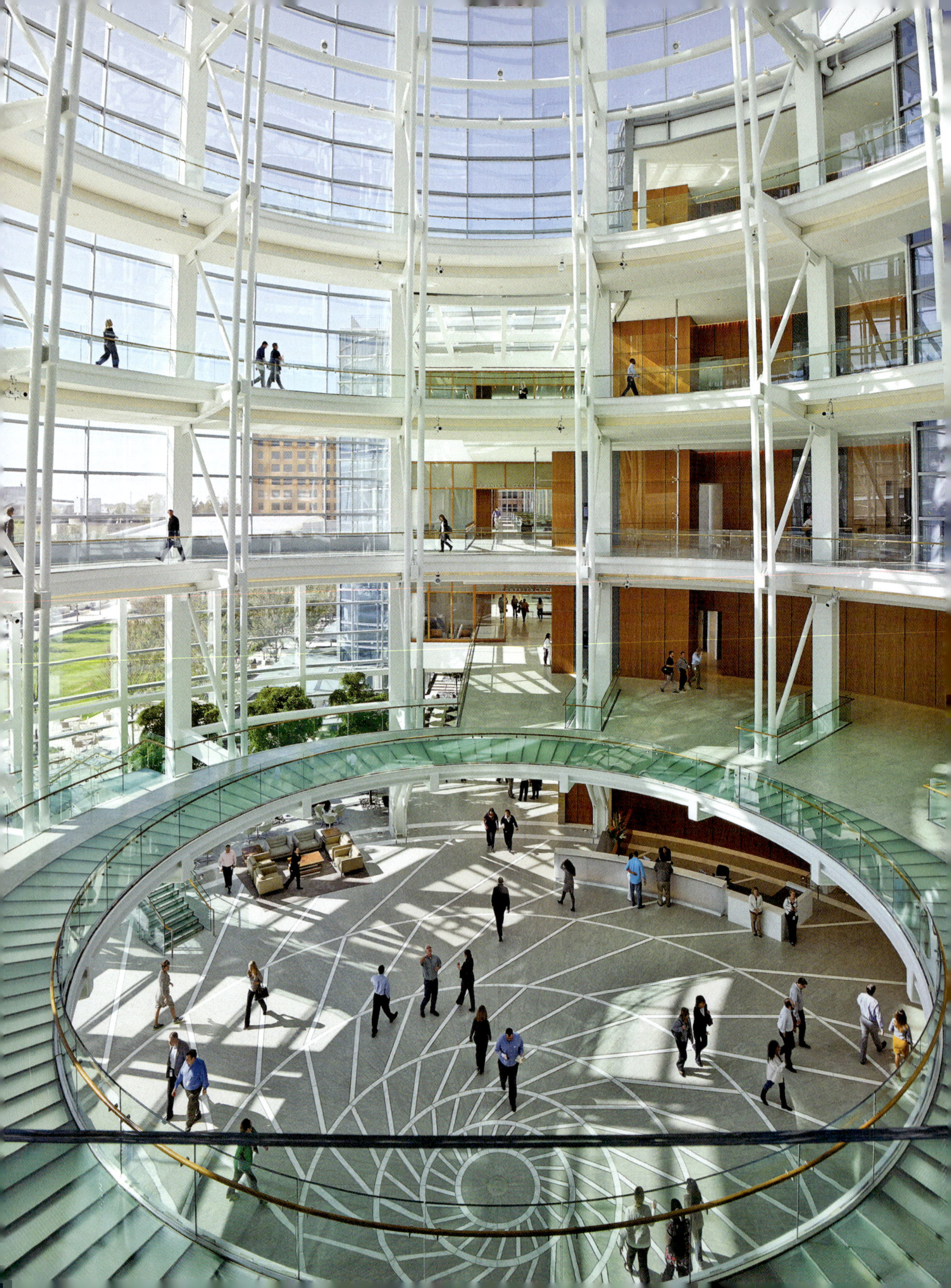

A grand civic-scaled space with glass walls, a series of balconies, and a sky-lit roof, the six-story Rotunda serves as the entrance and connecting hub for the entire complex—and a dramatic setting for special events and civic gatherings.

the synergy between Devon's chairman and the Pickard Chilton design principal as key to what was achieved, through mutual trust built through accessibility. "Accessibility to the design principal was critical," explains Kimker. "I don't believe we could have gotten this design and this impact without it."

The Hines company, acting as Devon's development manager, was comfortable working with Pickard Chilton in light of the mutual trust that had previously been cultivated between the developer and the architects. "Mutual trust is very important to us," says Hines's Jerry Lea. "You can usually figure out not too far into the relationship whether you'll get it or not." In the case of Devon, Pickard Chilton's cultivation of mutual trust with Hines was already established, which helped the client, development manager, and architect to arrive at a design that works for everyone on the team. In a career that spans four decades, Lea has observed that an architect might present a design that is beautiful, but inefficient. "I'm looking for the architect to trust me" when told that the design falls short of being innovative *and* of the highest quality for that market, Lea explains.

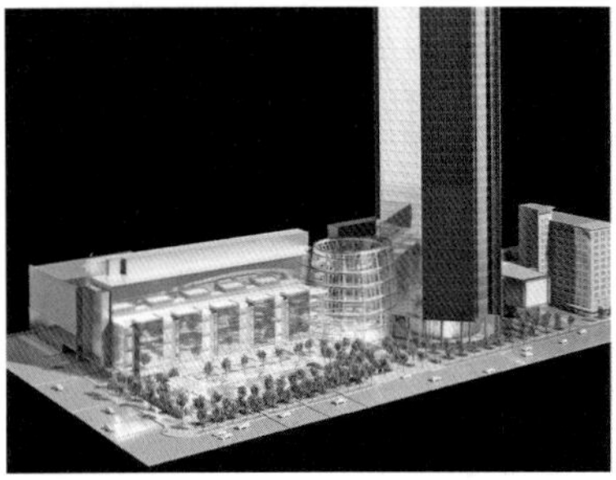
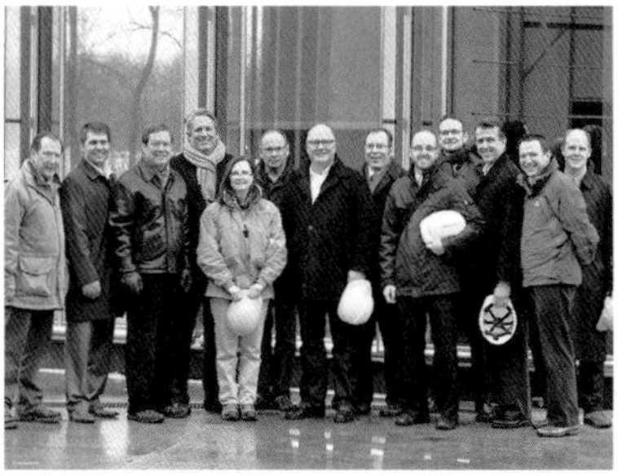
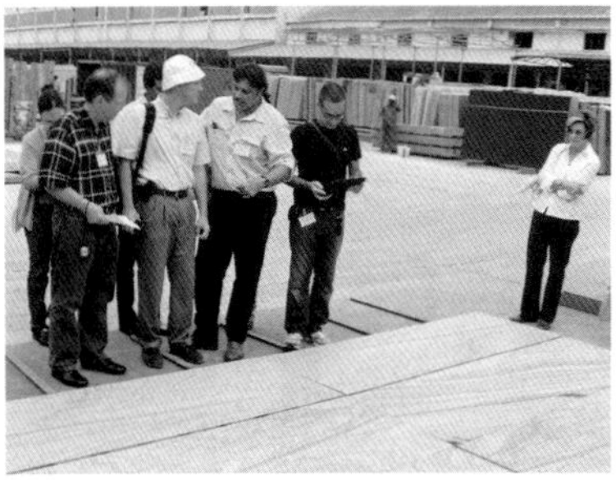
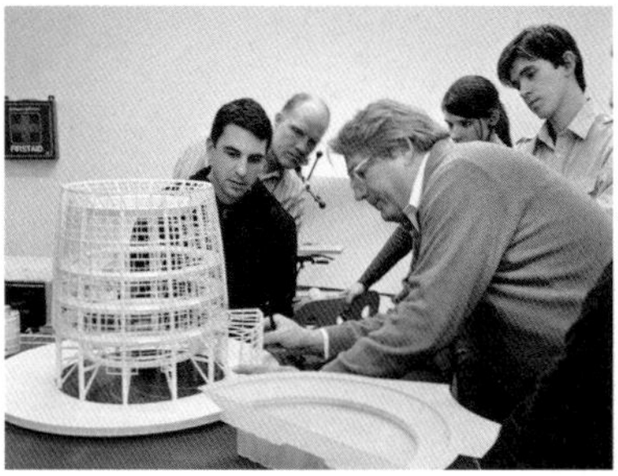

← Images of the highly collaborative design and construction process of Devon Energy Center.

↓ Bird's-eye view axonometric pencil drawing of the entire Devon Energy Center.

→ Presentation model built for the public unveiling of the Devon Energy Center.

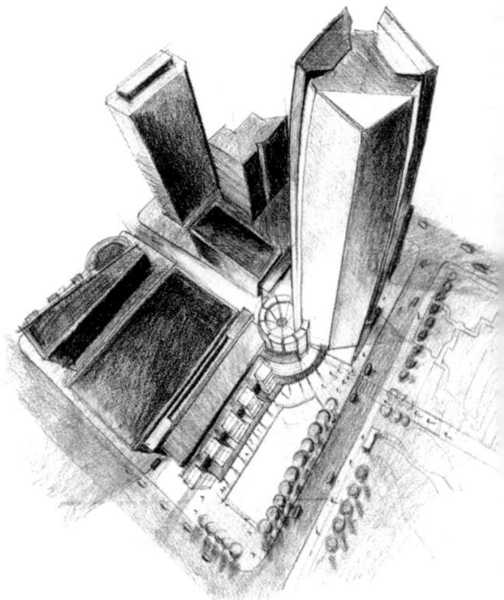

Mutual trust should also enhance the working relationship between the architects and the various consultants on the project. Kimker saw this demonstrated firsthand. "I had not always seen design teams work together well," says Kimker, "but in this case, I was just amazed," particularly how the architects led the synergy of the team, which helped to build mutual trust throughout. According to Kimker, the architects created a partnership with each of the team members, "The interiors team,

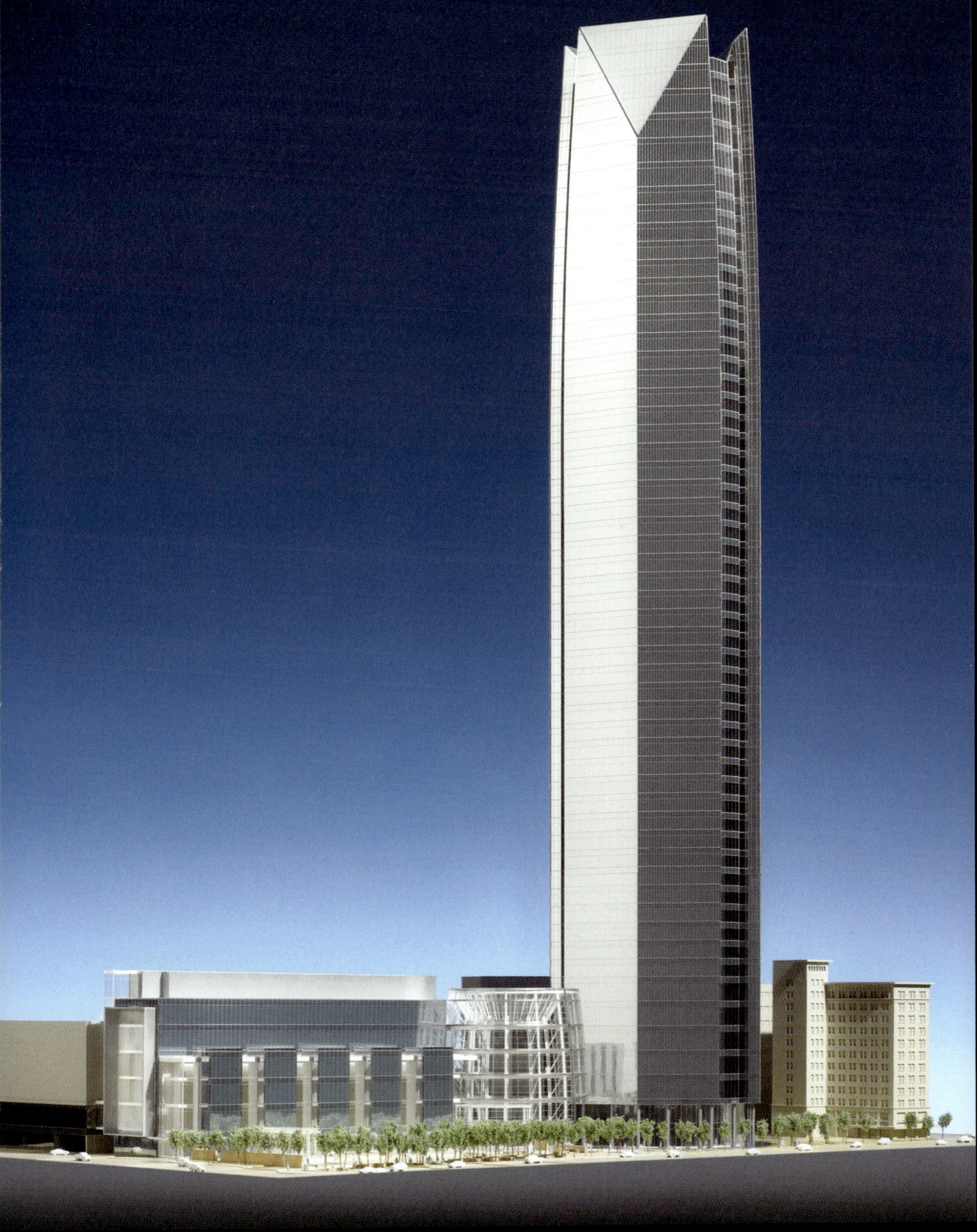

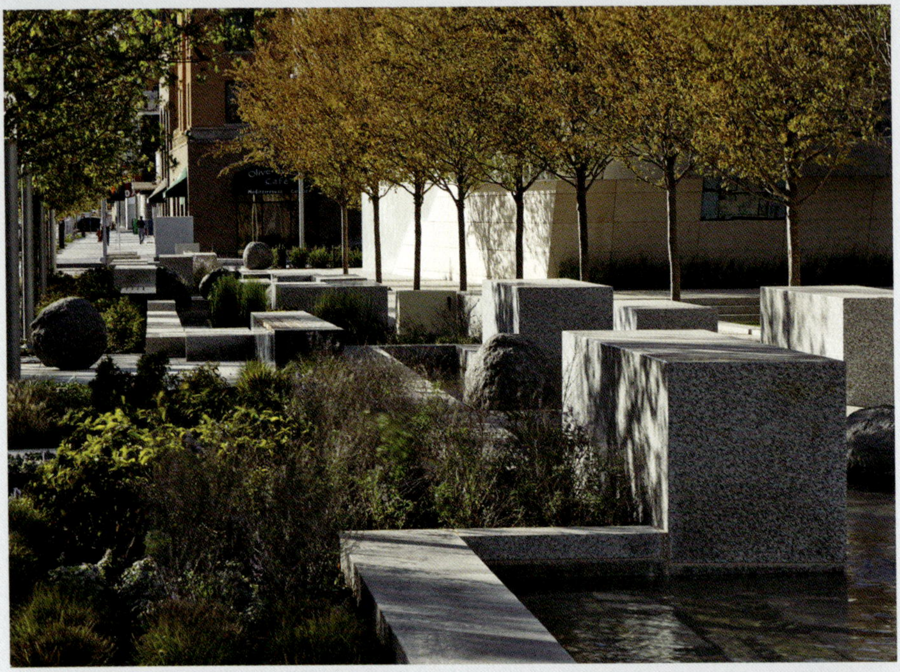

A series of pools, planters, and stone boulders along Sheridan Avenue create an engaging street edge.

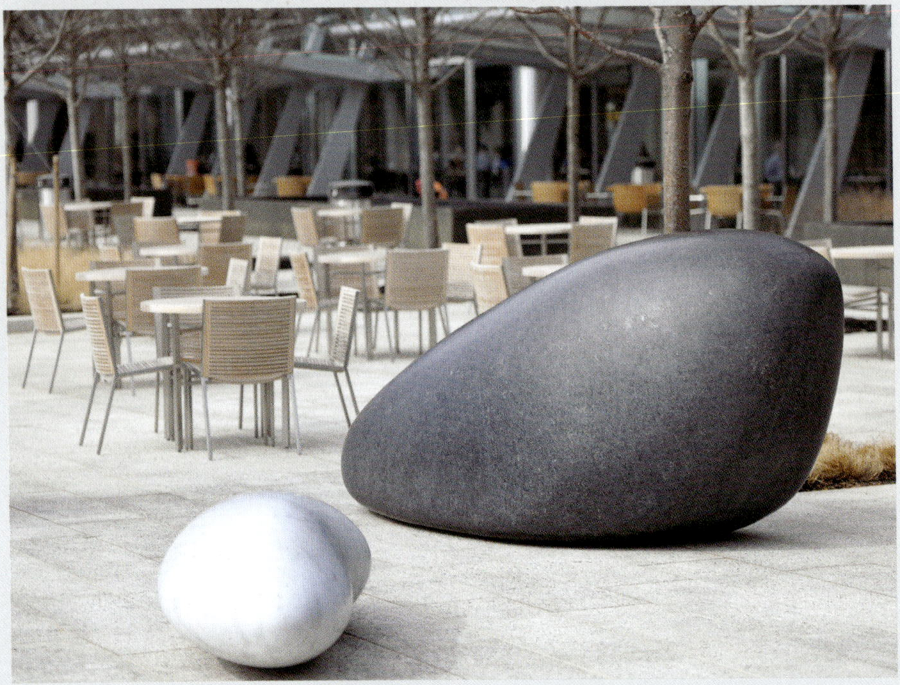

the landscape architect, the lighting consultant, even the snow and ice consultants and bird consultants were taken in and considered and their thoughts and comments were of value," explains Kimker. As team leaders, the architects nonetheless were self-deprecating, acting in a kindly and respectful manner toward other team members. During project meetings, the architects requested that various consultants present their particular approach to the design. Such willingness to call upon consultants to enlighten the entire team is possible only when there is shared mutual trust among team members.

"It became infectious," says Kimker. "If you interviewed other members of the team, you would find that most would say, 'We will probably never work on another project like this again.' In addition to being outstanding from a design perspective, this team was fun. We traveled together benchmarking, visiting material suppliers, and reviewing mock-ups. We had dinners together. It was amazing to watch. I was at every meeting, and I did not see a single moment of angst or anger among the team members. It was truly special."

Mutual trust allows … a design to develop in a direction that neither the architect nor the client might have expected.

DEVON ENERGY CENTER
OKLAHOMA CITY, OKLAHOMA

Completion 2012
3 million gross square feet / 280,000 gross square meters
LEED for New Construction Gold

Devon's new world headquarters serves as a focal point for the company and for Oklahoma City. Characterized by civic-scaled spaces, the corporate headquarters brings Devon's local workforce together in a single state-of-the-art facility. A six-story glass rotunda with interior balconies serves as the entrance and connecting hub for the entire complex — and a dramatic setting for special events. The five-story podium houses the conference and training centers and employee amenities. The indoor Galleria includes dining areas overlooking the new park and landscaped plazas that are key elements in the overall site strategy.

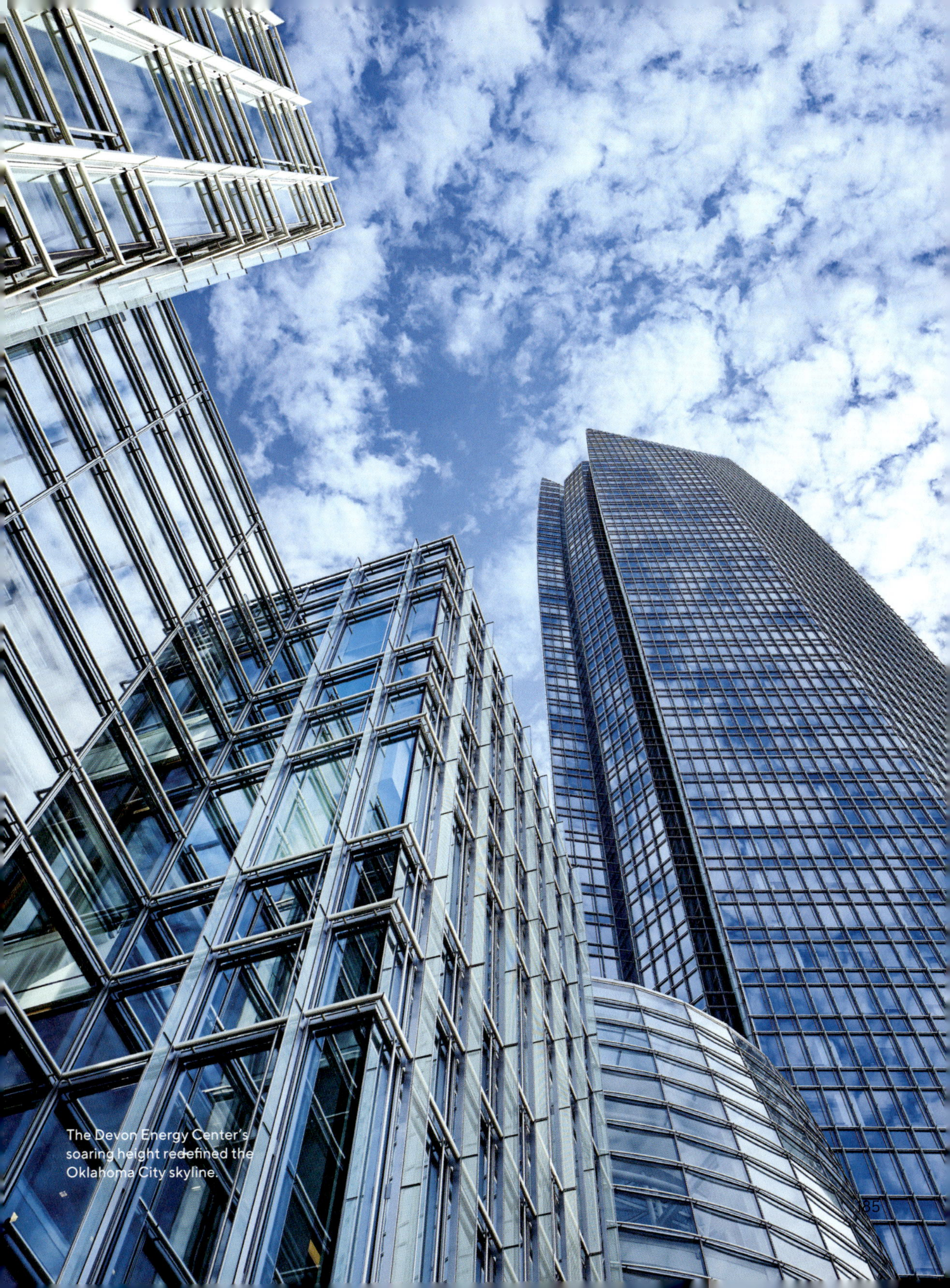

The Devon Energy Center's soaring height redefined the Oklahoma City skyline.

The highly articulated mullion system integrates solar shading and night lighting and adds richness and texture to the exterior.

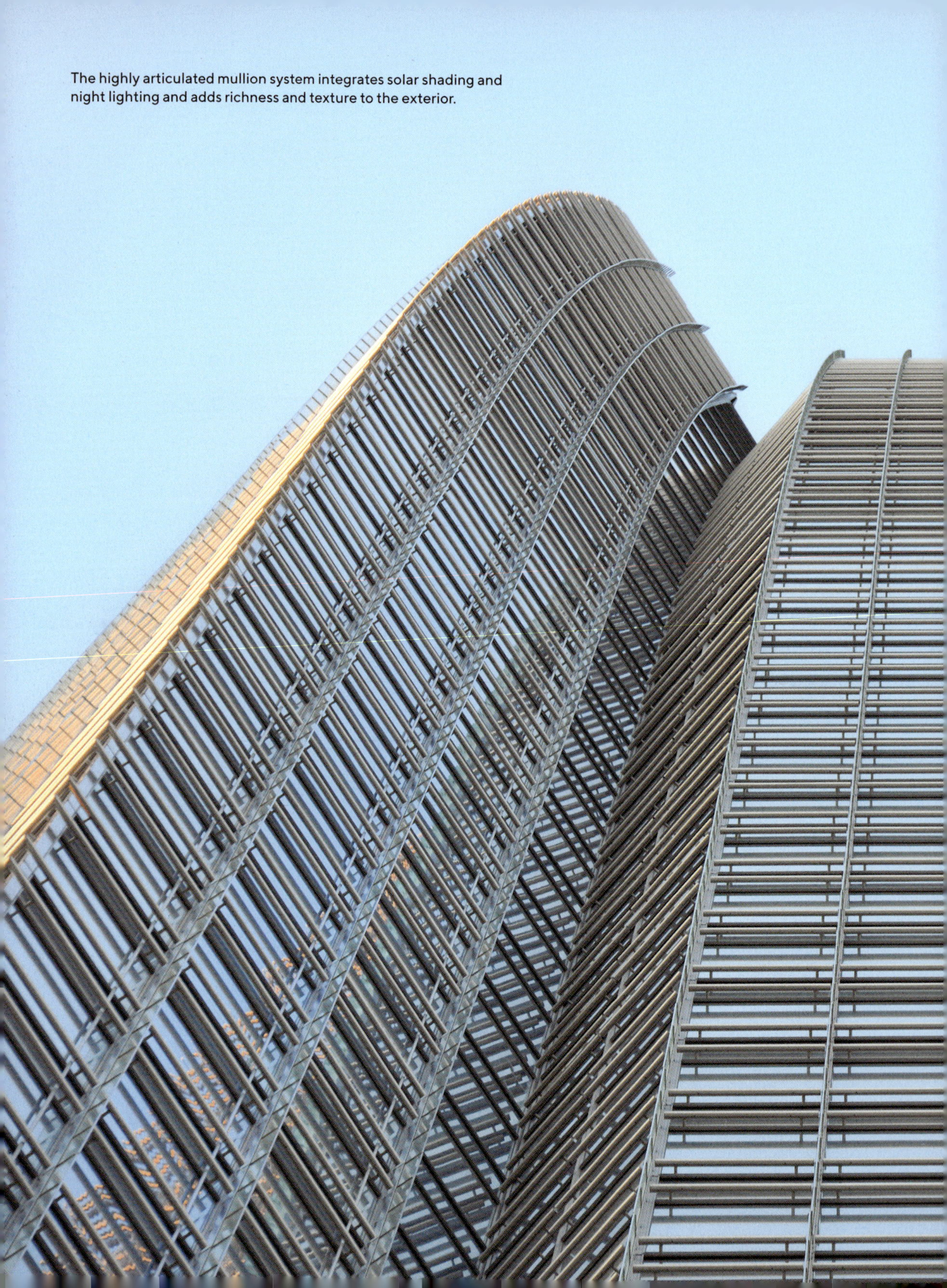

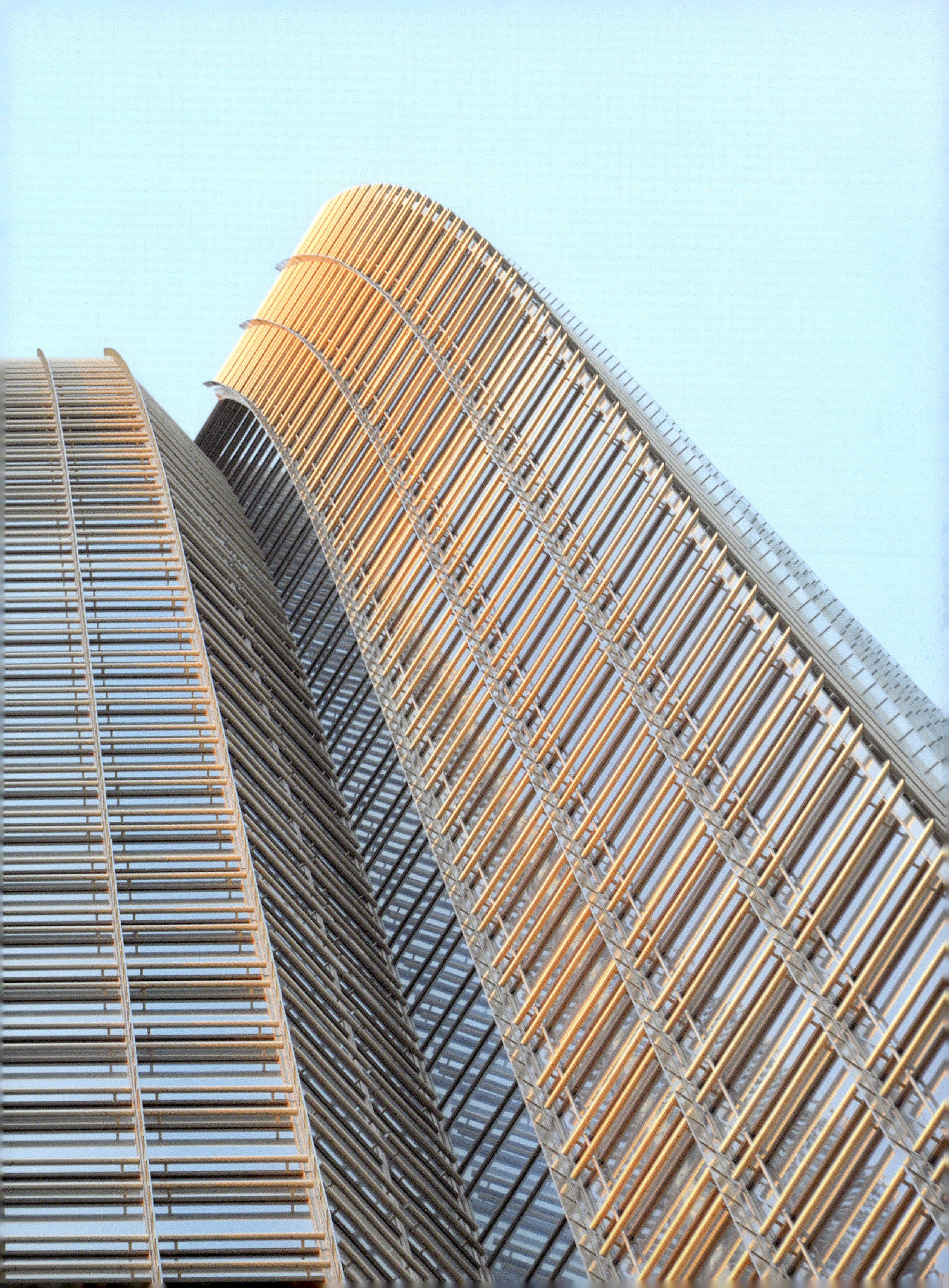

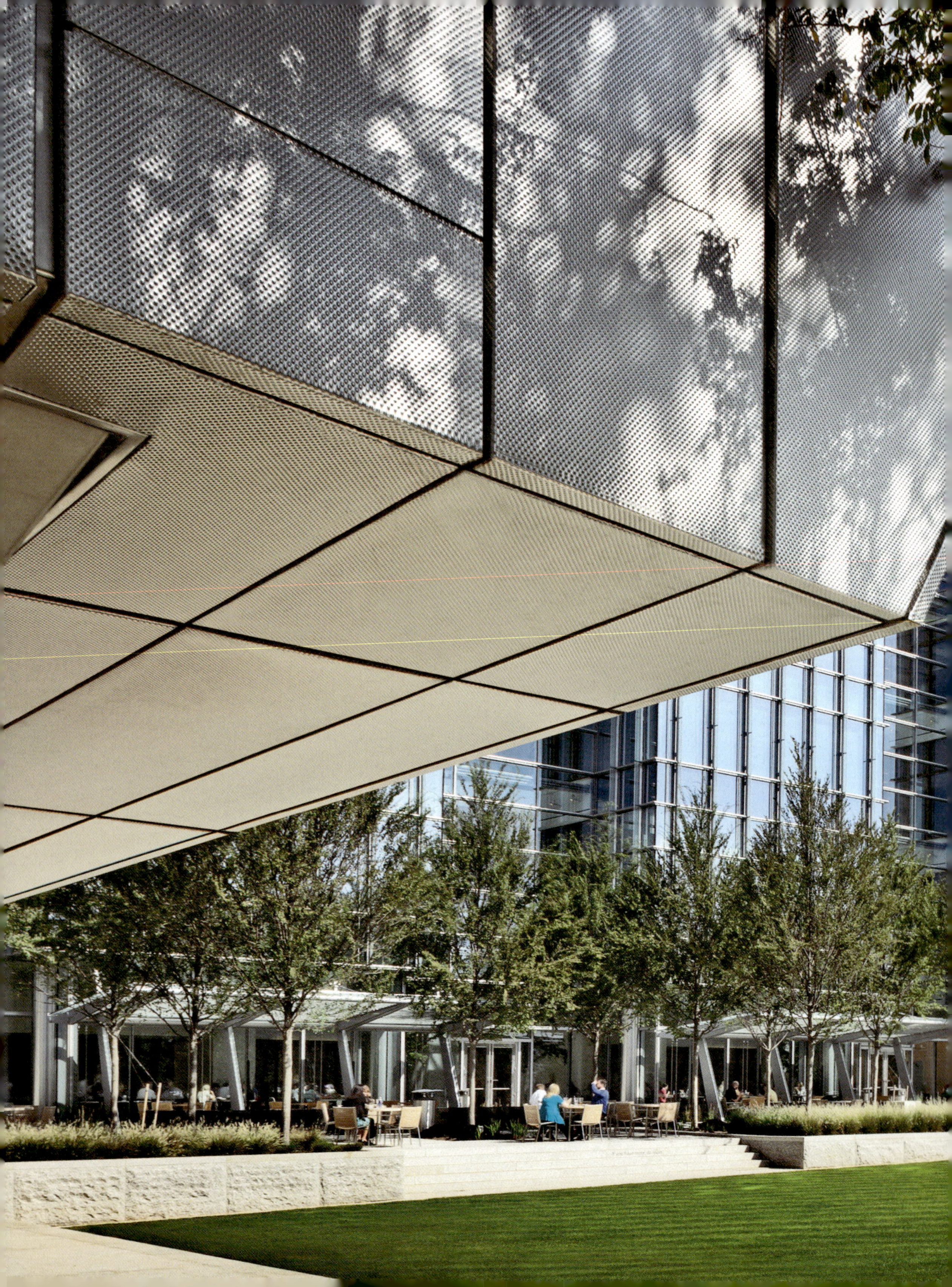

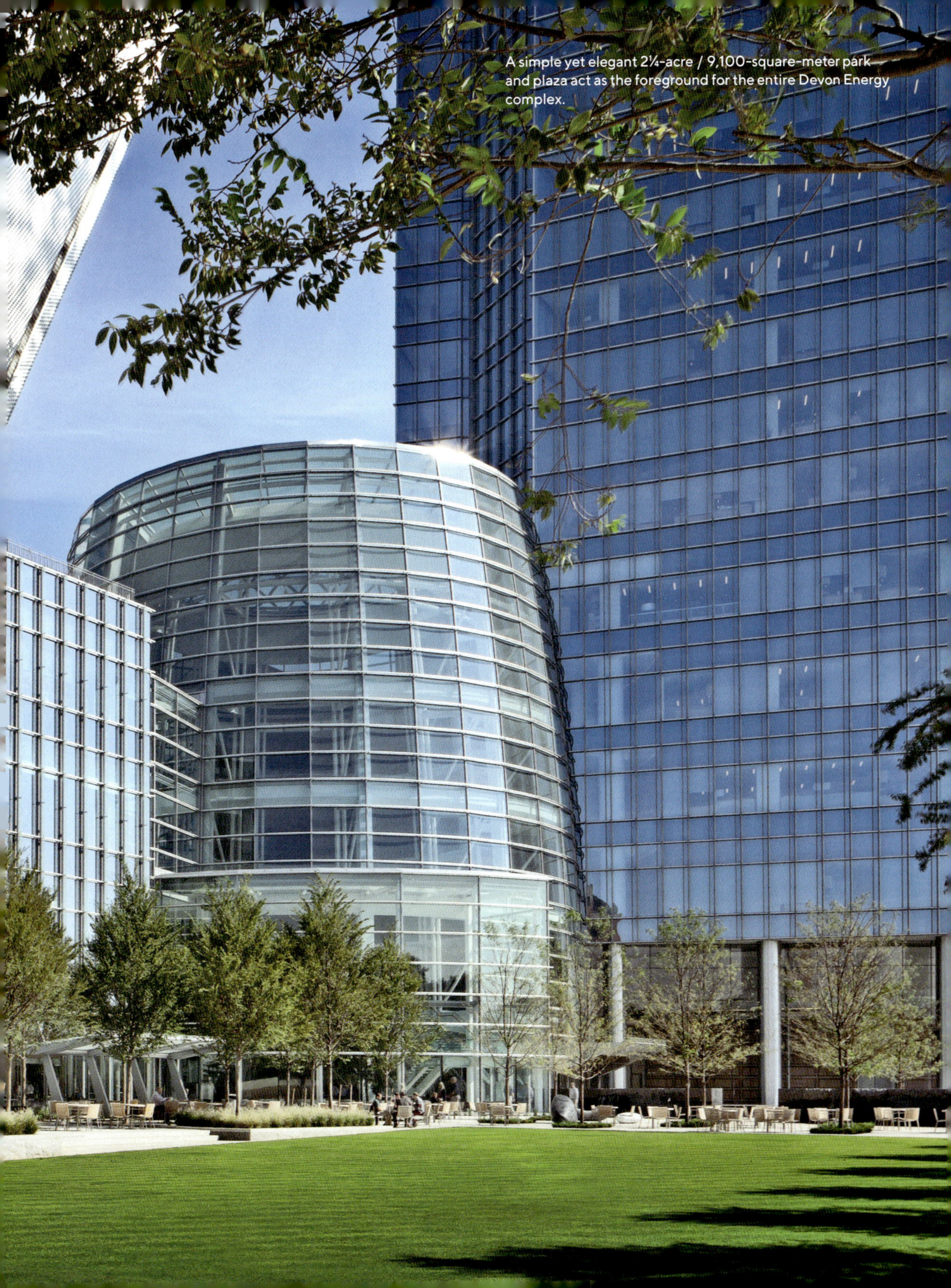

A simple yet elegant 2¼-acre / 9,100-square-meter park and plaza act as the foreground for the entire Devon Energy complex.

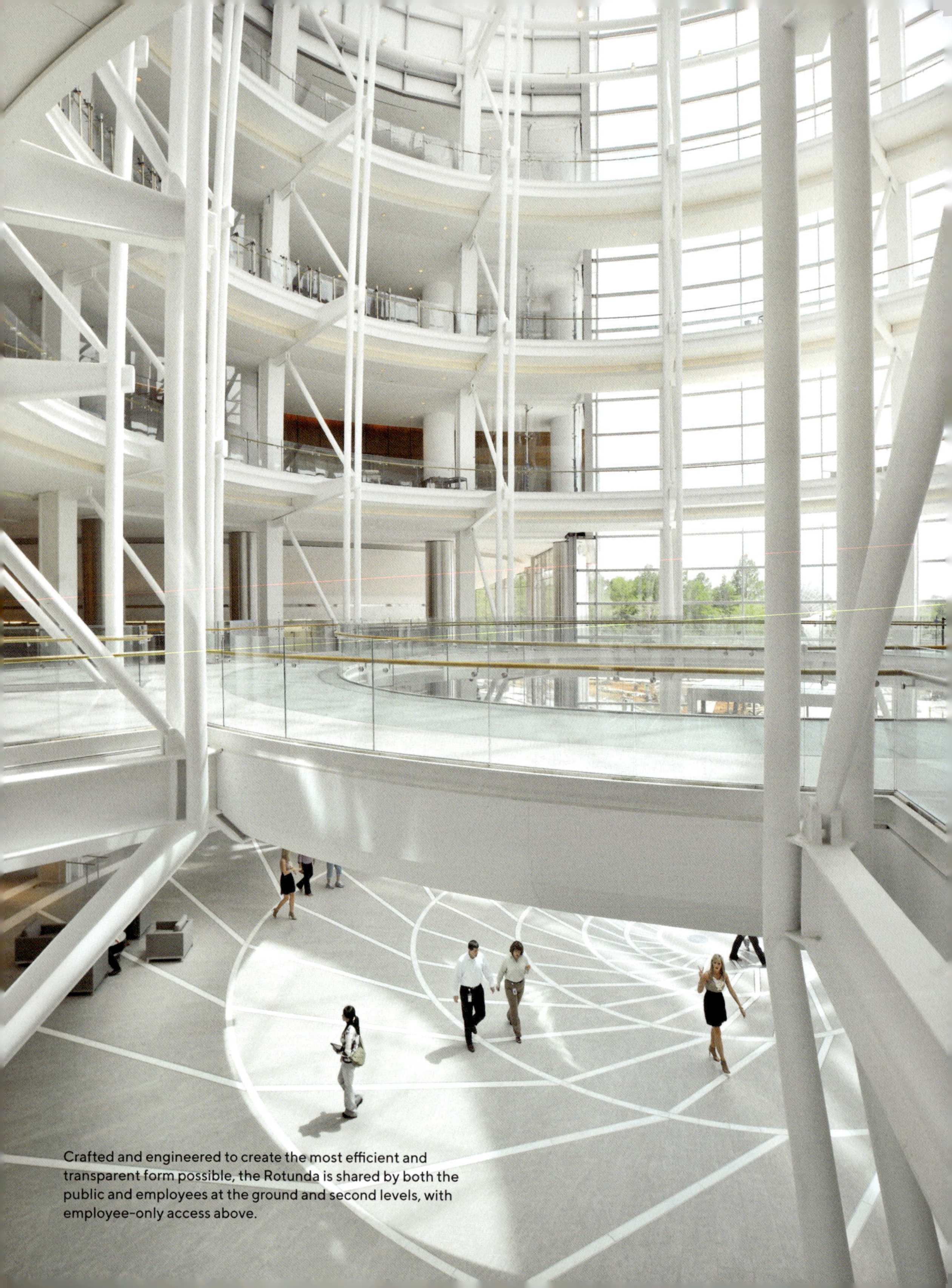

Crafted and engineered to create the most efficient and transparent form possible, the Rotunda is shared by both the public and employees at the ground and second levels, with employee-only access above.

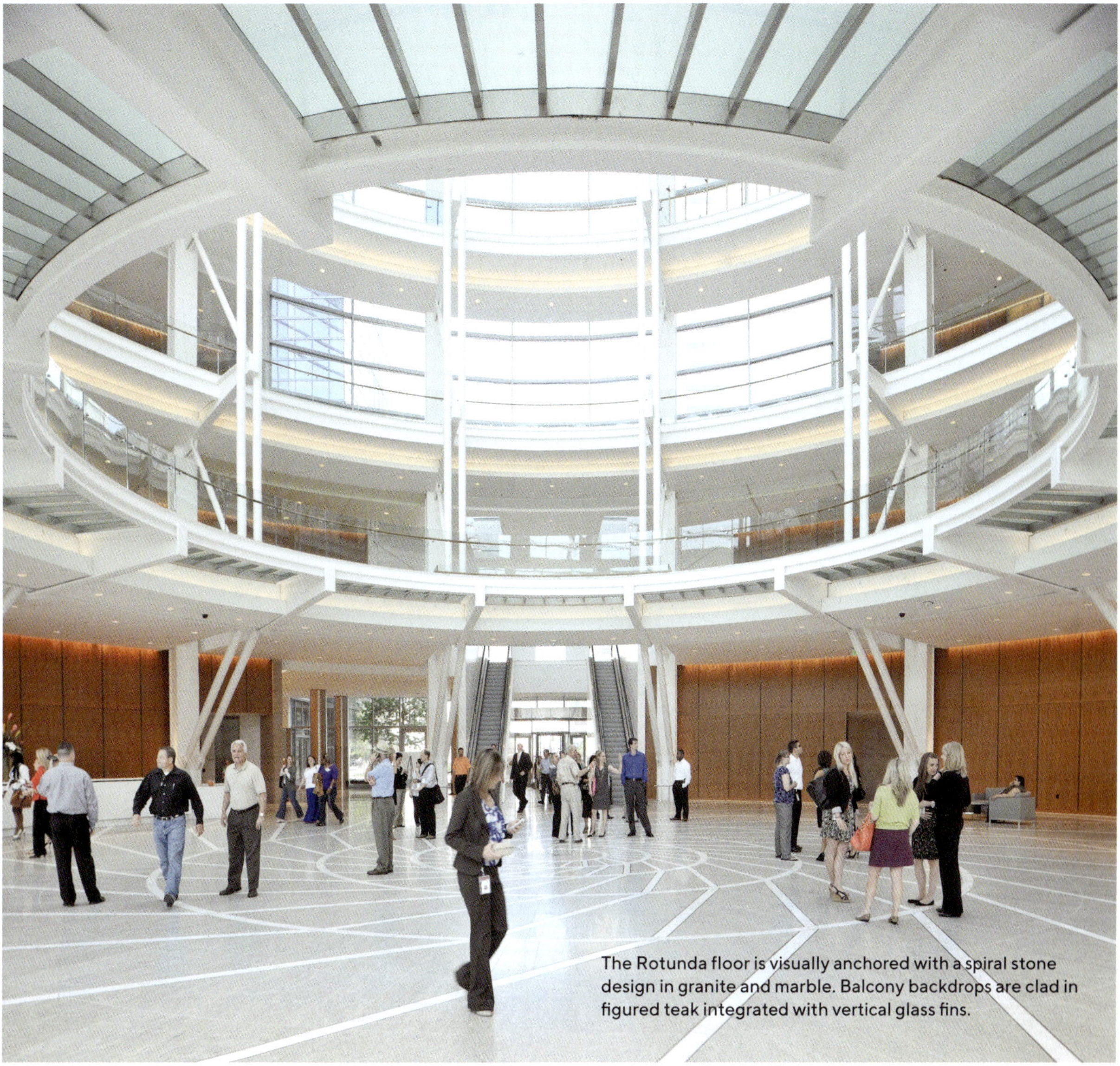

The Rotunda floor is visually anchored with a spiral stone design in granite and marble. Balcony backdrops are clad in figured teak integrated with vertical glass fins.

The indoor Galleria includes dining areas overlooking the new park and landscaped plazas that are key elements in the overall site strategy.

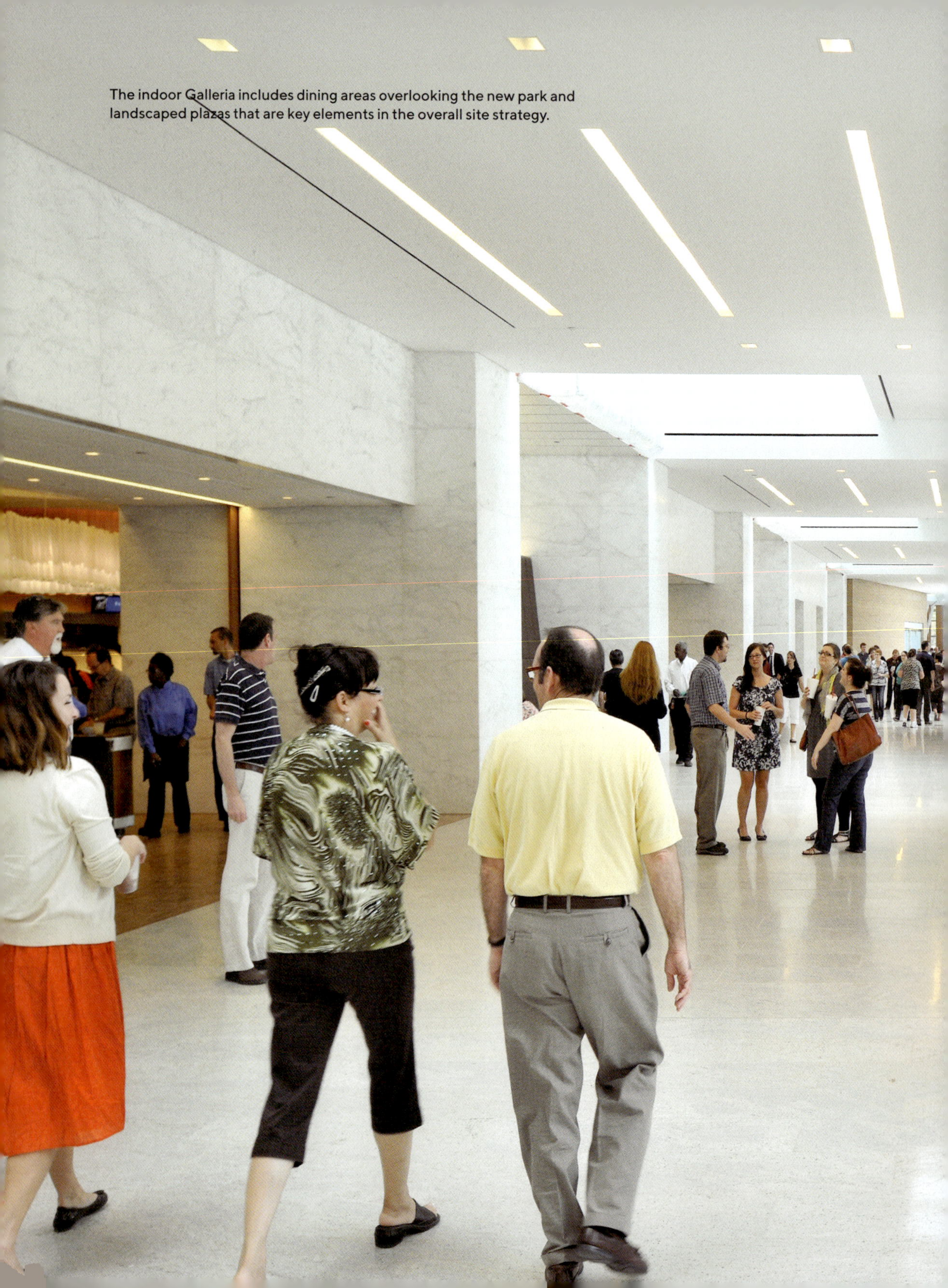

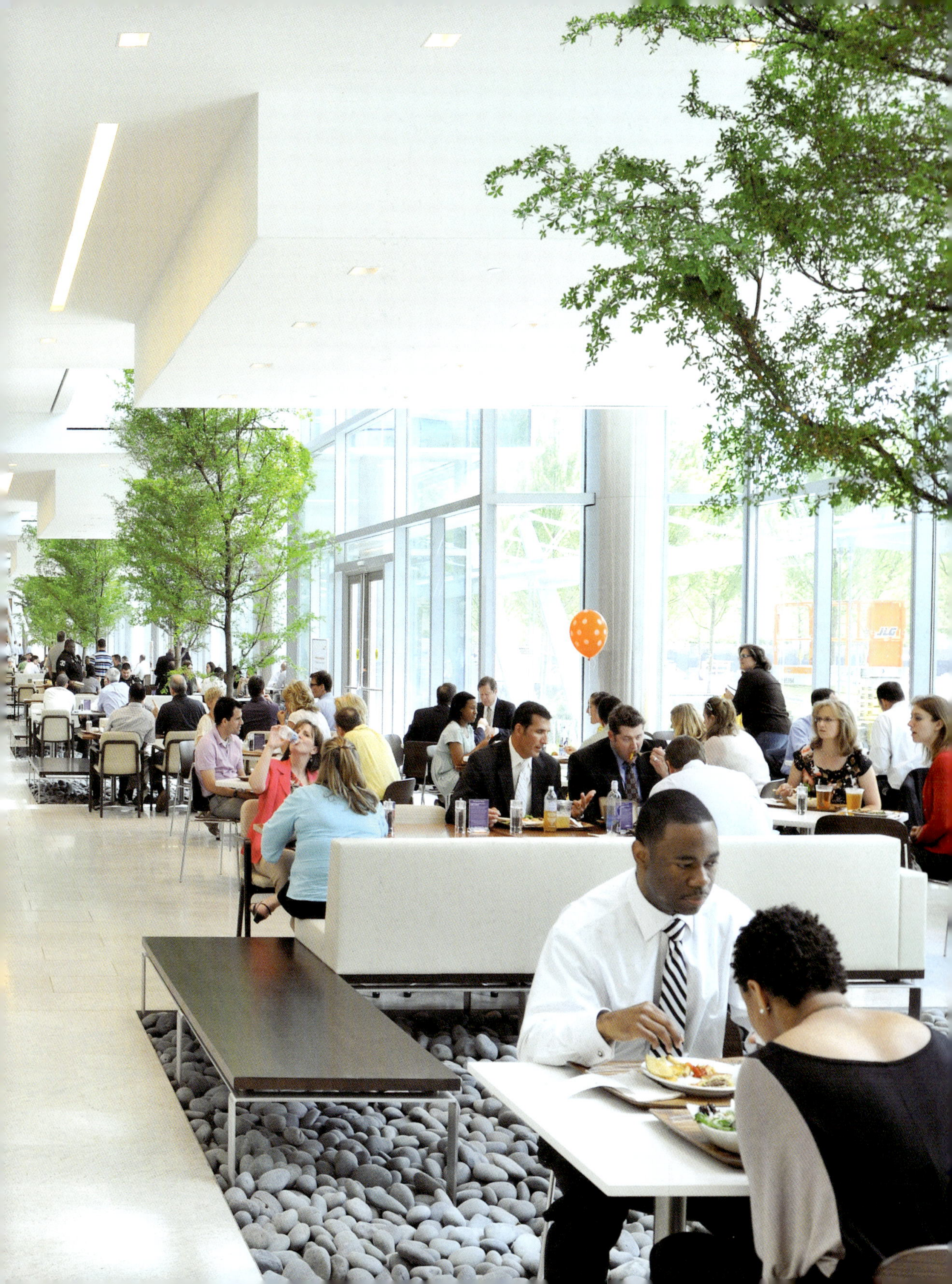

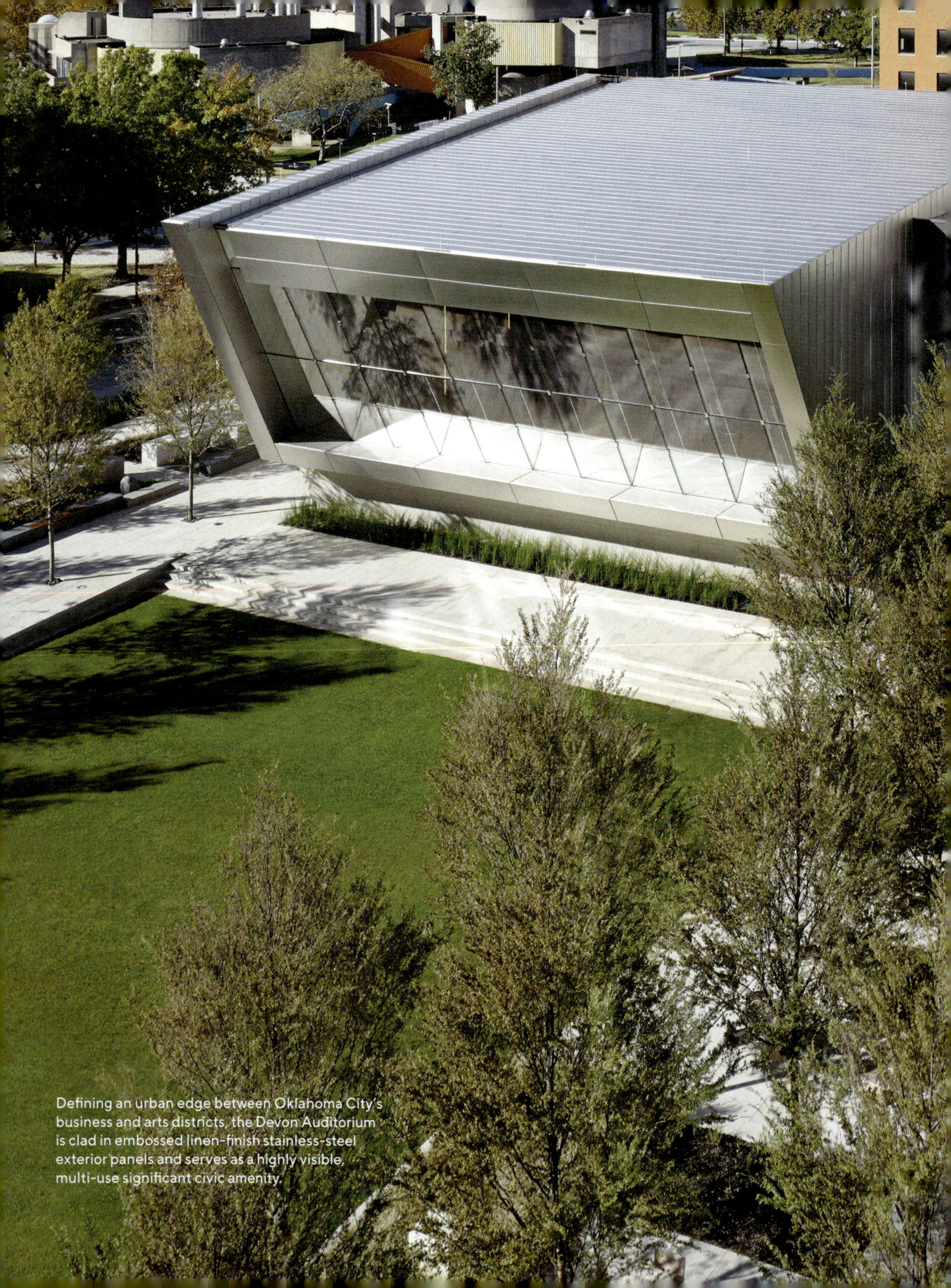

Defining an urban edge between Oklahoma City's business and arts districts, the Devon Auditorium is clad in embossed linen-finish stainless-steel exterior panels and serves as a highly visible, multi-use significant civic amenity.

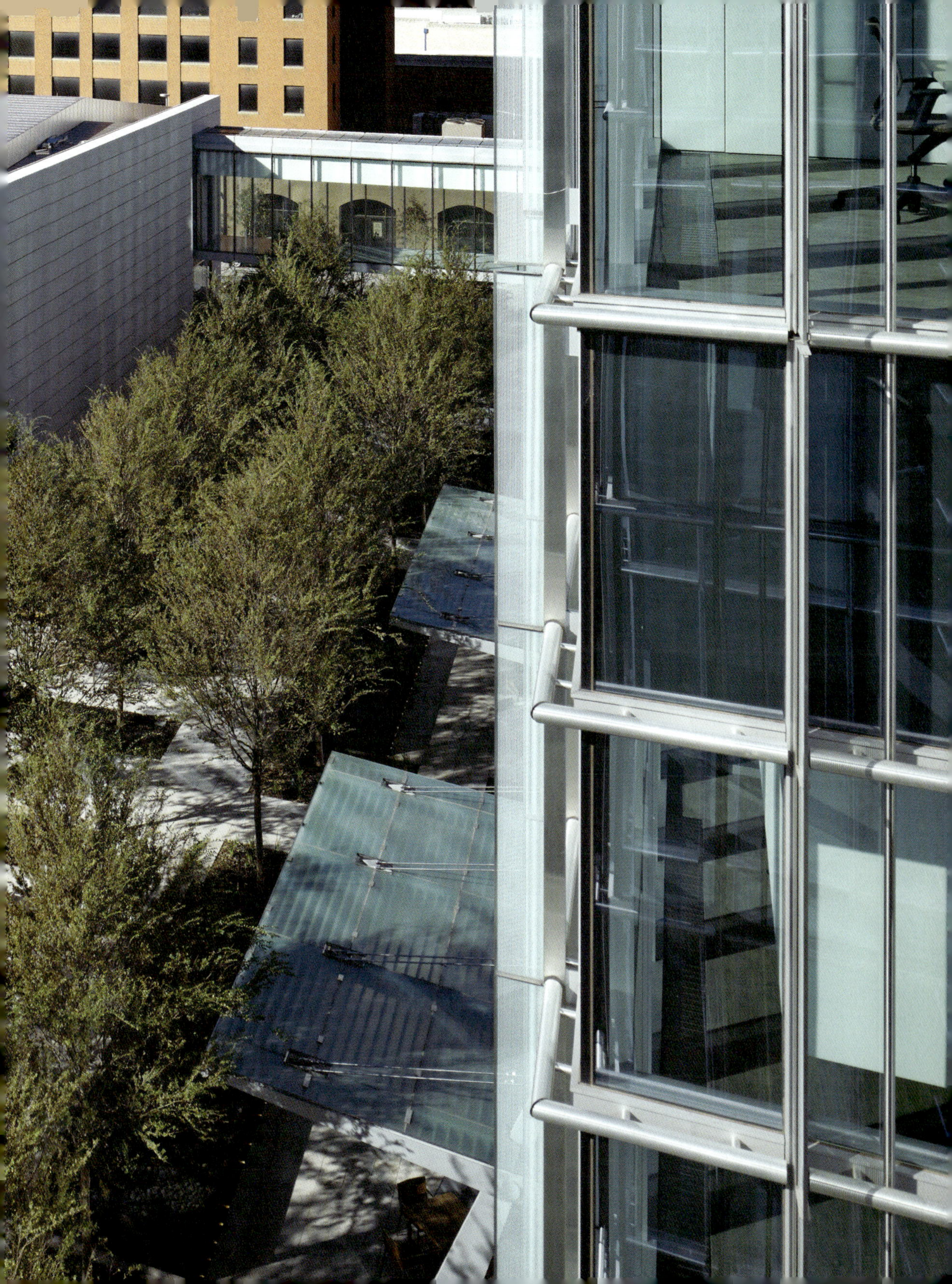

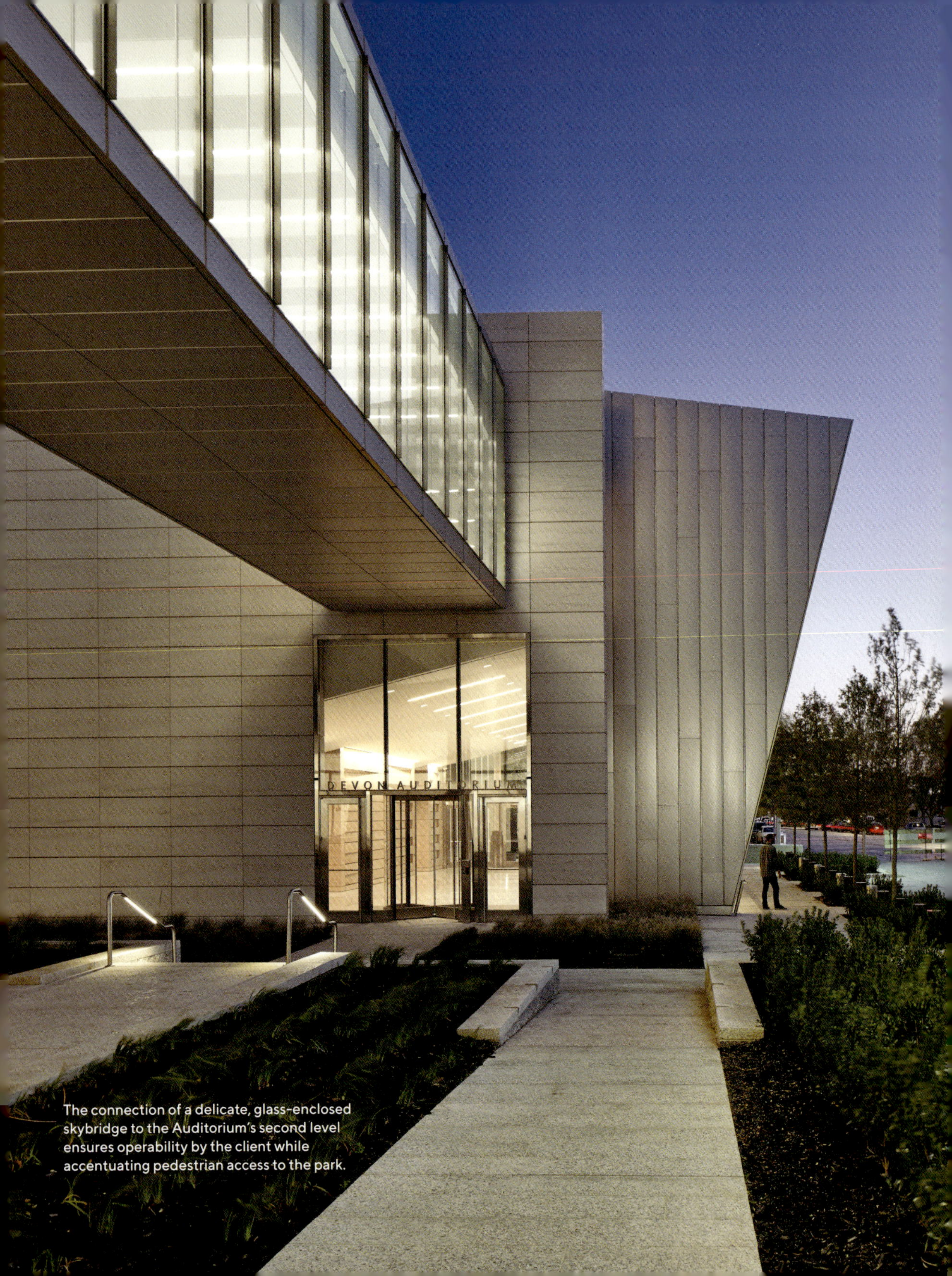

The connection of a delicate, glass-enclosed skybridge to the Auditorium's second level ensures operability by the client while accentuating pedestrian access to the park.

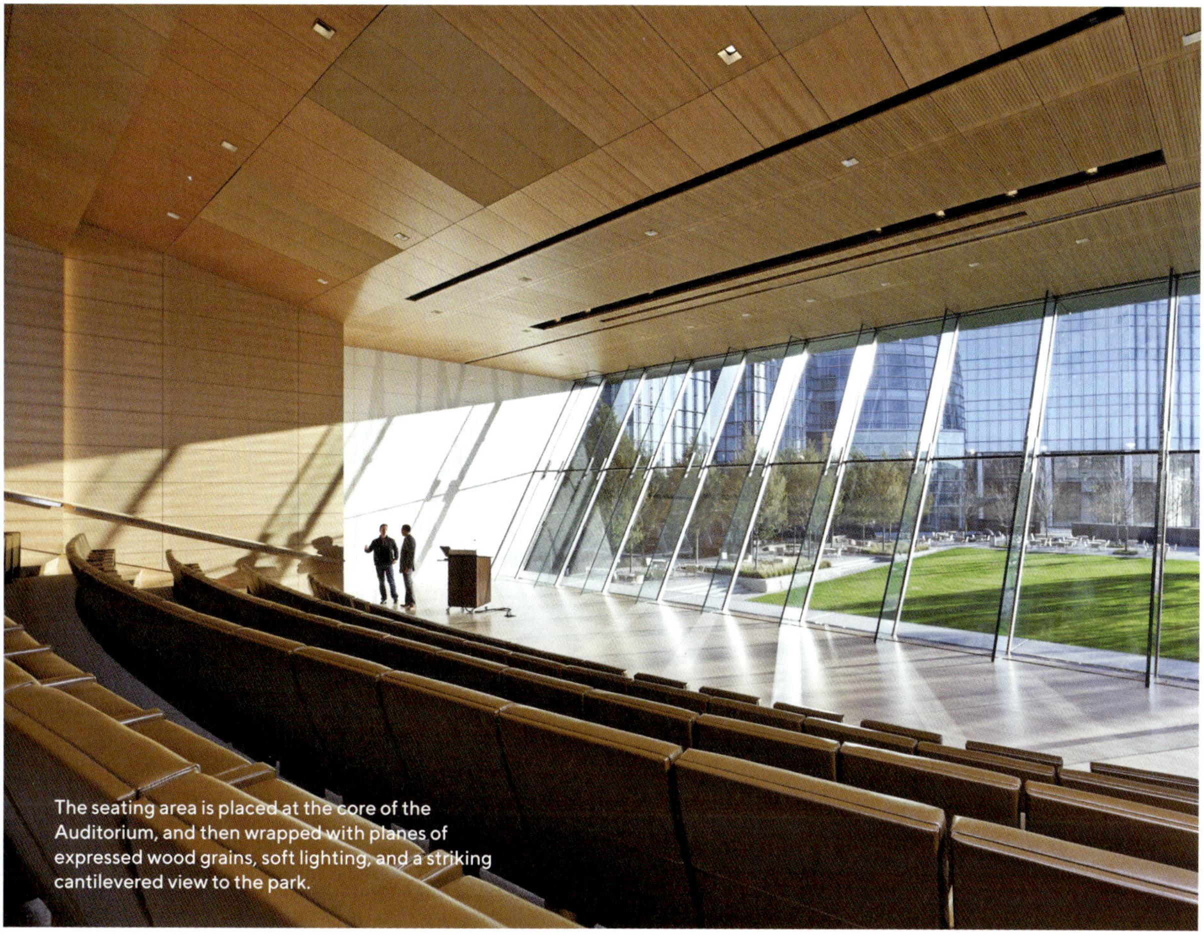

The seating area is placed at the core of the Auditorium, and then wrapped with planes of expressed wood grains, soft lighting, and a striking cantilevered view to the park.

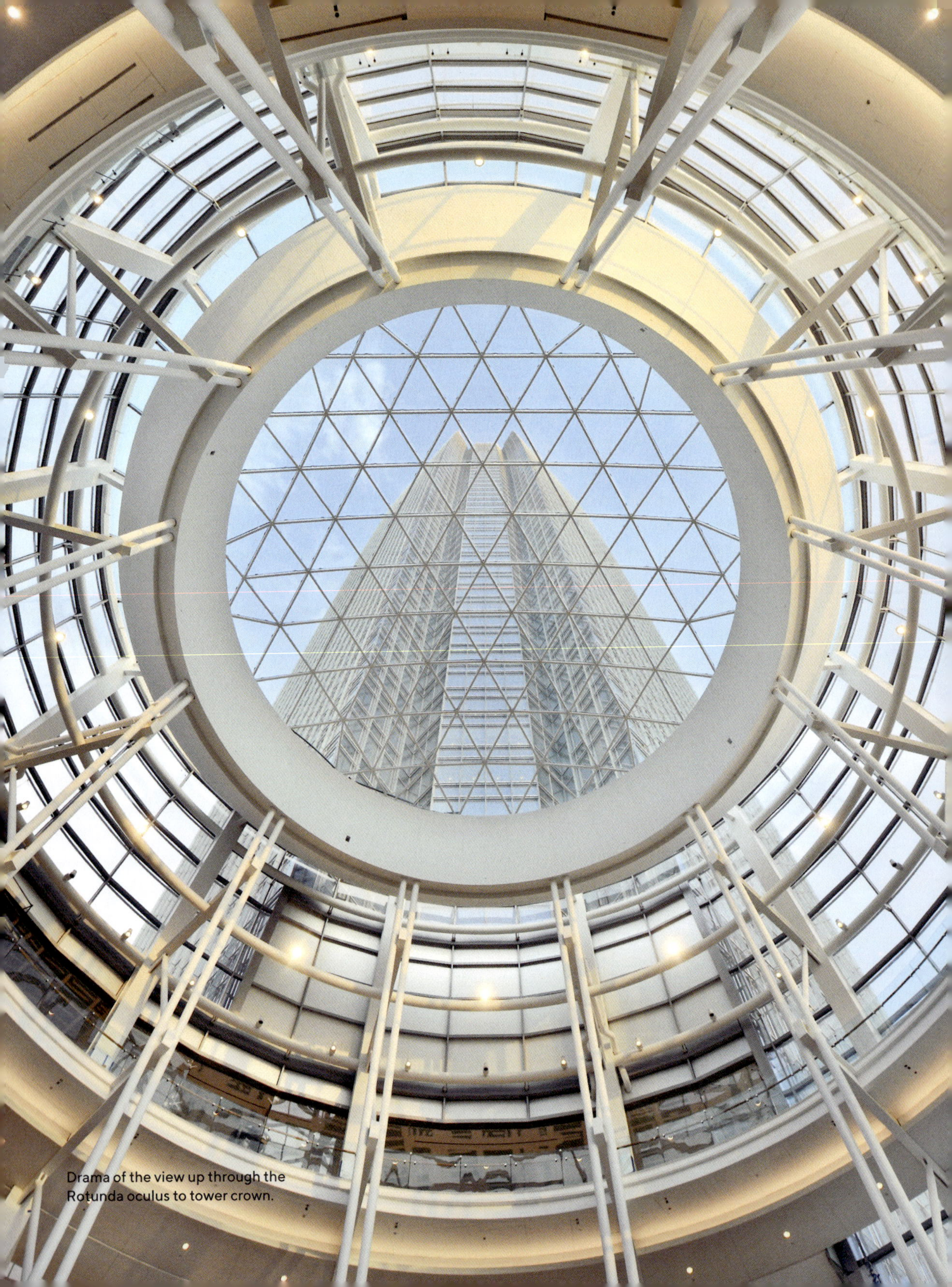

Drama of the view up through the Rotunda oculus to tower crown.

"Accessibility to the design principal was critical. I don't believe we could have gotten this design and this impact without it."

Klay Kimker
Vice President of Administration, Devon Energy

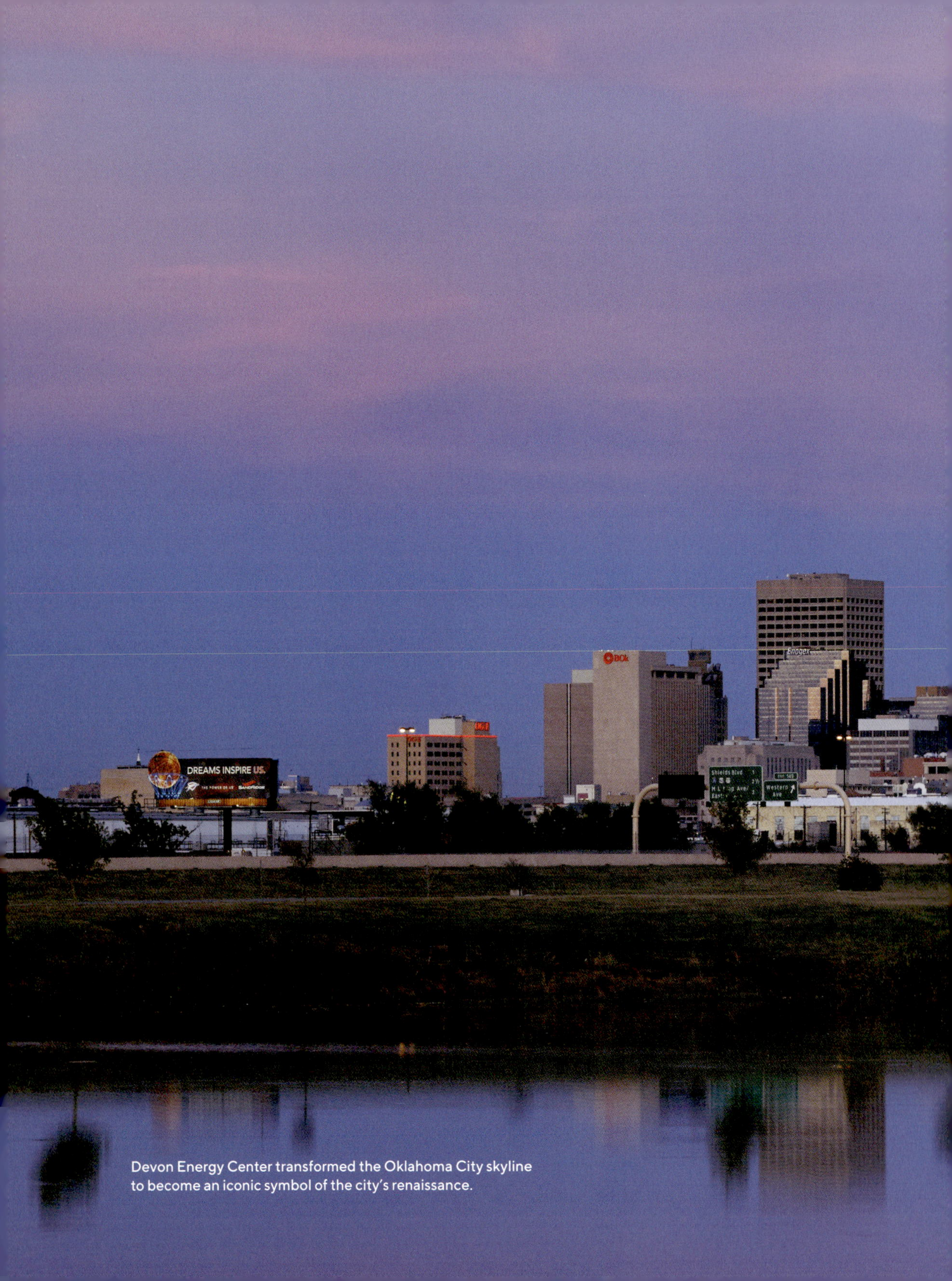

Devon Energy Center transformed the Oklahoma City skyline to become an iconic symbol of the city's renaissance.

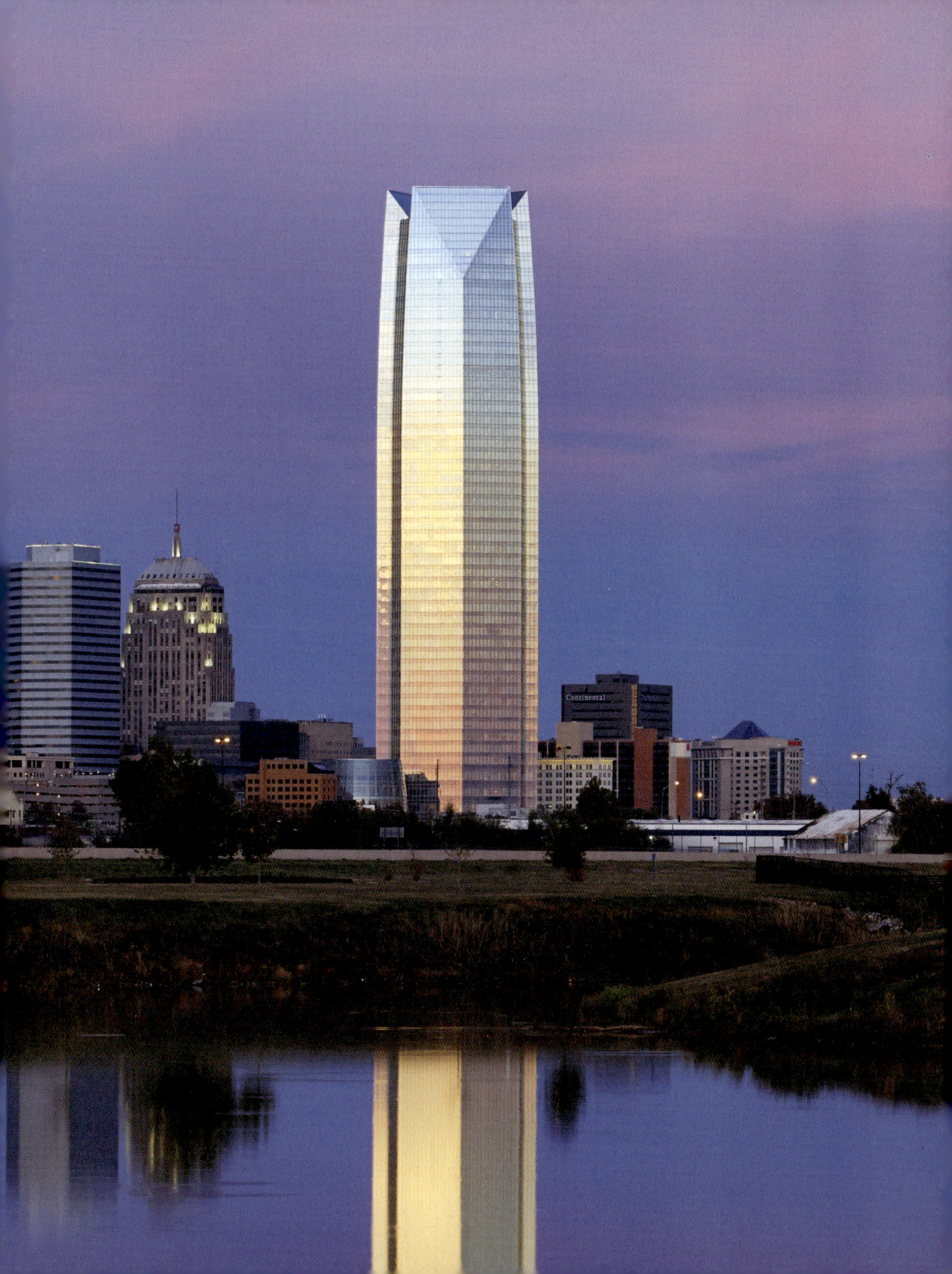
Continental

Time and Place

BARACK H. OBAMA MAGNET UNIVERSITY SCHOOL

City of New Haven
New Haven Public Schools
Southern Connecticut State University
Gilbane
Pickard Chilton
JCJ Architecture
Giordano Construction
Michael Horton Associates
Consulting Engineering Services (CES)
Freeman Companies
Simpson Gumpertz Heger
BVH
A.M. Fogarty
OLA Consulting Engineers
cmkLEED
McFarland Kistler & Associates
Jaffe Holden Acoustics

PLIENINGER STRAẞE 140 DEVELOPMENT

Hines
P140 PropCo S.à.r.l.
ARP ArchitektenPartnerschaft Stuttgart
Glück Landschaftsarchitektur

Ultimately, the architect, working through the design process with his or her client collaborator, seeks to create architecture that is just the right solution for its time and its place. This continues the tradition of such architects as Eero Saarinen, Kevin Roche, and Cesar Pelli, who always saw the architecture they created as particular to a time and to a place, responding to the culture, the current historical circumstances, and the spirit of the place in which it was designed. Pelli described designing within such parameters as creating "the art of the possible." The architect accepts the facts and limitations of the project head on—without ignoring them, trying to change them, or circumventing them—so that the result is an authentic response to the reality given, while it aspires to some greater end within the circumstances of its time and place. Such an approach guards against the development of "signature styles" that many architects employ as a way to brand their design work. It is impossible to be faithful to the special time and place of a design with a signature style, which is why Pickard Chilton has never developed one (and neither did Saarinen, nor Roche, nor Pelli).

Detail of west façade of the Barack H. Obama Magnet University School showing fenestration strategies that create visual interest while maximizing views to West Rock Ridge State Park and Sleeping Giant State Park.

As a continuation of the Saarinen/Roche/Pelli lineage, Pickard Chilton's design approach is to pursue the art of the possible as it reflects the time and the place. As the architects describe it, one tries to capture the culture for the time in which one is designing. It becomes an interpretive process. Or the architect might be designing for a time that has yet to transpire, for the client's future. Such architecture can be seen as a threshold to a client's new sense of self, of a new culture. This leads one to ask, how do the client's own values align with the importance of time and place in the firm's architecture? How does the architect work with the client in seeking an architectural solution that is just right for its time and place—not only its physical attributes, but also in response to the societal and historical context? Can architecture be both timeless and reflect the time in which it was created? How do clients express time

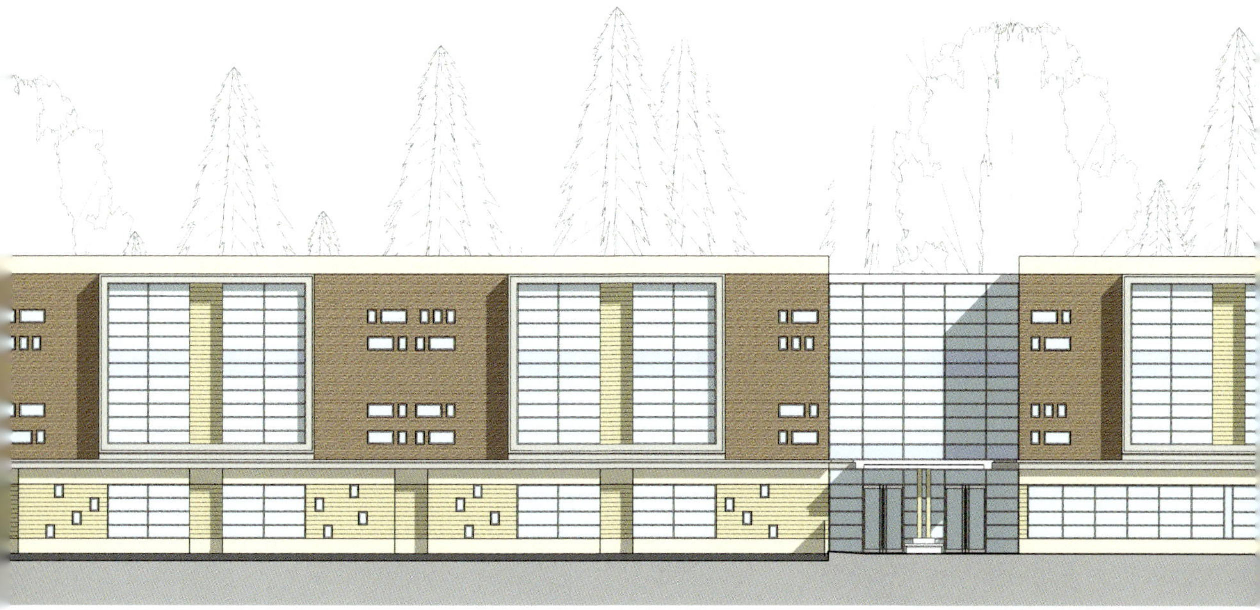

and place as a value? How is time and place expressed in architecture?

The design of a magnet school, set within the heart of a college campus in New Haven, Connecticut, responds to an existing place, its architecture, and the nature that surrounds it. According to Carolina Cudemus, who served on the project as deputy director for the local school system, the Barack H. Obama Magnet University School reflects the prevailing architecture of its place on the Southern Connecticut State University campus. But it's playful at the same time, with its small, dot-and-dash windows that suggest Morse Code messages.

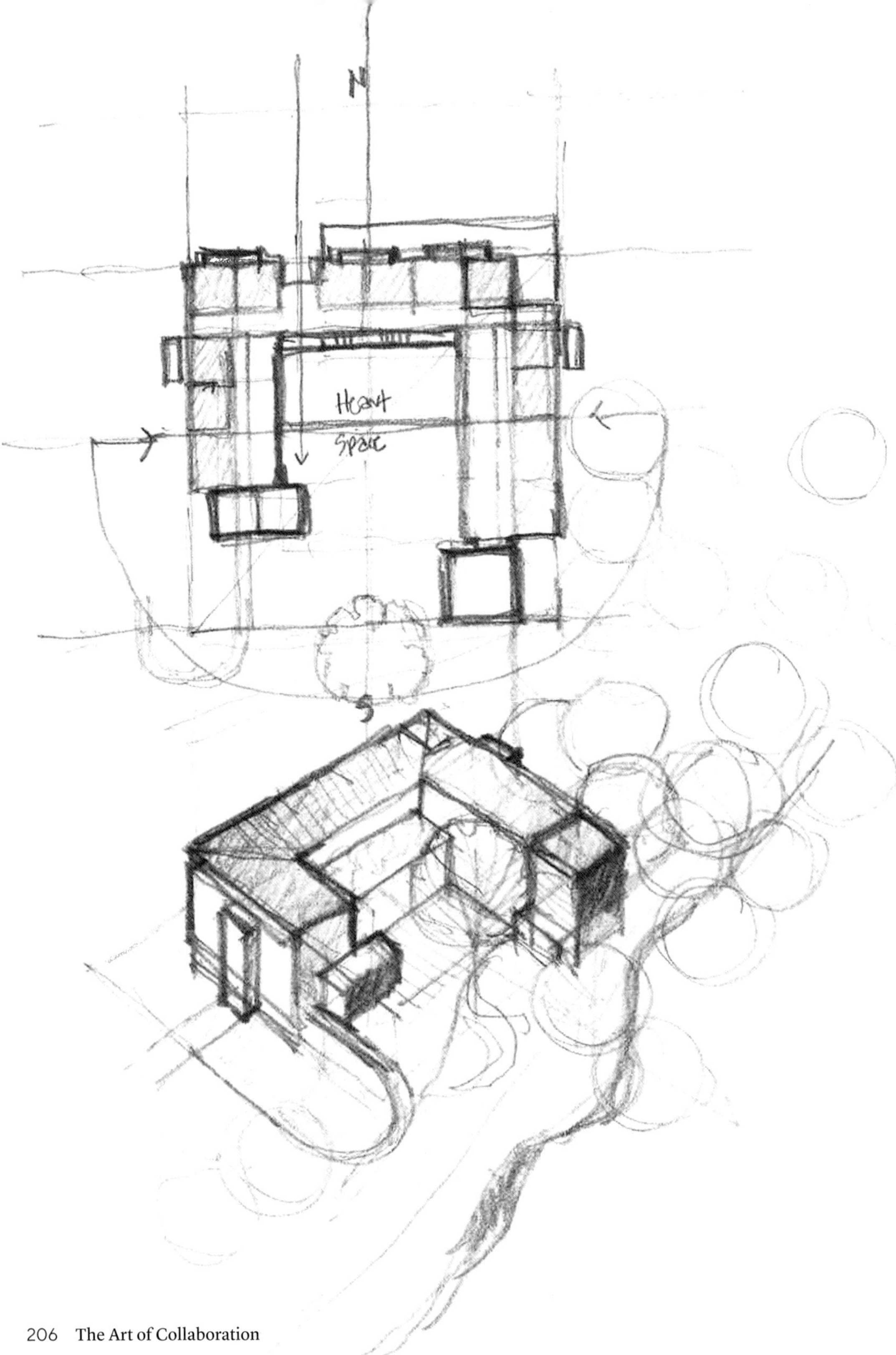
N
Heart
Space

← Early conceptual sketches exploring potential massing strategies on the site.

→ Senior Associate Nancy Clayton (second from left) at one of many community input meetings.

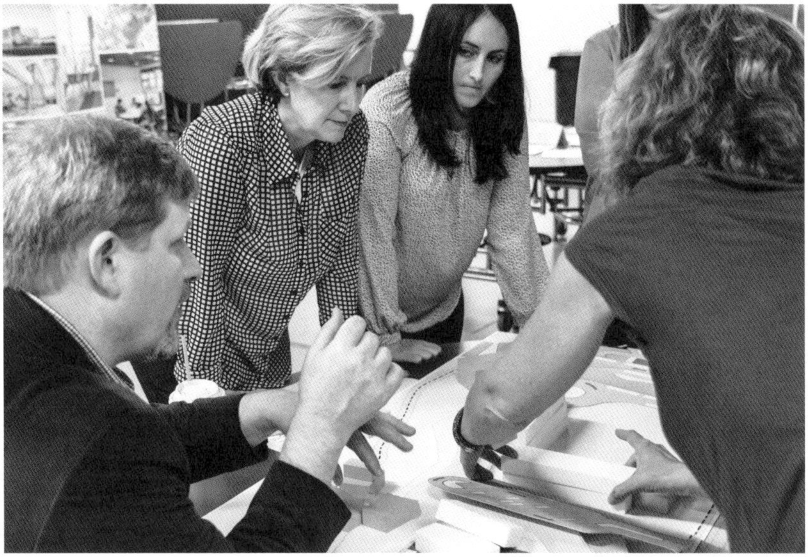

According to Cudemus, the school had to reflect the desires of New Haven educators and the university's physical plant staff, while giving the architects and their team freedom of design expression. "They listen carefully, very carefully," says Cudemus of the architects during the process of design. They inserted the building into the site to protect the privacy of nearby buildings, preserve parts of the surrounding nature, and frame views of distant natural landmarks, including Sleeping Giant State Park and West Rock Ridge State Park. The design underscores and celebrates the special visual qualities of the place.

The interior of the school reflects the needs and personalities of the people who are learning there—students from pre-Kindergarten to fourth grade. Great emphasis is placed on delivering natural light through the generous lobby and to classrooms and assembly areas. Splashes of color are used throughout the interior as well as on the exterior, where the natural wood base is topped by a band of vibrant red above which the upper floors appear to float.

A continent away, the master plan and multi-building design in Stuttgart, Germany, of Plieninger Straße 140—an urban office campus to be built on the perimeter of the city—is an example of one driven by the conditions of its place and time. Ecological building performance is key to the design, as it is to the locale. For example, local codes govern deep penetration of daylight into employee work spaces—workstations can be no more than 23 feet / 7 meters away from a window. The ecological imperative of building in this place governs the master plan, which incorporates a generous open green space and water feature that wind their way between two phalanxes of relatively low-rise buildings that reinforce the sustainable design.

→ Diagram illustrating the Plieninger Straße 140 development's urban connectivity and pedestrian circulation.

↘ Plans for Phase 2 and Phase 3.

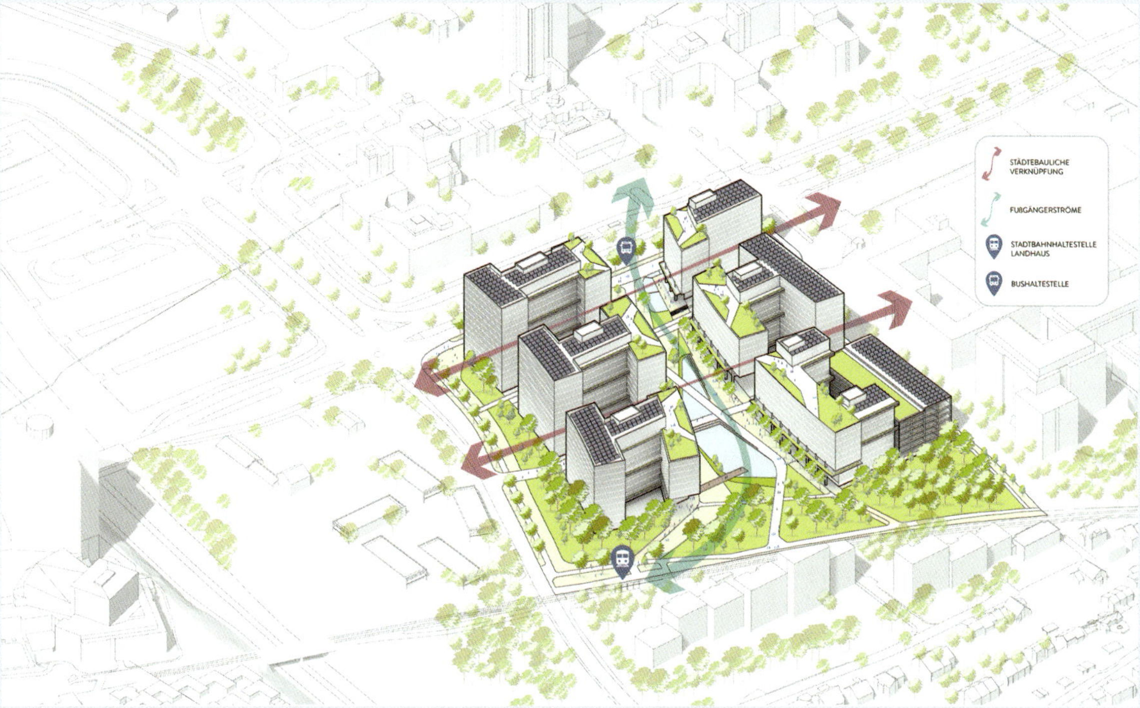

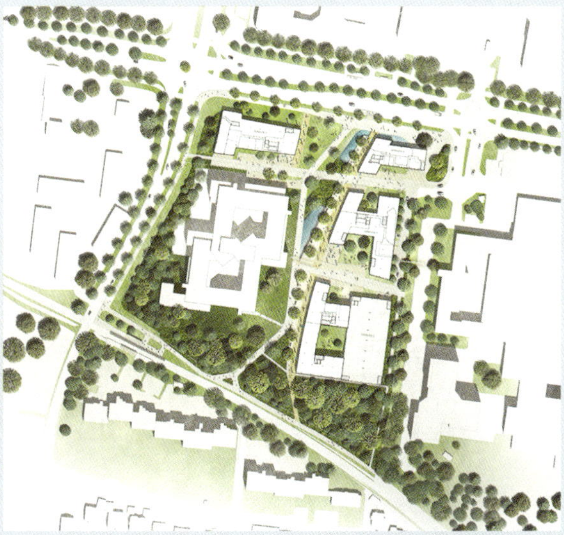

Phase 2 ground-level plan with the existing building at the bottom left side of the site.

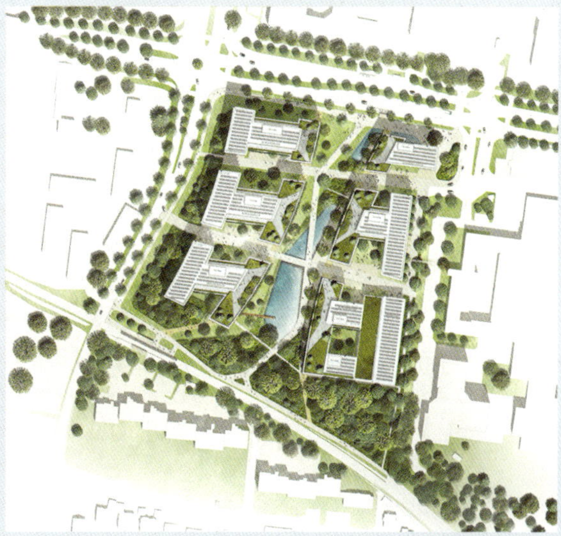

Phase 3 roof plan of full build-out of entire development.

Michael Topham, a Senior Advisor for Hines Europe (which is developing Plieninger Straße 140), notes that the design is reflective of its time and place in the German municipality, as is the case in most European-based developments. "Local weather is a big factor," explains Topham, in shaping sustainability concerns. "In Europe, the place (community, municipality, and capital) that funds a project is driven by a much higher sense of sustainability. There is more interest in natural sunlight and fresh air through operable windows, less reliance on air conditioning."

Adaptability to the passage of time is becoming a greater issue in architectural design, according to Topham. The lines between working, living, and recreational environments are in flux; blending these realms is becoming more commonplace. "The speed of change is greater," explains Topham, "within 20 years a building still has to be adaptable and reusable, recycled faster, because how people work and live are quickly changing." He observes that the recent global health crisis demonstrates how rapidly new patterns of working, living, and recreating can emerge. "Architecture that's truly timeless will be one that changes with time."

→ Office plans maximize the perimeter working area to create high-value space with access to daylight and natural ventilation from operable windows.

↘ Cross section illustrating lobby through-connection that traverses the changing grade of the site and interconnects with the interior courtyard.

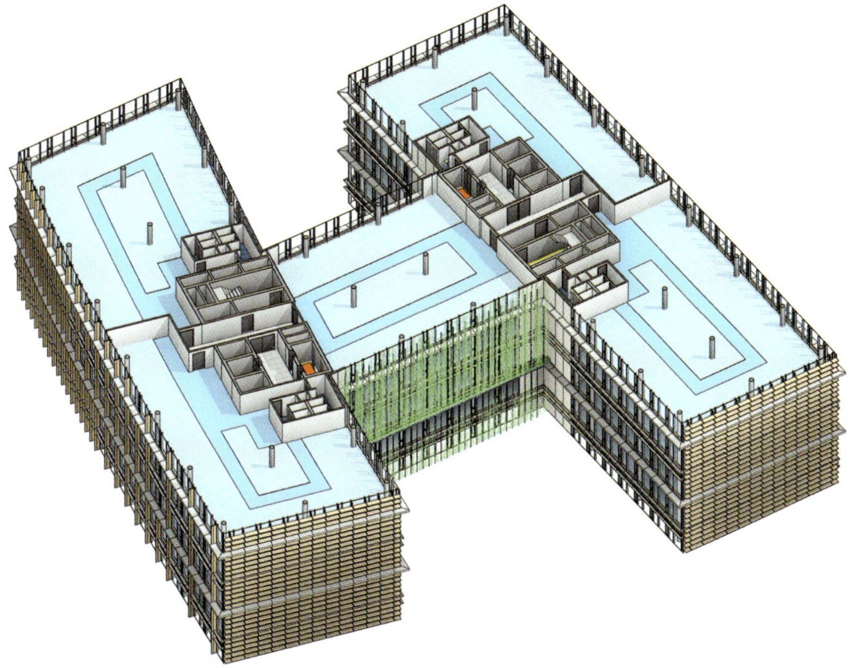

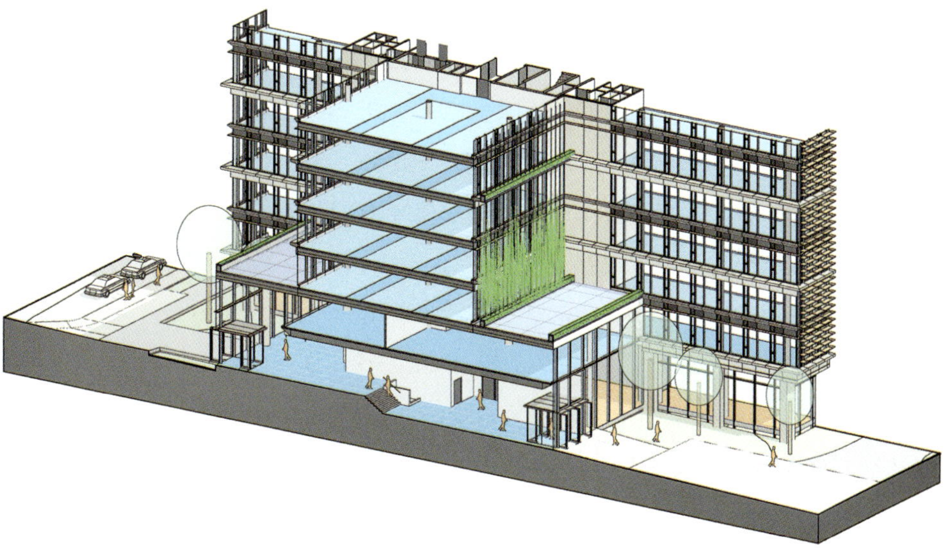

The design celebrates the special visual qualities of the place.

BARACK H. OBAMA MAGNET UNIVERSITY SCHOOL NEW HAVEN, CONNECTICUT

Completed 2020
63,000 gross square feet / 5,850 gross square meters

Located on the campus of Southern Connecticut State University (SCSU), the new Barack H. Obama Magnet University School is a New Haven Public School for 490 Pre-K through fourth-grade students. It will serve SCSU's School of Education as a "laboratory school" for students preparing to be teachers. The design captures daylight and views to create positive learning environments, embraces the forest to engage students with nature, respects its neighborhood, and synergizes with SCSU.

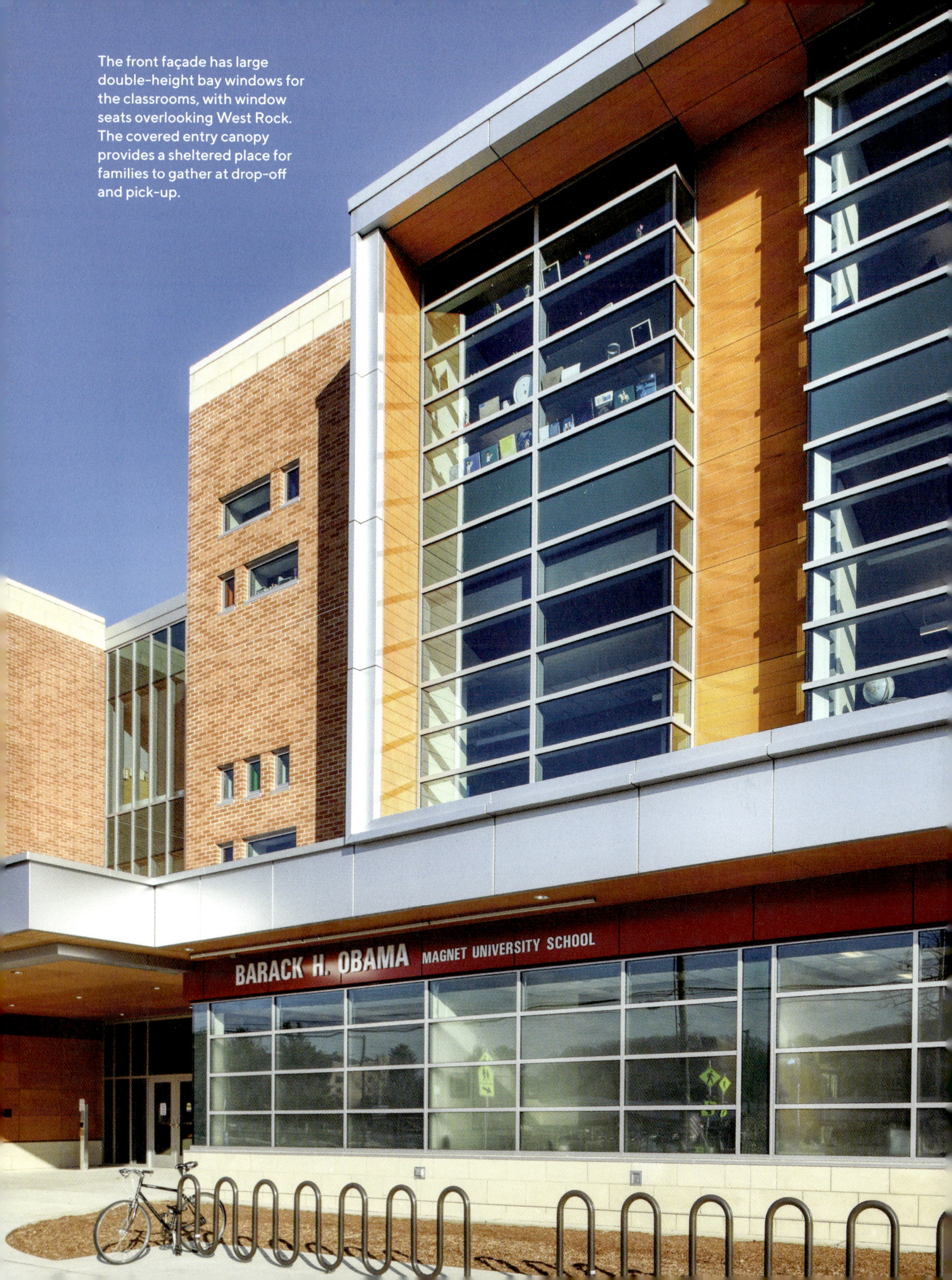

The front façade has large double-height bay windows for the classrooms, with window seats overlooking West Rock. The covered entry canopy provides a sheltered place for families to gather at drop-off and pick-up.

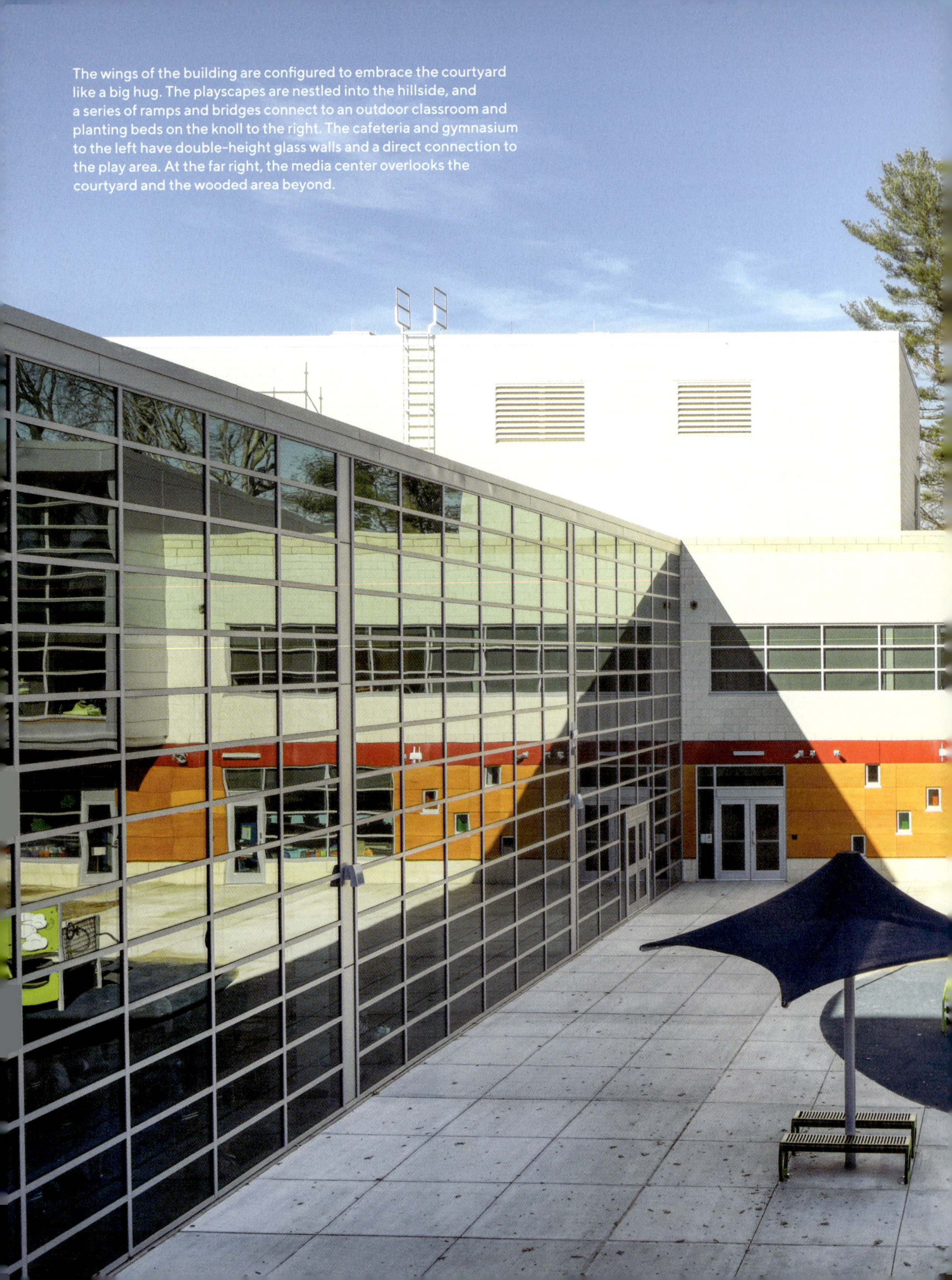

The wings of the building are configured to embrace the courtyard like a big hug. The playscapes are nestled into the hillside, and a series of ramps and bridges connect to an outdoor classroom and planting beds on the knoll to the right. The cafeteria and gymnasium to the left have double-height glass walls and a direct connection to the play area. At the far right, the media center overlooks the courtyard and the wooded area beyond.

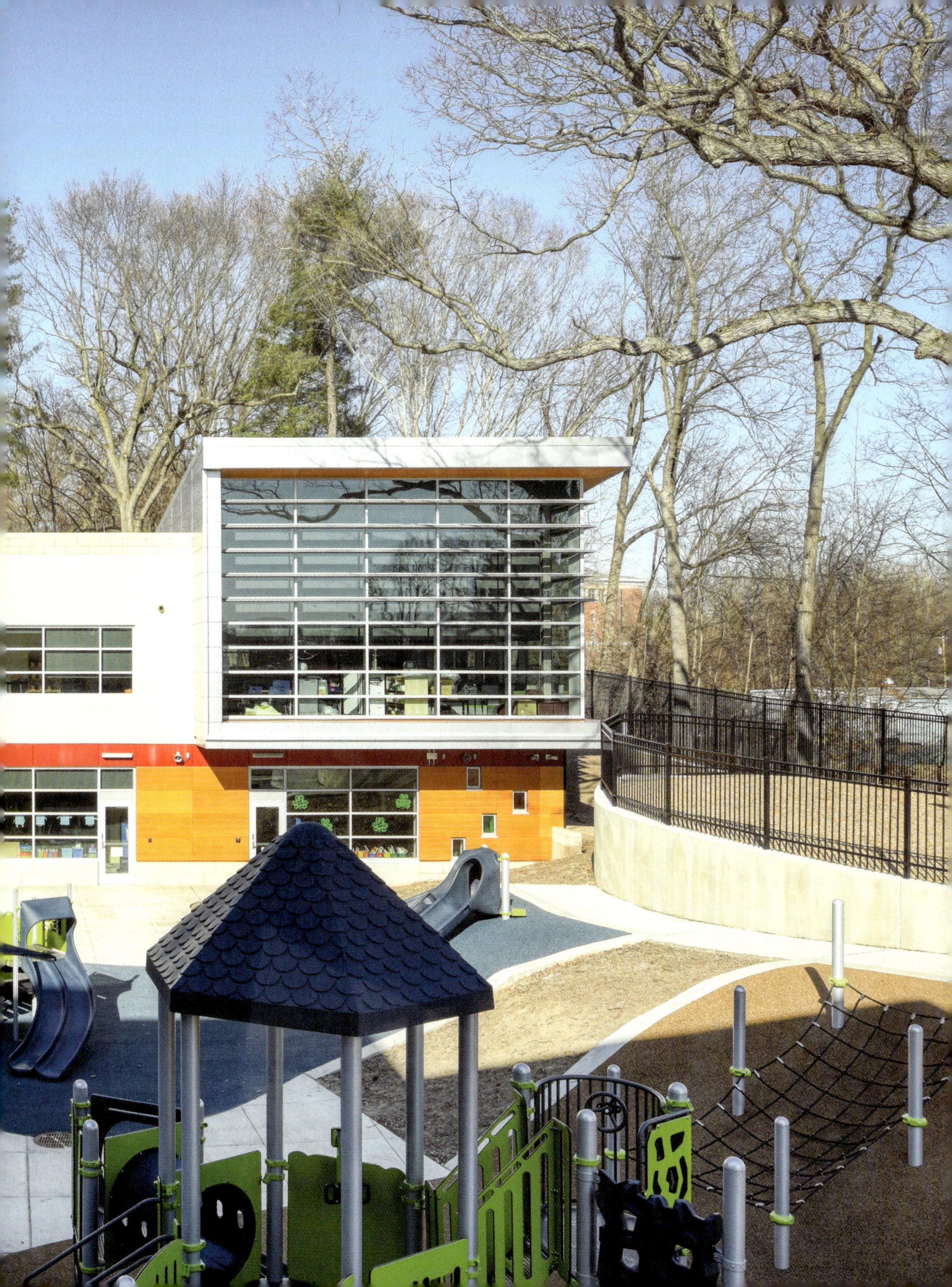

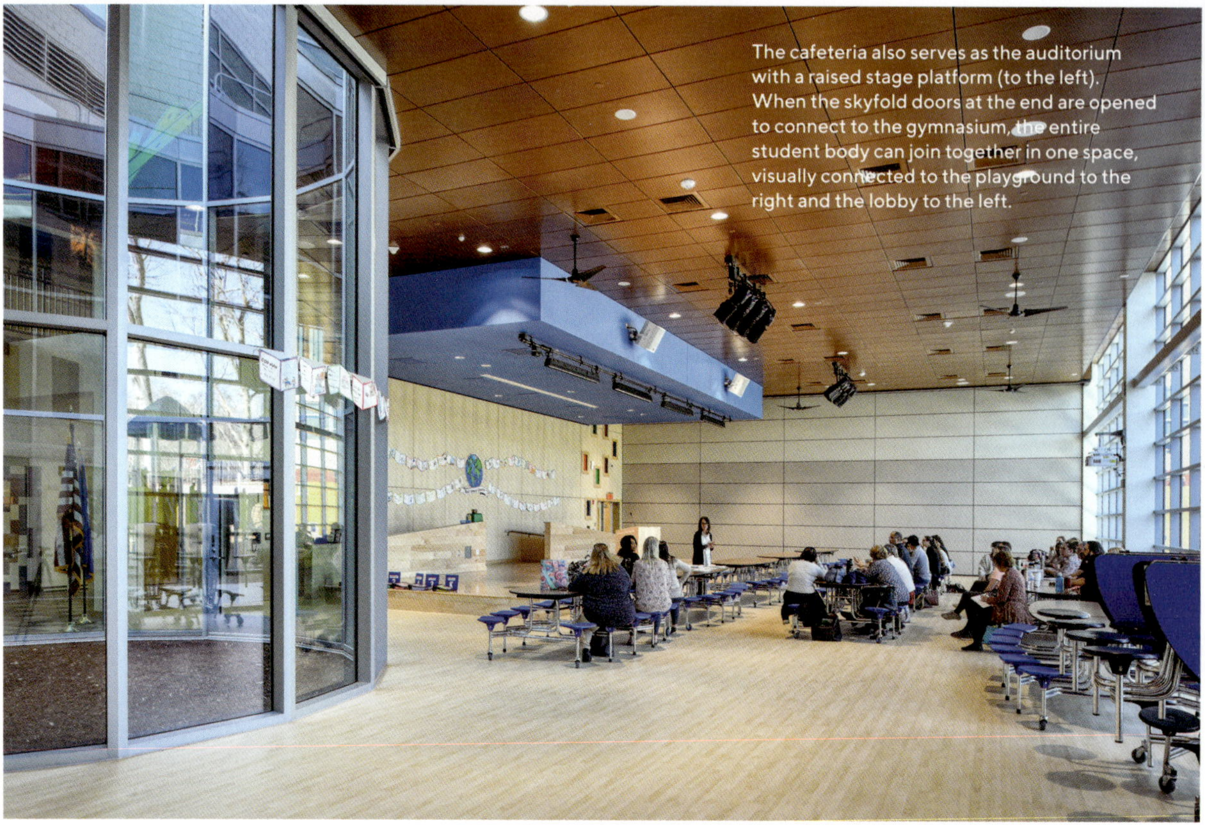

The cafeteria also serves as the auditorium with a raised stage platform (to the left). When the skyfold doors at the end are opened to connect to the gymnasium, the entire student body can join together in one space, visually connected to the playground to the right and the lobby to the left.

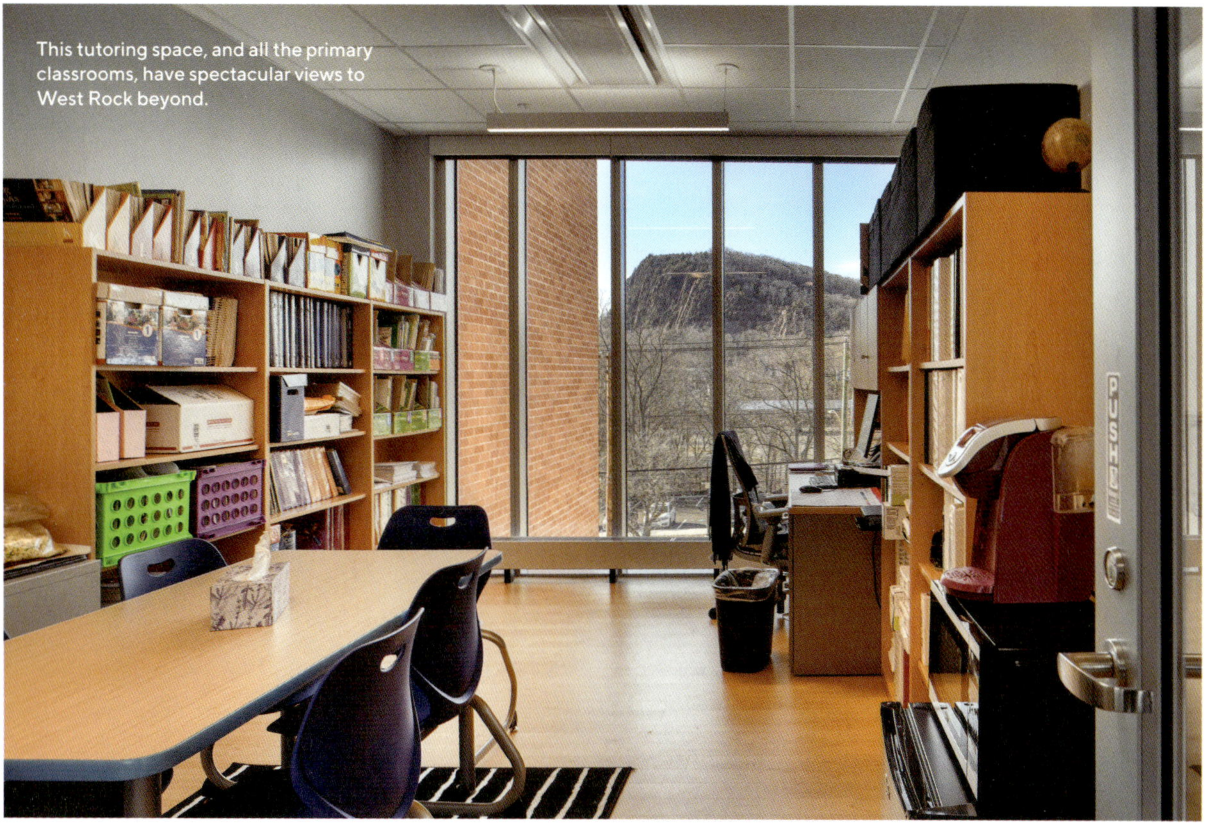

This tutoring space, and all the primary classrooms, have spectacular views to West Rock beyond.

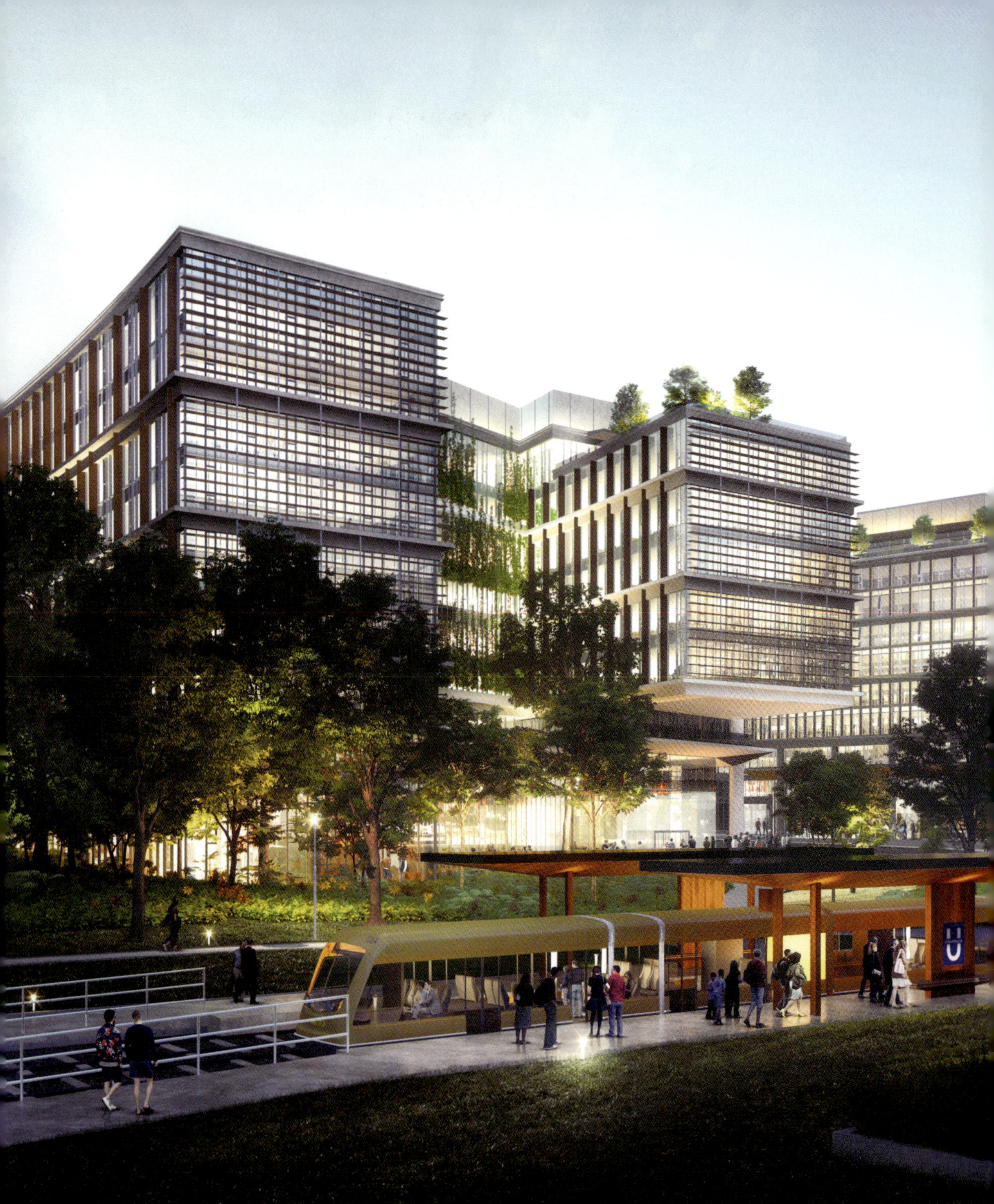

Building detail illustrating approach to enclosure treatments and immediate adjacency to transit

“Architecture that’s truly timeless will be one that changes with time.”

Michael Topham
Senior Advisor, Hines International

PLIENINGER STRAßE 140 DEVELOPMENT
STUTTGART, GERMANY

In Design
1.35 million gross square feet / 125,000 gross square meters
Pickard Chilton’s largest development in Europe to date

After an invited international competition, the Pickard Chilton–led team was selected to master plan and design an urban development at Plieninger Straße 140 in Stuttgart. The objective was to envision a sustainable, high-quality, and future-oriented urban development that maximizes landscape open space while integrating the broader urban context. The resulting three-phase master plan yields a development with 1.35 million square feet / 125,000 square meters of above-ground gross floor area across six high-performance buildings.

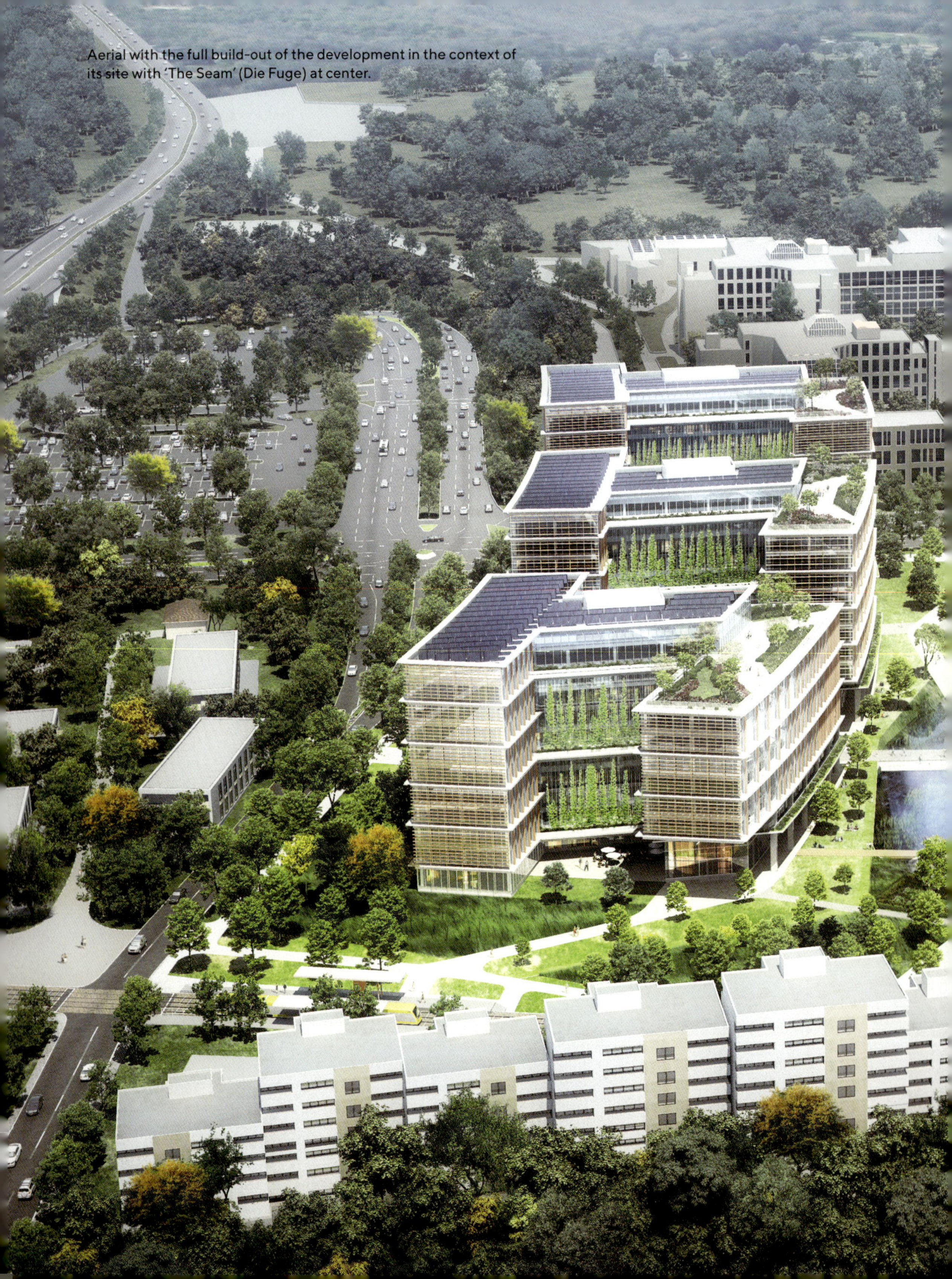

Aerial with the full build-out of the development in the context of its site with 'The Seam' (Die Fuge) at center.

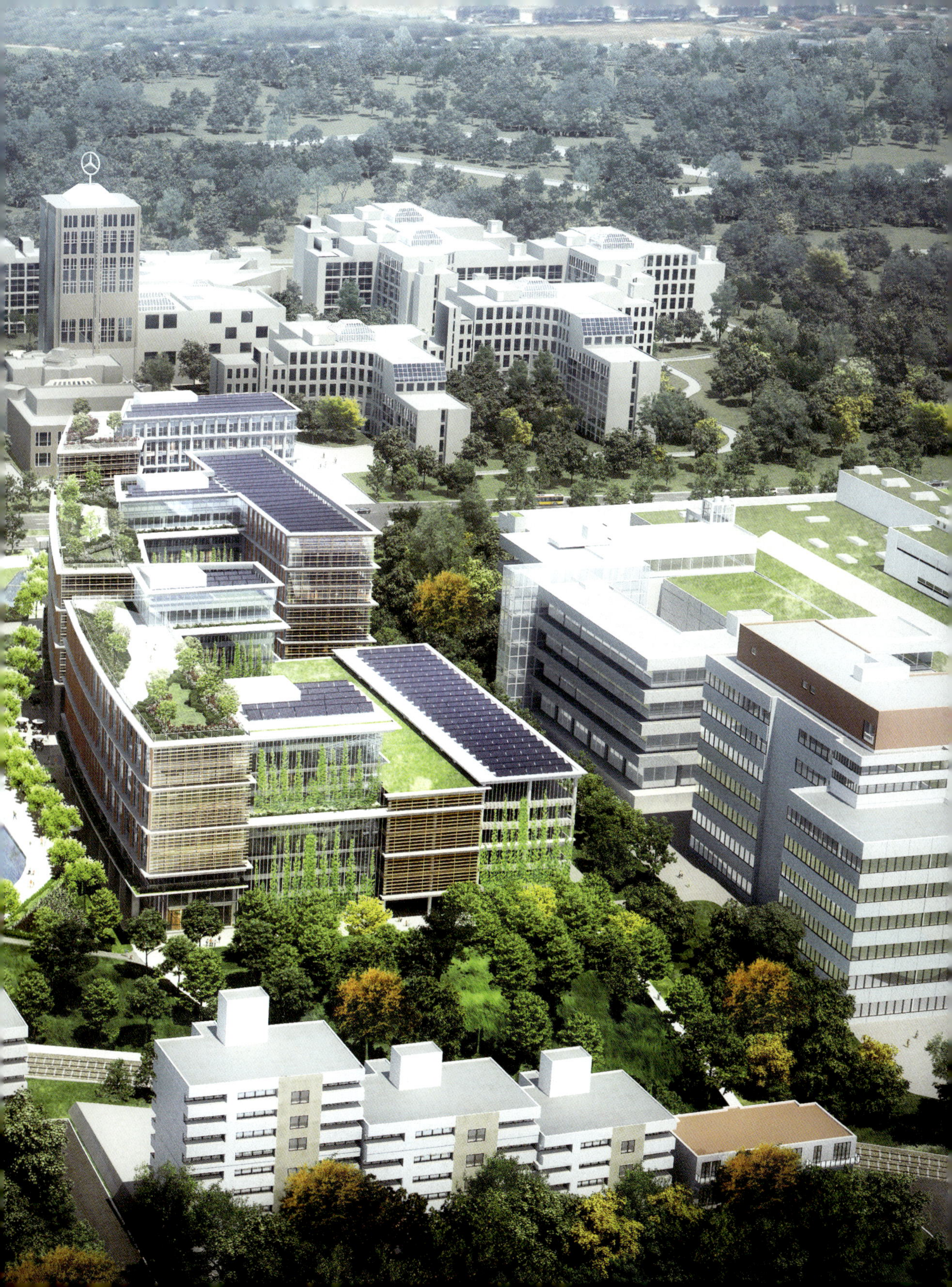

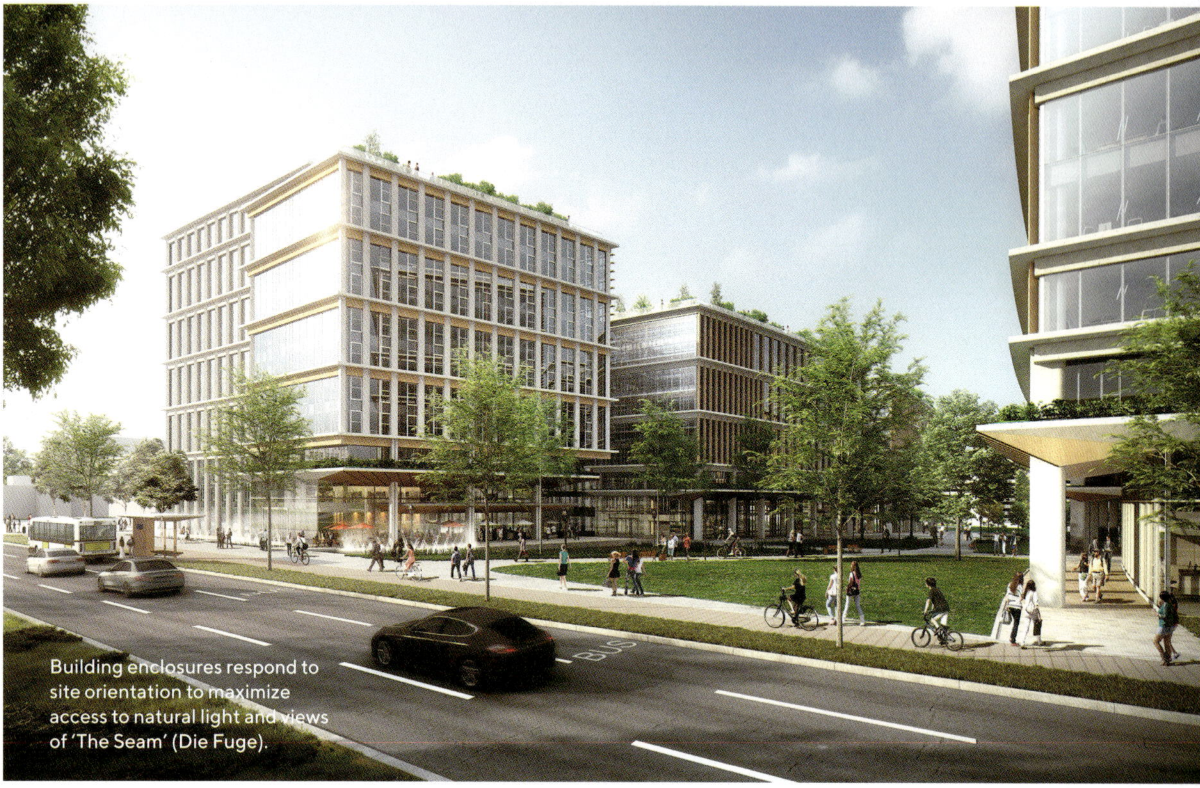

Building enclosures respond to site orientation to maximize access to natural light and views of 'The Seam' (Die Fuge).

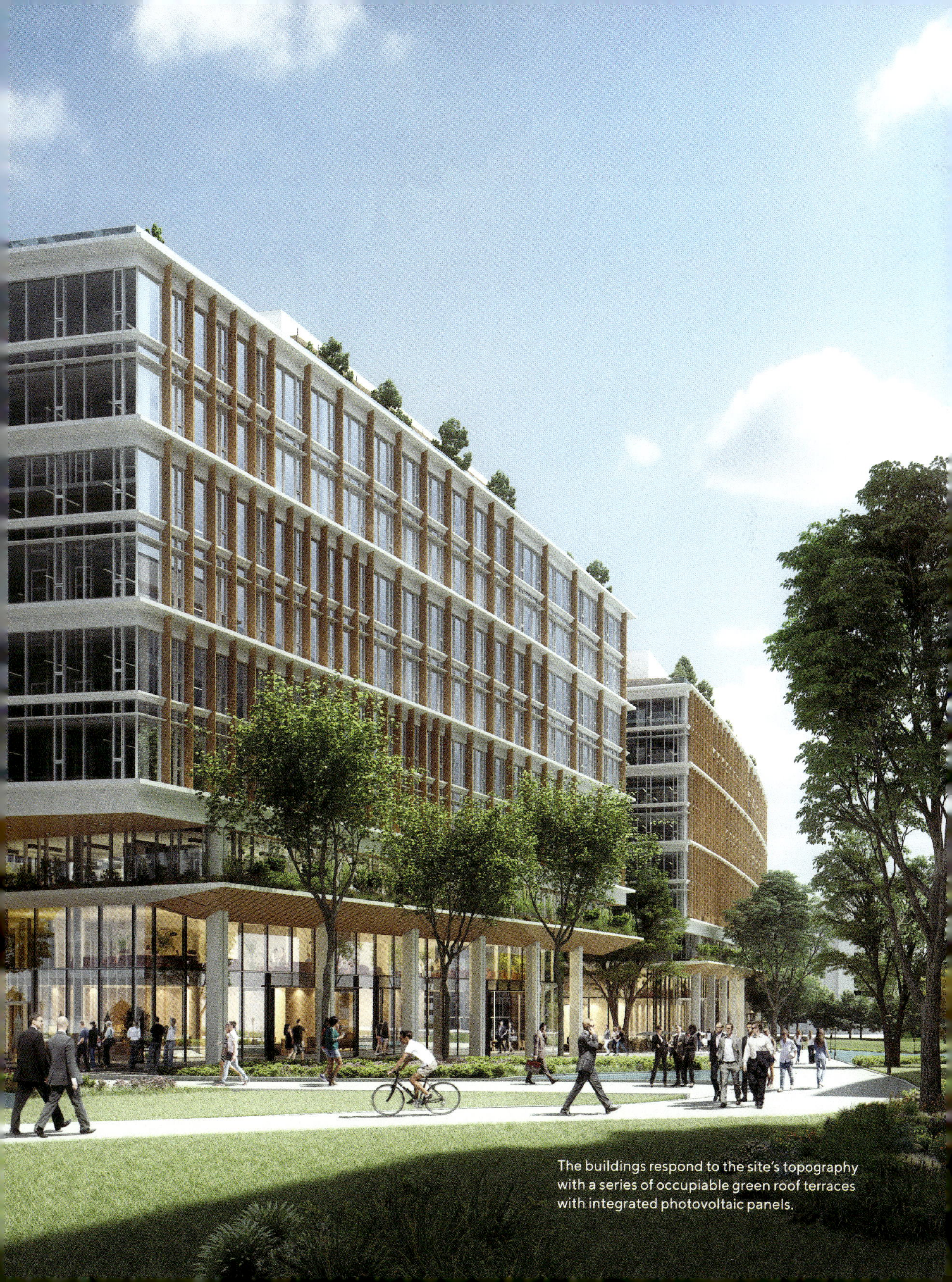

The buildings respond to the site's topography with a series of occupiable green roof terraces with integrated photovoltaic panels.

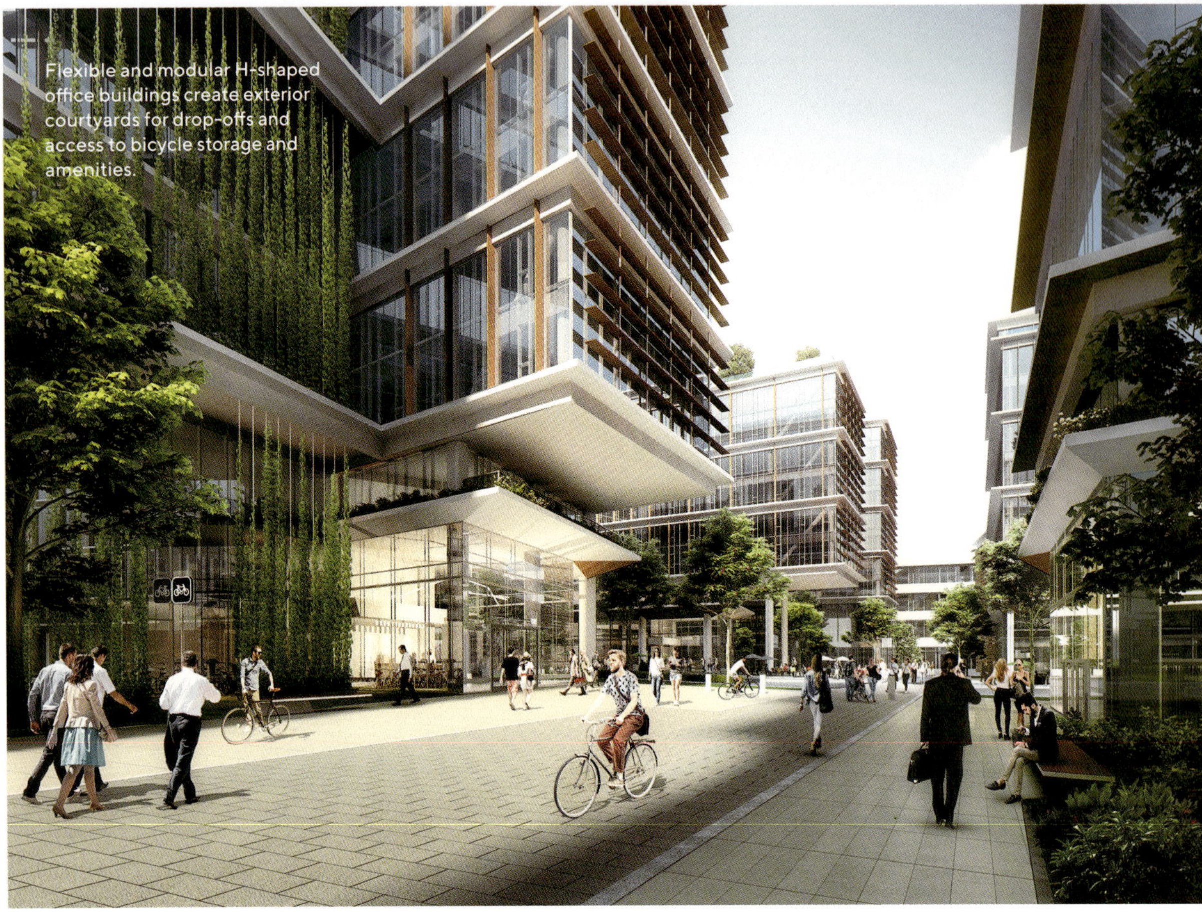
Flexible and modular H-shaped office buildings create exterior courtyards for drop-offs and access to bicycle storage and amenities.

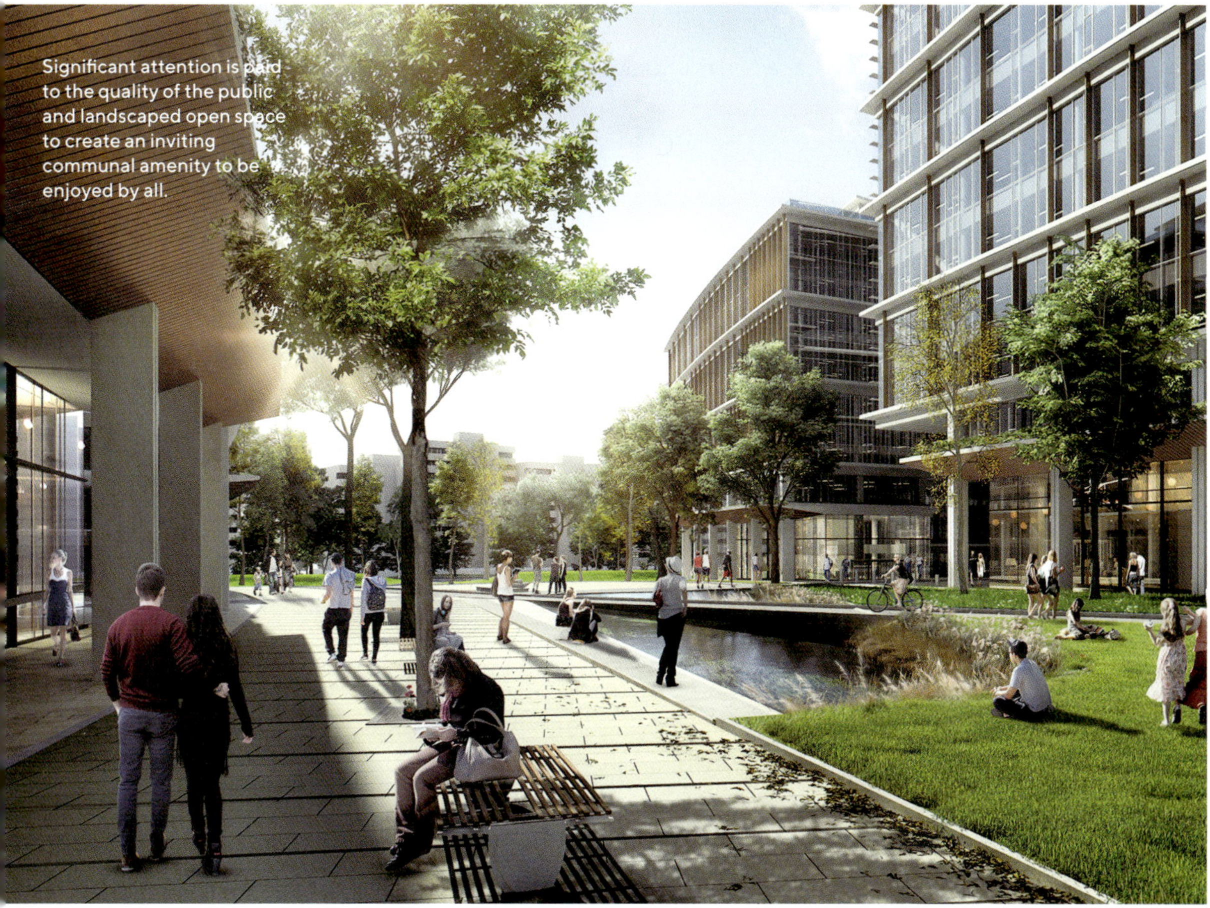

Significant attention is paid to the quality of the public and landscaped open space to create an inviting communal amenity to be enjoyed by all.

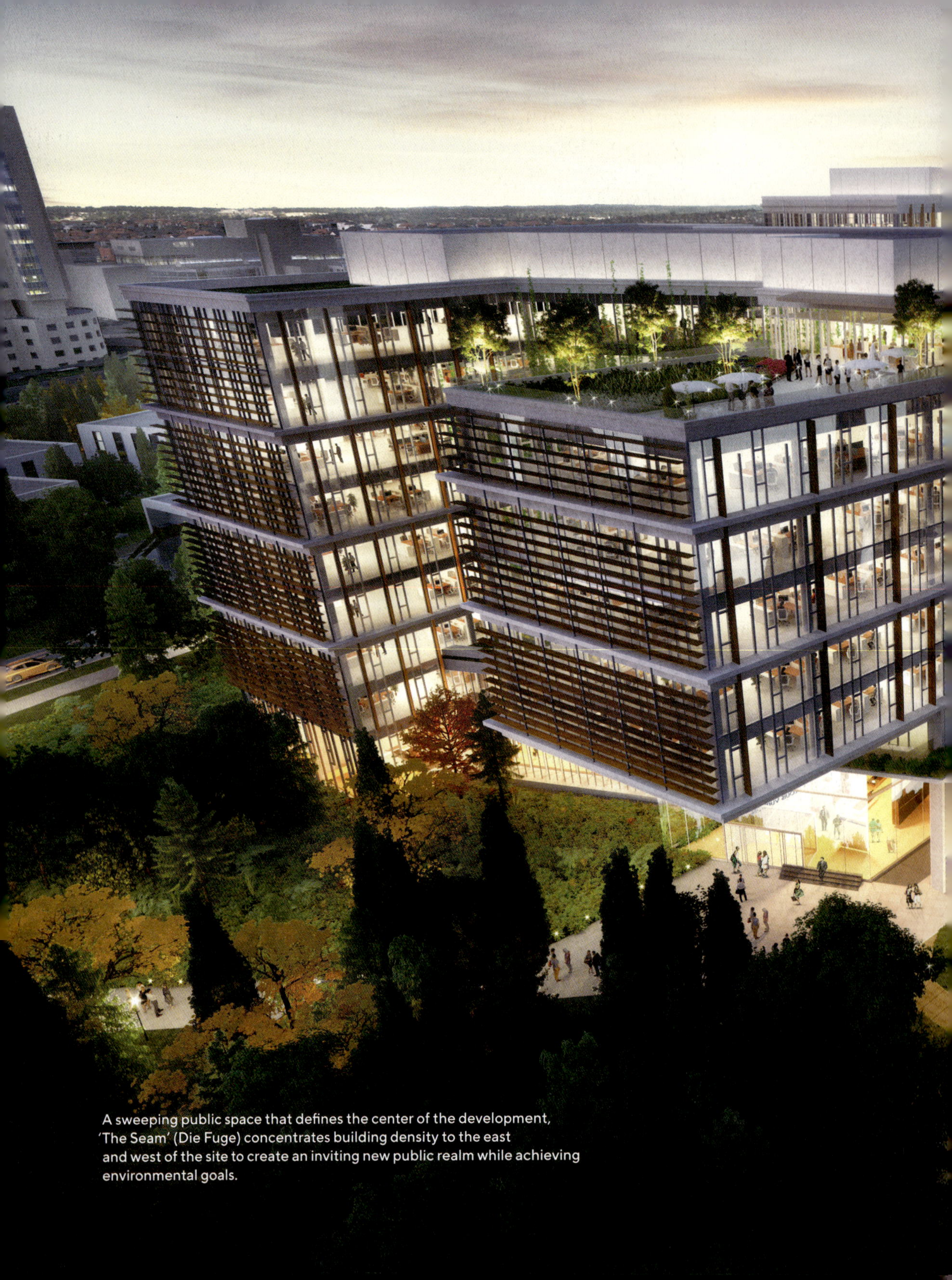

A sweeping public space that defines the center of the development, 'The Seam' (Die Fuge) concentrates building density to the east and west of the site to create an inviting new public realm while achieving environmental goals.

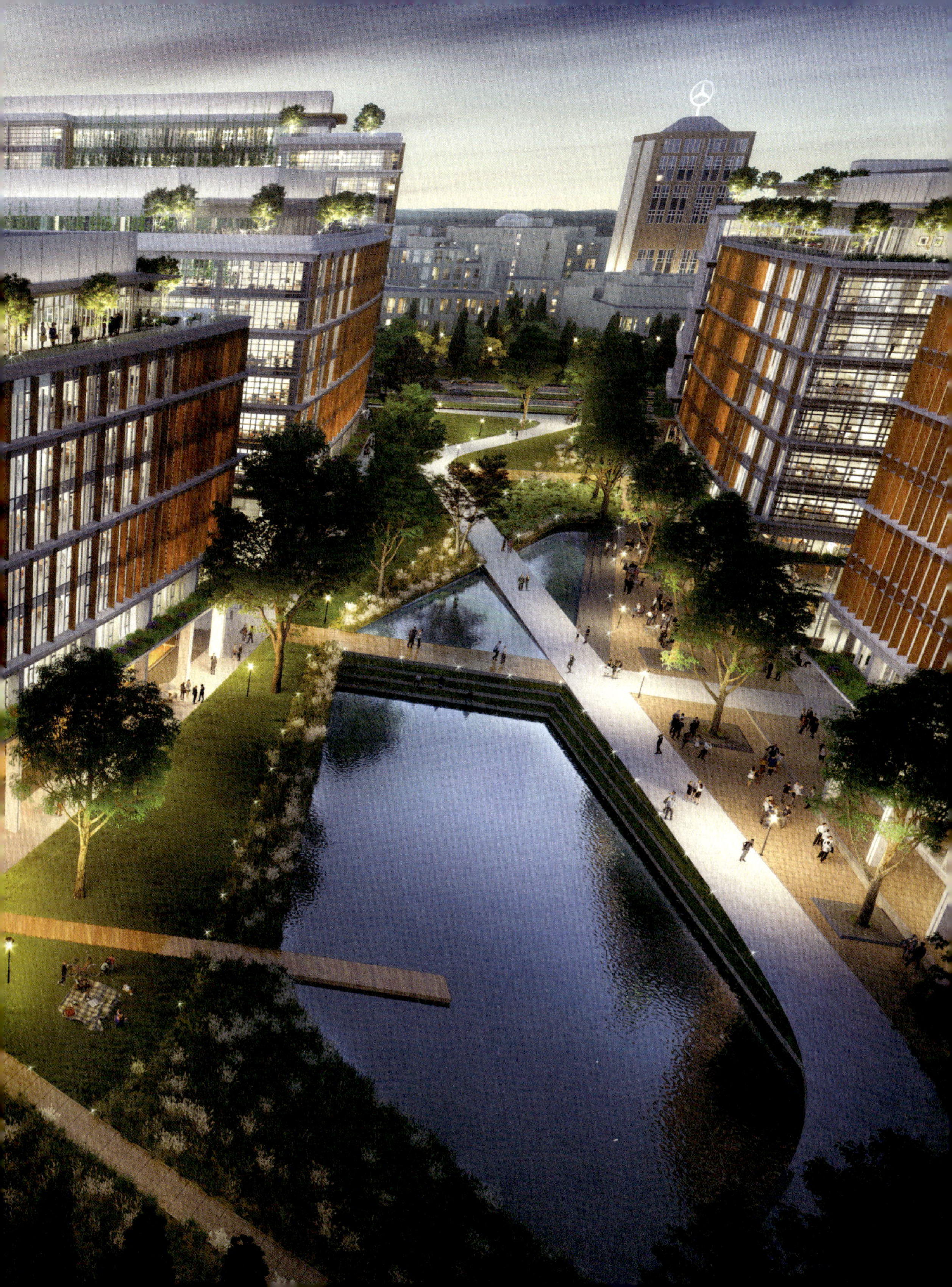

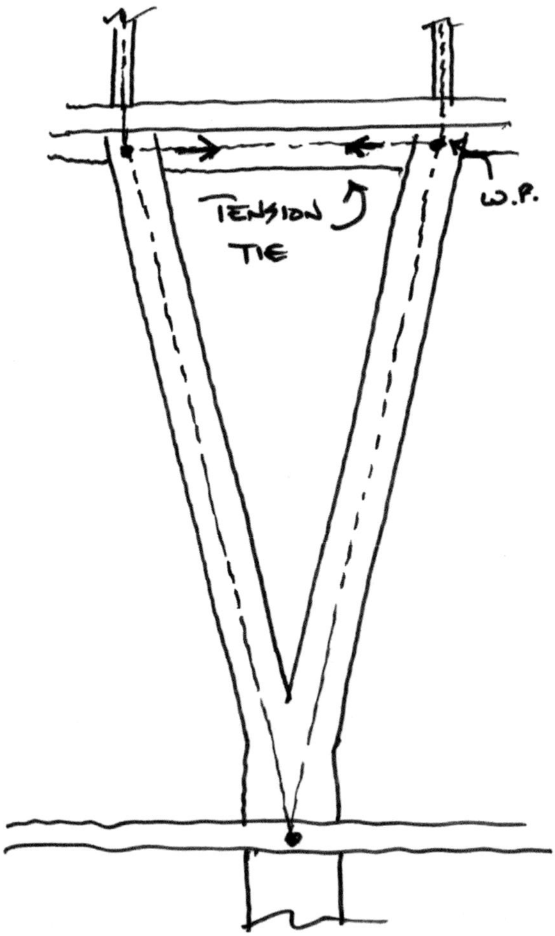

2+U

Afterword

Developing Relationships That Matter

Ron Klemencic

The creation of buildings requires the input of countless professionals, each skilled in their own discipline. Envisioning, designing, and constructing the greatest, most respected, and revered buildings requires more—that special magic between the owner, architect, and consultants whose sum total is far greater than that of the individual inputs. To consistently realize greatness is the profound gift of few. Pickard Chilton, led by Jon Pickard, Bill Chilton, and Tony Markese, are among this rarest breed.

Greatness in building design is found at the intersection of art and science. Art stirs the human soul and inspires emotion. Science rationalizes the laws of nature to achieve a desired outcome. The greatest buildings combine art and science in a seemingly effortless way. The outcome is a building that inspires, motivates, and encourages people to be at their best.

For many, this intersection is ellusive. In fact, it may never be discovered or achieved. For a few, the intersection is understood and respected but is not consistently found because it requires the paths of all project participants to find a common meeting place.

Most rarely, the intersection is a fundamental axiom of practice. The intersection is not simply a crossing of paths, but a merging of ideas in concert with one another. Synonymous with creating the most amazing jazz music where each musician contributes their own skill and inspiration resulting in magical combinations of sound—such is the collaboration with Pickard Chilton. Building owners, managers, consultants, and builders are encouraged to bring their unique skills and talents, each contributing to the ensemble, from which arises an extraordinary building.

Series of study models exploring the forms of the Y columns.

Fundamental to this merging of ideas is respect and trust. Through the consistent practice of respect for the ideas and inputs of others, a foundation is laid. Through dialogue, careful listening, and a constant quest to understand, a framework of trust is established. With trust comes inspiration and daring. With inspiration and daring comes transformation—something new—something better than before. The ability to repeat this process time and time again is where Pickard Chilton shines brightest.

I have had the unique honor and pleasure of collaborating with Pickard Chilton for more than 20 years. Each experience is among the most fulfilling and satisfying of my career. Their profound respect for the skills and talents of those around them, combined with their true and sincere desire to understand and synthesize, all underpinned by a modest and humble leadership style, inspires everyone to perform at their best. After completing a project together, we can all barely wait for the next adventure!

Collaborating with Pickard Chilton is much more than designing and constructing a building—it is a profoundly enriching and fulfilling experience. Developing relationships that matter is the core of Pickard Chilton's incredible success.

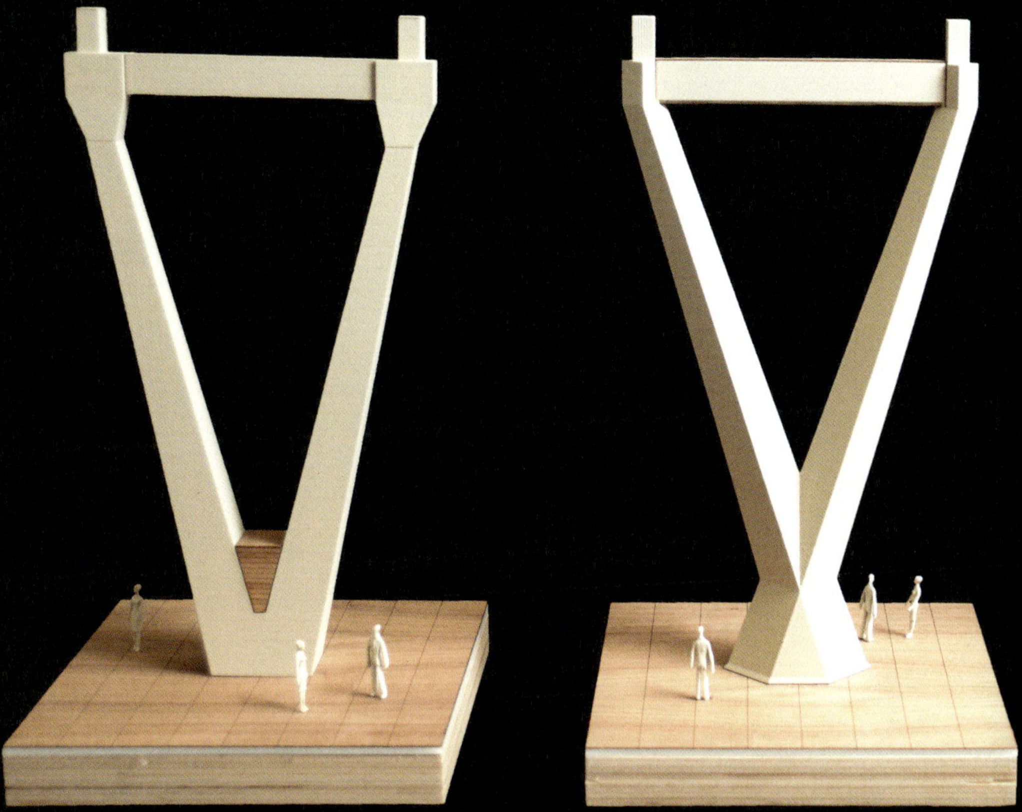

Index of Projects

Eaton House p 32

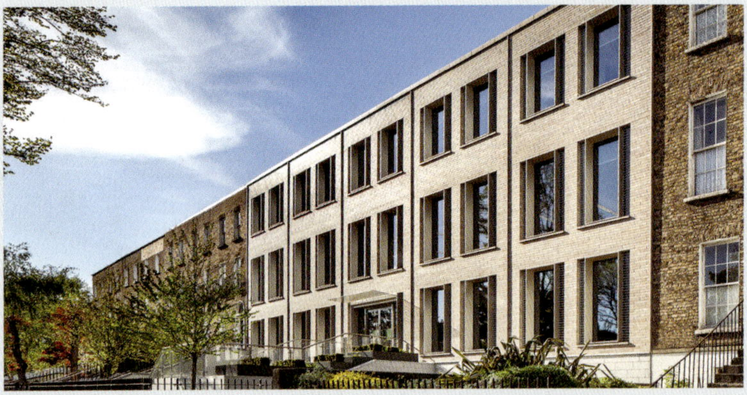

The RO p 52

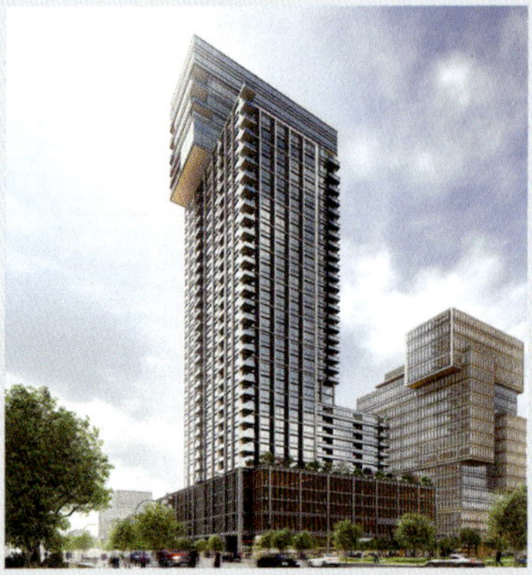

T3 RiNo p 86

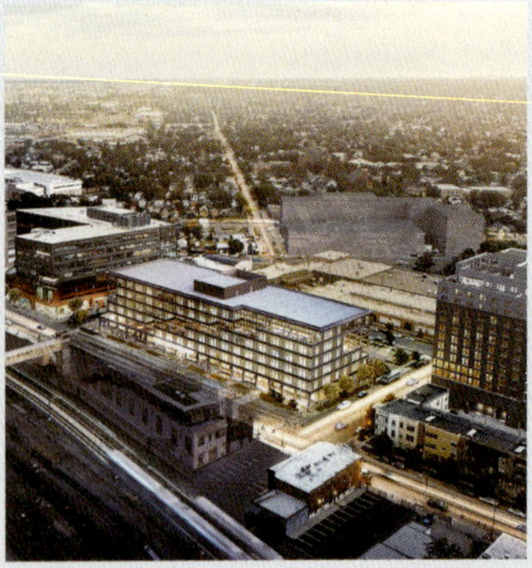

1144 Fifteenth Street p 94

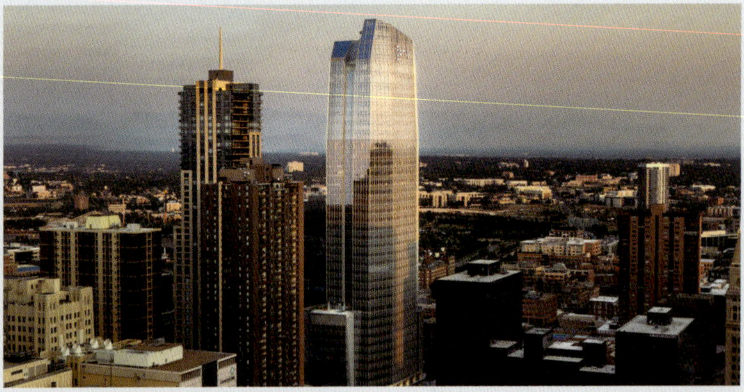

Global Gateway Shinagawa p 154

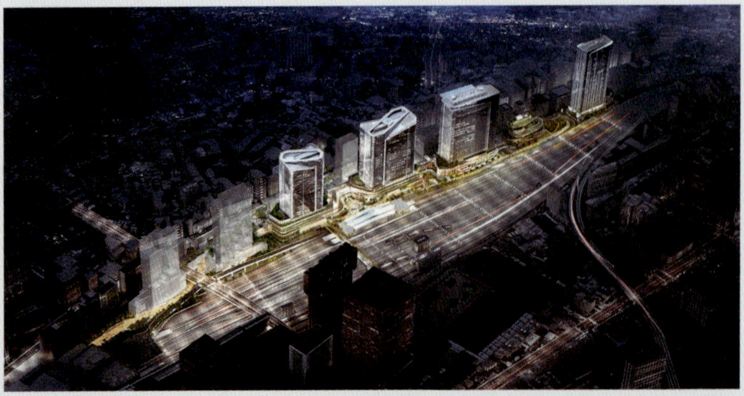

325 Main—Google Cambridge Headquarters p 166

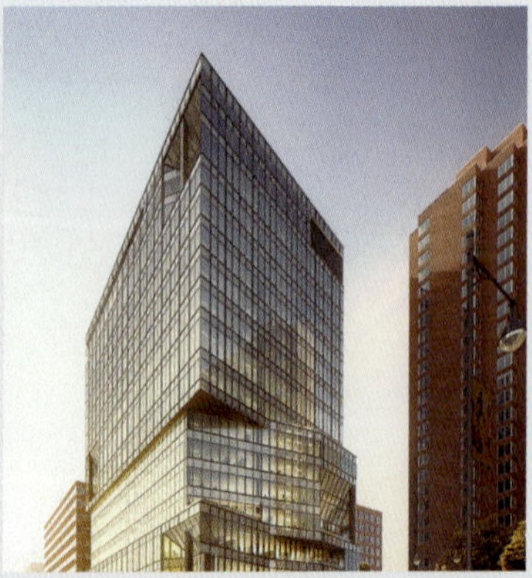

2+U p 58

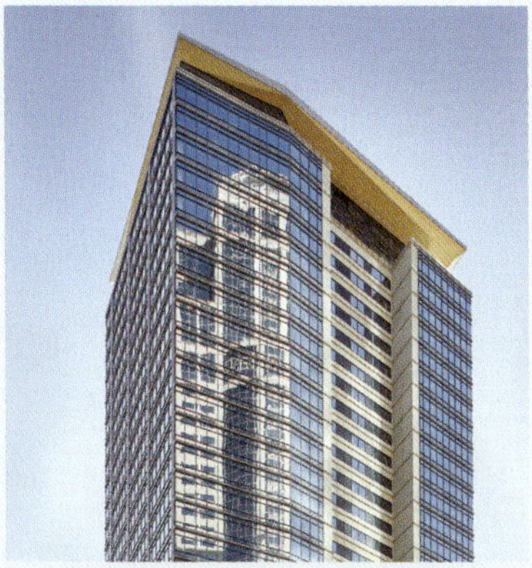

The Eight p 68

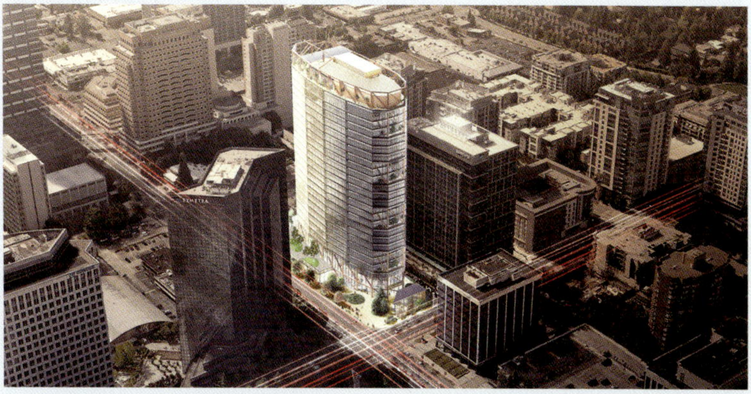

Devon Energy Center p 184

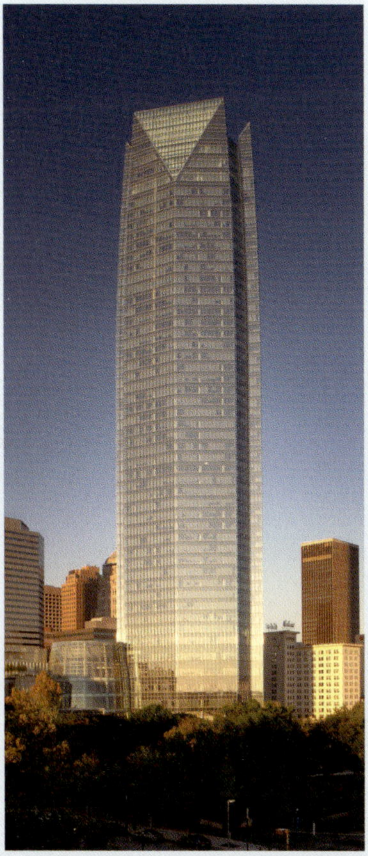

Minnesota Senate Building p 116

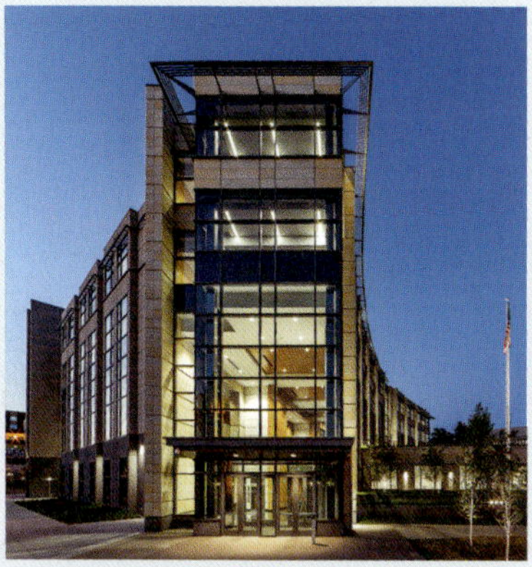

CalPERS Headquarters Complex p 124

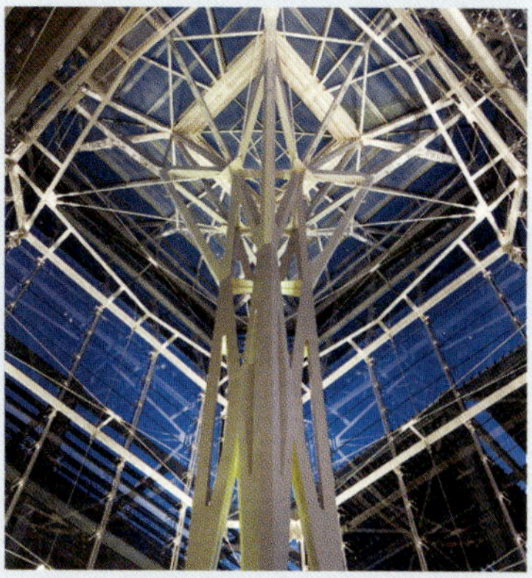

Barack H. Obama
Magnet University School p 212

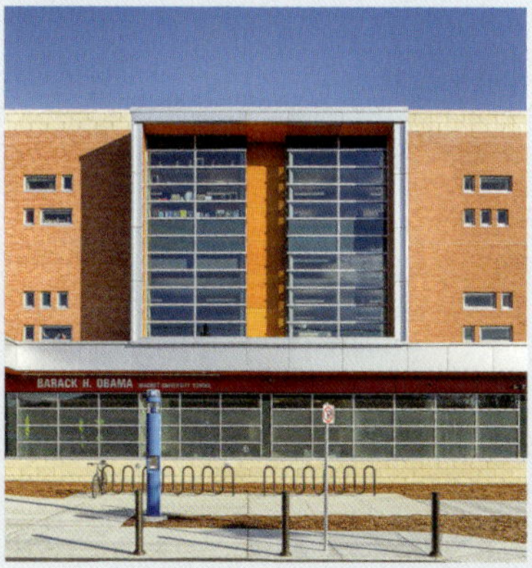

Plieninger Straße 140
Development p 218

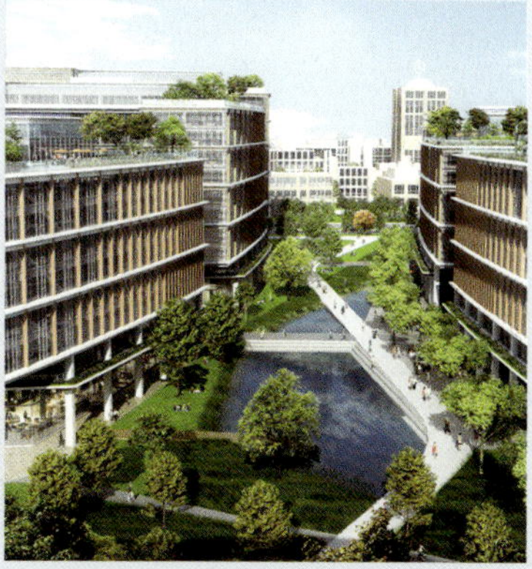

Acknowledgments

The Art of Collaboration is a candid record of how we work as a design studio. We trust it provides clients and partners with whom we collaborate, as well as students and architects, an understanding of what underpins our design process.

Collaboration and our connection to others are as important as the places we design and build. We are committed to serving our clients in more effective and innovative ways based on the tenets this book defines.

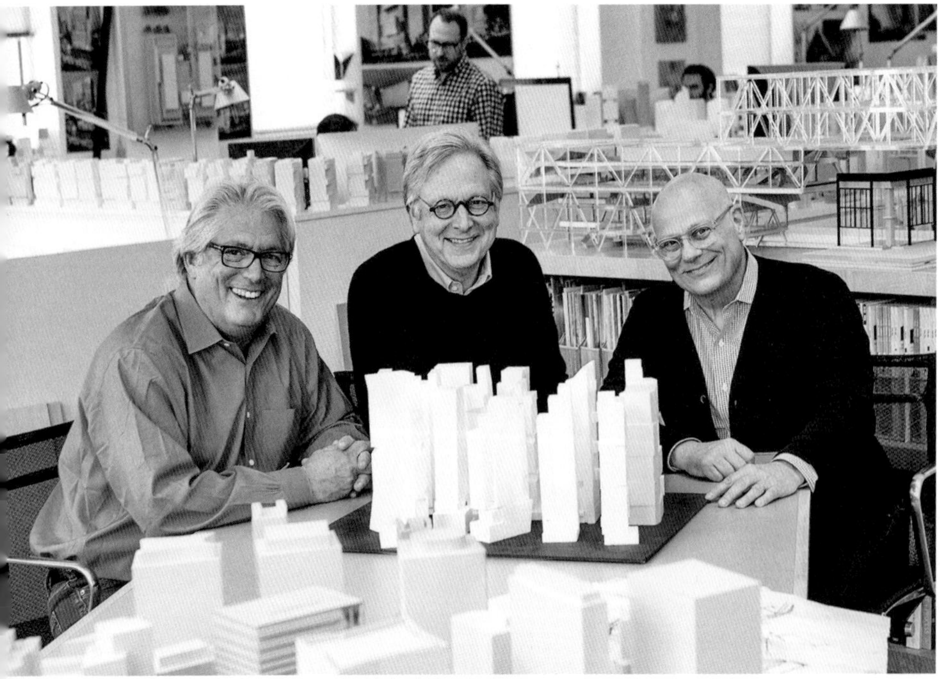

The Art of Collaboration is fundamentally a synthesis of the studio's commitment to serving our clients with uncompromising dedication. We are deeply honored by those clients who graciously and generously offered insightful and candid input for Michael J. Crosbie's thoughtful essays. While we were not able to solicit input from each of our clients, we believe these voices collectively represent the studio's body of work, with a diversity of project types, culture, scale, challenges, and solutions.

We extend our appreciation to our collaborators who helped realize this book, including clients, partner architects, consultants, and our studio colleagues.

We are indebted to our mentors for their seminal influence on our design process. Most importantly, we are grateful for the trust our clients have placed in Pickard Chilton to help them realize their vision and aspirations.

Jon Pickard FAIA, RIBA, *William D. Chilton* FAIA, RIBA, *Anthony J. Markese* FAIA, RIBA

AUTHOR AND CONTRIBUTORS

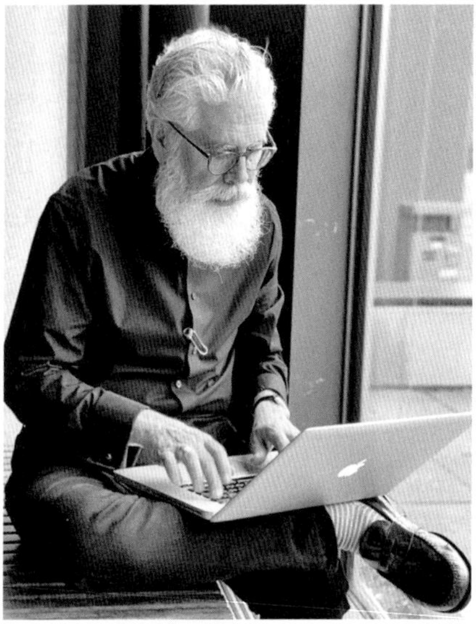

Michael J. Crosbie, Ph.D., FAIA, is a writer, educator, and architect. He earned degrees in architecture from The Catholic University of America, where in 2015 he was the Walton Visiting Critic and Professor in Residence. He has lectured at dozens of architecture schools in the United States and abroad. The author of, contributor to, and editor of more than 70 books on architecture and design (including five books for children), Dr. Crosbie has served as an editor of *Progressive Architecture* and *Architecture* magazines, and the journal *Faith & Form*. He has authored hundreds of articles appearing in publications and digital media around the world. He is Professor of Architecture at the University of Hartford, where he teaches a course on architecture and film. Dr. Crosbie is a winner of the Edward S. Frey Memorial Award, bestowed by the American Institute of Architects, and is a member of the AIA College of Fellows. He has practiced with architecture firms in Connecticut, where he is a registered architect.

Cesar Pelli, FAIA, founded the firm Cesar Pelli & Associates in New Haven, Connecticut, in 1977 (now Pelli Clarke Pelli Architects), the year he became the Dean of the Yale School of Architecture. Scores of design awards have recognized his architecture around the globe. In 1997, his design for Malaysia's Petronas Towers was completed, making them the tallest in the world — a title they held for seven years (they are yet the tallest twin towers in the world). Pelli is the author of the book *Observations for Young Architects* (Monacelli). In 1995 he was awarded the Gold Medal, the highest honor bestowed by the American Institute of Architects. He authored this book's Foreword shortly before his death.

Thomas Fisher, Assoc. AIA, is a Professor in the School of Architecture, Director of the Minnesota Design Center, and former Dean of the College of Design at the University of Minnesota. The former Editorial Director of *Progressive Architecture* magazine, he was recognized in 2005 as the fifth most-published architecture writer in the United States. He has written or edited 11 books, 70 book chapters or introductions, and more than 450 articles in professional journals and major publications. His research focuses on urban design, strategic design, human-centered design, and ethics and the built environment.

Ron Klemencic, Hon. AIA, is Chairman and CEO of Magnusson Klemencic Associates (MKA), a structural and civil engineering firm with offices in Seattle and Chicago. He was recognized by the Council on Tall Buildings and Urban Habitat with the Fazlur R. Khan Lifetime Achievement Medal. In 2019, he won *Engineering News Record Magazine*'s Award of Excellence. He has led initiatives that have led to improvements to the design and construction of buildings through his role as a Director of the Charles Pankow Foundation. In addition, Klemencic has been inducted into the National Academy of Construction, National Academy of Engineering, and recognized by the American Institute of Architects as an Honorary Member.

IMAGE CREDITS

PAGE 4 © Peter Aaron/OTTO
5 Courtesy of James Lambiasi Architect
6 Pickard Chilton
7 Pickard Chilton
8 © Lifang
9 Pickard Chilton
12 © Balthazar Korab
14 Courtesy of James Lambiasi Architect
18 © Joe Aker/Aker Imaging
23 Pickard Chilton
27 Courtesy of Dublin City Archive
28 (left to right) Pickard Chilton; Pickard Chilton; © David Sundberg/Esto
31 © David Sundberg/Esto
32 © David Sundberg/Esto
34 © David Sundberg/Esto
36 © David Sundberg/Esto
37 © David Sundberg/Esto
38 © David Sundberg/Esto
42 Pickard Chilton
45 Pickard Chilton
47 © Benjamin Benschneider
48 Pickard Chilton
50 © Benjamin Benschneider
52 © Lifang
54 © Lifang
55 © Lifang
56 © Lifang
59 Courtesy of Skanska USA Commercial Development
60 © Benjamin Benschneider
62 © Benjamin Benschneider
63 © Benjamin Benschneider
64 © Benjamin Benschneider
65 © Benjamin Benschneider
66 © Christopher McClure
67 © Benjamin Benschneider
68 Pickard Chilton
70 Pickard Chilton
71 © Steelblue
72 Pickard Chilton
74 Pickard Chilton
78 Pickard Chilton
80 Pickard Chilton
81 © Steelblue
82 Pickard Chilton
83 © Steelblue
87 © Steelblue
88 © Steelblue
89 © Steelblue
90 © Steelblue
92 © Neoscape
94 © David Sundberg/Esto
96 © Raul J. Garcia/Astula
97 © David Sundberg/Esto
98 © David Sundberg/Esto
100 © David Sundberg/Esto
101 © David Sundberg/Esto
102 © Ryan Dravitz
106 © David J. Oakes, Chief Photographer, Minnesota Senate
108 Pickard Chilton
109 Pickard Chilton
110 Pickard Chilton
113 Pickard Chilton
114 © Peter Aaron/OTTO
115 Pickard Chilton
116 © Paul Crosby
118 © Paul Crosby
120 © Paul Crosby
121 © Paul Crosby
122 © Paul Crosby
125 © Keith Baker
126 © Peter Aaron/OTTO
128 © Peter Aaron/OTTO
129 © Peter Aaron/OTTO
130 © Peter Aaron/OTTO
132 © Peter Aaron/OTTO
133 © Peter Aaron/OTTO
134 © Peter Aaron/OTTO
139 Utagawa Hiroshige. (8th month of 1857). *Shinagawa Susaki, No. 83 from One Hundred Famous Views of Edo* [Woodblock print]. Brooklyn, New York: Brooklyn Museum. Gift of Anna Ferris.
141 (left to right, from top row) Pickard Chilton; Pickard Chilton; Pickard Chilton; Courtesy of James Lambiasi Architect; Courtesy of James Lambiasi Architect; Pickard Chilton; Courtesy of James Lambiasi Architect; Courtesy of James Lambiasi Architect; Courtesy of James Lambiasi Architect; Courtesy of Tripod Studio
142 Courtesy of James Lambiasi Architect
143 Pickard Chilton
144 Pickard Chilton
146 Pickard Chilton
148 Pickard Chilton
149 Pickard Chilton
150 Pickard Chilton; © Bob Handelman; Pickard Chilton
151 Pickard Chilton
152 Pickard Chilton
155 © Atchain
156 © Atchain
158 © Lifang
159 © Lifang
160 © Atchain
161 © Atchain
162 © Atchain
164 © Atchain
167 © Lifang
168 © Lifang
170 Pickard Chilton
171 © Lifang
172 © Lifang
177 Pickard Chilton
178 © Alan Karchmer
180 Pickard Chilton
181 © Jock Pottle Photography
182 © Alan Karchmer; Pickard Chilton
185 © Alan Karchmer
186 Pickard Chilton
188 © Joe Aker/Aker Imaging
190 Pickard Chilton
191 Pickard Chilton
192 Pickard Chilton
194 © Alan Karchmer
196 © Alan Karchmer
197 © Alan Karchmer
198 Pickard Chilton
200 © Alan Karchmer
205 Pickard Chilton
206 Pickard Chilton
207 Pickard Chilton
209 Pickard Chilton
211 Pickard Chilton
213 Pickard Chilton
214 Pickard Chilton
216 Pickard Chilton
217 Pickard Chilton
218 © Lifang
220 © Lifang
222 © Lifang
223 © Lifang
224 © Lifang
225 © Lifang
226 © Lifang
228 © Magnusson Klemencic Associates
231 Pickard Chilton
232 (left to right, from top row) © David Sundberg/Esto; © Lifang; Courtesy of Studio216; © David Sundberg/Esto; © Lifang; © Lifang
233 (left to right, from top row) © Benjamin Benschneider; Pickard Chilton; © Joe Aker/Aker Imaging; © Paul Crosby; © Peter Aaron/OTTO; Pickard Chilton; © Lifang
234 © Bob Handelman
236 Courtesy of Imdat As

Published in Australia in 2021 by The Images Publishing Group Pty Ltd
ABN 89 059 734 431

OFFICES

Melbourne
6 Bastow Place
Mulgrave, Victoria 3170
Australia
Tel: +61 3 9561 5544

New York
6 West 18th Street 4B
New York City, NY 10011
United States
Tel: +1 212 645 1111

Shanghai
6F, Building C, 838 Guangji Road
Hongkou District, Shanghai
200434
China
Tel: +86 021 31260822

books@imagespublishing.com
www.imagespublishing.com

The Images Publishing Group Reference Number: 1541

NATIONAL LIBRARY OF AUSTRALIA

A catalogue record for this book is available from the National Library of Australia

Title: Pickard Chilton: The Art of Collaboration
ISBN: 9781864708516

Design by Jenny Chan/Jack Design (www.jackdesignstudio.com)

This title was commissioned in IMAGES' Melbourne office and produced as follows:
Editorial Georgia (Gina) Tsarouhas, *Production* Nicole Boehringer, *Thanks to* Jeanette Wall

Printed by Graphius nv, in Belgium, on 150gsm Magno Volume art paper

FSC www.fsc.org MIX Paper from responsible sources FSC® C014767